# SHOP PROJECTS

## BASED ON

# COMMUNITY PROBLEMS

BY

MYRON G. BURTON, A.B., M.S.

DIRECTOR OF VOCATIONAL AND MANUAL-TRAINING INSTRUCTION IN THE PUBLIC SCHOOLS OF KANSAS CITY, MISSOURI

GINN AND COMPANY

BOSTON · NEW YORK · CHICAGO · LONDON
ATLANTA · DALLAS · COLUMBUS · SAN FRANCISCO

PAGE

Introduction to Section III .................. 112
Sleeve Board .................. 113, 114, 115, 116
Water Wheel .................. 117, 118, 119, 120
Window Box .................. 121, 122, 123, 124
Miter Box .................. 125, 126, 127, 128
Picture Frame .................. 129, 130, 131, 132
Dishcloth Rack .................. 133, 134, 135, 136
Book Shelves .................. 137, 138, 139, 140
Sled .................. 141, 142, 143, 144
Saw Horse .................. 145, 146, 147, 148
Hatchet and Hammer Handle .................. 149, 150, 151, 152
Suggestions for Community Research..... 153
Review Questions and Problems .................. 154, 155

Introduction to Section IV .................. 156
Wash Bench .................. 157, 158, 159, 160
Nail or Screw Tray .................. 161, 162, 163, 164
Candlestick .................. 165, 166, 167, 168
Hand Mirror .................. 169, 170, 171, 172
Flower Pot Stand .................. 173, 174, 175, 176
Bird House .................. 177, 178, 179, 180
Wagon Jack .................. 181, 182, 183, 184
Seed Corn Tester .................. 185, 186, 187, 188
Evener and Singletree .................. 189, 190, 191, 192
Farm Gate .................. 193, 194, 195, 196
Suggestions for Community Research..... 197
Review Questions and Problems .................. 198, 199

Introduction to Section V .................. 200
Shoe Polishing Box .................. 201, 202, 203, 204
Tabouret .................. 205, 206, 207, 208
Foot Stool .................. 209, 210, 211, 212
Folding Game Table .................. 213, 214, 215, 216
Stepladder .................. 217, 218, 219, 220
Automobile Creeper .................. 221, 222, 223, 224
Shop Tool Case .................. 225, 226, 227, 228
Work Bench .................. 229, 230, 231, 232
Cow Stanchion .................. 233, 234, 235, 236
Chicken Brooder .................. 237, 238, 239, 240
Suggestions for Community Research..... 241
Review Questions and Problems .................. 242, 243

| | PAGE |
|---|---|
| Introduction to Section VI | 244 |
| Porch Swing | 245, 246, 247, 248 |
| Jardiniere Stand | 249, 250, 251, 252 |
| Tool Chest | 253, 254, 255, 256 |
| Piano Bench | 257, 258, 259, 260 |
| Magazine Rack | 261, 262, 263, 264 |
| Telephone Stand and Stool | 265, 266, 267, 268 |
| Medicine or Shaving Cabinet | 269, 270, 271, 272 |
| Cedar Chest | 273, 274, 275, 276 |
| Writing Desk | 277, 278, 279, 280 |
| Library Table | 281, 282, 283, 284 |
| Suggestions for Community Research | 285 |
| Review Questions and Problems | 286 |
| Supplement | 287 |
| Chapter I. Mechanical Drawing— | |
| Introduction and Definitions | 288 to 290 |
| Drawing Outfit | 291 to 294 |
| Lettering | 295, 296 |
| Problems | 297 to 307 |
| Chapter II. Tool Processes— | |
| Squaring Stock | 308 to 312 |
| Gauging | 313, 314 |
| Boring | 314, 315 |
| Sandpapering | 317 to 319 |
| Nailing | 321 to 323 |
| Rafter and brace cuts | 324, 325 |
| Reading and Writing Dimensions | 325 |
| Lumber Measure | 325, 326 |
| Chapter III. Varieties of Timber— | |
| Introduction | 327 to 330 |
| Hardwood Trees | 331 to 340 |
| Softwood Trees | 340 to 343 |
| Lumber and Methods of Sawing | 343 to 346 |
| Drying and Shrinkage of Lumber | 346, 347 |
| Chapter IV. Wood Finishing — | |
| Painting | 348, 349 |
| Cabinet Finishing | 349, 350 |
| Staining | 350, 351 |
| Filler | 351, 352 |
| Wax Finish | 352, 353 |
| Shellac Finish | 353 to 355 |
| Varnish Finish | 355 to 357 |
| Care of Finishing Materials | 357 |

| | PAGE |
|---|---|
| Chapter V. Principal Joints Used in Woodwork | 358 to 371 |
| Chapter VI. Tools and Tool Sharpening— | |
| Saws .............................. | 372 |
| Rip Saws .......................... | 372, 373 |
| Cross-Cutting Saws ................ | 373, 374 |
| Saw Filing ........................ | 374, 375 |
| Care of Saws ...................... | 375 |
| Planes ............................ | 375 |
| Parts of the Plane ................ | 376 to 378 |
| Sharpening Planes ................. | 379 |
| Sharpening Chisels ................ | 381 |
| Sharpening Knives ................. | 382 |
| Care of the Sharpening Equipment....... | 382 |

## ALPHABETICAL INDEX OF PROJECTS.

| | PAGE |
|---|---|
| Automobile Creeper....... | 221 |
| Bench Hook ............... | 49 |
| Bird House ............... | 177 |
| Book Rack ................ | 77 |
| Book Shelves ............. | 137 |
| Box Kite ................. | 37 |
| Bracket Shelf ............ | 61 |
| Bread or Meat Board....... | 69 |
| Broom Holder ............. | 45 |
| Camp Stool ............... | 73 |
| Candlestick .............. | 165 |
| Cedar Chest .............. | 273 |
| Chicken Brooder .......... | 237 |
| Child's Swing ............ | 89 |
| Coat Hanger .............. | 41 |
| Cow Stanchion ............ | 233 |
| Dishcloth Rack ........... | 133 |
| Drawing Board ............ | 81 |
| Evener and Singletree ..... | 189 |
| Farm Gate ................ | 193 |
| Feed Scoop ............... | 57 |
| Flower Pot Stand .......... | 173 |
| Flower Trellis ............ | 105 |
| Fly Trap ................. | 93 |
| Folding Game Table ....... | 213 |
| Foot Stool ............... | 209 |
| Hand Loom ................ | 33 |
| Hand Mirror .............. | 169 |
| Harness Rack ............. | 101 |
| Hatchet and Hammer Handle. | 149 |

| | PAGE |
|---|---|
| Jardiniere Stand .......... | 249 |
| Library Table ............. | 281 |
| Magazine Rack ............ | 261 |
| Match Box ................ | 25 |
| Medicine or Shaving Cabinet. | 269 |
| Milking Stool ............. | 97 |
| Miter Box ................ | 125 |
| Nail or Screw Tray ........ | 161 |
| Necktie Rack ............. | 29 |
| Piano Bench .............. | 257 |
| Picture Frame ............ | 129 |
| Porch Swing .............. | 245 |
| Saw Horse ................ | 145 |
| Seed Corn Rack ........... | 53 |
| Seed Corn Tester .......... | 185 |
| Shoe Polishing Box ........ | 201 |
| Shop Tool Case ........... | 225 |
| Sleeve Board ............. | 113 |
| Sled ..................... | 141 |
| Stepladder ............... | 217 |
| Tabouret ................. | 205 |
| Telephone Stand and Stool... | 265 |
| Tool Chest ............... | 253 |
| Wagon Jack ............... | 181 |
| Water Wheel .............. | 117 |
| Wash Bench ............... | 157 |
| Windmill ................. | 85 |
| Window Box ............... | 121 |
| Work Bench ............... | 229 |
| Writing Desk ............. | 277 |

# PREFACE

MODERN educators have come to realize that the only avenue of approach to the child's mind is through the light of his experience, therefore recent text-books are being so arranged as to utilize the things with which the child comes in contact outside of school as well as in the classroom in guiding him into new fields of knowledge.

Under the old school the plan of the text-book was to arrange the subject-matter in a logical and scientific way, giving but little consideration to the immediate interest of the child, or to the natural steps of his development. This so-called logical arrangement placed the paramount consideration on a skillful organization of the great store of racial subject-matter, and was no doubt quite satisfactory to the learned scholar or the mature mind provided with a broad field of experience.

A more vital consideration of the natural unfolding of the child's mind has created a great interest in what has been called the "psychological" arrangement of subject-matter. The psychological order of presentation means that the subject-matter is to be constantly handled and shaped in accordance with the developing thought of the child. This thought of course cannot be identical in any two children, due to their unequal ability and unlike experiences. This psychological plan of presentation, followed to the extreme, may result in random thought with but little central idea, thus following no particular channel, and consequently failing to arrive at any definite goal.

Ironclad advocates of the old school of logical thinking (fortunately but few of them are left at present) maintain that but little consideration should be given to the individual student, but that the mathematically correct and absolutely sequential logic of the subject should be the master in prescribing the order of procedure in all school tasks.

On the other hand, over-enthusiastic champions of the psychological doctrine are too prone to ignore the logical side entirely and allow their efforts to be wasted in rambling, and thus really give their students absolute command of nothing which will function in future adjustments.

These two extremes are the paths which lie open to any author when he undertakes the preparation of a text-book. While the logical arrangement has been almost slavishly followed in some of the old line subjects, it has asserted itself only to a very limited extent in the newer industrial lines. There have, however, been a few attempts at text-books and courses of study which have required students to follow a prescribed course in an absolute way, thus leaving no opportunity for the development of individual tastes, initiative and self-reliance. By far the greater risk, however, has been in the opposite extreme. Since there have been no definite standards nor prescribed courses by which industrial efforts can be measured, many teachers have neglected to check up their work with sufficient rigor. On account of the newness of handwork as a public school undertaking, there are as yet a great many difficulties to be confronted in following the natural development of the child and thus prescribing projects which will set forth the very best training for his particular case. Much of the indefinite, inaccurate, slipshod sort of work which is being done under the name of Manual Training apologizes for its existence by claiming that it is following the psychological trend.

Superintendents who have been accustomed to maintaining a high ideal of excellence in all their work have been not a little annoyed by the chaotic unmeasurable results in their industrial classes, but they have been told by the experts along the theoretical side of the work that the child should be allowed to unfold in his own way. Then when the class has been intrusted to an inexperienced, perhaps meagerly trained teacher, the superintendent sees that the fine theory of the psychological expert brings about intangible standards and indefinite results in the hands of the less capable teacher.

If handwork is to be made a real school problem, and is to have its highest educational value, it certainly must conform to the same rules of pedagogy which govern the other subjects. The mind does not undergo any transformation because the child happens to be in the shop or to have a saw or hammer in his hand.

In the preparation of this text, which is based upon many years of personal instruction and observation of all types of schools in several states, the effort has been to find a sane medium between the logical and psychological methods of presentation. Those who are familiar with the subject are well aware that there is a science in mechanics and a correct way to execute the most common and universal tool processes, and that there are fundamental principles as well defined as the principles of mathematics or the sciences. These mechanical processes and principles represent the best of the experiences of ages gone by, and if the learner expects to develop with economy of time and effort, he should profit by the racial experience and acquaint himself with the very best ways which time has demonstrated for carrying out the universal processes and principles.

On the other hand the experience of the child must be studied and respected. His apperceptive powers constitute the only means by which we can be hopeful of his interpreting his surroundings. With this idea in mind this text has been designed to deal with the logical principles in a psychological way. Paradoxical as this may seem at first glance, a careful investigation of the text will reveal the fact that every project gives an opportunity for the presentation of mechanical principles to be employed in the making of a project which will appeal directly to the child's interest. Unlimited opportunity is offered for the development of the child's original taste and initiative in such portions of the projects as will permit of modification without violation of the principles.

In order to meet this widely varying condition of mind, in every section of the text a very extensive list of projects has been presented and kindred ones suggested, thus making it possible to claim the interest and attention of students of either city or country environment, and also care for the needs of those who are urging the making of practical things.

The preparation of this text was undertaken only after many years of teaching experience, and innumerable conferences with industrial instructors and other educators in various parts of the country.

As the text is submitted to the verdict of his fellow teachers, it is the sincere hope of the author that it will find a place where it may offer its share of real and tangible assistance to every conscientious influence which is earnestly endeavoring to give to our youth a form of education which will fit them for lives of useful service.

# COMMUNITY PROBLEMS

GREAT captains of industry, professional men and those who are giving their attention to various practical lines have recently raised a great criticism on the public schools because, as they claim, the things taught in school fail to empower the students to meet the demands of business life. Even our strongest advocates of the cultural doctrine are ready to admit that these criticisms are not entirely without foundation. Modern educators are beginning to see that too many of our school problems have no vital connection nor practical application in community life, so in recent years there has been a great wave of enthusiasm sweeping over the country for a more utilitarian policy in our public schools. Rather than concoct mathematical conundrums or enigmas of language, which serve only as mental gymnastics in the classroom, it is just as cultural and far more economic to take some of the great problems of the community and, through typical projects, teach the students how to investigate and find a solution to the things which they will soon be called upon to control.

As soon as a student leaves school he ceases to make problems for the sake of keeping himself busy in their solution. The process is now reversed and he is not only brought face to face with ready-made problems calling upon him for a solution, but is surrounded beyond escape by a class of community problems which demand the full exercise of his capabilities. An unsuccessful meeting of these community problems and an incorrect solution may mean his loss of social standing, professional failure, financial reverse, moral disgrace, or possibly absolute extermination.

The fact that all students, regardless of ability and condition, will, in a very few years, be compelled to undergo this adjustment, makes it unnecessary to make any argument to show why community problems should constitute a vital portion of the school curriculum.

The industrial work through its Manual Training, Agriculture, Home Economics and other practical lines, offers a most excellent opportunity of employing the students' natural interest and the inherent disposition toward activity in working out projects which are typical of the great community problems. For illustration: the great problem of sanitation is demanding universal attention and no one could claim a liberal education without understanding the theories, and being able to follow the modern rules of sanitary living. The theory of sanitation may be taught in an old line physiology class, but it can be made to function not only in methods of thinking, but in the formation of habits of action, in the class of Home Economics.

The community demands that a boy be taught proper care and respect for neat and orderly arrangement in his home life. An unlimited amount of advice on this subject may avail but little. However, if the boy is given the experience of making some of the practical things, such as a coat hanger, a broom holder or other equipment required to carry out these theories, he is practically sure to have the ideas everlastingly instilled into his nature.

A perusal of statistics showing how rapidly civilization is becoming centralized in our cities makes it necessary for the community to concern itself with the problem of showing in an effective way how the boy may become interested and profit by remaining on the farm. No amount of theory or poetry regarding "lowing herds," "sighing boughs" and "sweet-perfumed meadows" will prove effective in the solution of this problem unless the boys are taught how to approach the subject of agriculture and make it pleasant as well as profitable. This sort of interest can be inculcated only by the early experience in doing realities in agriculture and agricultural mechanics. The boy who makes and uses a seed corn tester will have a better comprehension of seed testing than a boy who merely reads of the value of seed selection.

Throughout this text the prevailing idea is to present only such projects as may be made typical of some community problems which are worth while. To be sure there are certain projects which in themselves are designed particularly to appeal to boyish tastes (the kite, for example), yet this project is replete with possibilities for the study of the great modern subject of air-craft, and by studying some of the references following the introductory statement an unlimited interest can be aroused.

The introductory statement at the opening of each lesson is intended to give some conception of the community problem from which the project is taken. It is not the intention to take up these various discussions in such a way as to give the child a complete comprehension of the great value of the community problem, but merely to introduce the idea and offer a few references for outside reading which the teacher may use as his time and inclination may dictate.

There is being much said these days about the idea of correlating the industrial work with the particular activities of local interest. This is sometimes misunderstood by the inexperienced, who think that in a community where a certain occupation prevails this occupation should be taught to the exclusion of all others. There can be no greater mistake than this, if our grammar grade students are to have a well-rounded education. It may even be said that the fact that a certain occupation prevails may be argument for its receiving less attention in the school, for the students will no doubt get an opportunity to come in contact with what it has to offer without much school assistance. Of course in purely vocational work the opposite view of this question might prevail, but in these days of a constantly shifting population we must not think that every boy who lives within the shadow of a blacksmith shop is destined to become a blacksmith.

The greatest obligation of the school is to give to each student such training as will enable him to find his proper place in his environment, and throughout this text it has been the design to draw a sufficient number of typical projects from the community interest to appeal to the widely varying inclinations and tastes of individual students and at the same time to guide them sufficiently so that their time will not be wasted in aimless effort.

# SUGGESTIONS TO TEACHERS

THE following suggestions to teachers are intended to give a broad conception of the underlying principles upon which this text is founded, and to offer means by which it can be made most effective in the hands of the students. It is not the intention to curtail the possibilities, nor any of the originality or initiative of the teacher, but rather to relieve him as much as possible of the drudgery and minor detail which falls to the lot of one who must be a constant source of information and advice to his classes.

In practically all other school subjects the teacher has the advantage of placing in the hands of his students some sort of literature from which they may gather the essential facts of the subject-matter. In proper justice to the industrial instructors, as well as to the students, these classes should be provided with some means by which they may gather pertinent information and direct these activities by their own powers of research. This will conserve the teacher's time and energy, allowing it to be devoted to the more important function of studying the case of each individual student, and then prescribing work suitable to serve his need.

This book is arbitrarily divided into six sections and each section presents ten projects in detail and offers suggestions for three or four times as many more. It is not the idea that any one student should be required to make every project in each section, but rather to set forth an abundance of work from which the teacher may direct the choice of the student after considering his personal taste and individual needs. But little attempt is made to grade the projects of each section and present them in the order of the sequence of processes, but rather to offer a series of projects which present kindred principles or which offer an opportunity of appealing to the varying tastes of the students. The sections, however, are sequential from the standpoint of difficulty. When a student has completed one project, by careful consideration of the finished product and the capability of the student, the teacher should advise him regarding what project he is next to undertake. In making this selection the wishes of the student should have careful consideration and also the selection should be made in such a way as to give him further training on the particular processes which he did not do satisfactorily in his last lesson. For illustration: if in making the matchbox the student has not shown sufficient ability in the use of the coping saw or in planing parallel edges, he might be given the whiskbroom holder for his second lesson and be encouraged to undertake a design which would re-employ these principles.

It will be observed that in each section there are offered projects of such a nature as to appeal to the interest of any boy, whether of the city or of the country. There are also projects of purely boyish interest from the standpoint of amusement, as well as some things which will be of value to him in his room.

The introduction to each section should be carefully perused so the instructor may have a fairly clear idea of what it embodies. He should also acquaint himself with the processes involved in each project before allowing a student to begin it. A student who has not sufficiently mastered the work of one section should not be allowed to pass to the next, but should be given further work either from the regular lessons set forth or from the "suggestions employing similar principles" until he has proven his capability of undertaking the more advanced section. It is not absolutely necessary that all the students of the class be working on projects from the same section at the same time; in fact, too much emphasis cannot be laid upon the matter of giving to each student the work best adapted to his personal development regardless of what the other members of the class may be doing at that time.

On the opening page of each lesson is given a halftone illustration to enable the student to visualize the essential points of the thing which he is about to make. The illustrations will also be found valuable in guiding the students and the teacher in making selection of lessons to be undertaken. The bill of material is given in detail on the same page with the cut, so that as the student thinks of each piece on the bill he may glance at the illustration and thus see its exact application in the finished product. This does not necessarily mean that the stock must be furnished to the student in the number and dimension of pieces given in the bill. It may sometimes be convenient and desirable to furnish the stock in bulk, from which the student is to cut the necessary bill. No definite instructions can be given on this point because of the widely varying conditions in different schools.

The kind of wood suggested for each lesson is not necessarily the only kind which is suitable, but in most of the projects considerable latitude is possible, and such material as is available may be used. But if a substitution is made the student should be told, so he may familiarize himself with whatever kind he is using. In order that the student may have an opportunity of knowing about the tree, its characteristics, nature, function, etc., and may also have certain guiding points in its identification, the references to the supplement are given in each lesson. Students should be required to turn to this supplement and read the discussion of the particular kind of wood which they are using. This reading may be done outside of the shop period or at any other time which the teacher may dictate. It should not, however, be allowed to go by unobserved.

On this same page of each lesson will be found an "introductory statement." The purpose of the introductory statement is to help the student to realize that there is a great community problem in which he should be interested, and that the project which he is about to undertake is a means toward the solution of this problem. Any student will approach his work with greater enthusiasm, wiser judgment and consequently better educational value if he sees that it is a reality, or that it is typical of some of the activities which are going on about him. It is not the purpose of the introductory statement to do anything more than to arouse an interest by suggesting that the community problems exist, as but little space can be devoted to a general discussion of these problems. However, references are given to government bulletins, text-books, magazines and other sources of information to which the student may turn for broader information on the subject. It is urgently advised that these references be followed as far as at all possible, because they will thus unfold a vast field of practical industrial information to the students. Many of these publications can be had without expense and the others can be purchased at a reasonable price; they should therefore be secured for the library and made the nucleus of the equipment for industrial research. It will be found an excellent plan to assign various topics to different students for special reports. This will also supply material for supplementary reading and furnish themes for composition work.

The entire design of the book is not merely to set forth a few plans and drawings for the construction of shop projects, but to give the work the broadest possible application, and thus develop the most points of contact with the various industrial activities of the community.

On the second page of each lesson will be found a simple working drawing for the making of the project as shown in the photograph. These working drawings have been so constructed as to be free from unnecessary technicalities, and to leave as much latitude as possible for the exercise of the judgment of the student. In fact, it has been the effort to make the drawings absolute only in so far as the principles are concerned. On the latter portion of the page will be found "suggestions for original designs." It is not the thought that these suggestions shall cover all of the possibilities which might enter into the construction of the lesson, but they are intended to show the student opportunities and to give him different types upon which he may base his judgment for an original idea. Many teachers may choose to have their students make complete working drawings of their own. In this case it would be well to study the working drawing set forth in the lesson and discuss the various ideas given under the suggestions, pointing out very carefully just which parts will permit of variation without violation of principles. After this sort of consideration (and not before) the students might be called upon to prepare their own working drawings.

The entire spirit throughout this text is to make only absolute principles ironclad, and to leave the way open for every point which will admit of the introduction of the personality of the student. The teacher may quite frequently, particularly if he has had good training and long experience, have other methods that are just as good and possibly even better for his particular class than those set forth in the book, and in such instances he should most certainly feel at liberty to weave his own suggestions into the product of the shop. There are so many possibilities in the various lines of mechanics that no text-book can presume, nor would it be desirable to pretend, to set forth all of the possible and proper ways of doing a piece of work.

On the third page of each lesson will be found "working specifications." The purpose of these specifications is to guide the student so he will undertake his work systematically and will follow his efforts consistently. No attempt is made to show him how to perform each operation nor to "feed him with a spoon" on processes where the exercise of his own capability is most desirable. However, for each process there are references to the supplement, where there will be found, clearly set forth by halftone illustrations and simple discussion, definite methods of performing each operation. It is the idea that where a student is capable of doing the work without assistance it would be detrimental to his best progress to offer him unnecessary aid. However, it is very essential that a means of relief should be available if occasion arises where a student is in need of such help. This will be found a great assistance to the teacher who, when he finds a boy incorrectly performing any process, may simply direct him to turn to the supplement and correct his error. This will place the boy on his own resources, will develop his power of research and instill habits of self-reliance. It is needless to say that the teacher's time will be thus saved to an extent which will increase his capacity many fold. These references will apply also to the subject of tool-sharpening, wood-finishing and drawing.

There is such a wide difference of opinion regarding the relation of drawing to shop work that it is difficult for a text-book to be so prepared as to conform to the ideas of all instructors. For that reason, while throughout this book working drawings are presented, yet in the supplement considerable attention is devoted to the subject, and sufficient material is offered for the average teacher to be able to direct such work in mechanical and shop drawing as should accompany the industrial subjects in the grades for which this text is intended. There is no limit to the amount of geometric construction which may be offered in mechanical drawing work; however, in order to make this work as practical as possible, abstract problems have been reduced to the minimum and the production of shop drawings has been emphasized. It is left to the option of the teacher as to whether this drawing work is to be taken up as a separate subject and given a specific period per week, or whether it should be given as a part of the shop work and each student be required to prepare his own drawings for each project before undertaking it.

For the staining and the finishing of the models only a few suggestions are given, for it is felt that this matter should be left very largely to the taste of the student and the judgment of the teacher who best understands local conditions. Instead of giving specific instructions for the finished work on each lesson, references are made to the supplement for the kind of finish which would be appropriate. The matter of color and number of coats and fineness of polish is merely suggested and left for its final decision to the instructor in charge.

Under the heading, "Original Projects Employing Similar Principles," there will be found a number of suggestions which will furnish additional kindred work which may be utilized as local conditions suggest. There may be adept students or those who wish to work extra hours for whom these suggestions will be found quite beneficial. No attempt is made to furnish drawings or illustrations, but simply a few guiding suggestions are given for the purpose of directing the attention of the student to the principles which should be observed. For undertakings of this character it will be necessary for the students to work out their own designs and make their complete working drawings. These projects will offer possibilities for home work, for contests on outside efforts and for the making of things which may be used in school exhibits or auction sales, which are sometimes resorted to in assisting to raise money. Students should be encouraged to give considerable attention to these original projects, but care must be exercised on the part of the teacher to prevent violation of principles, and the students should be led to see that their originality must cover only such points as will admit of modification without destroying the function of the article. For illustration, in making a T-square, the shape, length, width and thickness of the head, also the dimensions of the blade, are largely matters of personal choice, but that the edges of the blade and of the head must be perfect, straight lines, and must be set at right angles are absolute principles which the originality of the maker cannot in any way modify. In almost every project there are some such absolute principles which are inviolable, and these (and these alone) are the things upon which this text endeavors to be ironclad.

The review questions and problems found at the close of each section are given as an aid to the teacher in developing the correlation between the industrial work and the other subjects, particularly with the arithmetic. These problems are not all arithmetical, however; they deal with number conception, not with the idea of presenting the problems under a classified head, as they are often found in arithmetic, but so arranged that they will test the judgment of the student and make him feel that he is dealing with real questions rather than that he is handling problems which were made only for the sake of furnishing him something to do. These problems will serve as a guide in preparing as many others as the time and needs of a particular class may dictate.

The "suggestions for community research" constitute the connecting link between the work of the shop and the activities of the home and the community. The teacher should lay great emphasis upon this work, for there is no other way by which so much community interest can be aroused as by having all of the students constantly on the alert to gather information from the activities about them and carry it into the schoolroom. Parental support can be most heartily enlisted and the good will of the community acquired by having the students enter into this co-operative plan of civic development.

The reference work indicated in this text will give the students a margin of technical information which they may impart to their parents and neighbors in return for their practical ideas and experience, and thus every factor of the community will profit by the encouragement of this research work. This movement is replete with possibilities in connection with reports and discussions in which both students and patrons might participate, in parent-teachers' clubs, farmers' institutes and other community gatherings. There is no way more sure nor more economic in making a good citizen of a boy than to develop his interests in community problems during the period of his plastic age.

# INSTRUCTIONS TO STUDENTS

IN undertaking this shop work you will find many things which are a little different to the regular recitation work to which you have been accustomed in the other subjects. Here you will have a chance to learn by doing as well as by thinking, and also to use some of the experience which you have had at home and elsewhere. There are so many activities going on about you that you are constantly meeting with many different kinds of material; the purpose of this work will be to help you to understand those things.

Shop work is not merely to furnish you employment for your hands, but to teach you to think as well as work, for skillful work comes only from hands that are properly guided by the mind. There are so many valuable and interesting things presented in these lessons that you have a chance to select such things which you desire to make. But before making your selection you should discuss it with your teacher. After you have made a selection and commenced a piece of work, complete it to the very best of your ability before leaving it. Sometimes a student wants to leave a piece of work before it is done; this disposition encourages very bad habits and is sure to develop a boy into an unsuccessful business man if it is continued. Always complete a task when you undertake it, even though you may find some portions of it a little difficult.

In every lesson there are illustrations showing you just how the finished product will appear. The bill of material tells you exactly what lumber, hardware and other supplies are necessary in making the article. The material may not be furnished to you in exactly the number of pieces and sizes given in the bill, but with a little thought you will be able to cut the required pieces from stock lumber. In cutting from stock always be very careful to avoid wasting material. Always read over the bill and look at the picture and see if you can tell for which portion of the article each piece is intended.

The introductory statement on the first page should be very carefully read, for this will give you an idea of the purpose of the thing which you are to make and you will thus see that it is valuable from a practical standpoint. The references given at the bottom of the page are of great importance, not so much in training your hand as in teaching you to think accurately and to understand some of the great questions which are so important to men who are running the affairs of the world. If you have access to a good library you will be well paid for the effort of looking up all these references and studying them in detail. It would be an excellent plan to keep a notebook and write notes on such articles as are of particular interest. This information will be quite valuable in a very few years, when you are called upon to earn your way in the world and compete with men who are carrying on the activities of your community.

On the next page of each lesson you will find complete working drawings showing the shape and dimensions of every piece. You must not expect to understand a drawing perfectly at the first glance; it will require careful study of every drawing to be able to make your work as it should be. If you do not understand how to read drawings, turn to the chapter on mechanical and working drawings and study this chapter very carefully, for it will enable you to understand just how the drawings are made. All shop drawings are made on the same principles. The purpose of this chapter is to explain those things to you.

On the lower portion of this drawing space is given a number of ideas which you may use if you desire. This does not mean that the ways given on this page are the only ways in which an article can be made, but these are some of the ways which are quite often used. In many of the lessons you may be able to pick out some original plan which you will desire to use; it would be well for you to discuss your plan with your teacher, or possibly your parents, or some one who has had experience, and find out the good and poor points in your plan. If you work out a plan of your own, it would be very desirable for you to make a complete working drawing before undertaking the work. Your teacher will no doubt advise on this matter.

The working specifications on the next page are intended to assist you in making each part. These specifications do not attempt to tell you everything which you are expected to do. You are left to think for yourself. The references given in parentheses refer to the chapters in the supplement at the close of the book. If you are told to perform any sort of tool operation and do not understand it, turn back to the supplement and you will find an explanation, and possibly illustrations showing you exactly how this particular process should be executed. You should study these explanations very carefully and perform the processes accordingly. Do not fail to look up all of the references so you can be sure that you are handling your tools properly.

The suggestions for optional projects employing similar principles are intended to awaken your thought and to furnish you something to do during outside periods or home work. The principles which you gather from these lessons should be made valuable to you in your practical everyday life. If you will think very carefully you will notice that each suggestion guides you in the making of things which will be quite useful; they are of course not exactly like the things which you have made in the shop, but they employ the same principles, and you should be able to make them without any difficulty.

The real value which you get out of this work will depend very largely upon your ability to make useful articles about your home. The making of any one project in itself might not be of any great importance to you, but what you learn in making that thing may save you a great many dollars. Keep this in mind and try to learn as much as possible from whatever you are making; you can do this only by giving it your best attention and doing it the very best you know how. Some students have the habit of going to the teacher and asking whether a piece of work is 'good enough.' No piece of work is good enough unless it is the very best that you can do. Keep in mind that if you expect a piece of work to be beautiful and perfect when completed it must be correctly done from the very start. A little error in the beginning of a piece of work is quite likely to be evident when the thing is finished. The time to commence being careful is when you begin the project.

Another important thing which you are to learn from this work is the value of having a place for everything and keeping it in its proper place. There is no one subject in school which will give you such an excellent opportunity to show that you have habits of orderly arrangements. Always keep your tools in the proper place on your bench. See that your tools are kept sharp and clean. When you are through with your bench, remove the scraps, put the tools in the proper places and brush the dust from your bench. A business man would not want to employ a young man who has careless habits. The only way to develop habits of neatness and care is to practice such things in all of your work.

Be sure that you do not overlook the suggestions for community research. These suggestions will guide you into some of the most interesting things in connection with your school work.

There will be a great many things found out in this research work which will be worth while to enter in your notebook. You may not now see the value of keeping a notebook, but you will appreciate it after a few years.

The questions and problems are intended to point out to you some things worth remembering. So even though some of these questions and problems may seem a little difficult, it will be well worth your while to think about them and find the solution. It is not the things that are easiest done that give us most strength, so, even though some of the things may be difficult, approach them with a good will and determination and you will soon be quite proud of the results.

You should equip yourself, if possible, with a bench and some tools in some sort of shop so that you could do work at home. It does not require a separate building nor very much space; a corner in the garage, tool shed, barn or basement would answer very satisfactorily. You could make your own bench, following the instructions given in this text, and it would not require very much expense to equip yourself with the necessary tools. You no doubt could find some of the tools about your home; they would probably be satisfactory if put in good condition. Remember that one of the principal things in the use of tools is to have them sharp and free from rust, and kept where you can find them without loss of time. From time to time you could add a few tools to your stock, and in the course of a year or so be well supplied with the necessary tools for ordinary tasks.

Your parents would no doubt rather pay you for making a screen window or repairing a door or doing some other such task, and allow you to have the money for tools, than to have a mechanic come and do it. Possibly you may never care to become a carpenter or a woodworker of any sort, but nevertheless it will always be quite valuable to you to be able to handle tools with skill and to have a knowledge of good work when you see it.

A knowledge of the different kinds of wood and how they are finished will also be quite valuable to you. This information may save you a great many dollars in the purchase of furniture some time during your life.

# INTRODUCTION TO SECTION I

IN this section will be found an introduction to elementary tool processes and the simpler hand tools. The laying out tools, such as the ruler, try-square and marking gauge are introduced. The plane, hammer, saw, coping saw, brace and bit, screwdriver, wood file and sandpaper are brought in with easy applications of their use.

The projects of this section are all soft wood models and should thus give the student but little difficulty in executing tool processes. While not all of the projects are identical in processes set forth, yet they are so planned and presented as to deal with such principles as the student should master early in his work.

It is strongly advised that each student be required to make his own working drawings after making a careful study of those given and of the suggestions for optional design.

The assembling work throughout this section will be found very simple, consisting of no mortise and tenon or other difficult joints. The staining and polishing is largely optional, but can be very satisfactorily done by referring to the references in the supplement, where detailed instructions are given for this work.

The home research work following this section is not limited to the interest aroused by these projects, but is based on a broader view, which may be derived from the references. As many as possible of these should be given careful study and some discussion in class.

Before a student is ready to leave this section he should be able to read and interpret simple working drawings. He should be able to make accurate measurements with the ruler, to use the try-square in scoring and in testing edges, to regulate and adjust his plane and to plane a straight edge. He should have but little difficulty with the marking gauge and should have had sufficient experience with the ripsaw and cross-cutting saw to be able to use them without developing incorrect habits. He should have acquired sufficient judgment to be able to use a hammer, boring tools and screwdriver in simple assembling work.

If the student has acquired a high ideal of excellence in this first section, and understands that each process must be executed to the very best of his ability before undertaking another one, the particular processes covered by the section need not be a matter of deep concern.

# MATCH BOX

MATERIALS.

Basswood (Chap. III., Par. 31).

1 pc. 1/4"x4"x8 1/2" S 2 S Back.
3 pcs. 1/4"x2 1/4"x9" S 2 S Sides, front and bottom.
1 pc. sandpaper 2"x2".
20-3/4" No. 18 brads.

## INTRODUCTORY STATEMENT.

We all know that it is an excellent plan to have a place for everything and then see that things are kept in their proper places. A great deal of valuable time can be saved by being able to find what you want when you want it.

Some things can be carelessly laid about without any great danger, but this is not true of matches; if left in an improper place they may be the cause of great damage.

This match box will be very valuable for home use in furnishing a handy and safe place in which to keep the supply of matches. It should be hung on the wall, not too close to the stove or heat pipes and high enough to be out of the reach of small children.

If we could know how many buildings are destroyed by fire every year because of carelessness, we would understand why every one should do his part in preventing this needless waste.

---

**References:**

"How Matches Are Made," Industries of Today, by Lane. Ginn Co., Publisher.
"American Inventions and Inventors," by Mowry. Silver-Burdett Co.
"The Match"—Stories of Useful Inventions, by Forman. The Century Pub. Co.
Fire Prevention, Crocker. Dodd, Mead & Co.
Protection Against Fire, Bird. Hurd & Houghton.
Fire Department Journal, New York City.

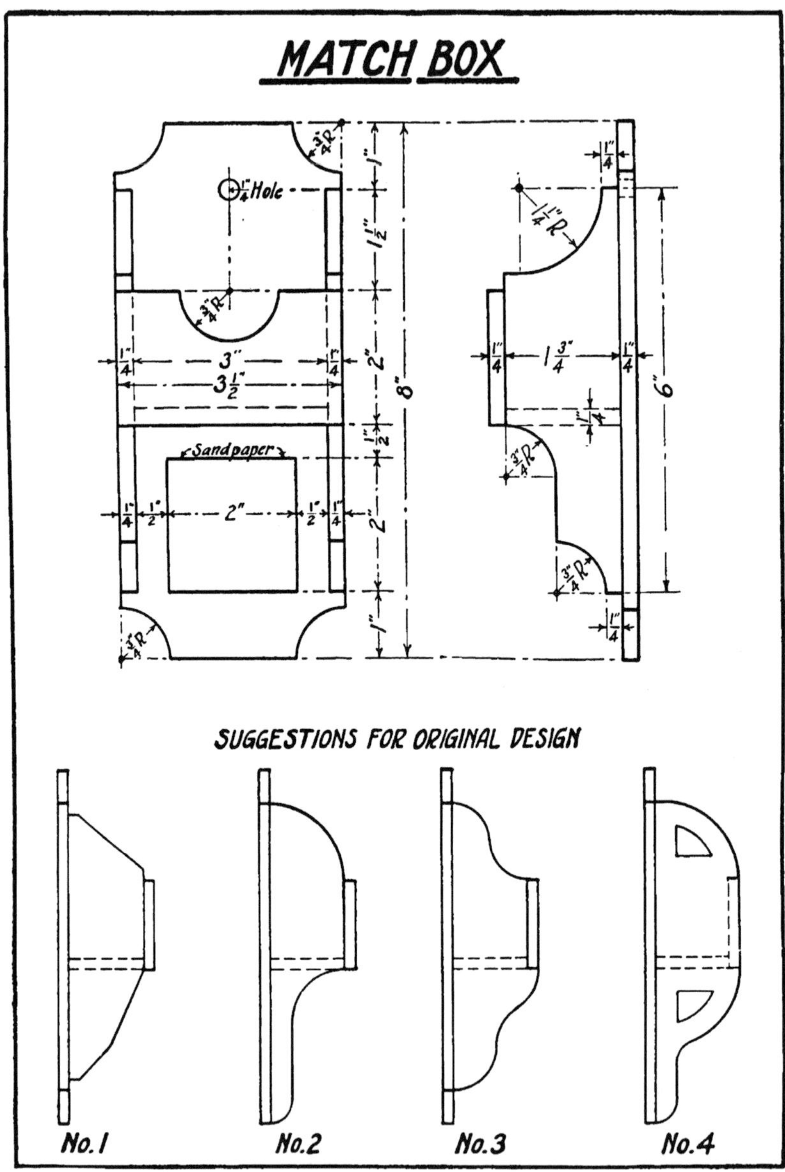
MATCH BOX
1/4" Hole
3/4" R
1 1/4" R
3"
3 1/2"
Sandpaper
2"
1"
1 1/2"
8"
6"
1 3/4"
SUGGESTIONS FOR ORIGINAL DESIGN
No. 1
No. 2
No. 3
No. 4

# MATCH BOX SPECIFICATIONS

## THE BACK.

Select the best side of the back piece for the working face. As this material is furnished S 2 S (planed or smooth on two sides), you will not need to plane the surface. Mark this, the Working Face (Chapter II., Paragraph 2).

Plane one edge perfectly straight (Chapter II., Paragraph 4). Gauge the exact width on both surfaces (Chapter II., Paragraph 6); carefully plane to the gauge lines.

Lay out the design which you are to use for the back. If you are to use the one given in the working drawing, be sure to make the measurements carefully, and lay it out very accurately. Saw out with the coping saw, smooth the edges with the wood file and sandpaper.

## THE SIDES.

Two of the pieces $\frac{1}{4}''$ by $2\frac{1}{4}''$x9" are for the sides. If you do not wish to use the design given in the drawing, draw a design of your own before attempting to lay out the sides. Plane one edge of one of the pieces of material perfectly straight, and use this for a working edge (Chapter II., Paragraph 4). Make all measurements from this edge and lay out the design for the side. Saw out with the coping saw and smooth the edges as you did the back piece. Make the second piece exactly like the first.

## THE BOTTOM AND FRONT.

The piece $\frac{1}{4}''$x$2\frac{1}{4}''$x9" is large enough to make both the bottom and front of your match box. Plane one edge perfectly straight and square (Chapter II., Paragraph 4). Plane one end perfectly square (Chapter II., Paragraph 5); measure and cut the length of the bottom. Gauge the width of the bottom (Chapter II., Paragraph 6). This, you will notice, is exactly the same as the width of the side.

## THE FRONT.

Plane one edge of the front for a working edge (Chapter II., Paragraph 4). Square one end (Chapter II., Paragraph 5); measure and cut the length of the front. Be sure to cut it perfectly square. Gauge the width of the front piece and plane to the gauge line (Chapter II., Paragraph 6). Lay out, cut and smooth the half-circle in the front piece.

## ASSEMBLING.

Test the two sides to be sure they are exactly the same width. Try the front piece, and see if it is just as long as the back piece is wide. Make sure that the bottom is perfectly rectangular and exactly the same width as the sides. The match box is to be assembled with plain butt joints (Chapter V., Paragraph 60) fastened with brads. The edges, however, should be spread with a very little glue. Do not use too much or it will spread out and soil the outside surfaces of the joints. You will have to be very careful in driving the brads to prevent splitting out (Chapter II., Paragraph 21).

## FINISHING.

When the match box is completely assembled, clean it all over. It may be necessary in some places to take off a very thin shaving with a sharp plane. With the sandpaper and wood file make sure that the edges are perfectly even and all the surfaces free from glue, tool marks or soiled places. The match box should have a finish of some sort, which you may choose for yourself. It might be stained a desirable color (Chapter IV., Paragraph 54), and shellaced (Chapter IV., Paragraph 57). If you wish it to be the natural color of the wood, it should be given one or two coats of shellac.

**Optional and Home Projects Employing Similar Principles.**

## COMB CASE.

1. A very pretty comb case may be made after the same fashion as this match box. It would have to be wider so the box would receive a long comb.

## LETTER BOX.

2. In using this plan for a letter box, it would be necessary to make the box deeper and wider to provide room for long letters and papers. The material should be thicker.

## WRENCH OR GREASE BOX.

3. In the tool shed or garage a box of this kind will be found a great convenience in furnishing a place for the wrenches, oil can or grease box.

## WHISK BROOM HOLDER.

4. A very satisfactory whisk broom holder could be made by leaving out the piece which forms the bottom, making the front a little wider and setting the sides so they would be somewhat closer together at the bottom than at the top.

# NECKTIE RACK

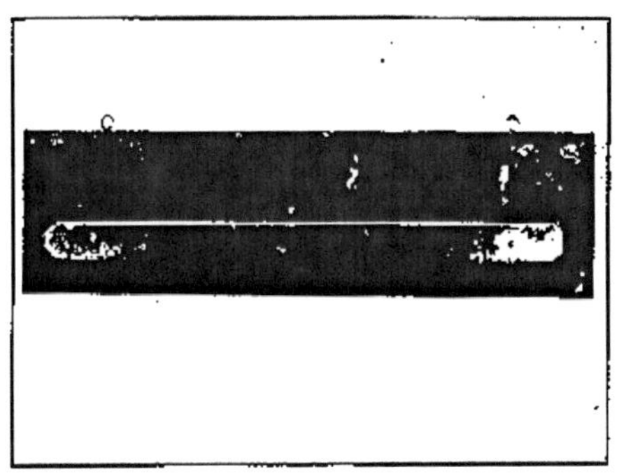

MATERIALS.

Basswood (Chap. III., Par. 31).

1 pc. 3/8"x4 3/4"x16 1/2" S 2 S Back.
1 pc. 3/8"x1 1/2"x 8" S 2 S Brackets.
1 pc. 1/4"x1 1/4"x14 1/2" S 2 S Cross rod.
2-3/4" No. 6 R. H. brass screws.
2 screw eyes, No. 114.
6-1" brads, No. 17.

INTRODUCTORY STATEMENT.

It is a very great convenience to keep the things of daily use where they can be had without any loss of time or patience. Successful business men say that the boy who learns to be careful and orderly in his daily habits has learned the greatest secret of business success.

While the necktie rack provides a handy place for one's ties, so they can always be found when wanted, it also helps to keep the ties smooth, free from wrinkles and in good condition for wear.

Do not forget that the value of this article, like most all conveniences, depends upon what use you make of it. Try to make it so perfectly that in appearance as well as in service it will be an attractive article for your room.

---

References:

Handicraft for Handy Boys, Hall. Lathrop, Lee & Shepard Co., Boston.
Boys' Make at Home Things, Bailey. Frederick A. Stokes, Pub.
The Boy Craftsman, A. Neely Hall. Lathrop, Lee & Shepard Co., Boston.
Trees That Every Child Should Know, Rogers. Doubleday, Page & Co.

# NECKTIE RACK

SUGGESTIONS FOR ORIGINAL DESIGN

No. 1

No. 2

No. 3

No. 4

# NECKTIE RACK SPECIFICATIONS

## THE BACK.

The piece 3/8"x4 3/4"x16 1/2" is for the back of your necktie rack. It is furnished S 2 S, so it will not be necessary for you to plane your surface; however, you can sandpaper it to make it perfectly smooth and clean (Chapter II., Paragraph 17). If you have made an original design for the back you should lay out your design on this board and then cut it out. If you are following the drawing given, first plane one edge of the board perfectly straight and square for a working edge (Chapter II., Paragraph 4). Square one end, plane it perfectly smooth with the block plane (Chapter II., Paragraph 5). Measure the length which the back is to be; square off this end and plane smooth with a block plane. Gauge the width and plane to the gauge line (Chapter II., Paragraph 6). With your lead pencil and ruler, or pencil and finger, gauge a pencil line all around the edges for the chamfer (Chapter II., Paragraph 7-8).

## The Brackets.

Lay out a design for the end brackets. This design should be laid out carefully on a piece of paper before you attempt to draw it on your material. The suggestion for original designs will give you a number of ideas from which you should be able to work out something of your own. This design should be drawn freehand, or with the use of a ruler and compasses. It might be well to cut out one bracket, and use it for a pattern in laying out the other one to make sure that the two are exactly alike. These brackets may be cut with a coping saw. The edges and surfaces must be made perfectly smooth with a wood file and sandpaper.

## THE FRONT STRIP.

Plane one edge perfectly straight and smooth (Chapter II., Paragraph 4), gauge the width with the marking gauge (Chapter II., Paragraph 6). Carefully plane to the gauge line. Cut it the proper length and shape the ends.

## ASSEMBLING.

The brackets are to be fastened to the back piece with glue and brads from the back side. Test with a try-square and be sure that the brackets stand straight up and down, and exactly the same distance from each end. The front piece is to be put on with two round head screws. You should bore a hole through the front piece for the screws. Make the holes just large enough to receive the body of the screw. With a brad awl, make holes to start the screws into the brackets. When the screws are tight, they should stand with their eyes either straight up and down or straight across. Whenever screws are used as a part of the decoration of a piece of work, care should be taken to have the screw slots all stand parallel or in straight lines.

## FINISHING.

You may stain your necktie rack a desirable color (Chapter IV., Paragraph 54). Be sure to stain the back side as well as the front side on all pieces. In this way you can prevent warping. It also makes the work much neater in appearance. Finish with shellac (Chapter IV., Paragraph 57) or wax finish (Chapter IV., Paragraph 56). Insert the two screw eyes, as shown in the drawing.

**Optional and Home Projects Employing Similar Principles.**

## RIBBON RACK.

1. This same idea might be used to make a very pretty ribbon rack; if desired the back might be shaped or carved with some decorative design.

## TOWEL ROD.

2. By constructing the back and sides of heavier material, possibly 5/8″ or 3/4″, and using a round rod, which might be a piece of 3/4″ dowel, a very satisfactory towel rod could be made.

## TOWEL ROLLER.

3. By making a round tenon on each end of the rod and making the holes in the brackets large enough for it to turn easily, a towel roller may be constructed.

## PAPER RACK.

4. By making the side brackets considerably longer, and using two or three strips across the front, and providing a bottom, this same plan can be used in making a paper or magazine rack to hang on the wall.

# HAND LOOM

MATERIALS.

Basswood (Chap. III., Par. 31), or any soft wood.

2 pcs. ¾"x1¾"x12" S 2 S Ends.

2 pcs. ⅜"x1½"x13" S 2 S Sides.

8 dozen 1" No. 17 brads.

## INTRODUCTORY STATEMENT.

One of the oldest and most important of all industries is the art of weaving. Before people understood how to make cloth in this way clothing was made principally from hides of animals, and even after the process of weaving was begun it had to be done entirely by hand on very rude looms.

Cloth is made by various ways of plaiting threads; these threads usually run at right angles to each other and are known as warp and woof threads. The warp threads extend the long way of the cloth and are therefore parallel with the selvage edge; the woof threads extend across the warp threads from one selvage edge to the other.

This hand loom may be used to illustrate the principle of weaving by which all of our clothing is made today. You will find it very interesting to look up some of the following references regarding this very important industry:

---

**References:**


What Can Be Done in a Hand Loom, by Mabel Priestman, in American Homes and Gardens Magazine, June, 1909.

Cotton Weaving, by R. Marsden. Geo. Bell & Sons, New York, Pub.

Hand Loom Weaving, Mattie Phipps Todd. Rand-McNally, Pub.

"The Textile Industry"—The Origin of Invention, Mason. Charles Scribner's Sons, Pub.

Silk, Its Origin and Culture, The Corticelli Mills, Florence, Mass.

The Silk Worm and Its Silk. Belding Brothers & Co., Chicago, Ill.

Silk and Silk Manufacture. Cheney Brothers, South Manchester, Conn.

How the World Is Clothed, Carpenter. American Book Co.

The Tree Book, Rogers. Doubleday, Page & Co.

# HAND LOOM

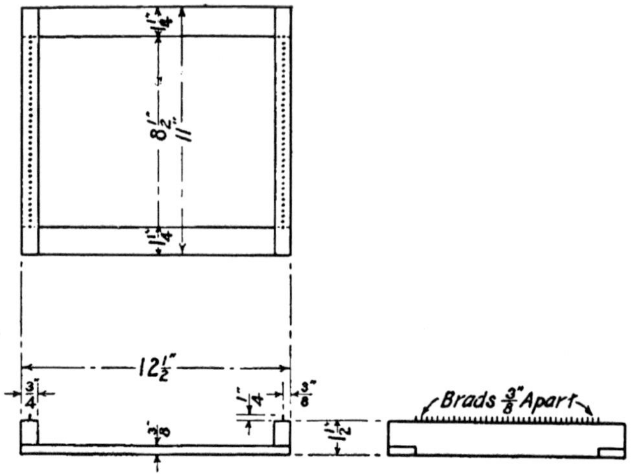

SUGGESTIONS FOR ORIGINAL DESIGN

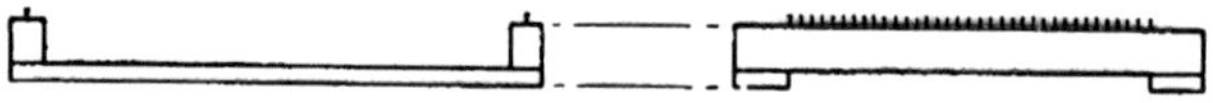

No. 1

No. 2

# HAND LOOM SPECIFICATIONS

## ENDS.

As the material is furnished S 2 S, you will not need to plane the surfaces. Plane one edge of the end pieces (¾"x1¾"x 12") perfectly straight and square (Chapter II., Paragraph 4). With the marking gauge, gauge the width of this piece on both surfaces (Chapter II., Paragraph 6). Carefully plane to the gauge line. Plane one end perfectly square (Chapter II., Paragraph 5). Measure the length and square off the other end. In small pieces of material a wood file is often used instead of the block plane in smoothing the ends.

## SIDE STRIPS.

Plane one edge of the side strips perfectly straight and square (Chapter II., Paragraph 4). With the marking gauge, gauge the width on both surfaces, and plane carefully to the gauge line (Chapter II., Paragraph 6). Square one end (Chapter II., Paragraph 5). From this end measure the length and square the other end. Make the two side pieces exactly the same length and the same width. The side pieces may be nailed on to the ends, as shown in the first suggestion for original design, but it will be very much stronger if you will follow the drawing in gaining, or notching, the end pieces into the side pieces. These gains should be cut so that the side pieces will exactly fill them.

## ASSEMBLING.

This piece of work is to be assembled with glue and brads. Use a very little glue and spread evenly so it will not spread out, and soil the outside surfaces of your work. Test it with a try-square, and be sure that you assemble the work perfectly square. After the work is completely assembled, clean and smooth all the surfaces with the wood file and sandpaper (Chapter II., Paragraph 17). Do not destroy the corners in sandpapering. Fine workmen are always careful to respect the corners of their work, taking great care not to rub them off with the sandpaper.

## FINISHING.

This piece of work should be finished with shellac. You may stain it if you desire, but it is not necessary. Shellac will keep the wood clean and free from dirt (Chapter IV., Paragraph 57).

When the finish is thoroughly dry, with a pencil and finger, gauge a line (Chapter II., Paragraph 8) for the brads on each end piece. Set the compasses with their points as far apart as the distance between the brads, and step off the spaces on each line. The sharp points of the compasses will make convenient holes in which to start the brads. Drive the brads into the end pieces, as indicated in the drawing. These brads are to hold the warp thread for the weaving. The brads must be very carefully driven, exactly the same distance apart, so they will stand in a straight line.

**Optional and Home Projects Employing Similar Principles.**

## QUILTING FRAMES.

1. The plan of a rectangular frame made of strips can be used in making simple quilting frames. The frame should not be permanently assembled, but fastened at each corner by a large nail, or wooden pin dropped through holes in the strips. There should be several holes in each strip so the size of the frame may be adjusted.

## CURTAIN STRETCHERS.

2. Curtain stretchers may be made on this same plan of a rectangular frame. Some arrangements should be made for adjusting the size of the frame. This may be done by providing a long slot in one end of the strips, and assembling them with small bolts fitted with butterfly nuts. Each strip should have a straight row of small brads near its edge upon which to fasten the curtains.

# BOX KITE

## MATERIALS.

Pine (Chap. III., Par. 48) or any soft wood.

4 pcs. 5/16"x5/16"x30" S 2 S Corner strips.
2 pcs. 5/16"x5/16"x23" S 2 S Cross braces.
5 pcs. 5/16"x5/16"x12" S 2 S Braces.
Paper and string not furnished.

## INTRODUCTORY STATEMENT.

Almost everyone has had some experience with kites, but most people consider them merely interesting toys without realizing how much can be learned by studying different kinds of kites, how and why they fly and what these principles mean in modern inventions.

We all remember what Benjamin Franklin learned from his kite experiment, but in the last few years much more has been accomplished in the line of airships, most of which has been due to a knowledge of the science of kite flying.

There are many different styles and kinds of kites, but they all mount the air by the same general principles. By a little careful study and experimenting you can learn to make kites and fly them in a scientific and accurate way.

---

**References:**

The Construction and Flying of Kites, Miller. Manual Arts Press, Peoria, Ill.
Kitecraft and Kite Tournaments, Miller. Manual Arts Press, Peoria, Ill.
Kitecraft. School Arts Book, February, 1910.
Flying Machines, J. H. Alexander. David Williams Co., New York.
Building and Flying an Aeroplane, Hayward. Popular Mechanics Book Dept., Chicago.
Flying Machines, The Boys' Book of Inventions, Baker. McClure, Phillips Co.
Santos Dumont and His Airship—Stories of Inventors. Doubleday, Page & Co.
The Aeroplane, Boys' Book of New Inventions. Doubleday, Page & Co.
Practical Aeronautics, Hayward. American Technical Society, Chicago.
Our Native Trees, Harriet Keeler. Chas. Scribner's Sons.

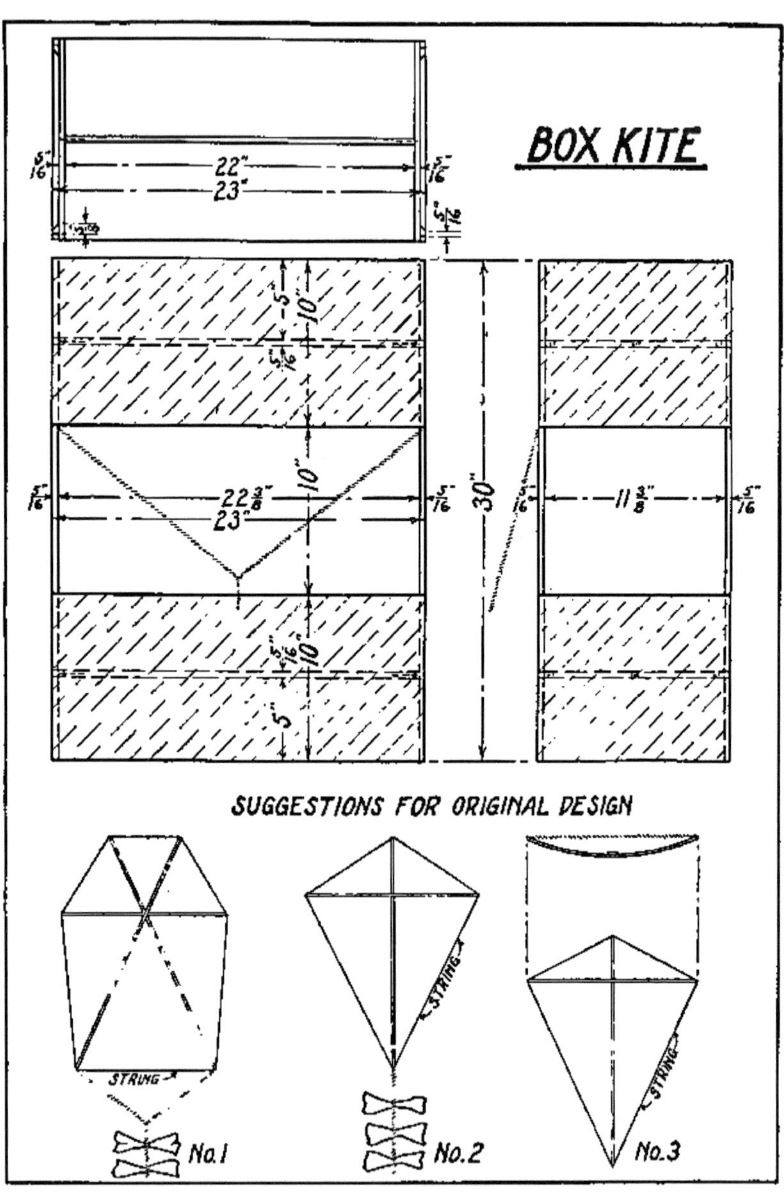
BOX KITE
22"
23"
5/16"
10"
5"
22 3/8"
30"
11 3/8"
SUGGESTIONS FOR ORIGINAL DESIGN
STRING
No.1
No.2
No.3

# BOX KITE SPECIFICATIONS

## THE CORNER STRIPS.

You will probably have to rip your kite strips from stock. If you do, select the best surface for a working face (Chapter II., Paragraph 2). Plane one edge perfectly straight and square for a working edge (Chapter II., Paragraph 4). With the marking gauge set to the proper distance, gauge the width of the strips on both surfaces of the material (Chapter II., Paragraph 6).

NOTE:—If your material is quite thin and soft, you may be able to split it after gauging it very deeply on both surfaces; if not, use a knife or saw. Plane the edge. In planing a thin strip you must be very careful to use a sharp plane set to take a very thin shaving or you may break the strip.

In like manner prepare all of the strips. Cut the four corner strips exactly the same length.

NOTE:—This kite is to be so assembled that it can be taken down and rolled up when not in use. The two side frames are fastened permanently with glue and brads, but these frames are attached to each other only by the bottom and top stretchers. These stretchers each have a brad driven in the end, and extending far enough to enter small holes in the side cross rails, thus holding the kite in shape.

## SIDE CROSS RAILS.

Make the four side cross rails the required dimensions. (Be sure they are exactly the same length). Fasten them to the corner strips with small brads; cut short blocks about 3/4" long, and glue them on the side cross rails against the corner strips to reinforce the joints. Do this on all the joints. Make the two side frames exactly the same size.

## THE PAPER COVERING.

Select a good tough paper (not too heavy). Cut a strip long enough to go entirely around the kite frame, allowing 2" for lapping. Cut it about 1½" wider than called for in the drawing so it may be turned over 3/4" on each edge. Lay the paper flat on the floor, or on a long table, spread an even coating of glue along each edge, covering a margin of about 3/4". Lay a string perfectly straight the full length of the paper about 3/4" from the edge, and fold the glued edge over the string, thus forming a very strong margin for the paper. Prepare both edges of each piece in similar manner.

Determine the length required to cover the kite frame and glue the ends of each piece of paper togther, forming a complete circular band of each. Be sure the two are exactly the same size.

## ASSEMBLING.

With a brad awl bore a small hole in the center of each side cross rail to receive the brads. Drive a brad in one end of one of the stretchers, place the side frames inside the paper bands, and with one end of the stretcher in its proper place, spread the kite into its desired shape and measure the length to cut this stretcher. Cut it long enough so that when in position the paper will be stretched perfectly smooth. In like manner cut the second stretcher. Insert brads in the second end of each stretcher.

## THE BRIDLE.

Attach the bridle to the corner strips, as indicated in the drawing; the strings may be simply tied around the corner strips in small notches to prevent slipping. A more substantial way of attaching the bridle is to use a piece of small, flat braid moistened in glue and wrapped around the corner strips so as to form loops to which the bridle may be attached.

### Optional and Home Projects Employing Similar Principles.

## PLAIN KITE WITH TAIL.

1. The plain flat kite with two or three sticks, may be made as shown in suggestions Nos. 1 and 2. This kind of kite requires a tail, which serves as a balance, and prevents darting. The bridle should be attached to each of the sticks a short distance from the central point; these strings are all brought together and tied a few inches from the face of the kite. The flying string is attached to this bridle.

## TAILLESS KITE.

2. The tailless kites are very interesting and the most difficult to make; they cannot be made flat like the kites which have tails, but must be considerably bowed, as shown in suggestion No. 3. The paper covering should be very loose. The bridle is attached on the outside of the bow; that is, so the wind blows against the rounding side of the kite as it goes up.

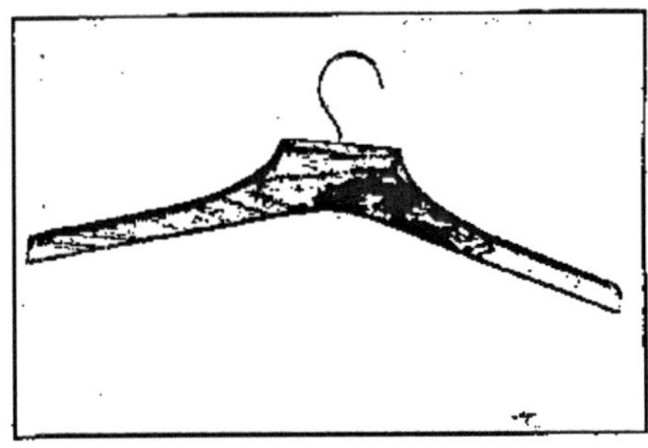

# COAT HANGER

MATERIALS.

Poplar (Chap. III., Par. 42) or any soft wood.

1 pc. ⅞"x4¾"x18" S 2 S Hanger.

1 pc. Cop. Bess. rod 5/32" x8" Hook.

1 Cop. washer 5/32".

## INTRODUCTORY STATEMENT.

A coat hanger should be more than simply a place to hang a coat; it should be so shaped as to keep the coat from wrinkling. This design provides a support for the collar, which is often omitted in a shop-made coat hanger. Notice in the picture that the top is not a continuous curve. If you will experiment by hanging the coat on a hanger made with a continual curve, and then on a hanger made like the illustration, you will see how much more satisfactorily this shape protects the form of the shoulders and collar of the coat.

A pole such as a dowel rod or a broomstick furnishes the most convenient arrangement for a wardrobe, because it will hold a great many coat hangers like this without crushing the garment. This pole is simply a horizontal rod placed at the convenient height and so none of the garments will touch the wall when they are hanging in position.

---

**References:**

Home Occupations for Boys. George W. Jacobs & Co.
Handy Book for Boys, D. C. Beard. Chas. Scribner's Sons.
Educational Woodwork for Home and School. Park-Macmillan Co.
The Boy Mechanic, Windsor. Popular Mechanics Co., Chicago, Ill.
Boys' Useful Pastimes, Griffith. Book Supply Co., Chicago.
Timber and Logging, How the World is Housed, Carpenter. American Book Co.

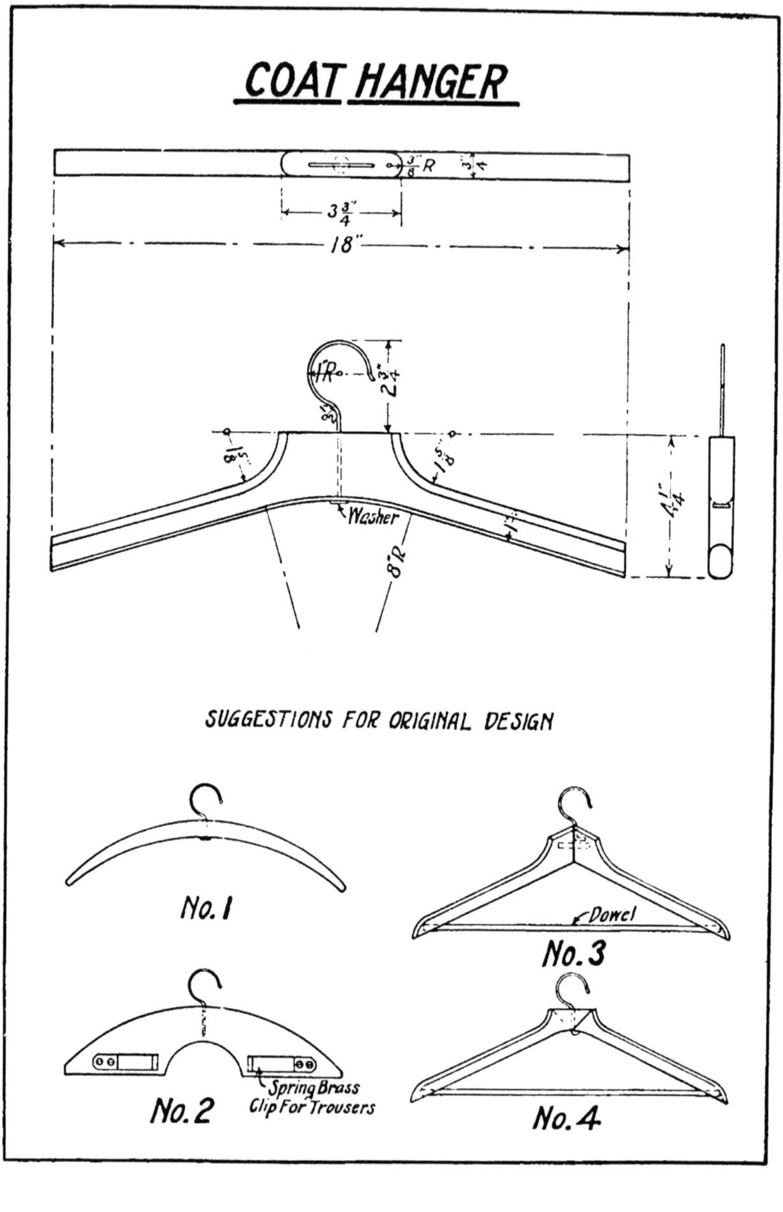

# COAT HANGER

$\frac{3}{8}$" R

$\frac{3}{4}$"

$3\frac{3}{4}$"

18"

1" R

$2\frac{3}{4}$"

$1\frac{5}{8}$"

$1\frac{5}{8}$"

Washer

8" R

1"

$4\frac{1}{4}$"

SUGGESTIONS FOR ORIGINAL DESIGN

No. 1

Dowel

No. 3

Spring Brass Clip For Trousers

No. 2

No. 4

# COAT HANGER SPECIFICATIONS

If this piece of material is furnished S 2 S, it will not be necessary for you to plane the surface, for it will be smooth enough for you to lay out your work. Select the best surface, and make it the working face (Chapter II., Paragraph 2) ; plane one edge perfectly straight and square (Chapter II., Paragraph 4) for a working edge. Plane one end perfectly square with the working edge and the working face (Chapter II., Paragraph 5). It will not be necessary for you to plane the other edge, nor the other end, but you should make all measurements from the working edge and working end. With a lead pencil, carefully lay out the work on the working face. You will see in the drawing that some of the curves are to be laid out with the compasses; some of these may be drawn free hand. You may use your own ideas in laying out this piece of work, but it is most important that you make the two sides of the coat hanger alike. Whatever curves you use must be the same on both sides. With the turning saw, or coping saw, saw as laid out. With the drawing knife, or wood file, carefully round all the curved edges of the coat hanger.

In the front view, as shown in the drawing, the inside line indicates where the round edge begins. You may leave a well-defined line here on each surface of the work, or round it down, making a perfect, continuous curve, as you see fit. Sometimes the under side of a coat hanger is not rounded; you may leave these edges square if you like. Be sure that you remove all irregularities, making the coat hanger perfectly smooth.

## THE HOOK.

You are to make your own hook from a piece of bessemer rod. (If you do not care to do this, you may purchase a screw hook from a hardware store). You will find it a very interesting piece of work to make your own hook. It is not a difficult task, and if you are careful you can easily do it. If your shop is provided with an iron cone, or a visc anvil, you can readily bend the bessemer rod the desired shape. If you do not have the cone, you might be able to find a small piece of old iron pipe, or other cylinder, which would answer very well. A round (cylindrical) piece of hard wood might be prepared on purpose for this work. Grasp the rod (near the end) firmly with the pliers, and form the hook by wrapping it around the cylinder. A few light blows with the hammer will complete the bending. Do not hammer the rod unnecessarily, as this will bruise and disfigure it.

Bore a hole in the coat hanger large enough to allow the rod to turn easily. Put the washer over the lower end of the rod, and with a few light blows of the hammer, rivet it in position. If this work is carefully done the coat hanger will turn on the hook, thus making it quite convenient in the hanging of garments.

## FINISHING.

With a clean piece of sandpaper, remove all tool marks, and finish with shellac (Chapter IV., Paragraph 57). The wood part should be given three or more coats, and when the last coat is perfectly dry it should be rubbed smooth with a piece of well worn sandpaper, moistened with linseed oil.

In the suggestions for original designs you will see ways of making coat hangers out of very small pieces of material. Nos. 3 and 4 can be made from narrow strips of material, but they require careful work in making the joints. No. 3 is joined with a dowel; No. 4 is a half lap joint.

## Optional and Home Projects Employing Similar Principles.

### SKIRT HANGER.

1. In modifying this plan to make a skirt hanger it would be necessary to change it only in length; it may be made as much shorter as desirable.

### SKIRT OR COAT HANGER MADE FROM A HOOP.

2. A very satisfactory skirt or coat hanger may be made from an old wooden hoop by attaching the hook, shaping the wood properly and covering it neatly with a remnant of silk, cretonne or any other suitable material. The hoop is sometimes wrapped with cotton batting before it is covered to give it a rounder appearance.

# BROOM HOLDER

MATERIALS.

Yellow Pine (Chap. III., Par. 48) or any soft wood.

1 pc. ¾"x3½"x9½" S 2 S Back.
1 pc. ¾"x3"x8" S 2 S Hanger.
2-1½" No. 10 F. H. B. screws.

## INTRODUCTORY STATEMENT.

The most usual place to find a floor broom is leaning somewhere in a corner with its weight resting on the straw. This helps to explain why so many brooms have their straws bent out of shape and in a poor position to do good work. If a damp broom is left standing with the weight on the straw it will quite likely be bent and when dry will remain in that unsatisfactory shape.

This illustration shows a broom holder which not only furnishes a place where the broom should always be found, but also avoids the difficulty just explained.

Some people claim that a broom should hang with the straw down in order to prevent any moisture which might be in it from draining into the body of the broom. This is not an important matter, for a broom should never be wet enough to drip when hung up.

---

**References:**

Brushes and Brooms, International Encyclopedia.
How to Make Common Things, J. A. Bower. E. S. Gorham, Pub.
Manual Training for Common Schools, Allen & Cotton. Manual Arts Press, Peoria, Ill.
Handwork for Boys, Pabst.
Broom Corn, Young Folks' Cyclopedia of Common Things, by Champlin. Henry Holt & Co.
The Book of Useful Plants, Julia Rogers. Doubleday, Page & Co., New York.
The Basket Maker, Luther W. Turner. Atkinson, Mentzer & Co., Chicago.
The Story of Lumber, Sara W. Basset. Penn Pub. Co.

# BROOM HOLDER

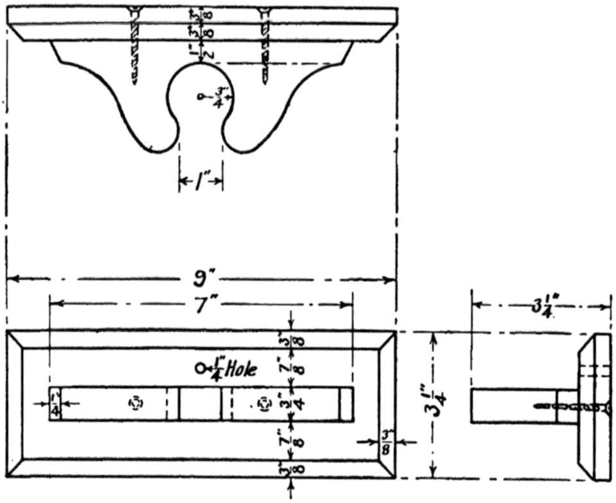

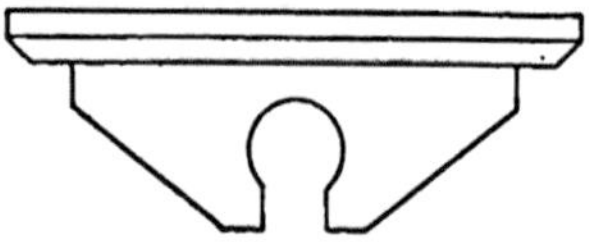

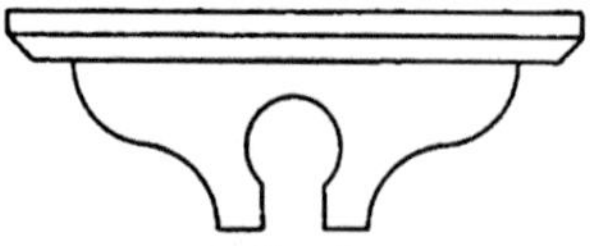

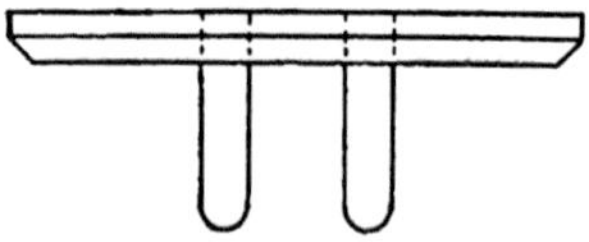

# BROOM HOLDER SPECIFICATIONS

## THE BACK.

As this material is furnished S 2 S, it will not be necessary for you to plane the surface. It should, however, be carefully smoothed with sandpaper (Chapter II., Paragraph 17). Select one surface for a working face (Chapter II., Paragraph 2). Plane one edge perfectly straight and square with the working face; mark this the working edge (Chapter II., Paragraph 4); prepare a working end (Chapter II., Paragraph 5). From the working end measure and cut the length given in the drawing. Carefully gauge the width on both surfaces (Chapter II., Paragraph 6); plane to the gauge line. With a lead pencil and ruler (Chapter II., Paragraph 7), or with the lead pencil and finger (Chapter II., Paragraph 8), carefully gauge for the chamfer. As this chamfer is to be cut entirely around this piece of material, you must gauge for it on all edges and entirely around on the working face. Form the chamfer by planing to these gauge lines (Chapter II., Paragraph 19). In planing a chamfer always be sure to leave sharp, well-defined corners. Do not give it a rounded appearance.

## THE HOLDER.

Prepare a working face (Chapter II., Paragraph 2); plane one edge perfectly straight and square and mark it the working edge (Chapter II., Paragraph 4). Plane one end perfectly square with the working face and working edge (Chapter II., Paragraph 5). In laying out your design, make all measurements from the working face and the working edge. Carefully lay out your chosen design on the working face. This may be partly laid out with the compasses and finished freehand. Be sure the two sides are alike. With the turning saw, coping or compass saw (if you have curves in your design) cut out the shape of the holder. Carefully smooth all of the edges with the wood file, and finish them with sandpaper. Make sure that you remove all tool marks and leave the edges perfectly square.

## ASSEMBLING.

This piece of work is to be assembled with glue and screws. Locate the holes for the screws, bore through the back piece with a bit large enough to allow the screws to go through easily (Chapter II., Paragraph 9); also bore the hanging hole. Use a smaller bit and bore in the holder to receive the screws. Be sure the holder stands perfectly square on the back piece.

## FINISHING.

When your work is assembled, with a sharp steel scraper (Chapter II., Paragraph 16) remove all rough places, pencil or tool marks. Sandpaper with a very fine, clean piece of sandpaper. Stain the work the desired color (Chapter IV., Paragraph 54). Finish with two or more coats of shellac (Chapter IV., Paragraph 57).

In small pieces of work like this all back parts should also be stained and shellaced.

### Optional and Home Projects Employing Similar Principles.

## TOOL RACKS.

1. This principle of using a back, with some special sort of holder attached, may be employed in a great many different styles of tool racks. By making the back very much longer and using a strip with a number of suitable holes in it for a holder, a very convenient rack may be provided for such tools as files, bits, screwdrivers and chisels.

## PANTRY WALL RACK.

2. A back made as long as desirable and provided with hooks, dowel pins, or even nails, will furnish a convenient rack for many things which are usually kept in the pantry. The particular style of hook or hanger may be selected to suit the articles to be hung.

## HAT RACK.

3. By making the back a little more elaborate, and perhaps adding some artistic effect in the way of a suitable design, a very satisfactory hat rack may be provided. The hangers may be made of wood, or some pleasing style of hook may be purchased.

# BENCH HOOK

MATERIALS.

Yellow Pine (Chap. III., Par. 48) or any soft wood.

1 pc. 7/8"x4¾"x19" S 2 S Base and blocks.
4-1½" No. 10 F. H. B. screws.

INTRODUCTORY STATEMENT.

While most work benches are provided with a vise in which to hold small pieces of material, yet a bench hook provides a very satisfactory means of holding small pieces of sawing in the absence of a vise; it also serves a great many purposes for which a vise cannot be used.

The bench hook should be kept hanging either on the leg of the bench or in some other convenient place, where it can always be had when needed. The proper use of a bench hook will prevent sawing the bench top or marring it with the chisel, for this bench hook is made wide enough to provide a good surface on which to do chiseling.

The bench hook shown in this lesson provides the sawing space on the right-hand side. If the hook is to be used by a left-handed person, the block should be set on in such a way as to leave the sawing margin on the left-hand side of the bench hook. A bench hook could be made with one right and one left-hand side.

---

**References:**

The Amateur Mechanic's Workshop. G. P. Putnam's Sons.
Elementary Woodworking, Edwin Foster. Ginn & Co.
The Handy Boy, A. Neely Hall. Lathrop, Lee & Shepard Co.
The First Book of Forestry, Ernest Thompson Seton. Doubleday, Page & Co.

# BENCH HOOK

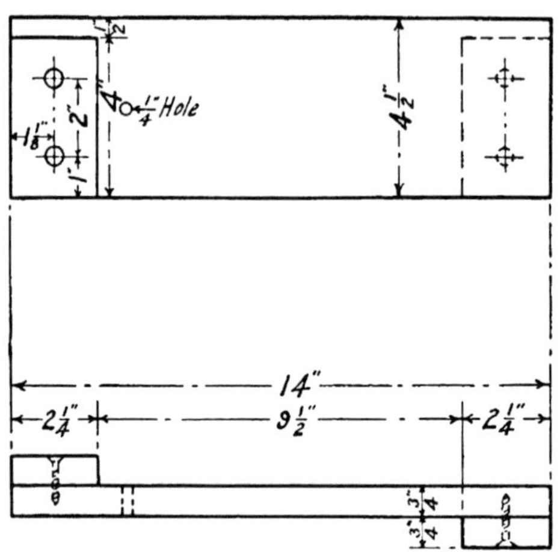


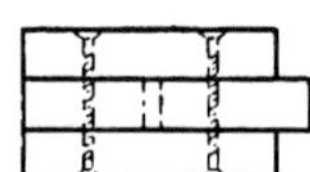

SUGGESTIONS FOR ORIGINAL DESIGN

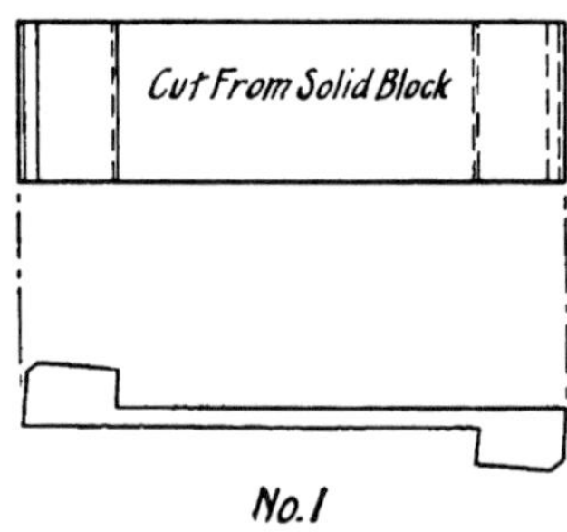


No. 1

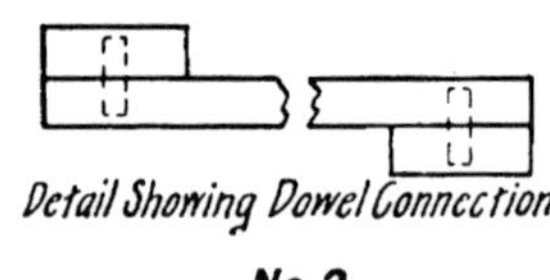

Detail Showing Dowel Connection

No. 2

# BENCH HOOK SPECIFICATIONS

## THE BASE.

If your material is furnished S 2 S (surfaced on two sides) it will not be necessary for you to plane the surface. Select one surface for the working face (Chapter II., Paragraph 2); plane one edge perfectly straight and square with the working face. Mark it the working edge (Chapter II., Paragraph 4). Plane one end perfectly straight and square with the working face and the working edge. Mark this the working end (Chapter II., Paragraph 5). Measure the length (14") from the working end; at this point square a line on the working face, square it around, and plane the end (Chapter II., Paragraph 5).

(NOTE:—The remaining material is to make the two blocks.)

Gauge the width 4½" on both surfaces (Chapter II., Paragraph 6); plane to the gauge line; leave all corners square and sharp.

## THE BLOCKS.

The two blocks are to be just alike (2¼"x4"). From the working edge gauge the width of one of the blocks (Chapter II., Paragraph 6); from the other edge gauge another line on the same surface. Fasten the material in the vise, and with a ripsaw rip between the two gauge lines. Plane to the gauge line on each block. With the try-square, carefully test each block on all edges and all corners; make them perfectly square.

## ASSEMBLING.

This is to be assembled with glue and screws (or with dowels if you care to follow the idea given in the Suggestions for Original Designs No. 2). If you use screws, bore through the block with a bit large enough to allow the screws to pass through (Chapter II., Paragraph 9). Countersink these holes so the heads of the screws will be slightly below the surface of the block. Hold the blocks (one at a time) in their proper positions, and with a brad awl, reaching through the holes, in each block indicate on the base where to bore for the screws. With a brad awl, or a small bit, make holes in which to start the screws. Spread a thin, even coating of glue on the side of the block which is to join the base. Fasten the blocks in place with screws. When the screws are tight they should stand with their slots in the same direction. It is a general principle of mechanics that wherever screws show the slots should stand in line.

## FINISHING.

When the work is assembled, clean it with sandpaper, making sure to remove any surplus glue that may have spread out of the edges of the joints. It may be necessary to plane the outside edges of the joints to make them perfectly even. Bore the ¼″ hanging hole, as indicated in the drawing (Chapter II., Paragraph 9). Finish with shellac (Chapter IV., Paragraph 57). This bench hook is a very serviceable article and should be used on your bench for sawing or chiseling purposes.

### Optional and Home Projects Employing Similar Principles.

## WALKING STILTS.

1. The principle of planing material straight and square, and of assembling with screws may be employed in a great many different articles about the home. For exercise and amusement it may be applied to the making of stilts. Plane two strong strips of any kind of sound material straight and smooth. They may be made as long as desirable, but should not be made too high for first experience. Prepare two triangular blocks by first making a rectangular block about four by eight inches, then sawing it diagonally. Fasten these blocks to the uprights (at the same height) with screws through the uprights into the blocks. A piece of strap iron or leather may be used to form a loop to help hold the foot in place.

## SWING BOARD.

2. After planing a board straight and square, it may easily be made into a swing board by providing notches for the rope. These notches can be best prepared by boring a hole very close to each end (perhaps within 1″ or 1½″ of the end) and sawing out a sort of "V" shaped notch to the hole.

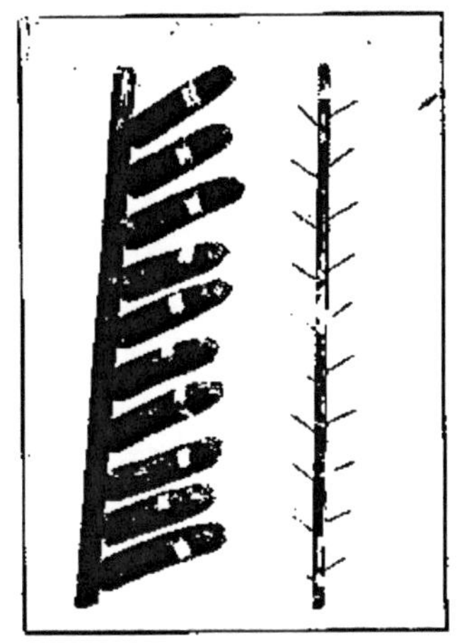

# SEED CORN RACK

MATERIALS.

Yellow Pine (Chap. III., Par. 48) or any soft wood.

1 pc. 7/8"x2"x36" Rough or S 2 S
10 nails, 10d common.

## INTRODUCTORY STATEMENT.

People who are interested in agriculture, or in fact in the growing of any sort of plants, are beginning to realize the value of planting only good seed. In order to produce excellent, high-yielding corn it is necessary to use seed from that sort of corn plant. Men who have made a scientific study of corn tell us that seed corn should be very carefully selected, taking into consideration not only the size, shape, kernel depth, variety and vitality of the ear, but also the proper characteristic of the mother plant. Seed corn should be very carefully stored during the winter where it will be free from rats and mice, dampness and other conditions which render it unfit for use.

This lesson shows you how to make a very convenient rack to hold ten or twenty ears. When it is filled with the selected corn it should be hung from a rafter or other timber in the barn or shed loft.

References:

U. S. Bulletin No. 229, The Production of Good Seed Corn.
U. S. Bulletin No. 409, School Lessons on Corn.
U. S. Bulletin No. 313, Harvesting and Storing Corn.
U. S. Bulletin No. 298, Food Value of Corn and Corn Products.
Book of Corn, Prof. J. R. Steward, Muncie Normal, Muncie, Ind.
The Book of Corn, Herbert Myrick. Orange-Judd Co., Publishers.
U. S. Bulletin No. 81, Corn Culture in the South.
U. S. Bulletin No. 199, Corn Growing.
The Tree Doctor. Davey.

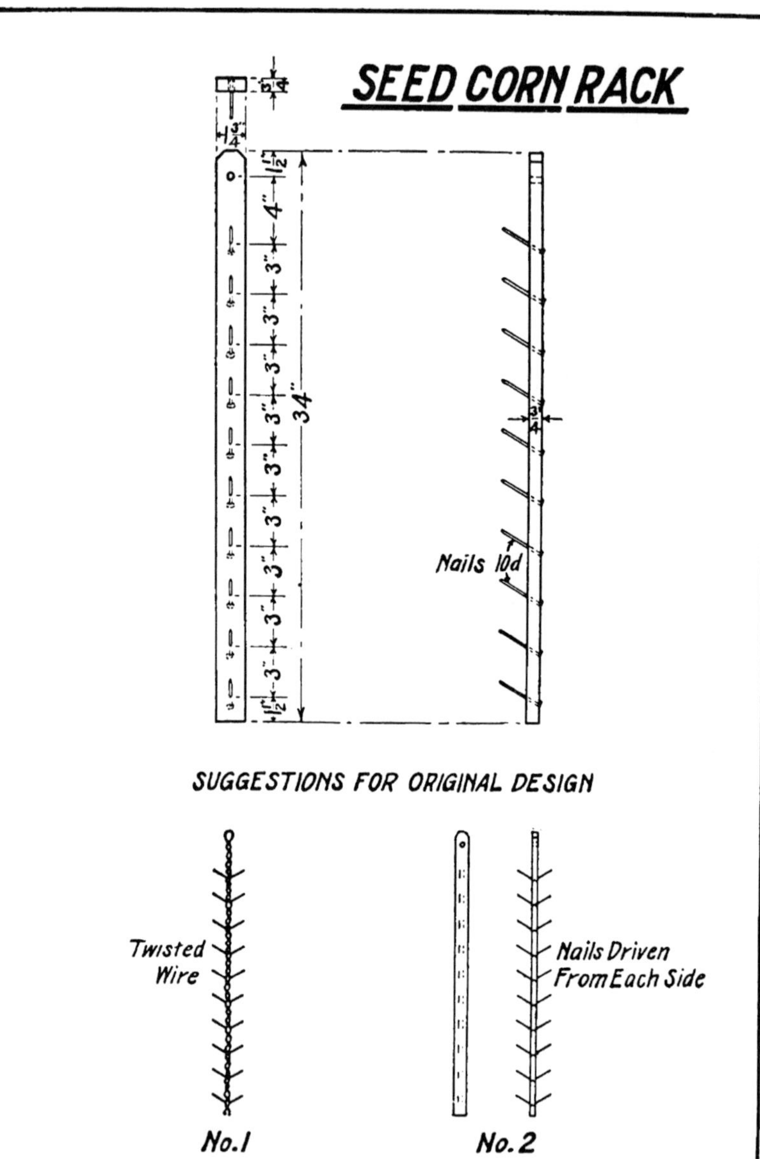
SEED CORN RACK
3/4
3/4"
1 1/2"
4"
3"
3"
3"
3"
3"
3"
3"
3"
3"
1 1/2"
34"
3/4
Nails 10d
SUGGESTIONS FOR ORIGINAL DESIGN
Twisted Wire
Nails Driven From Each Side
No.1
No.2

# SEED CORN RACK SPECIFICATIONS

As one of the principal things for you to learn in this lesson is to plane a long strip of material so it will be perfectly straight and square, you should perform each operation very carefully. If your material is furnished S 2 S, it will not be necessary for you to surface the sides; if not, first plane one surface smooth and straight for your working face (Chapter II., Paragraph 2). Plane one edge perfectly straight and square with the working face (Chapter II., Paragraph 4); mark this the working edge. With your try-square lay out, and with the back saw or panel saw saw one end perfectly square with the working face and the working edge; mark this the working end (Chapter II., Paragraph 5). With your marking gauge (held against the working edge) gauge the width on each surface (Chapter II., Paragraph 6). Carefully plane to the gauge line. From the working end measure the desired length and square off the end. Lay out and chamfer the upper corners, as indicated in the drawing.

This chamfer may be cut in a miter box, if your shop is provided with one, or you may lay out the regular half-pitch cut (Chapter II., Paragraph 24) with the large steel square, and from this cut set the T-bevel and use it in laying out. These marks should be squared across the edges with the T-square. Fasten the material in the vise, or hold it on the bench hook (Chapter II., Paragraph 5), and saw off the corners as laid out.

Bore the hole for the hanger (Chapter II., Paragraph 9). Lay out positions for the nails 3″ apart. To do this gauge a pencil line (Chapter II., Paragraph 7 or 8) in the center of the working face. Set the compasses with the points 3″ apart; step off the spaces on the pencil line to mark places for the nails. Holes should be bored with a small bit before attempting to drive the nails. Make sure that all the holes are bored at the same angle (Chapter II., Paragraph 12).

## ASSEMBLING.

With a sharp steel scraper, or a keen plane set to take a very thin shaving, remove all pencil or tool marks. Be sure to leave the corners perfectly straight and sharp. From the back side drive a nail through each hole (these nails will incline upward). Settle the heads slightly into the wood by one or two careful blows with the hammer. This will prevent the nail from pushing out when the corn is put in.

## FINISHING.

Although a fine finish is not required on a piece of work of this kind, yet it would be well to give it a coat of shellac (Chapter IV., Paragraph 57) or paint (Chapter IV., Paragraph 52).

**Optional and Home Projects Employing Similar Principles.**

## CLOTHESLINE POLE.

1. The principle of planing out a long, straight strip of material can be applied to a great many projects. The clothesline pole is such a strip cut to a desirable length, usually about 7 to 9 feet long. It should have a "V" shaped notch sawed in one end to receive the clothesline.

## TEN-FOOT POLE.

2. A ten-foot pole will be found quite convenient about the farm where measurements must occasionally be made. It consists of a straight pole, neatly planed, with the dimensions for feet, halves and quarters plainly marked. For convenience and accuracy, the last foot might be marked off in inches. A rod-pole could just as easily be made if desired.

## PLUMB BOB.

3. A plumb bob, or plumb rule as it is sometimes called, is a very handy tool where any kind of building work is going on. The only essential principle in its construction is the matter of getting the edges perfectly straight and parallel, and of gauging the testing line exactly in the middle. It should have a "V" shaped, or circular, fork in the lower end large enough to allow the weight or plummet to swing freely.

If desirable, and one is willing to exercise sufficient care, a very satisfactory spirit level may be made by getting a small level tube from the hardware store, and installing it in one edge of the plumb bob. The protecting plate over the tube may be made of a small piece of sheet brass, or it too may be purchased.

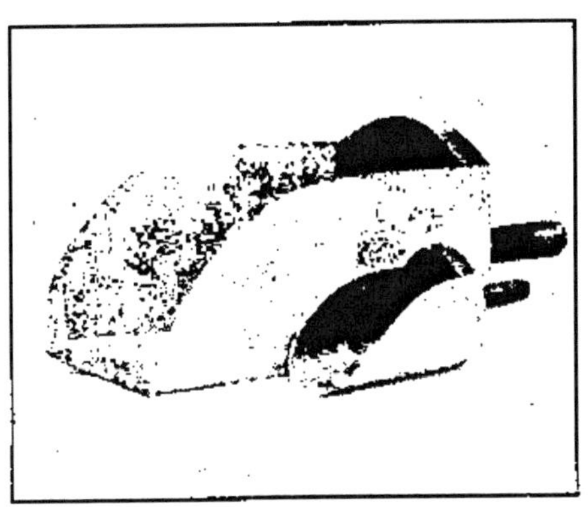

# FEED SCOOP

MATERIALS.

Poplar (Chap. III., Par. 42) or any soft wood.

1 pc. 7/8"x5½"x6½" S 2 S Back.

1 pc. 1⅛"x1⅛"x5½" rough Handle.

1 pc. galvanized 10"x15" Body of Scoop.

5 dozen ¾" No. 18 brads.

INTRODUCTORY STATEMENT.

Handy equipment is a great help in making everyday tasks lighter and more pleasant and much of this equipment can be provided without any particular expense.

In every home there are a number of purposes for which neat, well-made scoops would be convenient. The purpose for which the scoop is to be used will determine its size and shape. For house use, in salt, sugar or flour, the smaller neat size would be more appropriate; for use on the farm, in the barn or poultry house, larger and heavier scoops should be provided for handling ground feed and small grain. Such scoops could be made so as to serve as an approximate measure and thus enable one to feed accurate portions in making up rations.

---

References:

Tin Truth. Follansbee Brothers Co., Pittsburgh, Pa.
Tin—Source, Production and Manufacture. International Encyclopedia.
Tin, in Stories of Industries, Chase and Clow. Educational Pub. Co.
The Story of Iron, Elizabeth Samuel. The Penn Pub. Co.
U. S. Bulletin No. 99, Insect Enemies of Shade Trees.

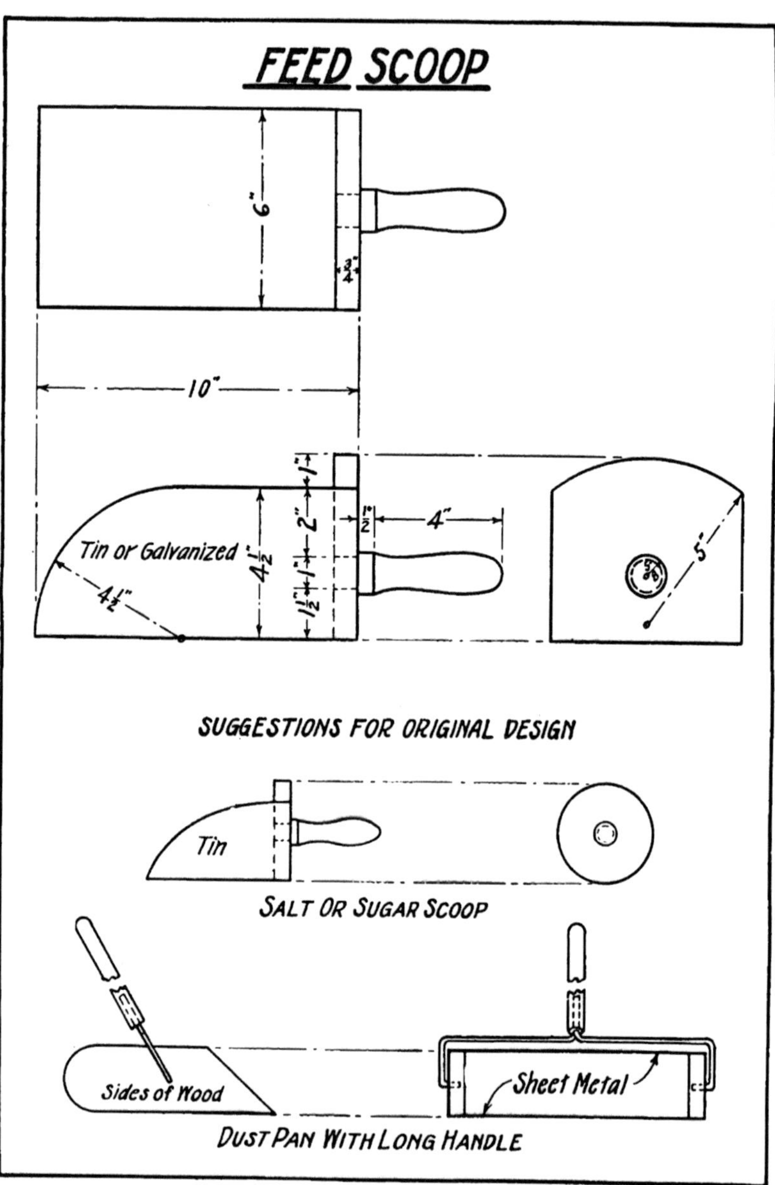
FEED SCOOP
6"
10"
1"
2"
4"
Tin or Galvanized
$4\frac{1}{2}$"
$4\frac{1}{2}$"
1"
$1\frac{1}{2}$"
$\frac{1}{2}$"
5"
SUGGESTIONS FOR ORIGINAL DESIGN
Tin
SALT OR SUGAR SCOOP
Sides of Wood
Sheet Metal
DUST PAN WITH LONG HANDLE

# FEED SCOOP SPECIFICATIONS

## THE BACK.

Plane one surface of this piece perfectly straight and smooth for a working face (Chapter II., Paragraph 2); plane one edge straight and square for a working edge (Chapter II., Paragraph 4). Square and saw, if necessary, and plane one end square with the working face and working edge for a working end (Chapter II., Paragraph 5). Measure and cut this piece the required length. With the compasses set to the proper radius, lay out the curve for the top edge of this piece, saw out with the coping or compass saw, and smooth with a sharp block plane or wood file. Locate and bore the hole for the handle (Chapter II., Paragraph 9).

## THE HANDLE.

In shaping a handle of this kind it is well first to make the material perfectly square (Chapter II., Paragraphs 2 and 4); next plane off the corners, making an octagon; then the corners should be planed off until the shape approaches a cylinder. A sharp knife may be used to make the curved shape to the handle. You must depend upon your eye and judgment very largely in shaping such a handle. Do not attempt to take deep shavings; cut away but little at a time, and keep turning the handle from side to side so you may be able to keep the curves the same on all sides.

## THE BODY OF THE SCOOP.

The body of this scoop is to be made of galvanized sheet iron; it will require a piece 10″ long, and wide enough to form the bottom plus the two sides (15″). With the square lay out an exact rectangle of this size, square pencil lines across it indicating where it is to be bent to form the corners; be sure these lines are just wide enough apart to receive the back which you have already made. With the compasses lay out the curves indicating where the corners are to be cut off. With tinner's snips, or an old pair of heavy shears, cut out the shape of the body as laid out. Place the sheet of galvanized iron between two straight-edged boards with the pencil line (for the corner bend) exactly even with the edge of the board; clamp in the vise and bend the sheet iron to a right angle. A few light blows with the hammer will complete the angle and make it perfectly square. Bend the other side in like manner.

## ASSEMBLING.

Glue the handle into the back; the end which extends through may be split and wedged, then sawed off even and planed smooth with the surface. Fasten the sheet iron body in position by nailing it with small brads (Chapter II., Paragraph 21).

## FINISHING.

Sandpaper the wood parts perfectly smooth (Chapter II., Paragraphs 16 and 17) and give them one or two coats of shellac (Chapter IV., Paragraph 57). With a file or piece of emory or sandpaper rub off any rough or sharp edges of the sheet iron which may be exposed in such a way as to cut one's hands.

## Optional and Home Projects Employing Similar Principles.

### SOIL SCOOP.

1. In connection with the class work in agriculture, where there will be a number of experiments calling for the handling of soils, a few scoops made in this way will be found very convenient. Discarded tin cans, such as baking powder, coffee or fruit cans may be used. Cut one end to the desired shape for the point of the scoop, the other end need not be removed; a wooden end should be shaped to fit this end snugly; it should be fastened in position (in the inside of the scoop) with brads into its edge; a screw through the wood (and the tin end) into the end of the handle will hold it firmly in place.

### DUST PAN.

2. A very convenient dust pan, which has the advantage of serving also as a sort of pail in carrying out the dust, can be made very easily in accordance with the Suggestions for Original Design. The two wooden sides are placed as far apart as one would desire the width of the dust pan to be and a continuous piece of sheet iron is bent around them and fastened with brads. A piece of heavy, stiff wire is bent and placed in holes in the sides to serve as a bail and a long handle of desired length is to be attached to this bail.

### WATERING OR FEED TROUGH FOR CHICKENS.

3. Following this same principle of construction a very satisfactory watering or feed trough for chickens may be made. Take a sheet of galvanized iron or tin of the desired size and turn up the two sides as far as the required depth of the trough; prepare wooden ends of the proper dimensions, and fasten them into position by brads driven through the metal. If it is to hold water, the brads must be very close together; the wood parts should be painted.

# BRACKET SHELF

MATERIALS.

Yellow Pine (Chap. III., Par. 48) or any soft wood.

1 pc. 7/8"x6¼"x21½" S 2 S
Top.

1 pc. 7/8"x7¼"x19½" S 2 S
Back.

1 pc. 7/8"x5"x10" S 2 S
Brackets.

12-6d finishing nails.

## INTRODUCTORY STATEMENT.

The bracket shelf is one of the best-known and oldest forms of equipment found in the home. This article of furniture admits of more variations in size, function and style than possibly any article found in house equipment. The old-fashioned long mantle above the fireplace was one form of bracket shelf. Other numerous forms serve various purposes, such as a place for the family clock, or in some instances a sort of "catch-all" for things which have no better place.

In designing a bracket shelf you should consider very carefully for what purpose it is to be used, and first of all make it sufficiently substantial to serve its purpose properly, then consider the point of making it attractive in appearance.

**References:**

Woodworking for Beginners, Wheeler. G. P. Putnam's Sons, New York.
Elementary Woodwork, F. H. Selden. Rand-McNally Co., Chicago.
Beginning Woodwork at Home and in School, Van Duesen. Manual Arts Press, Peoria, Ill.
Woodworking for Amateur Craftsmen, Griffith. Popular Mechanics Co., Chicago.
Our Trees, How to Know Them, Emerson & Weed. Lippincott Co., Philadelphia.

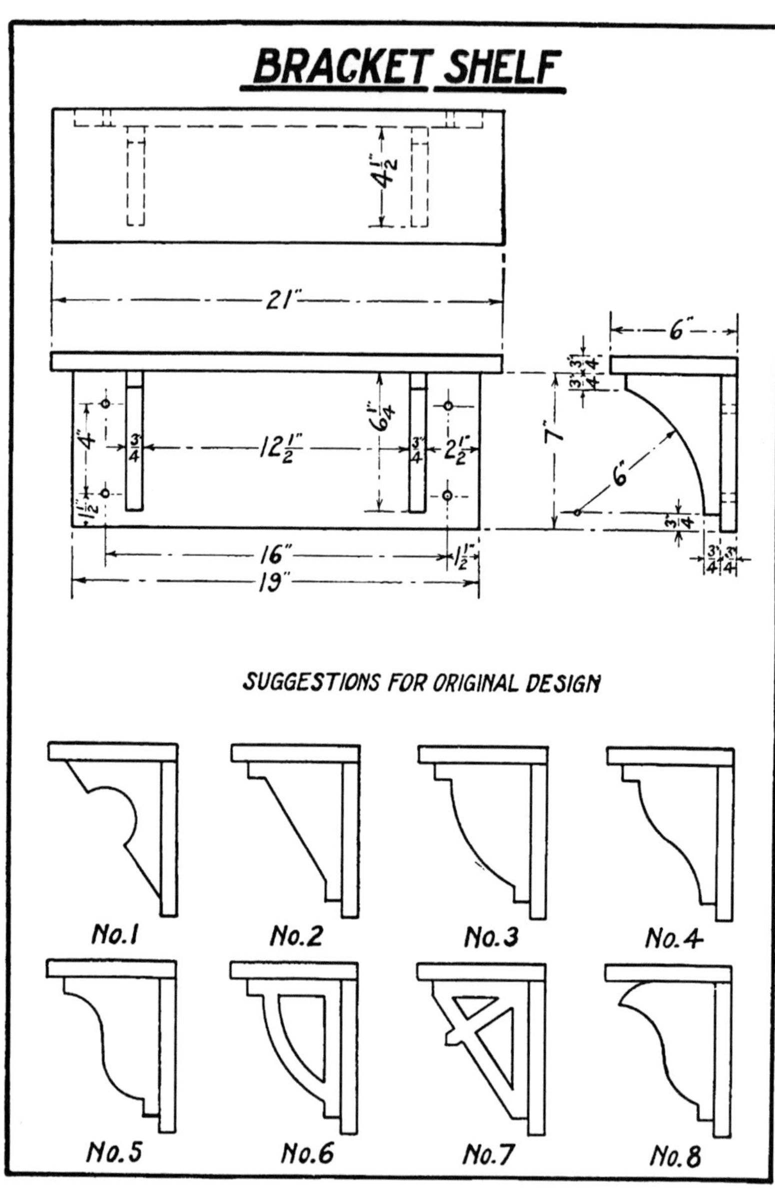
BRACKET SHELF
21"
19"
16"
12 1/2"
SUGGESTIONS FOR ORIGINAL DESIGN
No.1
No.2
No.3
No.4
No.5
No.6
No.7
No.8

# BRACKET SHELF SPECIFICATIONS

## THE BACK.

Select one surface for a working face (Chapter II., Paragraph 2). Plane one edge perfectly straight and square with the working face. Mark this the working edge (Chapter II., Paragraph 4). Plane one end exactly square with the working face and the working edge. Mark this the working end (Chapter II., Paragraph 5). Gauge the width (Chapter II., Paragraph 6) on both surfaces; plane to the gauge line. Measure and cut the length.

## THE TOP.

Plane one surface for the working face (Chapter II., Paragraph 2). Plane one edge perfectly square with the working face and mark it the working edge (Chapter II., Paragraph 4). Plane one end exactly square with both the working face and the working edge for the working end (Chapter II., Paragraph 5); measure and cut the length. Gauge the width (Chapter II., Paragraph 6) on both surfaces and plane to the gauge line.

## THE BRACKETS.

In the working drawing a very simple design is given for the brackets. Suggestions for Original Designs will give you a number of ideas from which you will be able to work out a design of your own. Make a drawing of your design. After you have worked out a design that is acceptable, use the ⅞″x5″x10″ piece to make the brackets. Plane one surface perfectly smooth and mark it the working face (Chapter II., Paragraph 2). Prepare a working edge (Chapter II., Paragraph 4). Plane one end exactly square with the working face for the working end (Chapter II., Paragraph 5). Note:—This board will be sufficiently long to make both brackets by reversing the pattern and using the material with economy. Lay out one bracket; carefully saw out this bracket with the turning, coping or compass saw. With a wood file and sandpaper make the edges perfectly smooth. Use this bracket for a pattern in laying out the second one. Make the second bracket exactly like the first.

## ASSEMBLING.

This work is to be assembled with brads. Be sure to set the brackets perfectly square and an equal distance from the ends. In driving the brads be very careful not to briuse the work with the hammer (Chapter II., Paragraph 21). With a nail set drive the heads a little below the surface so the holes can be puttied.

## FINISHING.

When the work is all assembled give it a final cleaning and smoothing with a sharp steel scraper (Chapter II., Paragraph 16) and finish with sandpaper (Chapter II., Paragraph 17). Be sure that all of the corners are left sharp and well defined. Bore the holes through which the hanging screws are to be placed. These holes should be 16" from center to center in order that the screws will strike the studding in an ordinary plastered wall.

If you do not expect your shelf to support a very heavy load, perhaps one screw at each end will be sufficient. Use your own judgment in this matter.

## FINISHING.

Give the bracket shelf a coat of stain of desirable color (Chapter IV., Paragraph 54). Finish with shellac (Chapter IV., Paragraph 57) or with wax (Chapter IV., Paragraph 56).

### Optional and Home Projects Employing Similar Principles.

## SHELF WITH TOWEL ROD.

1. By shaping the brackets so they will be a little wider at the lower end, and boring a hole about half or two-thirds through the thickness of each bracket, a rod for hanging a towel may be added. This rod may be made stationary, or one of the holes may be slotted so it can be lifted out, if desired.

## SHELF WITH DRAWER.

2. By designing the brackets properly a neat, shallow drawer may be constructed to fit between them; such a drawer should be carefully made, and so designed as to be in harmony with the general idea of the bracket shelf. The towel rod might also be added; for a lavatory not provided with a shaving cabinet, such a shelf would be very convenient.

# SUGGESTIONS FOR COMMUNITY RESEARCH

DID you ever think how much valuable information you may gather from the things which lie all about you? The people of your neighborhood are daily doing hundreds of things which you may sometime be called upon to do. You should therefore be interested in these activities and store up all the knowledge and experience you can.

There are farmers who, for a great many years, have been dealing with the problems of raising crops and farm animals and who, by this experience and hard work, have learned a great many things which they would be glad to tell you. These things would not only be as interesting as any of the stories studied in school, but they would possibly be quite valuable later on in helping you to make a living.

The carpenters, blacksmiths, masons, painters and other mechanics have gathered a great store of knowledge and acquired considerable skill by spending many years in careful practice at their trades. While it would be impossible for them to give you any portion of their skill, because this can be obtained only by actual practice, yet they can tell you many things which will be worth while for you to know.

Throughout your life you will be compelled to use a great many different kinds of equipment in the way of tools, implements, furniture, and even houses, barns and bridges, so the more you can know about the materials of which such things are made, how they are produced and their care and use, the more intelligently will you be able to deal with them.

These suggestions for research work are to guide you in finding out by observation and inquiry some of the practical things which every boy should know. It is particularly important that you should learn how to approach men in a genteel and polite manner and learn to talk with them intelligently about different lines of work. Almost any intelligent and right thinking man is not only willing, but glad to offer advice and information to a boy who is earnestly trying to learn. Of course nobody likes a meddler nor one who asks foolish questions out of idle curiosity or impudence. Whenever you are visiting a man's place of business to gather information, remember that he is doing you a favor and that you should not fail to appreciate it and to thank him for it. One of the best ways to get courteous treatment is to be thoroughly a gentleman yourself.

1. Make a list of all the hardwood forest trees (those that shed their leaves each year) that you can find in your community. Perhaps your father or some man whom you know in the neighborhood, who is familiar with the different kinds of trees, will be willing to go with you on a tree-examining excursion. When a tree has once been named and pointed out to you, study it very carefully so you will be able to recognize trees of its kind afterward. Notice the size of the tree, the general shape of the trunk and the branches, the nature of the bark, the color and exact shape of the leaves, and any flowers, fruit or nuts which it may bear. You cannot hope to remember the different kinds of trees unless you study their characteristic features.

2. On your tree excursion did you find any damaged, unhealthy or otherwise disfigured trees? What seemed to be the cause of the improper condition of the tree? The matter of caring for trees and of doctoring them has become quite a science; you will find it very interesting to see how the tree surgeon cuts out the rotten portions and fills the cavity with cement, very much as a dentist treats a tooth. Perhaps you can find where some work of this kind is going on or has been done in your community. It is not a very difficult task, and by carefully studying the references given in this text you might be able to undertake somé simple work of this kind with the help of your father or teacher. Make a list of all the influences which damage shade trees and suggest whatever remedies you can find for these difficulties.

3. Do you know of any one near your school who has a loom for weaving carpets or rugs? If you do, visit the place and find out all you can about weaving. Notice particularly how the stripes and the figures are woven. Do you know of anything produced in your locality which is used in the making of any kind of cloth? Some communities furnish a great deal of material from which the clothing of the world is made; other communities produce principally food materials. You will find it interesting to list and classify the products of your community. Possibly there are some articles manufactured in your city which are neither for food nor clothing, but which serve as equipment in aiding in the production of both. A wagon factory, for illustration, produces neither food nor clothing, but its wagons are very important in handling material for each.

4. Visit a number of farmers and ask them to explain to you how they select their seed corn. You will probably find that a large majority of them simply go to the crib and pick out the

ears which they consider the best. Can they in this way know much about the mother plants which produced the chosen ears? From the references given, of what value is the knowledge of the mother plant? By careful inquiry from a number of farmers, find the average yield of corn per acre in your neighborhood. If the average acre yield throughout the United States last year was twenty-six bushels, was your community above or below the average? The farmers will no doubt be interested in finding some way of increasing their yield.

5. What hand tools do you have in your home? Are they kept sharp and in good condition for use? Visit a carpenter's shop and ask the carpenter to let you examine his stock of tools; talk to him about the care and use of tools, and see whether you think that your tools, in their present condition, would be satisfactory for a man who is working at the carpenter's trade. What have you learned from this visit which you think is worth while?

6. Did you ever see a broom being made? While most brooms are now made by machinery, yet it is not uncommon to find a broom maker who does his work largely by hand. Perhaps you will have a chance to visit such a shop. If you do, find out all you can about "broom straw." Is there any broom corn raised in your neighborhood? If not, find the reason; would it be a profitable crop in your locality?

## REVIEW QUESTIONS AND PROBLEMS.

1. What is meant by a Working Face, a Working Edge, a Working End?

2. What is the purpose of the Marking Gauge? How should it be used? In what other ways can gauging be done?

3. How can you tell whether the edge of a piece of material is perfectly straight?

4. In what order would you give the dimensions of a piece of lumber?

5. What tools do you use in laying out work? Name as many as you can.

6. Name all the cutting tools which you have used thus far.

7. What is meant by assembling a piece of work? How many different means of assembling have you used?

8. What is the purpose of staining a piece of work? What is the purpose of shellac? Why is paint preferable on work which is exposed to the weather?

# INTRODUCTION TO SECTION II

BY the time the student has reached this section he should be able to understand the three regular views of the working drawing. The purpose of this section is to review and develop the principles and processes set forth under Section I. There will also be found the introduction of some processes which have not been previously set forth. The use of dowels in gluing up work is introduced and should be carefully impressed because of its common application. This work will make a very severe test of the pupils' ability in planing edges perfectly straight and square.

This section also offers some easy exercises which can be successfully carried out by less skillful students. For the more adept students there will be found certain exercises which, while they do not introduce any difficult joints, will call for very accurate thinking, particularly in the assembling work. This will be found especially true in the flytrap lesson.

Students should not feel that they are able to omit the references to the supplement. These references should be continually studied in order that each student may have before him constant ideals for the use of tools, and thus avoid forming any bad habits. It is very much easier to form correct habits at the start than it is to reform them after the incorrect habits have been established.

If the students have not been required to do tool-sharpening in Section I, they should be led to see the importance of this work by this time. They should be required to turn to the supplement and study the methods of sharpening chisels and planes. Students must learn quite early that it is impossible to do good work with dull tools.

This section offers an opportunity to do some very excellent work in finishing. The bread-cutting board is especially adapted to this purpose, and it will be found very interesting and attractive, as well as valuable from the practical standpoint, to have the students work out a fine shellac finish on this piece of work.

If the students have not been enthusiastic about the preparation of their own drawings, by making the drawing board as presented in the instructions, an interest may be aroused. The making of a T-square is not presented in the regular lesson, however; it can be readily made from the illustrations given with the drawing board and it will be found very interesting, particularly for the more skillful students.

# BREAD OR MEAT BOARD

MATERIALS.

Black Walnut (Chap. III., Par. 44) or Gum (Chap. III., Par. 37) or any dark wood.

2 pcs. 1"x2¾"x14½" S 2 S

Oak (Chap. III., Par. 29) or Maple (Chap. III., Par. 41) or any light-colored wood.

1 pc. 1"x5"x14½" S 2 S
1 pc. ¼"x10" dowel rod.

INTRODUCTORY STATEMENT.

The cutting of bread or meat, which must take place in every home, calls for some sort of cutting board. The size and shape of the board are not important features, but there are a few points which should be carefully observed. The boards should be made of some kind of hard wood, preferably maple or birch, but there are a number of other kinds of wood that will be very satisfactory. Wood used for this purpose should be free from any natural odor and as close-grained as possible so as to be non-absorbent. The board should have no cracks or decoration which would make it hard to keep clean. A board made of several pieces glued together is most satisfactory because it is less likely to warp.

---

**References:**

Maple, Maple Sugar and Syrup, U. S. Bulletin No. 252.
Familiar Trees, Mathews. Appleton Pub. Co., New York.
Timber and Timber Trees, Laslett. Macmillan Co.
Wood Finishing, Staining, Varnishing and Polishing, Hasluck.

## BREAD OR MEAT CUTTING BOARD

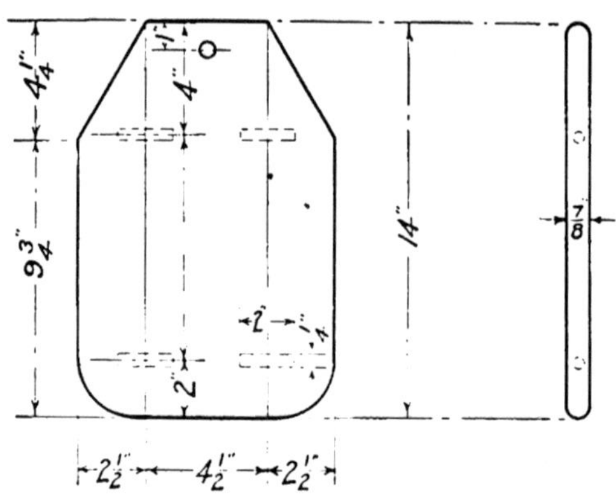


SUGGESTIONS FOR ORIGINAL DESIGN

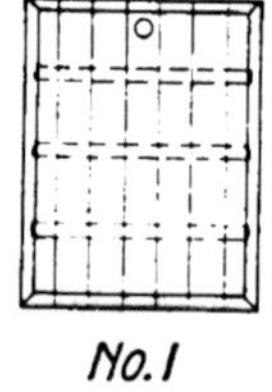
No. 1

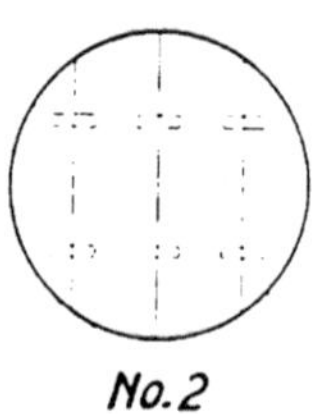
No. 2

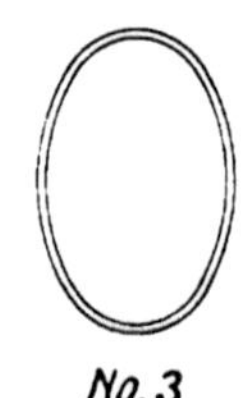
No. 3
STEAK OR FISH PLANK

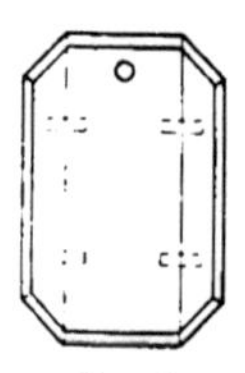
No. 4

# BREAD OR MEAT-CUTTING BOARD SPECIFICATIONS

This board is to be made by gluing together the three boards, as you will note from the illustration the light-colored piece is to be used in the middle with a dark piece on each edge.

## THE LIGHT-COLORED PIECE.

As this material is furnished S 2 S, and as you will have to resurface it after it is glued up, it is not necessary to plane the surface now. Select the best surface and mark it the working face (Chapter II., Paragraph 2). Carefully plane one edge perfectly straight and square with the working face (Chapter II., Paragraph 4). With the marking gauge or pencil and ruler gauge the width of the board (shown in the drawing), (Chapter II., Paragraphs 6 or 7). Carefully plane to the gauge line. It is not necessary to cut the length of this board at this time. That can be done after the work is assembled.

## THE DARK-COLORED PIECES.

Plane one edge of each of the dark strips perfectly straight and square (Chapter II., Paragraph 4). Lay the boards in position on your bench top, and press them closely together to make sure that the joints will fit perfectly. If they do not fit perfectly, determine what the difficulty is, and with a sharp plane, set to take a very thin shaving, plane them until they will make a very tight joint. These boards are to be joined with dowels, as indicated in the drawing. Locate the points where the dowels are to be and lay out for them (Chapter II., Paragraph 18) ; carefully bore for the dowel (Chapter II., Paragraph 13). Cut the dowels the right length (make sure they are not too long or the work will not assemble properly).

## ASSEMBLING THE WORK.

Glue the dowels in one edge of the center piece. Spread an even coating of glue on the edges which are to be joined. Carefully drive one dark piece down on the dowels. In like manner dowel the other dark-colored piece on the other edge. Place the material in a clamp, and tighten it securely; leave it until the glue has had time to dry (at least twelve hours).

## SURFACING THE BOARDS.

Both surfaces of the board are to be planed perfectly smooth (Chapter II., Paragraph 2). Plane the board to the desired width (make sure that the dark-colored pieces are exactly the same width). Square the boards the desired length. Lay out and cut the desired shape of the board. With the lead pencil and finger gauge entirely around the board on both surfaces for the chamfer or the round (Chapter II., Paragraph 8). Carefully plane to the gauge line, using the block plane for the end grain work (Chapter II., Paragraph 19). When the desired shape is completed, finish the surface of the board with a steel scraper (Chapter II., Paragraph 16). Do the final smoothing of the surface with very fine sandpaper (Chapter II., Paragraph 17). The round edges may be sandpapered as you would sandpaper a cylinder (Chapter II., Paragraph 15). Bore the hanging hole (Chapter II., Paragraph 9).

## FINISHING.

The board should be given the desired finish with shellac (Chapter IV., Paragraph 57).

### Optional and Home Projects Employing Similar Principles.

## DOUGH BOARD.

1. This plan of constructing a wide board by joining several narrow ones may be used in making a mixing board for dough. The boards should be perfectly fitted so there will be no cracks; the size of the board is immaterial, however it should be large enough for practical service, perhaps as much as 16"x18" or 18"x20". It should have cleats on each end to prevent warping; it would be well to have them fastened with a tongue and groove joint. Basswood, poplar or maple would be suitable wood.

## CHOPPING BOARD.

2. A heavy, smooth board is often needed for chopping meats or vegetables. This board should be made of some kind of hard wood, such as oak or maple. It should be joined perfectly, without rough places or indentations of any sort. A large staple might be driven in the face side near one edge, and left extending ½" or ¾"; by placing the point of a long kitchen knife in this staple the knife could be held steady while the chopping was being rapidly and safely done.

# CAMP STOOL

MATERIALS.

Yellow Pine (Chap. III., Par. 48) or any soft wood.

4 pcs. 7/8"x 1½"x22½" S 2 S Legs.
2 pcs. 7/8"x 1½"x13½" S 2 S Top strips.
3 pcs. ½"x12" dowel rod.
1 pc. canvas for seat 15"x16".
1½ dozen 8-oz. carpet tacks.

INTRODUCTORY STATEMENT.

The value of a camp stool can be fully realized only at crowded gatherings, picnics or camping parties, and yet occasions often arise in almost any home where a camp stool is convenient, particularly at lawn or porch parties. In designing a camp stool you should keep in mind the fact it is to be used for a seat and will likely have pretty rough usage; it should therefore be strong enough to stand the strain.

The plan given in this lesson is the standard way of making a simple camp stool. The method given in the suggestions allows the stool to close perfectly flat, but in order to do this it is necessary to leave out one of the cross rods between the legs.

**References:**

Harper's Camping and Scouting. Harper & Bros., Pub., New York.
The Outdoor Handy Book, D. C. Beard. Chas. Scribner's Sons.
The Field and Forest Handy Book, D. C. Beard. Chas. Scribner's Sons.
Boat Building for Amateurs, Adrian Neison. Frederick Drake Pub. Co., Chicago.
Timber, Bulletin No. 10 of U. S. Forestry Service.
Book of Woodcraft, Ernest Thompson Seton. Book Supply Co., Chicago.
Harper's Outdoor Book for Boys. Harper & Bros., New York.

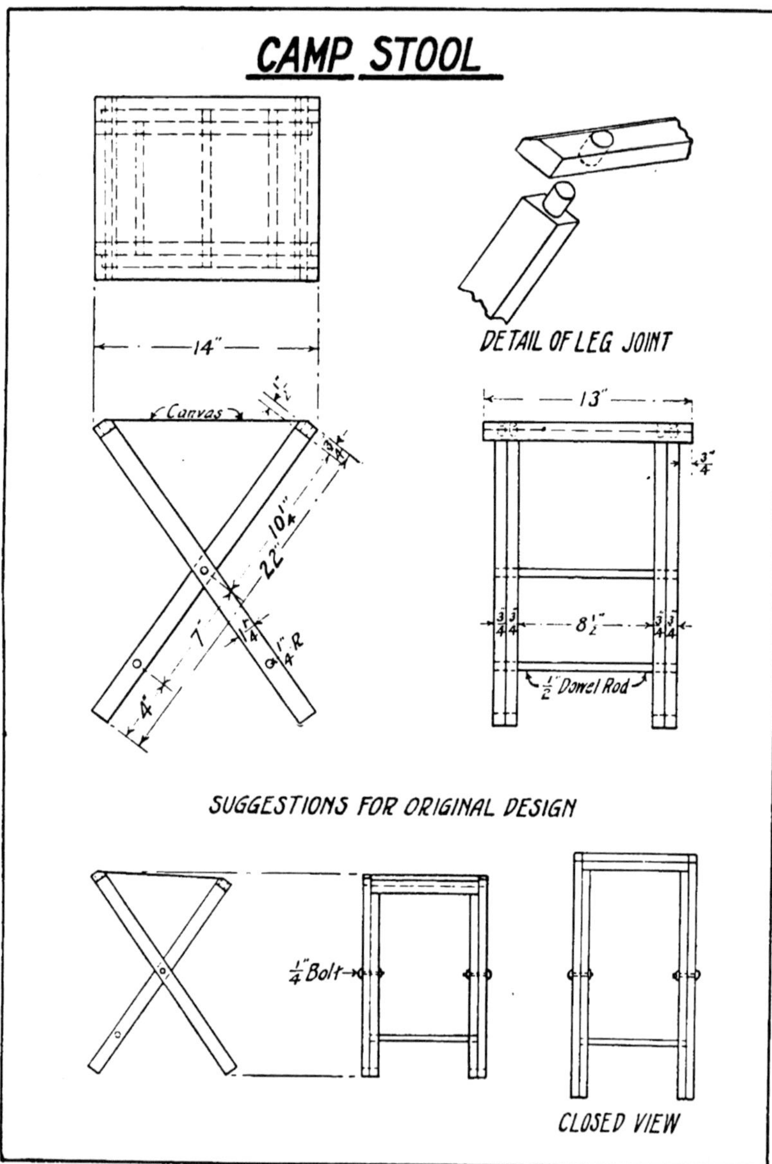
CAMP STOOL
DETAIL OF LEG JOINT
14"
13"
Canvas
10¼"
22"
7"
4"
¼" R
8½"
½" Dowel Rod
SUGGESTIONS FOR ORIGINAL DESIGN
¼" Bolt
CLOSED VIEW

# CAMP STOOL SPECIFICATIONS

## LEGS.

If you are cutting this material from stock, saw out a piece a little longer than the length of the leg shown in the drawing. Select the best side and mark it the working face. If it is S 2 S it will not be necessary to surface it (Chapter II., Paragraph 2). Plane one edge for a working edge (Chapter II., Paragraph 4). With the marking gauge, gauge the width of the leg on both surfaces of this board (Chapter II., Paragraph 6). Carefully rip just outside the gauge line and plane to the gauge line (Chapter II., Paragraph 4). Again prepare a working edge on the stock material, and in like manner lay out and make the four legs.

## CROSS PIECES AND JOINTS.

In similar manner rip out and plane to dimensions the two top cross pieces. The legs are to be joined to the cross piece with a round tenon construction (Chapter V., Paragraph 69). This tenon should be made ½″, ⅝″ or even ¾″ diameter. You may select a size which is the most convenient for the size of bit with which you expect to bore the hole. Locate the points where the holes are to be bored and bore the holes (Chapter II., Paragraph 9). Lay out and shape the round tenons (Chapter V., Paragraph 69).

Cut the legs the exact length as given in the drawing. Lay out and bore for the cross dowel rods (Chapter II., Paragraph 9).

## ASSEMBLING.

Assemble with glue. If desired brads may be driven through the leg in the stationary joints of the dowels, also into the top pieces. Be careful not to nail, or get any glue, on the dowel joints which are supposed to turn. With a sharp steel scraper (Chapter II., Paragraph 16) remove all pencil or tool marks.

## FINISHING.

If you desire to change the color of the wood, stain the desired color (Chapter IV., Paragraph 54); finish with one or two coats of shellac (Chapter IV., Paragraph 57).

## THE TOP.

The top is to be made of canvas. This is to be tacked on the outside of the top rail. The canvas should be turned under about

½" or ¾" on each side of the seat. This will give it strength. It should also be turned under slightly where it is tacked to prevent raveling and give it a neat appearance. Be careful to get it equally tight on each edge.

### Optional and Home Projects Employing Similar Principles.

#### FOLDING CHAIR.

1. A folding camp or porch chair can be made on almost exactly the same principles as the camp stool. The leg pieces should be considerably longer, with one pair extending high enough to form the back; from this back brace's should run down to the rear legs, and be joined with a long dowel which would rest in notches in the legs, thus providing means of adjusting the angle of the chair. The canvas would extend from the top round to the front one, forming both seat and back. Arms may be provided if desired.

#### FOLDING COT.

2. A folding cot, particularly adapted to outdoor sleeping or camping trips, may easily be made by using exactly the plan of the camp stool. The material should be heavier and the legs considerably longer; the cross rails between the legs would need to be about 6 feet long to provide sufficient length to the cot.

#### SAW BUCK.

3. In localities where wood is no longer used for fuel the saw buck has gone out of existence, but in some places there is enough wood to be sawed by hand to make it still worth while. It consists of a pair of strong legs (each made "X" shape, like the camp stool) fastened together at a distance of about 2½ or 3 feet with a heavy stretcher. This stretcher may consist of one piece rounded on the ends to enter holes in the legs, or it may be made of strips nailed on each side of the lower portion of the legs. The limbs, or pieces of wood to be sawed, are placed in the saw buck and, because of its "V" shape, are held perfectly solid at a convenient height to be sawed. Sometimes a temporary buck is made by driving stakes in the ground in an "X" shape over a small log, which thus braces them.

# BOOK RACK

MATERIALS.

Chestnut (Chap. III., Par. 35) or any hard wood.

1 pc. 5/8"x5 1/4"x28" Bottom and ends. S 2 S.

## INTRODUCTORY STATEMENT.

A small bookrack for use on a library or study table is very important in order to keep the books in shape for ready use. The length of the bookrack depends upon the number of books which it is intended to hold. The bookrack should be made of some kind of cabinet wood such as oak, walnut, cherry, mahogany or gum. It should be given a finish which will correspond with the finish of the furniture with which it is to be used. Innumerable designs have been worked out for bookracks, but you should try to put as much originality as you can in your piece of work. It is better to undertake a simple design and do it well than to attempt a difficult style and leave it showing marks of carelessness and inexperience.

**References:**

Handwork in Wood, Wm. Noyes. Manual Arts Press, Peoria, Ill.
Essentials of Woodworking, Griffith. Manual Arts Press, Peoria, Ill.
Instructions for Amateur Bookbinding. Craft Materials Guild, 119 La-Salle St., Chicago.
Harper's Indoor Book for Boys. Harper & Brothers, New York.
Seasoning of Timber, Bulletin No. 41, N. Y., 1902.

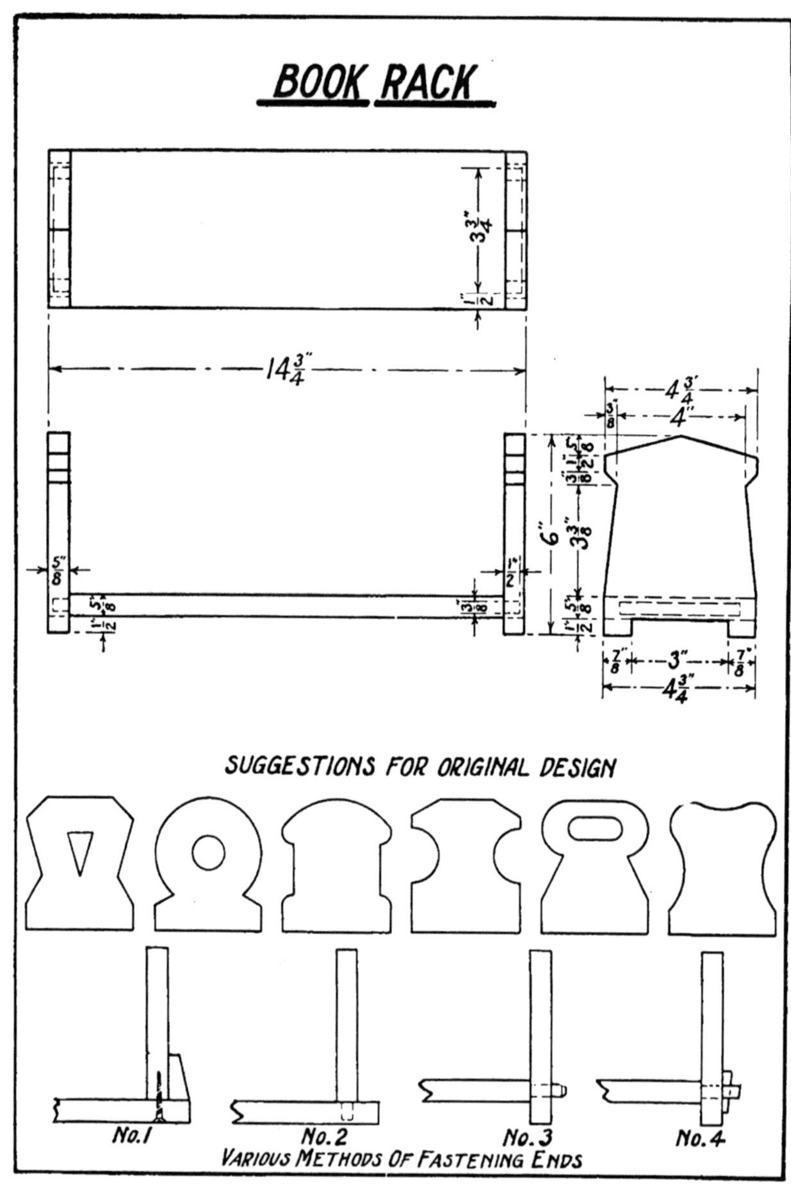
BOOK RACK
3 3/4"
1/2"
14 3/4"
4 3/4"
3/8
4"
5/8"
1/2"
3/8
1/2
5/8
3/8
6"
3 3/8"
1/2
5/8
3/8"
7/8"
3"
7/8"
4 3/4"
SUGGESTIONS FOR ORIGINAL DESIGN
No.1
No.2
No.3
No.4
VARIOUS METHODS OF FASTENING ENDS

# BOOK RACK SPECIFICATIONS

## THE BASE.

The entire material for the book rack may be cut from one piece of stock, ⅝"x5¼"x28". Select the best side of the material and plane it perfectly smooth for the working face (Chapter II., Paragraph 2). Plane one edge for a working edge (Chapter II., Paragraph 4). Prepare a working end (Chapter II., Paragraph 5); with the marking gauge (Chapter II., Paragraph 6) or with ruler and pencil (Chapter II., Paragraph 7) gauge the width of the base on both surfaces.

Since the ends and base are to be exactly the same width, you may gauge the full length of the piece of material; carefully plane to these gauge lines. Measure the length for the ends; with the try-square, square across the working face, cutting off pieces the right length for the ends (Chapter II., Paragraph 5).

## THE ENDS.

If you do not expect to use the design given in the working drawing, make a drawing of your own. This drawing should first be made on paper. Lay out and shape one of the ends; use it for a pattern in laying out the other; make the two exactly alike.

## MORTISING.

A wide mortise is to be cut in each end piece to receive the tenon on the end of the base (Chapter V., Paragraph 66). (Other methods of joining the ends and base are shown in the suggestions. Use one of these methods if you desire.)

## ASSEMBLING.

Assemble with glue and, if it seems necessary, two or three small brads may be driven through each end piece into the tenons (Chapter II., Paragraph 21). This, however, will not be required if the joints fit perfectly.

## FINISHING.

All broad surfaces should be carefully gone over with the steel scraper (Chapter II., Paragraph 16). All surfaces should be carefully sandpapered. Use great precaution not to round any of the sharp corners (Chapter II., Paragraph 17). Stain the book rack the desired color (Chapter IV., Paragraph 54). If desirable the book rack may be given a coat of filler (Chapter IV., Paragraph 55). It may be finished with a wax polish (Chapter IV., Paragraph 56) or with shellac (Chapter IV., Paragraph 57).

**Optional and Home Projects Employing Similar Principles.**

## POST CARD RACK.

1. In using this plan for making a post card rack the material should be somewhat thinner, perhaps $\frac{3}{8}''$ or even a little less. One of the fine cabinet woods should be used, such as walnut, cherry or mahogany. The base should be very much shorter than in a book rack; 4 or 5 inches would probably be long enough for an average-sized card rack.

## FOLDING BOOK RACK.

2. A very convenient folding book rack may be made by constructing a rectangular frame of the desired size for the base; this frame may be joined at the corners with the cross-lap joint; the end pieces should be made just wide enough to go inside the frame, and should be joined to it with a small piece of dowel rod, or a round head screw on each side. If these screws are properly placed the ends, when folded, will lie flat inside the rectangular frame, and when open will stand perpendicular, resting against the cross rails of the base frame.

# DRAWING BOARD

## MATERIALS.

Basswood (Chap. III., Par. 31) or White Pine (Par. 48).

| | |
|---|---|
| 3 pcs. 7/8"x6"x26" S 2 S Top. | 2 pcs. 7/8"x1 1/2"x16" S 2 S Cleats. |
| 1 pc. 1/4" dowel 12" long. | 10-1 1/4" No. 10 F. H. B. screws. |

## INTRODUCTORY STATEMENT.

The subject of drawing is continually growing in importance. When we think that before any piece of building or construction work can be undertaken it must first be drawn in perfect detail, then we begin to realize that this is a subject with which everybody should be somewhat familiar.

Every boy should be able to understand and to make simple working drawings. In order to make these drawings a drawing board is necessary.

The size of a drawing board depends upon the size of the drawings one intends to make; about 16 or 18 inches wide by 22 or 24 inches long is a very convenient size for ordinary work.

---

**References:**

Mechanical Drawing for Schools, Book 1. Atkinson, Mentzer & Co.
Mechanical Drawing for Schools, Book 2. Atkinson, Mentzer & Co.
Problems in Mechanical Drawing, C. A. Bennett. Manual Arts Press, Peoria, Ill.
Practical Mechanical Drawing Self-Taught, Chas. Westinghouse. Frederick Drake Co., Chicago.
Architectural Drawing, Edminster. David Williams Co., New York.
Practical Lessons in Architectural Drawing, Tuthill. David Williams Co., New York.
Junior Course in Mechanical Drawing, Thorne.
Elements of Mechanical Drawing, Titsworth.
Elementary Course in Mechanical Drawing, Chase.
A Practical Course in Mechanical Drawing, Willard. Pop. Mech. Co., Chicago.

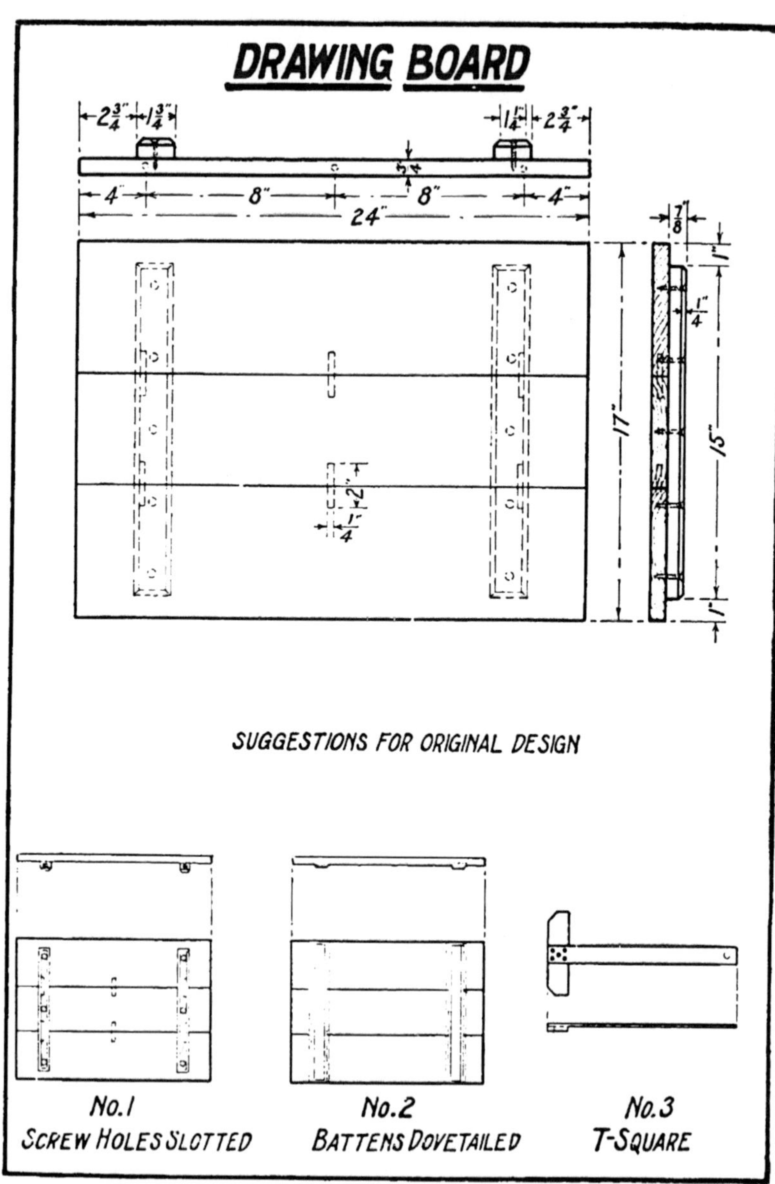
DRAWING BOARD
SUGGESTIONS FOR ORIGINAL DESIGN
No. 1
SCREW HOLES SLOTTED
No. 2
BATTENS DOVETAILED
No. 3
T-SQUARE

# DRAWING BOARD SPECIFICATIONS

The drawing board is to be made by gluing together three pieces (more pieces may be used if the material is narrow). As this board must be surfaced after it is completed, it is not necessary to plane a working face. Select the best side and mark it the working face (Chapter II., Paragraph 2). Plane the best edge of the first board perfectly square for a working edge (Chapter II., Paragraph 4). Plane one edge of the second board in like manner (Chapter II., Paragraph 4). Gauge the width on both faces (Chapter II., Paragraphs 6 or 7). Plane to the gauge line. Plane the best edge of the third board in like manner, then lay all of the boards in position on your bench top and examine the joints to see that they will fit perfectly.

## THE DOWELS.

By studying the drawing you will notice that the boards should be so assembled that the grain is reversed. Carefully lay out the dowels (Chapter II., Paragraph 18); bore for the dowels (Chapter II., Paragraph 13). Cut the dowels the required length. Be sure not to have them too long, as they will hinder the assembling. Glue the dowels into one board, then spread a thin coating of glue on the edges which are to come into contact, being sure that the boards are assembled with their face side up. Make both dowel joints in like manner and clamp securely.

## THE BATTENS.

Select the best side for the working face (Chapter II., Paragraph 2). Plane one edge for a working edge (Chapter II., Paragraph 4). With a marking gauge, gauge the width (Chapter II., Paragraph 6) and carefully plane to the gauge line. Square one end (Chapter II., Paragraph 5); lay out and cut them the proper length. Smooth these ends with the block plane (Chapter II., Paragraph 5). Lay out for the chamfer (Chapter II., Paragraph 8). Carefully plane to the gauge line. The battens should be fastened on with screws, as indicated in the drawing, or, if preferred, by the dove-tail method, indicated in No. 2 of the suggestions. If fastened on with screws, it is well to have the holes slotted slightly so, if the board shrinks or expands, the screws may slip in the slots and thus not bend the board out of shape.

## ASSEMBLING.

When the glue is dry carefully plane both surfaces of the drawing board and fasten the battens to the under side. Carefully plane and test the working surface of the drawing board (Chapter II., Paragraph 2). Plane one edge perfectly straight and square (Chapter II., Paragraph 4). With a large steel square square each end and finish with the block plane (Chapter II., Paragraph 5). The surface of the drawing board should be carefully finished with a steel scraper (Chapter II., Paragraph 16) and smoothed with fine sandpaper (Chapter II., Paragraph 17). It should be finished with one or two coats of shellac (Chapter II., Paragraph 57).

## T-SQUARE.

If you desire to make a T-square, you may easily do so by following the suggestions given in the drawing. The blades should be long enough to reach across your drawing board and the head should be 10" or 12" long. The blade should be about 1/8" thick and the head about 3/8". The blade and head must be assembled at a perfect right angle, or the T-square will be worthless. The top edge of the T-square must be a perfectly straight line.

## Optional and Home Projects Employing Similar Principles.

## MOLDING BOARD.

1. In connection with work in clay modeling and experiments with concrete a molding board is very necessary; such a board will afford a smooth working surface upon which to mix and mold the materials, and will also protect the desk or table tops. This board can be made any size, depending upon the material available and the projects to be worked out upon it. It should be about 1" thick, free from cracks and provided with strong battens on the under side.

## PLASTERER'S HAWK.

2. A plasterer's hawk will be found a very convenient article of equipment in conducting experiments with cement and plastering materials; it may also be made to serve a practical purpose about the home or farm. White pine is the most suitable wood for this project. The board should be made about 12" square and need not be more than 1/2" or 5/8" thick; it should be reinforced by having another board, somewhat smaller (perhaps about 9" square), fastened to its bottom side with the grain running at right angles (this will add strength and prevent warping). A cylindrical handle about 4" or 5" long is fastened to the bottom side.

# WINDMILL

## MATERIALS.

Basswood (Chap. III., Par. 31) or White Pine (Chap. III., Par. 48).

2 pcs. 7/8"x1¾"x 9" S 2 S Fans.
1 pc. 7/8"x 7/8"x21" S 2 S Shaft and upright.
1 pc. bright tin 5"x7".
2-1¾" No. 10 R. H. blue screws.
6-1" No. 17 brads.

## INTRODUCTORY STATEMENT.

In certain countries where the power of the wind is used in irrigating and in doing certain lines of work of this kind the windmill gets considerable study and attention. Most of us give but little thought to the direction or power of the wind, except when we occasionally see it turning a large fan on a wind pump.

This windmill which you are to make serves also as a weather vane and will thus indicate the direction as well as the force of the wind. Men who are studying the subject of flying machines have given great study to the same principles by which you are to construct this windmill.

The following references are worthy of careful study:

---

**References:**

Land of Dikes and Windmills; Our Little Dutch Cousins, McManus. L. C. Page & Co.
Windmills in a Country Below the Sea, Carpenter's Geographical Reader. American Book Co.
Harper's Outdoor Book for Boys. Harper & Brothers, Pub.
Harper's Machinery Book for Boys. Harper & Brothers, Pub.
Mechanical Toys Which a Boy Can Make, Geo. F. Johnson. Longmans, Green & Co.
First Book of Forestry. Ginn & Co.
History of Lumber Industry. U. S. Bulletin No. 34.

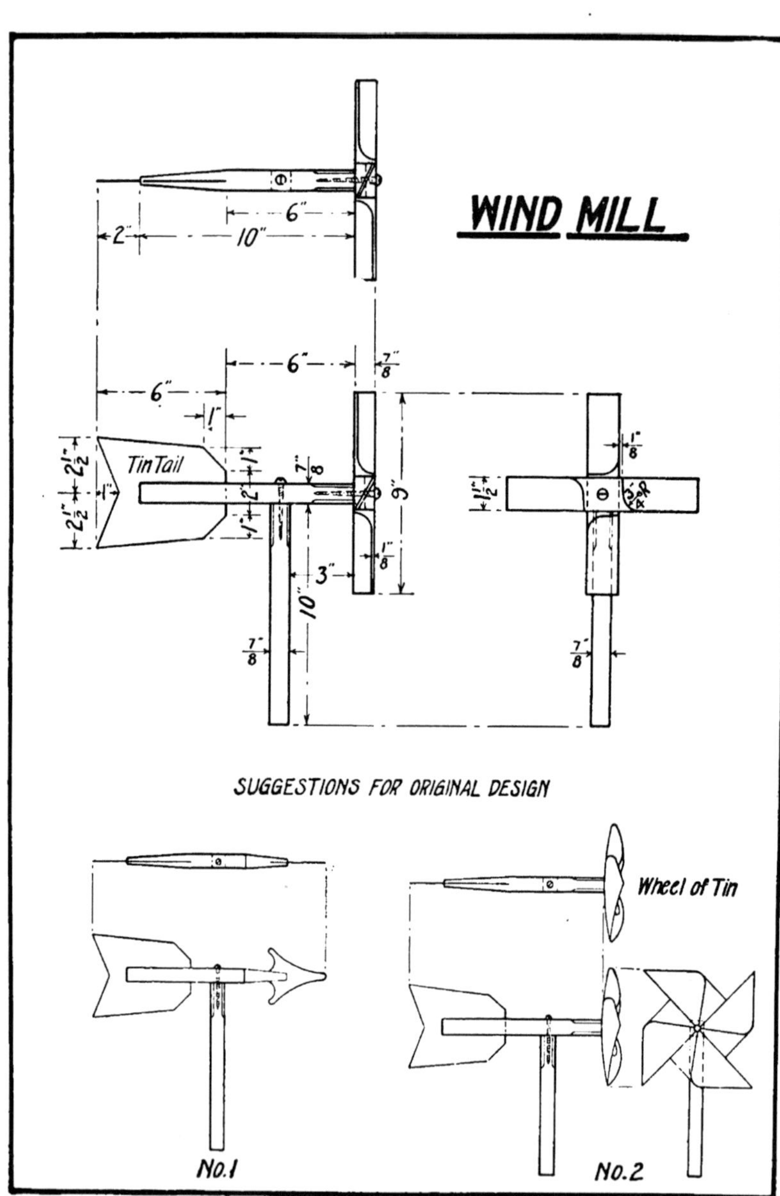
WIND MILL
6"
2"
10"
6"
7/8"
6"
1"
Tin Tail
2 1/2"
1"
2 1/2"
1"
7/8"
2"
1"
9"
1"
8
3"
10"
1"
8
1 1/2"
3/4"
7/8"
7/8"
SUGGESTIONS FOR ORIGINAL DESIGN
Wheel of Tin
No.1
No.2

# WINDMILL SPECIFICATIONS

## THE FANS.

As this material is furnished S 2 S, you will not need to plane the surface. Select the best surface and mark it the working face (Chapter II., Paragraph 2). Plane one edge for a working edge (Chapter II., Paragraph 4). Prepare a working end (Chapter II., Paragraph 5). Measure and cut the length of the fan, as shown in the drawing. In like manner prepare the other fan. Be sure these pieces are exactly the same size.

A study of the drawing will show you that these two pieces are to be put together with a cross-lap joint, crossing exactly at their middle (Chapter V., Paragraph 62). When the two pieces have been perfectly fitted, lay out the curves for the fan blades. This may be done with the compasses, or the curves may be drawn freehand. With the lead pencil and finger, gauge lines on the edges of each fan blade (Chapter II., Paragraph 8). Take the pieces apart, and with a sharp knife carefully whittle away the wood to the gauge line, forming a graceful curve.

## ASSEMBLING THE FAN.

When the fan blades are completed, fasten the cross-lap joint with small brads. These brads must be driven near the corners of the joint so as not to be in the way of boring the hole through the center. Locate the center (where the blades cross) and bore a hole (Chapter II., Paragraph 9) large enough to allow the screw to turn very freely.

NOTE:—When the windmill gets wet the wood will swell, and unless all holes, in which screws are to turn, have been bored apparently larger than necessary the joints will not turn.

## THE SHAFT AND UPRIGHT.

As the shaft and the upright are to be the same size, this piece of material should be planed the proper size before it is cut to length (Chapter II., Paragraphs 2, 3 and 4). You will notice that the end of the shaft is to be ripped to receive the tin tail. Gauge for the ripping on both sides of the shaft (Chapter II., Paragraph 6). Fasten the material in the vise and rip in the same manner as in sawing a tenon (Chapter II., Paragraph 14). Locate and bore the hole (Chapter II., Paragraph 9) for the screw which is to fasten it to the upright.

## THE TIN TAIL.

With lead pencil and ruler, lay out the shape of the tail. The tin may be cut with tinner's snips; if you do not have them, an old pair of shears will do very well. Fasten the tail in position by driving a few brads through the shaft and the tin.

## ASSEMBLING.

These parts are to be assembled with screws.

## FINISHING.

As this article is to be used out of doors, a coat of paint would be a good protection for it (Chapter IV., Paragraph 52). If desirable you may give the woodwork a coat of stain (Chapter IV., Paragraph 54).

### Optional and Home Projects Employing Similar Principles.

## HEAT WHEEL.

1. A paper heat wheel may be made on the same plan as shown in suggestion No. 2. Cut a perfect square of any kind of stiff, tough paper (not cardboard), mark the diagonals and cut on these lines from each corner toward the center; turn in the alternate corners, causing the wheel to take the shape shown in suggestion No. 2. Thrust a pin through each of these corners and the exact center of the wheel. Remove the pin and put it through these same holes from the other side; that is, so the head of the pin will be on the plane smooth side of the wheel; thrust the pin into the end of a small, softwood stick; the wheel can be made to stand in position by fastening the opposite end of the stick in a hot air register; the passing of the hot air will turn the wheel.

## CIRCULAR TIN WHEEL.

2. An easily constructed and very successful wind wheel may be made of a circular piece of tin. Almost any diameter will do, but about six or eight inches will be most convenient. Cut out a perfect circle of tin, find the center, and with the compasses lay out a small circle (about an inch and one-half in diameter); on the outside circumference step off equal spaces about one and one-half inches; from these points cut straight lines toward the center just to the inside circle; punch a smooth hole in the center; fasten to the end of a stick with a screw or a nail; twist each of the blades of the wheel so they will all stand at the same angle. It may require a little experimenting and adjusting to get them set so the wheel will turn satisfactorily.

# CHILD'S SWING

## MATERIALS.

Yellow Pine (Chap. III., Par. 48).

2 pcs. 7/8"x6"x12" S 2 S Bottom.
2 pcs. 7/8"x1½"x12" S 2 S Bottom battens.
7 pcs. 7/8"x1⅛"x12" S 2 S Rails.
1 pc. ½" dowel 30" long.
8-1½" No. 10 F. H. B. screws.
20 ft. 3/8" cotton rope (sash cord).

## INTRODUCTORY STATEMENT.

This lesson presents an easy but attractive and substantial way of making a swing which can be put up in the house or on the porch.

The seat may be upholstered with denim, canvas or imitation leather if the swing is to be used entirely indoors; the upholstering would not be desirable for outdoor use. If intended for outside use the seat should be reinforced with cleats, as indicated in the suggestions; the wood parts should also be well painted to protect them from the weather.

By using heavier material and making all the parts proportionately larger, and substituting small chain for the rope, a very excellent playground swing may be had.

---

**References:**

Rope. Upson Walton Co., Cleveland, Ohio.
Minnesota Bulletin No. 136, Rope and Its Uses on the Farm.
Minnesota Bulletin No. 33, Some Knots and Splices.
Flax, Hemp and Other Fiber Plants—Sixty Lessons in Agriculture. American Book Co.
Fiber Plants, the Book of Useful Plants, Rogers. Doubleday, Page & Co.
Cotton, Flax and Hemp; How the World Is Clothed, Carpenter. American Book Co.
Playgrounds and Parks; Health in Home and Town, Brown. D. C. Heath & Co.
Public Playgrounds, Day Allen Willie, St. Nicholas Magazine, May, 1909.
The School Playground, U. S. Bureau of Education, Bulletin 1912, No. 16.
Tree Planting on Rural School Grounds, U. S. Bulletin No. 134.

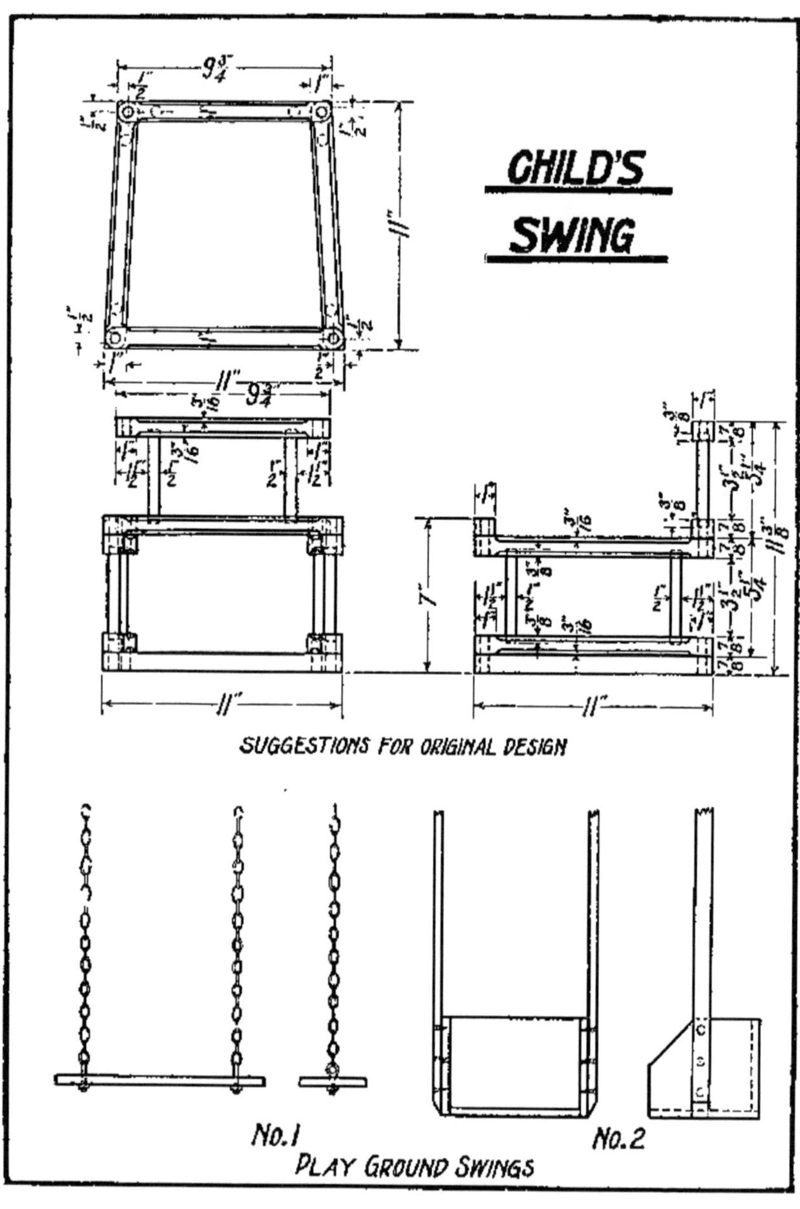
CHILD'S SWING
SUGGESTIONS FOR ORIGINAL DESIGN
No. 1
No. 2
PLAY GROUND SWINGS

# CHILD'S SWING SPECIFICATIONS

## THE BOTTOM.

The material for the bottom will probably be furnished in two pieces; if so, they should be joined with the dowel joint (Chapter V., Paragraph 72). Select the best surface of one board and mark it the working face (Chapter II., Paragraph 2). NOTE:—It will not be necessary to plane it now, for it will have to be replaned after the two pieces are glued together. Prepare a working edge (Chapter II., Paragraph 4). In like manner prepare the other bottom piece. Lay out (Chapter II., Paragraph 18) and bore (Chapter II., Paragraph 13) for the dowels. Make the glue joint and clamp securely. Leave the work clamped while you proceed with the other parts.

## THE SIDE AND BACK STRIPS.

You will probably have to rip these strips from a wider board. If you do, select a working face (Chapter II., Paragraph 2); prepare a working edge (Chapter II., Paragraph 4). With the marking gauge, gauge the width on both surfaces (Chapter II., Paragraph 6). Rip just outside the gauge lines. Plane to the gauge lines. In like manner prepare all the strips. NOTE:—In getting out a number of pieces from stock, be sure to prepare a working edge on the stock each time before attempting to lay out the required piece. Cut all the strips the required lengths, as shown in the drawing. Locate the places where the holes are to be bored. The holes for the dowels should not be bored entirely through. The holes for the rope should be bored through (Chapter II., Paragraph 9). Round the ends of each piece, and chamfer the corners, as shown in the drawing. Note that these chamfers do not extend the entire length of the strips, therefore you cannot make them with a plane. Lay them out (Chapter II., Paragraph 8) and cut them with a knife. Smooth with a wood file and sandpaper.

## THE DOWELS.

Dowels are to be used for the upright rails between the strips. Cut the required number the length indicated in the drawing. NOTE:—Dowel rods and small strips can be conveniently sawed in the square cut of a miter box.

## COMPLETING THE BOTTOM.

After the glue has had twelve to twenty-four hours to harden, remove the clamps and plane both surfaces (Chapter II., Paragraphs 2 and 3). In making this piece the desired shape it would be well first to cut it perfectly square, after which you can easily and accurately lay out the required shape. Bore the holes as required (Chapter II., Paragraph 9). If desired, battens about 1½" wide may be used on the under side of this bottom piece. They will add considerable strength and prevent warping.

## ASSEMBLING.

Glue the ends of the dowels into their proper positions in the side and back strips. Do not assemble with the rope until the finishing is completed.

## FINISHING.

With fine sandpaper remove all rough places. Stain the desired color (Chapter IV., Paragraph 54) and finish with two or three coats of shellac (Chapter IV., Paragraph 57). Assemble with the rope. Tie knots on the lower side of the bottom to prevent the rope from pulling out.

### Optional and Home Projects Employing Similar Principles.

## PLAYGROUND SWING.

1. A very suitable playground swing may be made of small chains fastened to a strong seat board with two eye bolts, as shown in suggestion No. 1. This sort of swing has the advantage of the seat board being held permanently in position. The use of the chain also makes it durable for outside service.

## BOX SWING.

2. A very simple and easily constructed swing may be made of a small dry goods box. Select a box which is made of sound material, and cut it the shape shown in suggestion No. 2. It may be hung with strips of wood or a small rope or chain, which should be attached to cross battens extending entirely across the under side of the box. One pair of ropes or chains, as the case may be, might be attached to the box near the top to prevent tilting over.

# FLY TRAP

MATERIALS.

Basswood (Chap. III., Par. 31).

8 pcs. 3/8"x1"x12½" S 2 S Sides.
8 pcs. 3/8"x1"x 7½" S 2 S Cross pieces.
5 pcs. ½"x¾"x9" S 2 S Top pcs.
8 pcs. ¼"x¾"x9" S 2 S Trim.
3 dozen 1" brads.
3 dozen ½" brads.
1½ dozen 3/8" corrugated nails.
1 yard 24" screen wire.
9 dozen small tacks.
1 piece 5/32" Bessemer rod 8" long.
2 screw eyes No. 114.
1 pair ¾"x¾" brass hinges.
1 small clasp.

INTRODUCTORY STATEMENT.

Recent investigation has proven that the common housefly is a very dangerous enemy to human life. The fact that it spreads disease and is in every way undesirable is sufficient reason why everybody should be as careful as possible to prevent its increase. One of the most successful ways to wage war on flies is to screen our homes so as to shut them out, and then leave no uncovered garbage pails or any other feeding places for them.

In cities where everybody has been interested in disposing of flies the results have been very encouraging. School children have helped wonderfully by engaging in fly-catching contests.

You can do a great practical good for your own home and community by making this flytrap carefully and using it throughout the fly season.

References:

The House Fly as Disease Carrier, L. O. Howard. Published by F. A. Stokes Pub. Co., New York.
U. S. Bulletin No. 459, and U. S. Bulletin No. 679, House Flies.
Insects and Disease, Doane. Henry Holt & Co.
Our Household Insects, Butler. Longmans, Green Co.
Household Insects and Methods of Control, Bulletin No. 3, Ithaca, N. Y.
U. S. Bulletin No. 155, How Insects Affect Health.
Fly Traps and Literature. International Harvester Co., Chicago.
Winter War on Flies, Willard Price, Technical World, February, 1915.
Our Insect Friends and Enemies, John Smith. J. B. Lippincott Pub. Co.

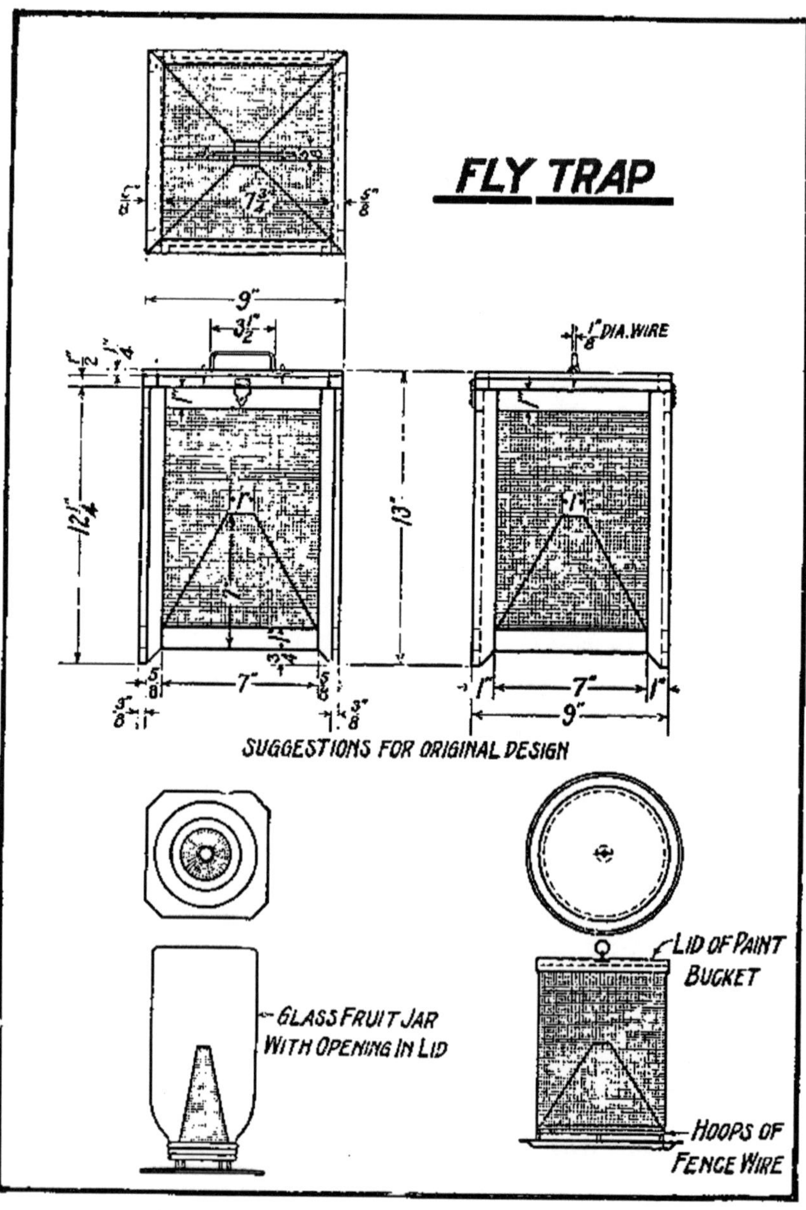

FLY TRAP
SUGGESTIONS FOR ORIGINAL DESIGN
1/8" DIA. WIRE
GLASS FRUIT JAR WITH OPENING IN LID
LID OF PAINT BUCKET
HOOPS OF FENCE WIRE

# FLY TRAP SPECIFICATIONS

## THE SIDE STRIPS.

You will probably have to rip your material from stock; select the best surface of your stock for a working face (Chapter II., Paragraph 2); plane one edge for a working edge (Chapter II., Paragraph 4). With the marking gauge, gauge the width of the strips on both surfaces of the stock (Chapter II., Paragraph 6). Rip just outside the line; plane to the gauge lines. Prepare all the side strips in like manner. Saw them the required length. Notice that on two sides of the fly trap, the side strips are narrower than on the other two sides. This is done so the four sides will be equal when assembled. Miter the lower end of each strip, as shown in the drawing.

## THE SIDE CROSS RAILS.

Rip out and plane the side cross rails in the same manner in which you have made the side strips. Cut all these rails the required length, as shown in the drawing. They may be easily and accurately sawed in the square cut of a miter box.

## ASSEMBLING THE BODY OF THE TRAP.

Each side is merely a rectangular frame. Lay two side strips flat on your bench top with the two cross rails in such position as to form a frame; make the angles square and fasten with corrugated nails (Chapter II., Paragraph 23). Assemble all sides in like manner. Cut screen wire the proper size and cover the inside of each frame; fasten the screen wire in position with small tacks. Assemble the four frames box fashion; they should be joined with a plain butt joint (Chapter II., Paragraph 60) at each corner; fasten with brads (Chapter II., Paragraph 21).

## THE LID.

The lid is a square frame (with a cross bar in the middle for the handle) joined at the corners with plain butt joints (Chapter V., Paragraph 60), fastened with brads. Square the stock for the lid (Chapter II., Paragraphs 1, 2, 3 and 4); cut each piece the required dimensions; assemble as explained; cover with screen wire. Strips of wood 1/4" thick are to be used as a trim on the lid, to cover the tacks and add to the appearance of the work; miter this trim at each corner (Chapter V., Paragraph 64); fasten it on with brads.

## THE INSIDE WIRE PYRAMID.

In order to cut the screen wire for this piece you should make a pattern of paper; if you will draw four triangles (each of the size of one side, as shown in the drawing) adjoining each other, you will have a correct pattern. Allow about an inch to make the lap; bend into proper shape; with a piece of the wire weave the open corner securely together; place in position and fasten with tacks. These tacks may also be covered with a trim just as you did the lid.

## THE HANDLE.

Bend the wire to form the handle; attach with two screw eyes. Fasten the lid in position with two small hinges and put on the fastening. Plane off uneven places if there are any. Stain some dark color (Chapter IV., Paragraph 54).

### Optional and Home Projects Employing Similar Principles.

1. A very satisfactory and convenient fly trap may be made of any ordinary glass fruit jar, as shown in the Suggestions. The entire central portion of the lid is cut out. A slender cone is made of screen wire with a small opening at the point. This cone may be attached to the lid by having a number of small holes punched around the opening in the lid, through which a small wire can be so woven as to bind the cone securely. A thin piece of wood, with four tacks or small nails, so driven as to extend slightly above the surface, will make a satisfactory base. In a trap of this kind the flies may be easily killed by pouring in boiling water.

2. An all-metal fly trap can be made from the lid of an old paint bucket, a few scraps of heavy fence wire and a piece of screen wire. The screen wire is rolled into a cylinder just as large as the bucket lid, which is to form the top. The screen wire cylinder is woven to the rim of the lid through small holes, as indicated in the drawing. A hoop of fence wire of the same diameter as the lid is attached to the other end of the cylinder, to hold it in shape. The inside cone of screen wire is attached to a second hoop of the same size as the first. The cone is placed in position, and if properly made will fit so closely that it will not require fastening. Small pieces of wire may be attached to form legs about a half-inch long. A sheet of tin, or an old pie tin will answer for a base.

# MILKING STOOL

MATERIALS.

Beech (Chap. III., Par. 32) or any hard wood.

1 pc. 1½"x9¼"x 9¼" S 2 S Top.
4 pcs. 1¼"x1¼"x12" S 2 S Legs.

## INTRODUCTORY STATEMENT.

The milking stool is usually such a rude, unsightly piece of equipment that it gets but little consideration and is often found dirty and poorly cared for. In the modern dairy many of the old-fashioned, dirty and unsightly pieces of equipment are giving way to things which are more convenient and more satisfactory from a sanitary standpoint.

This lesson shows how to make a milking stool on the same principles which any other stool should be made. The fact that it has four legs keeps it from falling over and getting unnecessarily soiled, also provides it with greatest strength. The height of the stool can be made to suit the desire of the one who is to use it.

This plan of making a stool is universal and can be used in making a bathroom, kitchen or office stool. Of course in making a high stool it would be necessary to provide cross rails to brace the legs.

---

**References:**

U. S. Bulletin No. 689, A Plan for a Small Dairy House.
U. S. Bulletin No. 413, Care of Milk on the Farm.
U. S. Bulletin No. 602, Clean Milk.
U. S. Bulletin No. 363, The Use of Milk as a Food.
U. S. Bulletin No. 32, Silos and Silage.
Minnesota Bulletin No. 130, Feeding Dairy Cows.
Forest Planting and Farm Management, U. S. Bulletin No. 228.

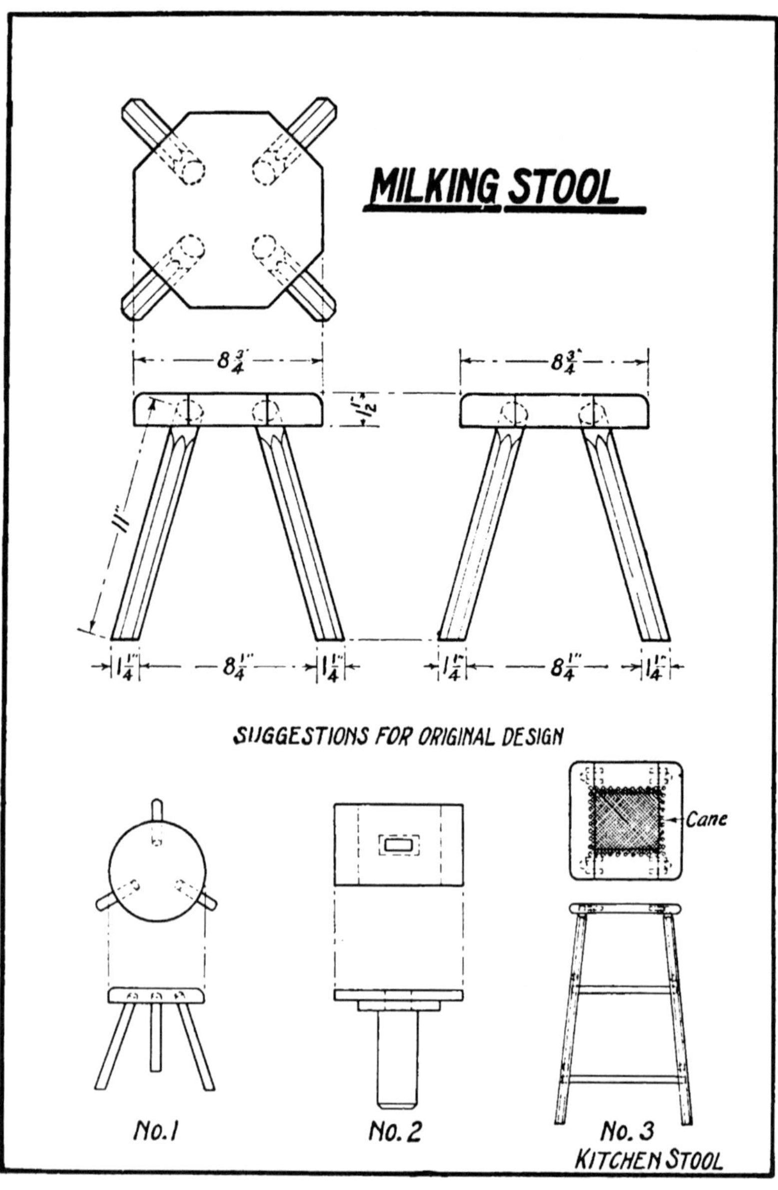
MILKING STOOL
$8\frac{3}{4}$
$8\frac{3}{4}$
$1\frac{1}{2}$"
11"
$1\frac{1}{4}$"
$8\frac{1}{4}$"
$1\frac{1}{4}$"
$1\frac{1}{4}$"
$8\frac{1}{4}$"
$1\frac{1}{4}$"
SUGGESTIONS FOR ORIGINAL DESIGN
Cane
No. 1
No. 2
No. 3
KITCHEN STOOL

# MILKING STOOL SPECIFICATIONS

NOTE:—This project can be made to serve either as a milking stool or a bathroom stool. If it is to be a bathroom stool it should have very careful workmanship, and should be painted white or enameled.

## THE TOP.

Select the best surface of the piece which is intended for the top and prepare a working face (Chapter II., Paragraph 2). If you are to use the design of top shown in the drawing, you will find it convenient first to make the material perfectly square, and then follow the directions for laying out an octagon given in Chapter 1, Problem 14. Saw out the octagon and plane all the edges perfectly square. The top edge may be rounded or chamfered (Chapter II., Paragraph 19). The holes which are to receive the legs are to be bored with a ⅞″ or 1″ bit, whichever you may have in the shop. Determine the angle which you wish to use (this can be done with the eye). Then set the T-bevel. Hold the T-bevel in such a position as to keep the bit at the proper angle while boring the holes (Chapter II., Paragraph 12). Do not bore the holes entirely through. In making a milking stool the holes are sometimes bored entirely through so the legs can be wedged in from the top side and sawed off even with the top.

## THE LEGS.

In making the legs, first plane the material perfectly square (Chapter II., Paragraphs 2, 3 and 4). They are to be made octagon shape by planing away the corners. These corners should be gauged with the lead pencil and finger (Chapter II., Paragraph 8). Carefully plane to the gauge line. The top end of each leg is to be rounded so it will enter the hole in top board. This may be done with a knife and finished with a wood file and sandpaper (Chapter II., Paragraph 15).

## ASSEMBLING.

Spread a little glue on the rounded ends of the legs and drive them into their places. When the work is all assembled, thoroughly clean it with a steel scraper and sandpaper. The bottom ends of the legs may be laid out the desired shape by setting the stool on a table top or level floor and laying out with the compasses; or this may be done by laying a ruler flat on the floor, and marking on the top edge of it all around the legs; saw on these lines.

## FINISHING.

If it is to be used for a milking stool it should be given a coat of paint of any desirable color (Chapter IV., Paragraph 52). If it is to be used for a bathroom stool it can be made very attractive by giving it two coats of white paint, and one coat of white enamel.

It is sometimes thought desirable to make a milking stool with only three legs so that it will sit level on an uneven surface. If you care to do this, follow No. 1 in the suggestions given.

## Optional and Home Projects Employing Similar Principles.

### COOKING STOOL.

1. It is usually desirable to have the school kitchen equipped with stools. These can be made on the same plan used in the construction of the milking stool. The top should be round, of the desired size, possibly 10″ or 12″ in diameter; the legs may be round, octagonal or square. They should be about 18″ long. There should be two cross rails between each pair of legs, as shown in suggestion No. 3. White enamel makes a very desirable finish for a stool of this kind.

### OFFICE STOOL.

2. An office stool may be made on the plan already given with the height changed to suit individual needs. The solid top may be used, although a more desirable plan is to construct a frame of four pieces neatly joined with dowels, as shown in suggestion No. 3. This frame may have a bottom woven of cane or may be covered with a patent imitation of leather, which can be purchased at any furniture store.

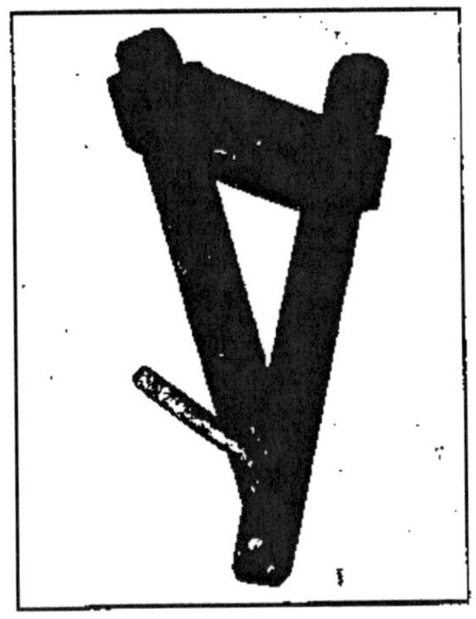

# HARNESS RACK

MATERIALS.

Oak (Chap. III., Par. 29) or any strong wood.

1 pc. 7/8"x2¼"x15½" S 2 S Back.
1 pc. 7/8"x2¼"x14" S 2 S Front brace.
2 pcs. 7/8"x2¼"x8" S 2 S Side braces.
1 pc. ¾"x6½" dowel rod.
12-6d finish nails.

## INTRODUCTORY STATEMENT.

If you visit a great many barns you will no doubt find that some people are very careless in their methods of caring for the harness. It is not uncommon to see harness laid on the barn floor, thrown carelessly in a corner or poorly hung on a nail, which is insufficient. Such methods not only cause considerable waste of time in handling the harness, but also bring about unnecessary damage.

The purpose of this harness rack is to provide a simple and easily made hanger which can be fastened to a wall or post and furnish a hanger which will keep the harness in good condition and always ready for use.

---

**References:**

Manufacture of Leather in Packing House Industries. International Library of Technology.
Leather; Stories of Industries, Vol. 2, Chase & Clow. Educational Pub. Co.
By-Products of the Meat Packing Industry. Swift & Co., Chicago.
Tanning and Preparation of Leather, Champlin's Cyclopedia of Common Things (p. 425). Henry Holt & Co.
Great American Industries, W. F. Rocheleau. A. Flanagan Pub. Co., New York.
How We are Clothed, Chamberlain. Macmillan Co., New York.
American Inventions and Inventors, Mowry. Silver, Burdette & Co., Chicago.
How the World is Clothed, Carpenter. American Book Co., Chicago.
The Farm Wood Lot, U. S. Bulletin No. 276.

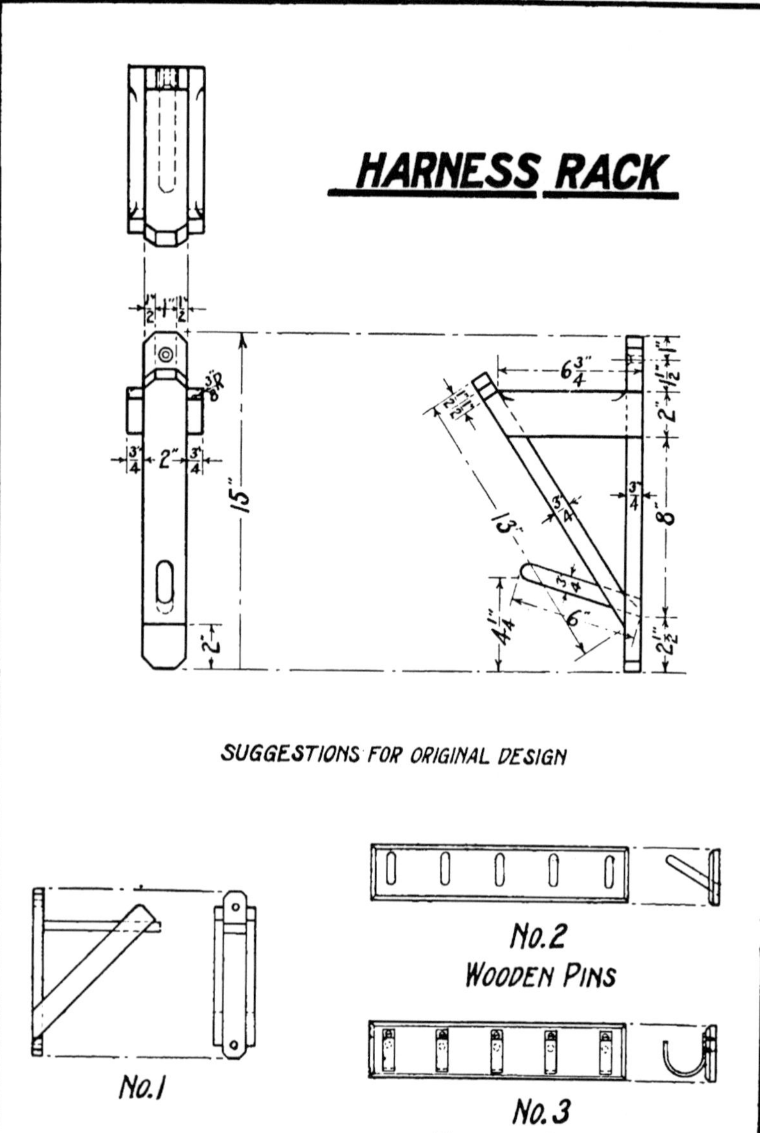
HARNESS RACK
SUGGESTIONS FOR ORIGINAL DESIGN
No.1
No.2
WOODEN PINS
No.3
HOOKS OF STRAP IRON

# HARNESS RACK SPECIFICATIONS

## THE BACK PIECE.

As this material is furnished S 2 S, it will not be necessary to surface it. Select the best side and mark it the working face (Chapter II., Paragraph 2). Plane one edge for a working edge (Chapter I., Paragraph 4). With the marking gauge, carefully gauge the width (Chapter II., Paragraph 6) and plane to the gauge line. Square one end (Chapter II., Paragraph 5). Lay out the length of the back piece, and cut this end perfectly straight. Chamfer the end as shown in the drawing.

## THE FRONT BRACE.

Select the best surface and mark it the working face (Chapter II., Paragraph 2). Plane one edge perfectly square for a working edge (Chapter II., Paragraph 4). With the marking gauge, set exactly as it was when you gauged the back piece, gauge the width (Chapter II., Paragraph 6) ; plane to the gauge line. Notice that the lower part of this piece is to be cut on an angle. About a third-pitch cut will be suitable for this angle. You may set your T-bevel to this angle (Chapter II., Paragraph 25). Lay out the angle on one edge of the material. With the try-square, square this line across the working face, and lay out the angle on the other edge to correspond with the first edge. Place the material in the vise and carefully saw on the lines. Measure the length shown in the drawing, and form the other end.

## SIDE BRACES.

Select the best surface of the piece from which the side braces are to be made, and mark it the working face (Chapter II., Paragraph 2). Plane one edge for a working edge (Chapter II., Paragraph 4). Gauge the width, as shown in the drawing (Chapter II., Paragraph 6) ; plane to the gauge line. This brace is also to be cut at an angle. This may be done after the work is assembled if you choose. At the other end these braces are to be cut square.

## THE DOWEL.

Measure and cut the dowel the length shown in the drawing.

## ASSEMBLING.

Nail the side braces in position shown in the drawing. Put the front brace in its position; nail through the side braces into it, making sure that you are holding it in such a position as to make the bottom end fit snugly against the back piece. With the try-square, test to make sure that the side braces are exactly at a right angle to the back piece. While holding in this position nail through the front brace into the back piece at each edge. Do not nail near the center because the nails will interfere with the boring for the dowel. Bore for the dowels with the bit inclined slightly up. This will give the pin an upward tendency. Notice that the pin extends through the brace and back piece. If necessary you may split the back end of the pin and wedge it to make it perfectly secure. Bore the hole for the screw upon which the harness rack is to hang (Chapter II., Paragraph 9). If you think necessary, you may bore another hole in the bottom of the back piece and thus provide room for two screws. This hanger may be placed on a post or on a flat surface.

## FINISHING.

Carefully scrape and sandpaper all surfaces. The top outside edges of the side braces should be chamfered and slightly rounded. This may be done with a pocket knife and wood file and finished with sandpaper. This piece of work may be finished with a coat of paint (Chapter IV., Paragraph 52) or it may be stained (Chapter IV., Paragraph 54) and shellaced (Chapter IV., Paragraph 57).

## Optional and Home Projects Employing Similar Principles.

### HARNESS RACK WITH DOWELS.

1. A very easily constructed harness rack may be made by boring a number of holes slightly on an angle, and driving in large dowels or wooden pins as hangers. A heavy board may be used for the base, or the holes may be bored directly in a post or beam of the barn.

### HARNESS RACK WITH METAL HOOKS.

2. Very substantial hooks may be made out of heavy strap iron or pieces of buggy tire. These pieces of metal should be cut the desired length then have two or three holes drilled near one end. These holes should be countersunk to receive the screw heads. Each piece should then be bent to form the hook, as shown in drawing No. 3.

# FLOWER TRELLIS

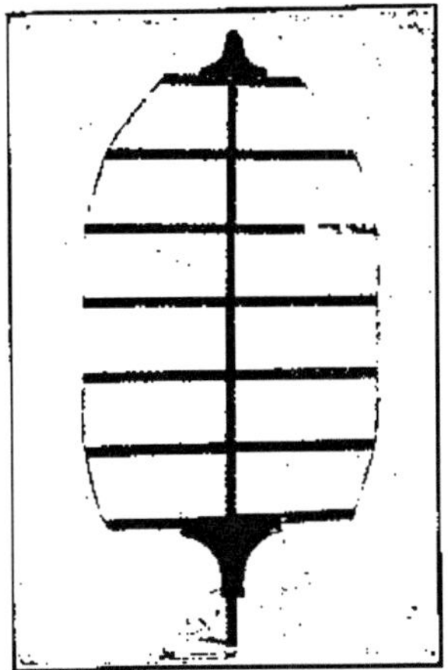

MATERIALS.

Yellow Pine (Chap. III., Par. 48) or any soft wood.

1 pc. ⅞"x2"x 5" S 2 S Upright.
7 pcs. ⅞"x1"x30" S 2 S Cross strips.
2 pcs. ¾"x5"x 7¼" S 2 S Brackets.
2½ dozen 6d finishing nails.
2 pieces soft iron wire 50".
16-¾" staples.

## INTRODUCTORY STATEMENT.

In a great many cities prizes are being offered and other inducements set forth to encourage people to keep their lawns clean and make their shrubbery attractive. It is not uncommon to see an otherwise beautiful rosebush or trailing vine showing neglect on account of the lack of some sort of support. A flower trellis made after the fashion shown in this lesson can be used to overcome this difficulty. In making a flower trellis you should consider the size, shape and weight of the bush for which it is intended and make it sufficiently strong and otherwise suited to that particular kind of bush. It is well to make the trellis larger than required so it can be used year after year. By making it of good material and doing the work accurately, then painting it, it can be made to add very much to the appearance of one's lawn or garden.

---

**References:**

U. S. Bulletin No. 185, Beautifying the Home Grounds.
U. S. Bulletin No. 91, Lawns and Lawn-making.
U. S. Bulletin No. 248, The Lawn.
New York Bulletin No. 2, The Flower Garden, Ithaca, N. Y.
Beautifying the Home Grounds; Sixty Lessons in Agriculture. Buffum & Deaver.
Our Garden Flowers, Keeler. Book Supply Co., Chicago.
Practical Forestry. Gifford.

# FLOWER TRELLIS

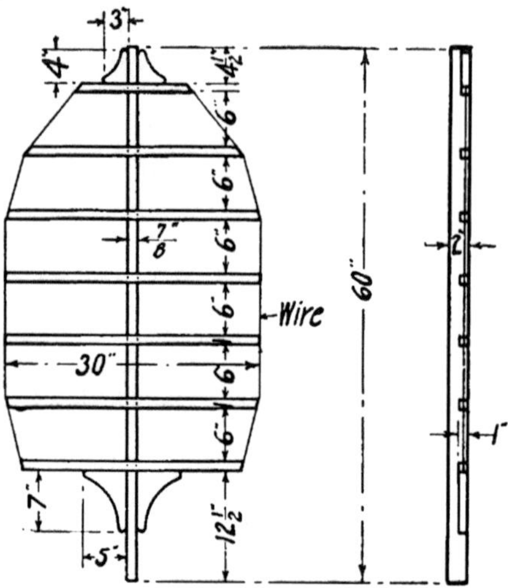


SUGGESTIONS FOR ORIGINAL DESIGN

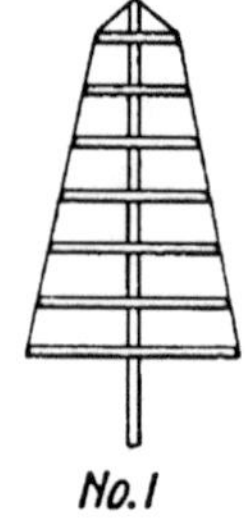

No. 1

No. 2

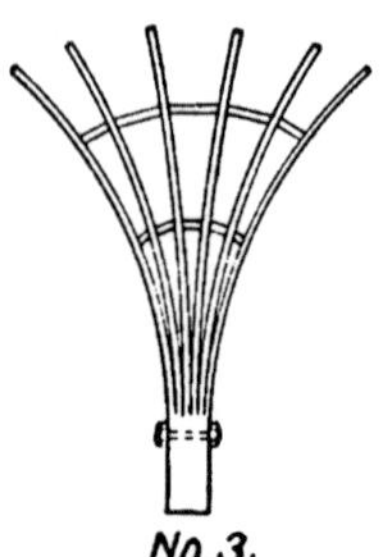

No. 3.

# FLOWER TRELLIS SPECIFICATIONS

## THE UPRIGHT.

As this material is furnished S 2 S, it will not be necessary for you to plane the surface. Select the best surface for the working face (Chapter II., Paragraph 2). Plane one edge perfectly straight as a working edge (Chapter II., Paragraph 4). With a marking gauge, gauge the width the entire length on both surfaces (Chapter II., Paragraph 6). Carefully plane to the gauge line. Prepare one end for a working end (Chapter II., Paragraph 5). Measure and cut the length (if desired the bottom end may be left considerably longer than indicated in the drawing so it can be pointed and driven in the ground. It is preferable, however, to drive heavy stakes into the ground and to fasten the flower trellis to it with nails or screws. This will avoid battering the top end in the driving process).

## THE CROSS STRIPS.

If you are cutting this material from stock it will be necessary to rip out the cross strips. In this case select the best surface of your stock for the working face (Chapter II., Paragraph 2). Carefully plane one edge for a working edge (Chapter II., Paragraph 4). With a marking gauge, lay out the width (Chapter II., Paragraph 6). Rip just outside the gauge line, and plane to the line. Again prepare a working edge on the stock material, and in the same manner lay out and rip the second strip. Continue this process until all the strips are provided. If the strips are provided properly ripped, all you will need to do is to prepare a working edge, and gauge the width as already indicated.

## ASSEMBLING.

Notice that the strips are to be gained into the upright their full size. Measure and lay out the spaces between the strips. With a try-square, square across the working edge of the upright where the gains are to be cut. Be very careful not to lay out the gains too wide, or the strips will not fill them and the joints will be bad. If your strips have been perfectly prepared they will be the same width, and the gains will all be cut exactly alike. If there is any variation, it will be necessary for you to test each strip to see that it will fit the gain laid out for it. In sawing for gains, saw just inside the pencil lines. With the marking gauge, gauge the depth of these gains on both surfaces of the upright. Do not gauge beyond the pencil lines, for this will leave an ugly mark on your upright. With the back saw, saw down to the gauge line, and with a sharp chisel cut out the wood between the saw kerfs. The bottom and top strips are to be cut a little shorter than the others so as to give the rack a pleasing shape; use your own judgment in this matter. The strips are to be fastened in place with nails (Chapter II., Paragraph 21).

## THE BRACKETS.

Lay out the brackets in any suitable design. Saw them out with the compass saw or coping saw, and carefully smooth the edges with a wood file. Fasten the brackets into position with nails, making sure they are perfectly square so as to make the strips stand square across the upright. The wire should be fastened with staples on the outer ends of the strips.

## FINISHING.

As this flower trellis is to be used out of doors, where it will be exposed to the weather, it should be well painted (Chapter IV., Paragraph 52) or given a good oil stain.

## Optional and Home Projects Employing Similar Principles.

### A METAL TRELLIS.

1. A very durable flower trellis may be made by bending a long piece of iron pipe to form a half-circle, or any other desired curve. The ends of the pipe should be driven in the ground deep enough to cause it to stand perfectly rigid. This framework should be neatly covered with poultry netting. With this style of trellis fancy and ornamental shapes may be worked out if desired.

### BENT WOOD TRELLIS.

2. A very interesting trellis may be made by ripping a wide board almost its full length, and spreading the strips into some pleasing shape, as shown in suggestion No. 3. A bolt should be put through the board edgewise to prevent splitting. The wood for this sort of trellis must be carefully selected. It must be straight grained; elm would probably be the most suitable.

## SUGGESTIONS FOR COMMUNITY RESEARCH.

No. 1. Do you know of a pattern-maker's shop in your community? If you do, visit it and ask the pattern-maker to show you the kind of drawings from which he works. Ask him to tell you how his blue prints are made. How much per week can a pattern-maker earn in your community? Is the pattern-maker's trade as important now as years ago? Find out all you can about this trade and decide whether it would be a promising occupation for a boy to learn. Is it likely that machinery will entirely take the place of handwork in pattern-making?

No. 2. Is the force of the wind used to do any kind of work in your neighborhood? Why is this true?

No. 3. Does your school have an outdoor playground equipment? Why? What portion of an outdoor playground equipment, which would be suitable for your school, could be made in the manual training shop?

No. 4. What measures are being taken in your home to dispose of house flies? Find out how the garbage and other waste matter about your home is disposed of. Do you think this is being done in the very best way to prevent the increase of flies? Discuss this question with your parents. Take home your fly trap and catch as many flies as possible. You would find it interesting to talk to your local physician about some of the causes and means of preventing typhoid fever.

No. 5. If possible, visit a dairy farm and get some one to tell you what improvements have been made in dairying in the past ten years. If you keep cows at your home, do you use the most modern methods of dairying? Why? Ask your parents for their opinions on these matters.

No. 6. Visit a harness shop and find out from the proprietor whether the demand for harness-makers is increasing or decreasing. How much per week does the average harness-maker earn? Would this be a good trade for a boy to learn? Why?

No. 7. How many different kinds of flowers, trees and shrubs (not counting garden vegetables) are you raising in your yard at home? What advantages are there in trimming shrubs and tying them neatly on well-made trellises?

No. 8. Visit a sugar camp and learn all you can about making maple sugar. How many kinds of maple grow in your community?

## REVIEW QUESTIONS AND PROBLEMS.

1. Why are dowels used in gluing together the edges of boards? How should the grain be turned in gluing together several narrow boards?

2. How may a piece of work be assembled without the use of nails, brads or screws?

3. How many feet of lumber in your drawing board? What would be the cost of this material at $60.00 per M.?

4. How much is the labor on your drawing board worth, counting the time which you have spent on it at 15 cents per hour? Figure any other project which you have made.

5. Make inquiry regarding any wind pump in your neighborhood and find out how many hours' work per week it saves the owner; at that rate how long will it take for the pump to pay for itself?

6. If the material for a book rack costs 15 cents, and you can sell it when completed for 65 cents, for how many hours' work would you be paid, counting your time worth 12½ cents per hour?

7. Why should a bread or meat board be free from cracks and perfectly smooth on all of its surfaces? Name four or five kinds of wood which would be suitable for such a board. Name some kind of wood which you think would not be suitable for this purpose. Why?

8. What features must receive careful attention in making a T-square?

9. What effect does dampness have on wood? How can wood which is to be exposed to the weather be protected?

10. What are some of the advantages and disadvantages of a three-legged milking stool? Of a one-legged stool?

11. How would you make a suitable finish on a kitchen stool?

12. What are battens, and why are they used?

13. What are some of the advantages of a flower trellis made of iron pipe and wire?

14. How can you tell a rip saw from a cross-cutting saw?

15. What are some of the advantages in keeping tools sharp?

16. How many tops for camp stools, as given in this section, can be cut from a square yard of canvas? What will be the cost of one stool top at the price charged at your local dry goods store?

REVIEW QUESTIONS AND PROBLEMS (Concluded).

17. Why are the hanging holes in a bracket shelf bored exactly 16 inches apart?

18. When screws form a part of the decoration on a piece of work, what should be their position?

19. About how many average-sized ears of corn, as raised in your community, are required to make a bushel?

20. In buying material less than one inch thick, how is the thickness considered? If it is more than one inch thick?

21. What are the regular widths of screen wire carried by your local hardware store? Find out the price per yard.

22. How is small rope like that used in the child's swing lesson usually sold, by the yard, bundle or pound? About how many yards of such rope are required to make a pound?

23. How can you test to make sure that holes are being bored perpendicularly?

24. How can you test to make sure that a number of holes are all being bored at the same angle?

25. What is meant by the "set" in a saw? Why is it necessary?

26. In sawing gains, on which side of the mark would you saw? Why?

27. In gauging the width of a piece of material, why should you gauge it on both surfaces?

# INTRODUCTION TO SECTION III

BY the time this section is reached students should be pretty thoroughly familiar with the more common elementary tool processes and should have but little difficulty in interpreting the working drawings. The use of the ruler, try-square and marking gauge in simple laying out work should be undertaken with considerable confidence.

The projects of this section will be found somewhat more difficult than those of the preceding sections, not so much in the matter of the introduction of difficult joints as in awakening and testing the judgment of the student in problems of assembling. No effort is made to give specific directions step by step for the assembling even of some of the more complicated projects, such as the water wheel and dishcloth rack. The matter of "getting together" the parts of a piece of work after all are correctly made presents the greatest possible opportunity for the exercise of the initiative of the student. The latitude which is left in this portion of the specifications is for the purpose of encouraging constructive thought.

The introduction of some hardwood projects will make a test of the students' ability along the line of certain tool processes which they may have performed with ease on soft wood. The fact that hard wood offers greater difficulties must not be made an excuse for less perfect work.

The simple miter joint is introduced in connection with the miter box lesson. Considerable emphasis must be laid upon this principle, for it has almost unlimited application in future work. Students should learn to lay out and cut this joint without the use of a box; when a knowledge of how to obtain the angle has been acquired, the assistance of the box may be employed in practical work.

By the time students have reached this stage in their work they should be taking considerable interest in finding home applications for the principles mastered at school; self-reliance will be greatly improved by the efforts on practical problems which are not under the constant dictation and supervision of the teacher.

An appreciation of the value of the drawing work must be instilled; whether the subject is given at a regular period or is studied incidentally with the shop work, it must have very careful and constant consideration.

# SLEEVE BOARD

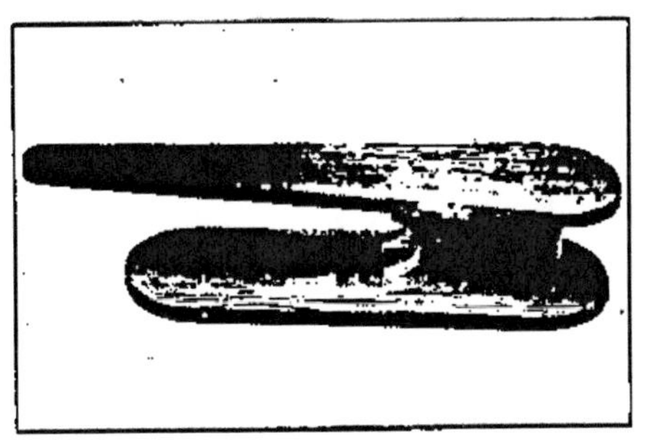

MATERIALS.

Yellow Pine (Chap. III., Par. 48) or any soft wood.

1 pc. ⅞"x5 "x24" S 2 S Top.
1 pc. ⅞"x5¾"x20" S 2 S Base.
2 pcs. ⅞"x4 "x 7" S 2 S Blocks.
8-1½" No. 10 F. H. B. screws.

## INTRODUCTORY STATEMENT.

This sleeve board offers a solution to the problem of pressing the sleeve of a garment without causing a crease. Some housekeepers consider a sleeve board a very important piece of equipment. It can be used in a number of ways in ironing and pressing. The pressing board may be covered with heavy muslin or whatever padding the user may desire.

**References:**

Educational Woodworking for Home and School, Park. Macmillan Co., New York.
Training in Woodwork, Tate. Northwestern School Supply Co., Minneapolis, Minn.
American Boy's Workshop, Kelland. Book Supply Co., Chicago.
U. S. Bulletin No. 173, A Primer of Forestry.

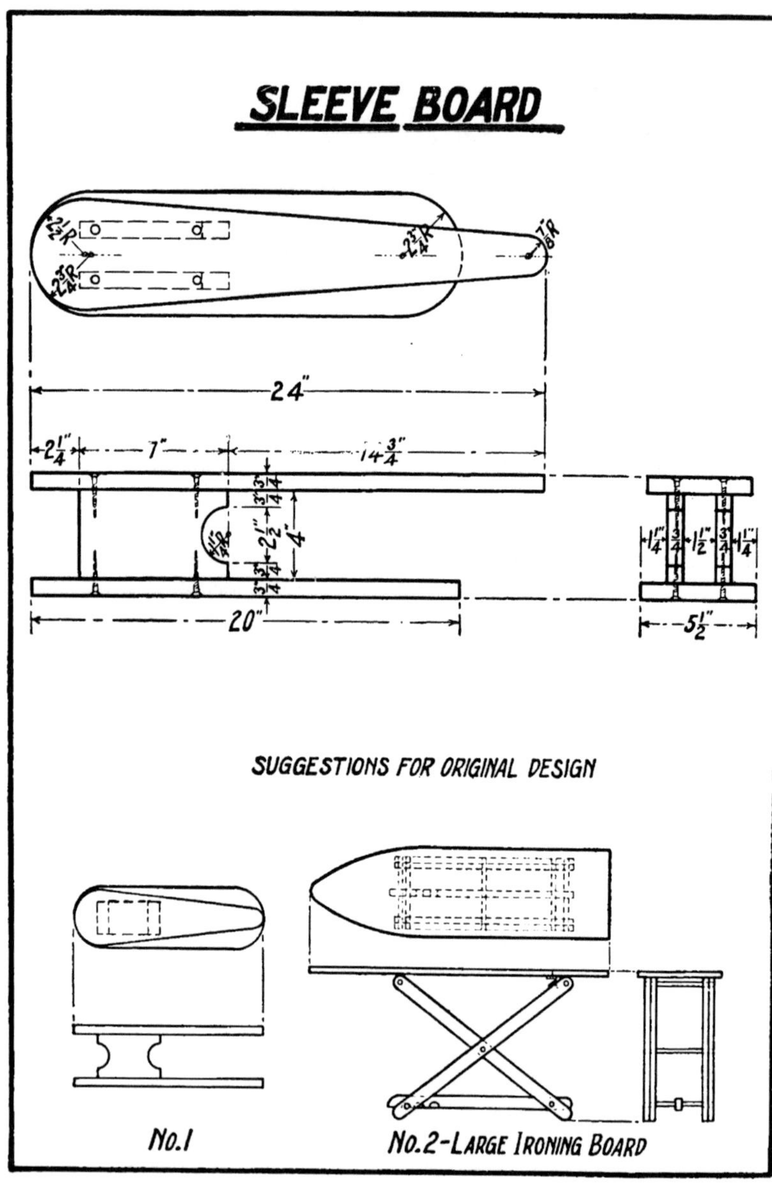
SLEEVE BOARD
24"
20"
SUGGESTIONS FOR ORIGINAL DESIGN
No.1
No.2-LARGE IRONING BOARD

# SLEEVE BOARD SPECIFICATIONS

## THE TOP.

Although this material is furnished S 2 S you should plane the surface with a sharp plane set to take a very thin shaving. Select the best surface for a working face (Chapter II., Paragraph 2). Plane one edge perfectly straight and square for a working edge (Chapter II., Paragraph 4). Prepare a working end (Chapter II., Paragraph 5); lay out and cut length of the top piece, as shown in the drawing. With the compasses set to the proper radius (shown in the drawing) lay out the shape of the top. With the compass saw cut the curves and with a rip saw finish sawing out the top. Carefully plane all the edges and make sure they are perfectly square with the working face. The round ends may be finished with a wood file.

## THE BASE.

Select the best surface for the working face (Chapter II., Paragraph 2). Prepare a working edge (Chapter II., Paragraph 4). Lay out and cut the base the shape and dimensions shown in the drawing. Make sure that the edges are planed perfectly square; finish the ends with a wood file and sandpaper.

## THE BLOCKS.

Select the best surface for a working face (Chapter II., Paragraph 2). Prepare a working edge (Chapter II., Paragraph 4). Cut the two blocks rectangular, the size shown in the drawing; with the compasses lay out the curve on one of the blocks (without changing the radius of the compasses); lay out the curve on the other block in the same manner. With the compass saw, saw out the curve in each block. Compare the blocks to make sure they are exactly the same size.

## ASSEMBLING.

This piece of work is to be assembled with screws. Be sure to bore the holes in the top and the base large enough to allow the screws to pass through freely (Chapter II., Paragraph 9). Countersink the holes so the screw heads will be slightly below the surface when they are driven in. In assembling this piece of work be very careful to have the top board stand exactly straight over the center of the base board.

## FINISHING.

With a sharp steel scraper (Chapter II., Paragraph 16) remove all pencil or tool marks from all parts of the work. Smooth perfectly with a clean piece of fine sandpaper (Chapter II., Paragraph 17). Give the work one or two coats of shellac (Chapter IV., Paragraph 57). Shellac the bottom of the base, the under side of the top and the inside of the blocks; these parts may not show, but shellacing them will prevent warping.

**Optional and Home Projects Employing Similar Principles.**

## SIMPLE PRESSING BOARD.

1. A simple pressing board to be used on the table can be very easily made of almost any kind of lumber. If two or more pieces are needed to make the required width, their edges should be neatly joined. Two or three battens should be attached with screws on the bottom side; a heavy piece of asbestos or a suitable metal stand for the iron might be fastened on the top side. The board should be covered with some suitable material.

## FOLDING IRONING BOARD.

2. Suggestion No. 2 presents an idea for a folding ironing board; this board is hinged to one pair of legs, leaving it free to raise at the pointed end. The notched strip across the bottom makes it possible to adjust the height and also to close it completely.

# WATER WHEEL

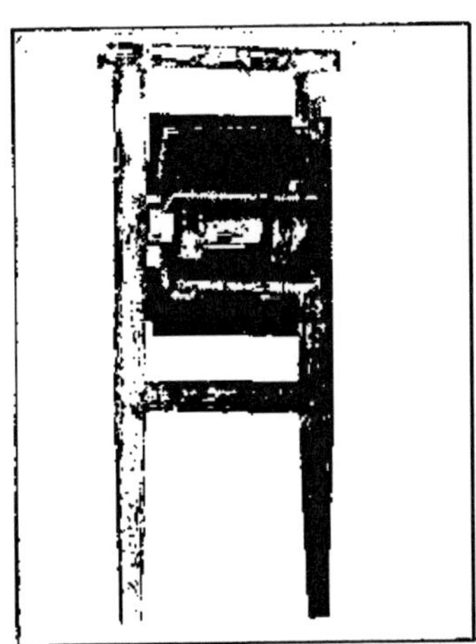

MATERIALS.

Oak (Chap. III., Par. 29) or any hard wood.

| | | | |
|---|---|---|---|
| 8 pcs. | ¼"x1¾"x4½" | S 2 S | Paddles. |
| 2 pcs. | ⅝"x4½"x4½" | S 2 S | Wheels. |
| 1 pc. | 1⅛"x1⅛"x 6" | | Cylinder. |
| 2 pcs. | ¾"x2"x15" | S 2 S | Sides. |
| 1 pc. | ¾"x2"x 7" | S 2 S | Top. |
| 1 pc. | ¾"x2"x 5" | S 2 S | Bottom. |

8-6d finishing nails.

INTRODUCTORY STATEMENT.

For hundreds of years water power has been used in driving the machinery of civilized man. When the invention of the steam engine was proven a success it was so general in its use that it threatened to take full place of water power. However, it has been proven that water power is very economical, and it is therefore being used in some of the largest power plants in the world. The great plants at Niagara Falls and Keokuk, Iowa, and in a great many other places, all depend on the same principle—that water flows down hill.

The water wheel given in this lesson will help you to understand in a simple way one of the earliest forms of using the force of water to turn a wheel. By experimenting with it in currents of water of different depth and different speed you will gain a great deal of information regarding water power.

---

References:

Boys' Book of Inventions, Roy S. Baker. McClure, Phillips.
Toys and Toymaking, George F. Johnson. Longmans, Green & Co.
Manual Training Toys for the Boy's Workshop, Moore. Manual Arts Press, Peoria, Ill.
Water Wheels, Young Folks' Cyclopedia of Common Things, Champlin, Henry Holt.
The Conservation of Water, John Mathews. Small, Maynard & Co., Boston.
Damming the World's Greatest Rivers, Rogers. Scientific American Supplement, August, 1912.
Harper's Machinery Book for Boys. Harper & Brothers, New York.
U. S. Bulletin No. 150, Clearing New Land.

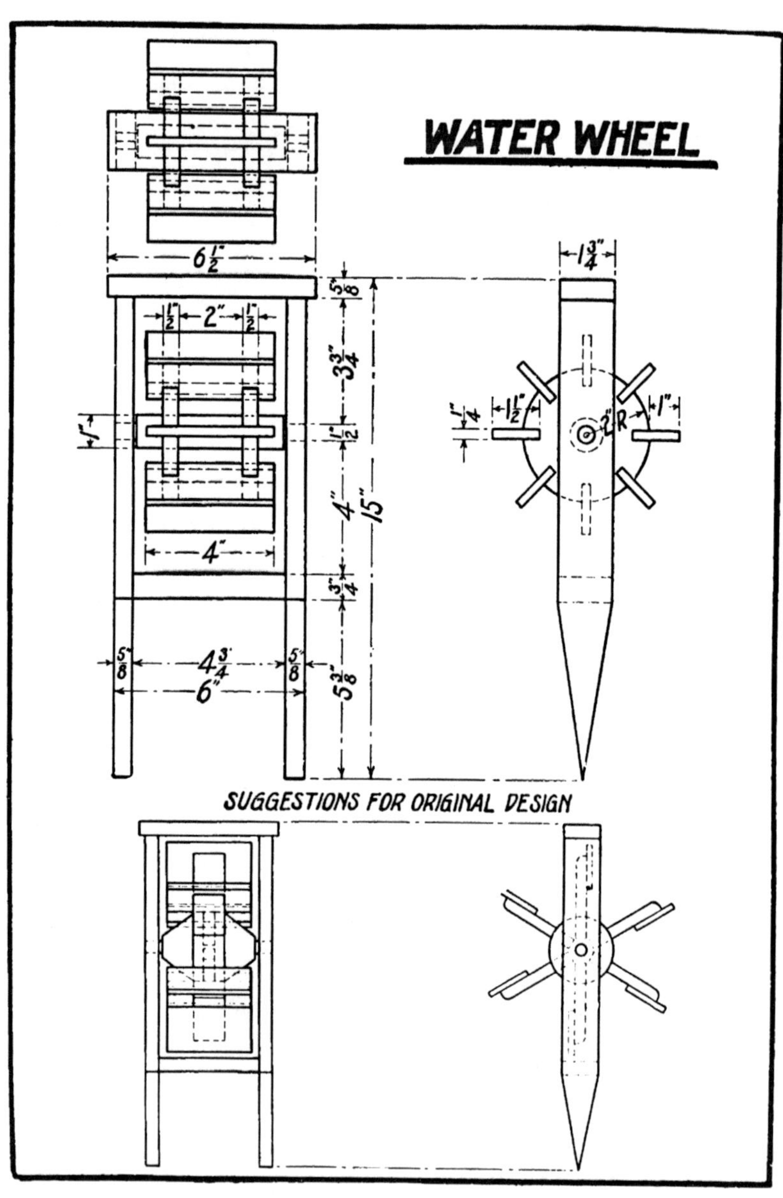
WATER WHEEL
6 1/2"
1/2"
2"
1/2"
5/8"
3 3/4"
1"
1/2"
4"
15"
4"
3/4"
5/8"
4 3/4
5/8
6"
5 3/8"
1 3/4"
1/4"
1 1/2"
2" R
1"
SUGGESTIONS FOR ORIGINAL DESIGN

# WATER WHEEL SPECIFICATIONS

## THE PADDLE.

If the material for the paddle is furnished in one long strip, you should make it the desired thickness and width before cutting off the separate pieces. Square this stock in the regular way (Chapter II., Paragraphs 1, 2, 3, 4 and 5). If the material is furnished you in short pieces, first plane out one paddle the desired dimension. To do this select the best surface and mark it the working face (Chapter II., Paragraph 2). Square one edge for a working edge (Chapter II., Paragraph 4). Gauge the width (Chapter II., Paragraph 6). Plane to the gauge line. Square one end (Chapter II., Paragraph 5); measure and cut the length. In like manner prepare the other paddles.

## THE PADDLE WHEEL.

The paddle wheel consists of two disks, which should be laid out with the compasses and sawed out with the coping or compass saw. Be sure to make the two wheels exactly the same size. After they are sawed out, file the edges perfectly smooth. Bore the center holes on the point where the compass rested in drawing the circles (Chapter II., Paragraph 9). The paddles are to be inserted in the paddle wheels by gains or dados. These should be cut at equal distances around the circumference of the wheels so the paddles will stand the same distance apart. Carefully lay out these gains equally distant. Gauge their depth with the use of the pencil and finger (Chapter II., Paragraph 8). Saw the gains down to the gauge line and chisel them out with a very sharp chisel.

## CYLINDER OR AXLE.

You are to plane a cylinder or axle which will fit the holes which you have bored in the paddle wheels. To plane this cylinder, first plane the stick perfectly square, then plane off the corners, making it an octagon. Again plane off the corners and continue planing off corners until it is as nearly round as possible. It can then be smoothed with a wood file and finished with the sandpaper (Chapter II., Paragraph 15). A round tenon is to be cut on each end of the axle (Chapter V., Paragraph 69).

## THE FRAMEWORK.

As this material is furnished S 2 S, it will not be necessary to plane the surface. Select the best surface and mark it the working face (Chapter II., Paragraph 2). Prepare a working edge (Chapter II., Paragraph 4). Lay out the two side pieces and make them the dimensions shown in the drawing. You will note from the drawing that these two side pieces are to be fastened in position by a bottom and top rail.

### ASSEMBLING.

Place the paddle wheel in position and see that it will turn very easily. You must remember that wood swells when it gets wet, and unless the turning joint is given considerable freedom it will not turn after the wood swells. Make it loose enough to allow a small brad to pass entirely around in the joint when the work is assembled. Carefully nail the frame together and test again to see that the wheel will turn very freely.

### FINISHING.

In as much as this piece of work is to be used in the water, it should have some sort of finish which will protect it. The easiest and best method of finishing it is to give it a good heavy coat of linseed oil and allow it to soak into the wood.

## Optional and Home Projects Employing Similar Principles.

### WATER MILL.

1. Make a water wheel as shown in this lesson, but let the axle extend about an inch beyond the frame on one side. Cut out a wooden pulley about 2½″ or 3″ in diameter and fasten it firmly on the extended axle. Groove the edge of the pulley. Construct a framework to hold as many wheels or pulleys as you desire; connect them to your water wheel with strong cord used as a belt.

### CORN STALK WATER WHEEL.

2. A simple water wheel which will furnish considerable amusement can be easily and quickly made of corn stalks. Select a corn stalk as nearly cylindrical as possible; cut a piece about 6″ or 8″ long for an axle. From another piece of stalk prepare eight or ten thin strips of the outside hard part about ¾″ wide and 3½″ or 4″ long. These pieces are to be used for paddles. In the center of the axle piece cut slits equally distant all around; insert one end of each of the paddle pieces to form a complete wheel.

Cut two forked limbs and smooth the forks inside to form bearings for the axle. Drive the forks into the bed of the stream just far enough apart to receive the ends of the axle.

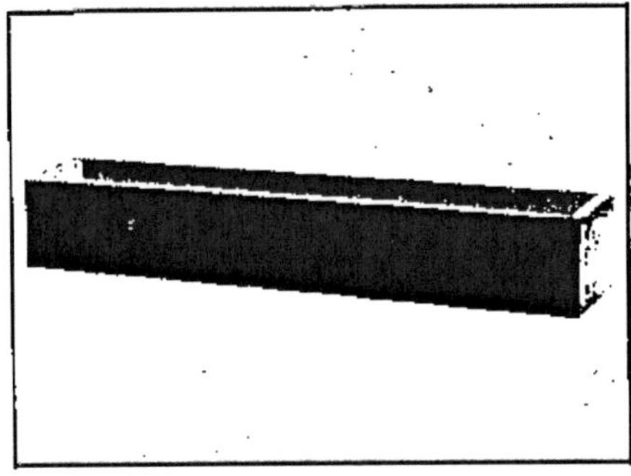

# WINDOW BOX

MATERIALS.

Poplar (Chap. III., Par. 42)
or any soft wood.

1 pc. 7/8"x6¾"x35" S 2 S
2 pcs. 7/8"x6"x37" S 2 S
2 pcs. 7/8"x6"x 6½" S 2 S
2½ dozen 6d finishing nails.

## INTRODUCTORY STATEMENT.

In cities where there is but little opportunity to come in touch with the beautiful green fields and bright flowers of the country, much has been done to give a cheerful and beautiful effect by encouraging the growth of plants and flowers in window boxes. Regardless of the surroundings, a pretty window box filled with growing plants adds considerably to the beauty of the home.

This box can be made of almost any kind of lumber. Even waste material from a dry goods box can be used if first-class material cannot be had. It should be carefully and neatly made then given at least two coats of good paint as a protection to the wood. Various ways have been devised for fastening window boxes in position; sometimes a small brace bracket is used under the box. An easy and simple way is to use small screen door hooks, thus fastening each end of the box to the window casing, allowing the weight of the box to rest on the window sill.

---

**References:**

A Garden City in a Country Village, Bessie M. Weed.
U. S. Bulletin No. 408, School Exercises in Plant Production.
U. S. Bulletin No. 218, The School Garden.
The Flower Garden, Bulletin No. 2, Ithaca, N. Y.
Lessons With Plants, Bailey. Macmillan Pub. Co.
U. S. Bulletin No. 157, The Propagation of Plants.
U. S. Bulletin No. 94, The Vegetable Garden.

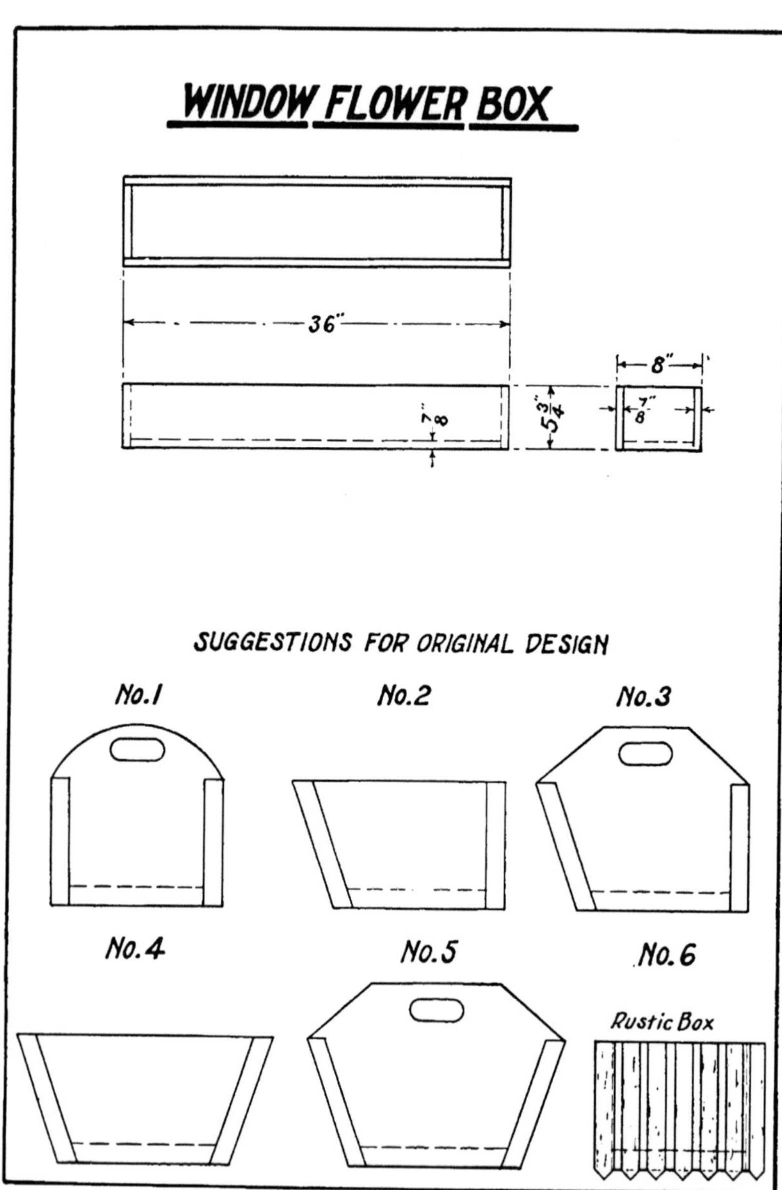
WINDOW FLOWER BOX
36"
8"
7/8"
5 3/4"
7/8"
SUGGESTIONS FOR ORIGINAL DESIGN
No.1
No.2
No.3
No.4
No.5
No.6
Rustic Box

# WINDOW FLOWER BOX SPECIFICATIONS

As this material is furnished S 2 S, it will not be necessary to resurface it.

## THE SIDE PIECES.

Select the best surface of one of the side pieces and mark it the working face (Chapter II., Paragraph 2). Plane one edge perfectly straight and square for a working edge (Chapter II., Paragraph 4). With the marking gauge (Chapter II., Paragraph 6), or with the lead pencil and ruler (Chapter II., Paragraph 7), gauge the width, as shown in the drawing; gauge on both surfaces. Carefully plane to the gauge line. Square one end (Chapter II., Paragraph 5). Measure the length, and in like manner square the other end. Prepare the other side exactly like this one.

## THE BOTTOM.

Select the best surface of the bottom piece and mark it the working face (Chapter II., Paragraph 2). Prepare a working edge (Chapter II., Paragraph 4). Gauge the width on both surfaces (Chapter II., Paragraphs 6 or 7). You will have to think carefully in determining the width of the bottom piece. The dimension in the drawing is from outside to outside of the box; it therefore includes the width of the bottom piece and the thickness of the two sides. Square one end (Chapter II., Paragraph 5). Measure and lay out the proper length. Notice that this bottom piece is to be cut enough shorter than the side pieces to receive the end pieces, therefore the bottom piece will be the thickness of the two ends shorter than the side pieces.

## THE ENDS.

Carefully square the stock (Chapter II., Paragraphs 1, 2, 3, 4 and 5). Lay out and cut one end the desired size. (Notice that the length of the end pieces is determined by the width of the bottom.) In like manner prepare the other end. Carefully compare the two end pieces to make sure they are exactly the same dimensions and perfectly square. NOTE: In any kind of box construction the opposite sides must be exactly the same length and all corners must be perfectly square or the box will not be rectangular when assembled.

## ASSEMBLING.

This work is to be assembled with nails (Chapter II., Paragraph 21). Finishing nails are recommended, because they have small heads and will therefore enable you to do a neater piece of work (6d common nails or slender-bodied box nails would be satisfactory, but they must be carefully used so the heads will not damage the appearance of the work).

## FINISHING.

After the box is assembled, with a sharp block plane set to take a very thin shaving, plane the outside of all the joints slightly, if necessary, to make them perfectly even. Finish with a sharp steel scraper (Chapter II., Paragraph 16). Sandpaper the entire surface (Chapter II., Paragraph 17). Inasmuch as this box is to hold dirt and will thus be kept moist almost constantly, it should have at least two coats of good paint, both inside and out. Paint it any desirable color (Chapter IV., Paragraph 52).

## Optional and Home Projects Employing Similar Principles.

### PORCH FLOWER BOX.

1. A porch flower box should be made the size and shape to suit the place for which it is intended. Where one side of the box is against the wall, the shapes shown in suggestions Nos. 2 and 3 are desirable. If both sides of the box are exposed, as is the case when used on a porch balustrade, the shapes shown in Nos. 4 and 5 would be preferable.

### RUSTIC FLOWER BOX.

2. A rustic flower box is always attractive and is not difficult to make. Prepare a strong, substantial box of the desired size; collect a number of limbs about 1½" in diameter; leave on the bark; rip them in two lengthwise and nail them to the box, covering it completely.

# MITER BOX

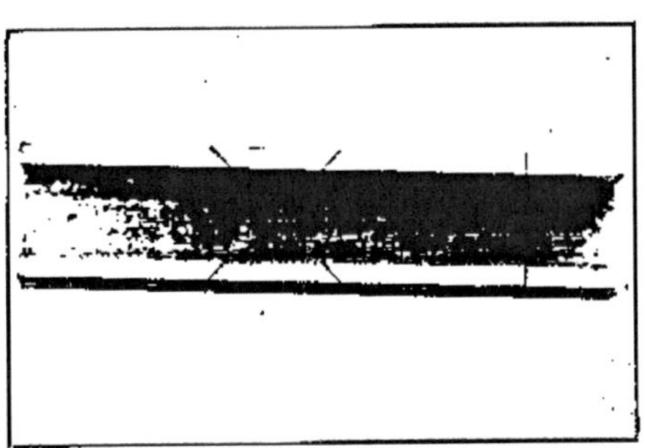

MATERIALS.

Poplar (Chap. III., Par. 42) or Yellow Pine (Chap. III., Par. 48).

1 pc. 1½"x3¾"x24½" S2S Bottom.

2 pcs. ⅞"x4"x24"½" S2S Sides.

10-1½" No. 10 F. H. B. Screws.

## INTRODUCTORY STATEMENT.

The use of the miter joint occurs so often in so many different kinds of construction work that every one needs to know how to lay out and cut a miter, but for the sake of speed, accuracy and convenience, where a number of miter joints are to be cut it is well to be provided with a miter box. An all-steel patent miter box can be bought from any tool dealer, but they are quite expensive.

The wooden miter box shown in this lesson is very inexpensive because it can be made of scraps of almost any kind of lumber. Its value depends upon its being sawed exactly on the true miter of 45 degrees.

If correctly made, this miter box will enable you to construct picture frames, window screens, and any other sort of rectangular frame.

**References:**

Elements of Construction, King. American Book Co.
The A, B, C of the Steel Square, Hodgson. The National Builder, Chicago.
Steel Square and Its Uses, Wm. Radford. David Williams Co., New York.
The Steel Square Pocketbook, Stoddard. David Williams Co., New York.
U. S. Bulletin No. 423, Forest Nurseries for Schools

# MITER BOX

SUGGESTIONS FOR ORIGINAL DESIGN

PICTURE FRAME CLAMP

# MITER BOX SPECIFICATIONS

## THE BOTTOM.

As this material is furnished S 2 S, it will not be necessary for you to resurface it. Select the best surface of the bottom piece and mark it the working face (Chapter II., Paragraph 2). Plane one edge perfectly straight and square for a working edge (Chapter II., Paragraph 4). As this piece of material is thicker than you have been accustomed to handling, you will have to take great care to make it perfectly square. Gauge the width on both surfaces (Chapter II., Paragraphs 6 or 7) and plane to the gauge line. Be sure that both edges are perfectly square or your work will not assemble properly.

## THE SIDE PIECES.

Select the best surface of one of the side pieces and make it the working face (Chapter II., Paragraph 2). Prepare a working edge (Chapter II., Paragraph 4). With the marking gauge or the lead pencil and ruler gauge the width, as shown in the drawing (Chapter II., Paragraphs 6 or 7). Plane to the gauge lines. Square one end for a working end (Chapter II., Paragraph 5). Lay out and cut the length. Prepare the other side in like manner.

## ASSEMBLING.

The two side pieces are to be fastened with screws to the edges of the bottom piece, making the bottom edge perfectly even. In assembling this work it would be advisable to put in one screw pretty close to the end of each side piece to hold the sides in proper position while you lay out the angle where the miter box is to be sawed. Then finish putting in the screws. Be careful not to place any of them where they will be in the way of the sawing. If you prefer, the miter box may be assembled with nails instead of screws, however it will not be so strong.

## LAYING OUT THE ANGLES.

The miter box should have one perfectly square cut. Lay it out with the large steel square, with the large blade held carefully on one edge of the box; with a sharp lead pencil lay out a square line across the top edge of each side piece. With the try-square square these lines down on the sides.

Lay out the half-pitch cut forming a letter "X" across the box. Lay out the half-pitch cut as explained (Chapter II., Paragraph 24). *You must make sure that this is accurate* or your miter box will be absolutely worthless. When the angles are laid out on the top edge of the two side pieces with the try-square, carefully square them down. Sawing these angles is the most particular part of your miter box construction. You should saw part way from one side and then turn the box around and saw from the other side. In sawing from the second side let the point of the saw follow in the cut made while sawing from the first side. By sawing very carefully you will be able to follow the lines.

## FINISHING.

With a sharp steel scraper remove all tool marks or rough places (Chapter II., Paragraph 16); finish with sandpaper (Chapter II., Paragraph 17). If desirable, the miter box may be given one coat of shellac. This will keep it clean and in good condition (Chapter IV., Paragraph 57). NOTE: Sometimes a miter box is made with one side wider than the other; in assembling such a box the sides are made even at the top, thus allowing one side to extend slightly below the bottom. This part can be held in the vise or against the edge of the bench top to hold the box solid when in use.

## Optional and Home Projects Employing Similar Principles.

### PICTURE FRAME CLAMP.

1. In assembling any kind of mitered frame a clamping device is very necessary. In the suggestions you will see the plan for a clamp which has a number of advantages. It can be used on almost any sized picture frame by adjusting the hand screws. It also affords an opportunity to resaw the miter joints if any of them require it.

# PICTURE FRAME

## MATERIALS.

Oak, plain or quartered (Chap. III., Par. 29).

2 pcs. 5/8"x2"x22" S 2 S
2 pcs. 5/8"x2"x18" S 2 S
12-1¼" brads.
2 screw eyes, No. 114.
Wire picture cord, 28".

## INTRODUCTORY STATEMENT.

Ever since pictures have been used as a means of decoration in the home of man the problem of providing suitable and artistic frames for their protection has been a matter of much study. A great many men spend their entire time making designs for picture frames and framing materials.

It would be almost impossible to give any rules which would serve as an absolute guide in designing all kinds of picture frames, but there are a few general principles which may be kept in mind. Frames should not be gaudy nor over decorative so as to detract from the picture. They should harmonize in size and color effect with the tone of the picture contained.

In order to become expert in the art of picture framing one would need to make a very careful study of interpretation of pictures.

References:

Picture Framing in Design and Construction in Wood, Noyes. Manual Arts Press, Peoria, Ill.
How to Study Pictures, Chas. H. Caffin. The Baker-Taylor Co., New York.
Picture Study in Elementary Schools, Wilson. Macmillan Co., New York.
A Child's Guide to Pictures, Chas. H. Caffin. The Baker-Taylor Co., New York.
The Book of Art for Young People, Conway. Adam & Black, publishers, London.
Famous Pictures, Barstow. The Century Co., New York.
How to Enjoy Pictures, Emery. Book Supply Co., Chicago.
Mounting and Framing of Pictures, Hasheck. Book Supply Co., Chicago.
U. S. Bulletin No. 358, Second Primer of Forestry.

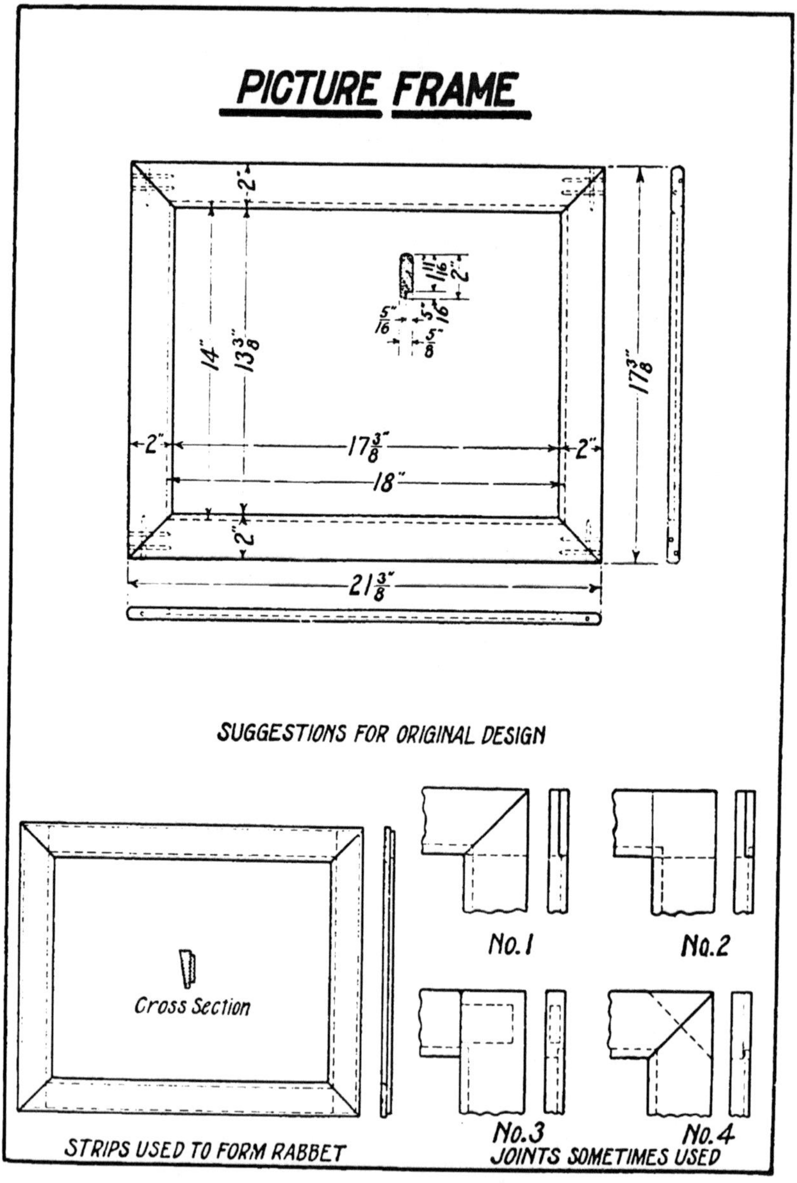

# PICTURE FRAME

2" 14" $13\frac{3}{8}$" $1\frac{11}{16}$" 2" $\frac{5}{16}$" $\frac{5}{16}$" $\frac{5}{8}$" $17\frac{3}{8}$" 2" $17\frac{3}{8}$" 2" 18" 2" $21\frac{3}{8}$"

SUGGESTIONS FOR ORIGINAL DESIGN

Cross Section

STRIPS USED TO FORM RABBET

No.1 No.2 No.3 No.4

JOINTS SOMETIMES USED

# PICTURE FRAME SPECIFICATIONS

## PREPARING THE STOCK.

Although your material is furnished S 2 S, it will be necessary for you to resurface it lightly with a very sharp plane. This will remove the marks of the machine planer with which it was originally dressed. Select the best surface and smooth it as directed for the working face (Chapter II., Paragraph 2). Carefully plane one edge for a working edge (Chapter II., Paragraph 4). With the marking gauge (Chapter II., Paragraph 6), or with the ruler and pencil (Chapter II., Paragraph 7), gauge the width on both surfaces; carefully plane to the gauge lines.

## FORMING THE RABBETS.

In picture frame material it is necessary to form a rabbet to receive the glass and the picture. If you have a regular rabbet plane, use it for this work; if not, you may use the grooving side of your matching plane; that is the side of the plane which has the single blade. Try this on a scrap of material until you see just how it can be done; a little experimenting will enable you to do it satisfactorily.

## CUTTING THE LENGTH OF SIDES AND ENDS.

If you have some special picture which you desire to frame, you should measure it and cut the lengths of your pieces to suit it. If not, you may follow the sizes given in the drawing.

The frame is to be joined at the corners with mitered joints; these are to be cut in the miter box which you have made. If you did not make the miter box and there is one provided in the shop, you may use it or lay out the half pitch cut (Chapter II., Paragraph 25) and then saw this angle by hand. This will be a little difficult, but if you are careful you can do it perfectly. After laying out the half-pitch cut once it is well to set the T-bevel to this angle and lay out the other pieces from the T-bevel. Remember, that in a rectangular frame opposite sides must be *exactly* the same length. The least variation will throw the frame out of square and ruin the joints.

## ASSEMBLING.

The joints are to be assembled with brads driven through the outside corners. This must be done with extreme care; you must not attempt to use large brads (Chapter II., Paragraph 21). NOTE: Before attempting to nail together the joints of the picture frame, lay it flat on your bench top or some other level surface to make sure that the joints will fit. This will determine whether opposite sides are exactly the same length and whether the joints are cut at a perfect half-pitch.

Sometimes in assembling a mitered frame mechanics nail together three joints, and if the last joint does not quite fit, they bring it as close together as possible, clamp it on the bench top with a scrap board under it and saw through the joint. The clamp holds the material from slipping, and the sawing through the joint makes it fit; it can then be brought together perfectly.

NOTE: In the miter box lesson a very excellent clamp for assembling frames is shown. This clamp makes it possible for a saw cut to be made in any joint that may require it.

### FINISHING.

After the frame is assembled, with a very sharp steel scraper (Chapter II., Paragraph 16), carefully smooth the outside surface; smooth all of the joints perfectly. If desirable, the outside corners of the frame may be slightly rounded or chamfered to suit your taste. With a piece of fine sandpaper (Chapter II., Paragraph 17), carefully smooth all of the surfaces. Stain the frame a desirable color to correspond with the picture with which it is to be used (Chapter IV., Paragraph 54). The picture frame should be given a coat of filler (Chapter II., Paragraph 55); one or two coats of shellac may be substituted, if you do not have the filler. Finish with shellac (Chapter IV., Paragraph 57) or with wax (Chapter IV., Paragraph 56).

## Optional and Home Projects Employing Similar Principles.

### FLY SCREEN.

1. The principle of a rectangular frame, assembled with plain mitered joints, is frequently and practically applied in the construction of a window screen. Measure a window at home and make a screen for it; stock 7/8"x2" or 2¼" is heavy enough for an average sized screen; any kind of soft wood is suitable; join with corrugated nails; after the screen wire is tacked on, trim with thin strips or flat moulding.

### HALL RACK.

2. A very attractive hall rack may be constructed on almost exactly the same principles as the picture frame; it should be made considerably heavier, and might have two or more cross mullions. The central frame should contain a mirror; artistic hooks of a desirable size and design should be properly placed on the frame and mullions.

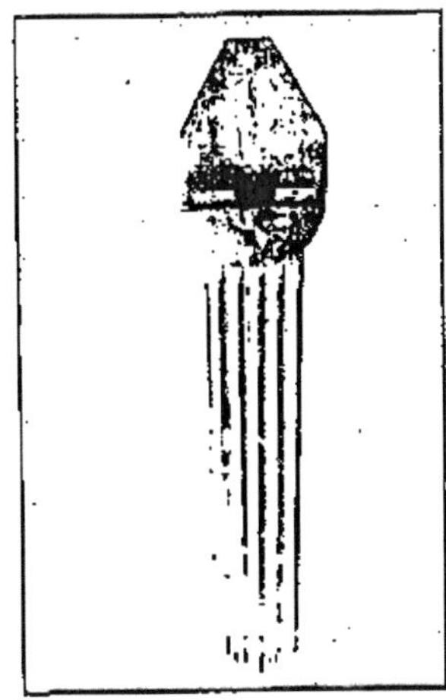

# DISHCLOTH RACK

MATERIALS.

Poplar (Chap. III., Par. 42) or any strong wood.

1 pc. 5/8"x6½"x 7" S 2 S Back.
2 pcs. 5/8"x3 "x 7" S 2 S Top and bottom.
5 pcs. 7/8"x 7/8"x21" S 4 S Hanger.
1 pair tight pin hinges 1¾"x1" (with screws).
6-1¾" No. 10 R. H. blue screws.
1 screen door hook and eye.

INTRODUCTORY STATEMENT.

Standards of cleanliness and sanitation demand that dishcloths should be properly cared for by being washed and dried. This means that some convenient method should be provided for thoroughly airing and drying the dishcloths. The old-time method of stretching a line across the room did the work very satisfactorily but was extremely inconvenient.

This dishcloth rack provides the means of hanging dishcloths in good condition and yet does not take up unnecessary room, because it can be unhooked and allowed to hang down out of the way when not in use. This rack should be hung on the wall near the stove or heat pipe.

References:

Home-Made Fireless Cooker, U. S. Bulletin No. 296.
How to Make an Ice Box, Radford's Details of Construction. Radford Architectural Co., Chicago, Ill.
North American Forests and Forestry, Brucken. G. P. Putnam's Sons.

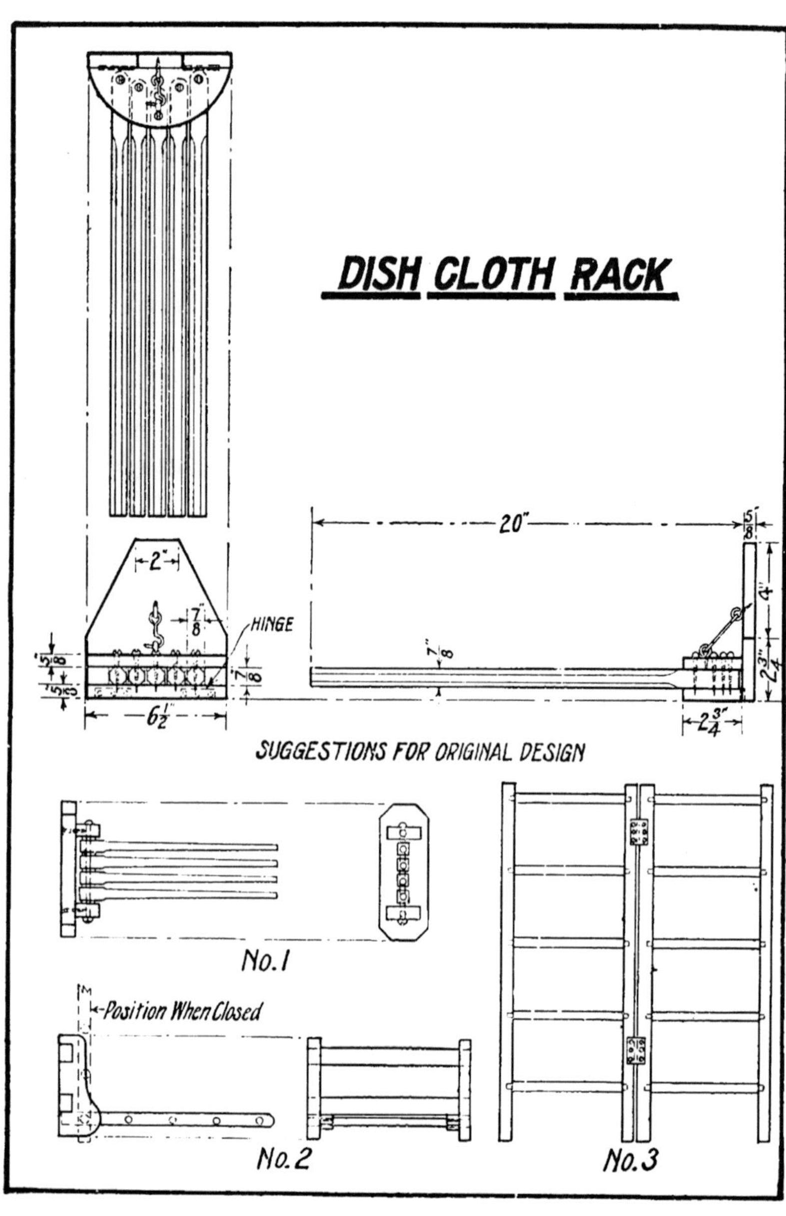
DISH CLOTH RACK
2"
7/8"
HINGE
5/8
5/8
7/8
6 1/2"
20"
5/8
4"
2 3/4"
2 3/4"
SUGGESTIONS FOR ORIGINAL DESIGN
No. 1
Position When Closed
No. 2
No. 3

# DISH CLOTH RACK SPECIFICATIONS

## THE BACK.

Select the best surface of the back piece, and mark this the working face (Chapter II., Paragraph 2), as it is already S 2 S you will not need to resurface it. Prepare a working edge (Chapter II., Paragraph 4). Lay out the design for the back (if you care to, you may make an original design for this piece) and saw it out; carefully plane all of the edges, making them perfectly square. Locate and bore the hole for the hanging screw (Chapter II., Paragraph 9); if desired, two screws may be used in order to hold the back perfectly solid; they should be placed one above the other so as to strike a stud when fastened to the wall.

## THE TOP AND BOTTOM PIECES.

Select the best surface of the top piece and mark it the working face (Chapter II., Paragraph 2). Carefully plane a working edge (Chapter II., Paragraph 4). With the compasses set at the proper radius; lay out the shape of the top piece. In like manner lay out the bottom piece. With the coping or compass saw, saw just outside the line. With a sharp block plane, or wood file, make these edges perfectly smooth and square with the working face. Notice that the length of the bottom piece must be exactly the same as the width of the back piece to which it is to be fastened with hinges. Hinge the bottom piece onto the back, as illustrated in the drawing. In setting a hinge, a gain should be cut in each piece deep enough to receive the hinge leaf, so it will be level with the wood.

## THE HANGER STRIPS.

You will probably have to rip these strips from stock. To do this, select a working face on your stock (Chapter II., Paragraph 2), plane a working edge (Chapter II., Paragraph 4); gauge the desired width on both surfaces (Chapter II., Paragraph 6). Rip just outside the gauge lines, and plane to the lines. In like manner rip out and plane the required number of strips. In preparing one of the hanger strips, first plane it perfectly square, the desired size (Chapter II., Paragraphs 2, 3 and 4), then plane it to the proper taper. With the lead pencil and finger, gauge for the chamfer on each corner (Chapter II., Paragraph 8). As the chamfer does not extend the full length of the strip, you cannot complete it with the plane. You will have to use a pocketknife or drawing-knife. Chamfer all of the corners equally so the end will be an octagon in shape. Be sure to leave the corners distinct and straight. In like manner prepare all the hanger strips. Near the larger end of each hanger strip bore holes for the screws (Chapter II., Paragraph 9). Be sure the holes for the screws are large enough to allow the screws to pass through freely.

### ASSEMBLING.

Notice that the center hanger strip is to be made stationary by having two screws. Each of the other strips will have but one screw. Fasten the center strip first, then place the other strips in position and lay out for the boring. Bore through the top with the same sized bit with which you bored through the hanger strips. Use a smaller bit to bore in the bottom piece, for the screws must tighten in it. After all the work is assembled, make sure that all the strips will spread easily. If they will not, remove the screws, and very slightly plane any of the strips which are too tight. When raised ready for use, the rack is to be held in position by a small hook and screw eye, as shown in the drawing; this hook should be sufficiently tight to hold the hangers rigid in a horizontal position; it may be tightened or loosened by turning the screw eye. It will require careful work to get this project properly assembled. You may have to experiment and adjust it somewhat.

### FINISHING.

With a sharp scraper (Chapter II., Paragraph 16), wood file and sandpaper, remove all pencil or tool marks; see that the work is perfectly smooth all over. It should be finished with shellac (Chapter IV., Paragraph 57).

## Optional and Home Projects Employing Similar Principles.

### WASH CLOTH RACK.

1. Suggestion No. 1 shows a very convenient plan of constructing a hanger which is particularly suited to the lavatory for a wash cloth rack. For this purpose it should be finished with white enamel.

### DISH TOWEL RACK.

2. No. 2 in the suggestion presents a simple plan for a folding rack. This will be particularly suitable in places where room is limited. It should be made of hard wood and neatly finished.

# BOOK SHELVES

MATERIALS.

Yellow Pine (Chap. III., Par. 48) or Oak, plain or quartered (Chap. III., Par. 29).

5 pcs. 7/8"x7 3/4"x33" S 2 S Shelves.
2 pcs. 7/8"x7 3/4"x52" S 2 S Sides.
3 dozen 6d finishing nails.

INTRODUCTORY STATEMENT.

To insure proper protection and arrangement of books, they should be kept in some sort of bookcase or shelves. Since a bookcase is rather expensive, a very satisfactory substitute can be provided by neatly made shelves. If desired these shelves may be provided with curtain rods and a curtain to protect the books from the dust.

While cabinet wood is preferable for this purpose, yet if the workmanship is carefully executed a very satisfactory shelf can be made from soft wood, particularly of yellow pine. The stain and finish should be made to correspond with the other furniture of the room in which the shelves are to be placed.

References:

Easy to Make Furniture, Crater and Holt. The National Builder, Chicago, Ill.
Woodworking for Amateur Craftsmen. The National Builder, Chicago, Ill.
Bench Work in Wood. Goss. Ginn & Co.
Wood and Forest, Noyes. Manual Arts Press, Peoria, Ill.

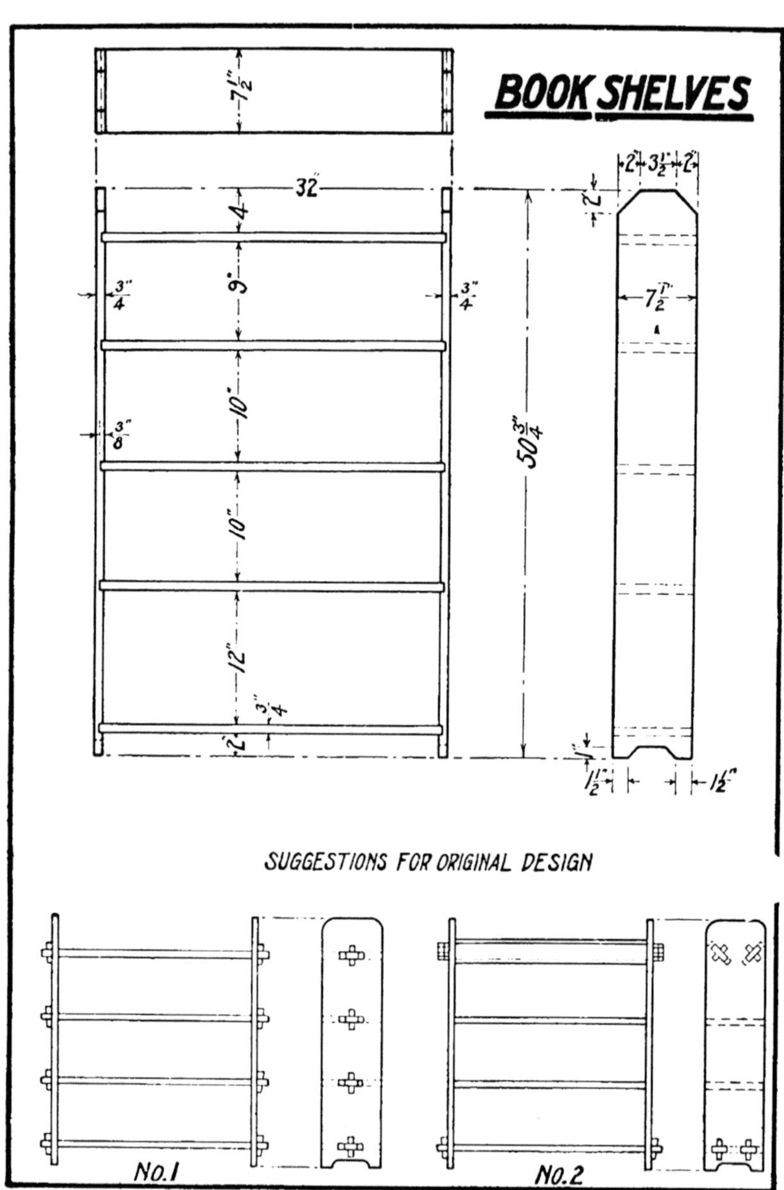
BOOK SHELVES
32"
4"
9"
10"
10"
12"
2"
50 3/4"
7 1/2"
3/4"
3/8"
2" 3 1/2" 2"
1 1/2"
SUGGESTIONS FOR ORIGINAL DESIGN
No.1
No.2

# BOOK SHELVES SPECIFICATIONS

## THE SIDES.

Select the best surface and mark it the working face (Chapter II., Paragraph 2). Prepare a working edge (Chapter II., Paragraph 4.) On a long piece of material of this kind planing the edges will require very careful work. With the marking gauge (Chapter II., Paragraph 6), or with the pencil and ruler (Chapter II., Paragraph 7), gauge the width of the side pieces on both surfaces; carefully plane to the gauge lines. Be sure that all edges are perfectly square. In like manner prepare the second side piece.

Lay out the bottom and top ends of one side piece, as shown in the drawing, or according to your own design. If you use an original design, first draw it on paper, then lay it out on your material. Carefully saw just outside the lines. With a wood file and block plane finish the edges, making them perfectly square and smooth. Make the second side just like the first.

Lay out the spaces for the shelves with the try-square; square these lines across the working face; lay out the gains on each side piece (Chapter V., Paragraph 61). The width of the gains is determined by the thickness of the shelves, for they must fill the gains snugly. It is well to lay out the gains a very little smaller than required, so you may thin the ends of the shelves slightly with a steel scraper, if necessary, in assembling. Use this piece as a pattern in laying out the gains on the other side piece. These gains must be exactly the same distance apart, or the shelves will not be level when the work is assembled.

## THE SHELVES.

Select the best surface of one shelf, and mark it the working face (Chapter II., Paragraph 2). Plane one edge for a working edge (Chapter II., Paragraph 4). Gauge the width on both surfaces (Chapter II., Paragraphs 6 or 7); carefully plane to the gauge lines; square one end (Chapter II., Paragraph 5). Lay out and cut the length, as indicated in the drawing. Prepare all the shelves in the same manner. If you desire you may change the length to suit your needs, but be sure all the shelves are exactly the same length.

## SURFACING.

Before the work is assembled, each piece should be carefully resurfaced with a sharp plane set to take a thin shaving. This will remove the marks left by the planing mill. All surfaces must then be finished with a sharp steel scraper to remove plane marks (Chapter II., Paragraph 16); the final smoothing should be done with very fine sandpaper (Chapter II., Paragraph 17).

## ASSEMBLING.

This work is to be assembled with finishing nails driven through the outside surface of the side pieces. Be very careful not to bruise the material. The nails should be uniformly spaced so, if the places where they are driven show, they will not mar the appearance of your work. Use the hammer as shown in Chapter II., Paragraph 21. With a nail set drive all nails slightly below the surface of the wood. The holes may be filled with putty, colored to match the stain you intend to use; or by careful work you may be able to cover them satisfactorily by putting a tiny drop of glue in each hole and sandpapering over it, allowing the wood dust to mix with the glue and fill the hole.

## FINISHING.

With a piece of fine sandpaper remove all pencil and tool marks. Stain the desired color (Chapter IV., Paragraph 54). If your book shelves are made of oak, a filler should be used (Chapter IV., Paragraph 55). Finish with shellac (Chapter IV., Paragraph 57), wax (Chapter IV., Paragraph 56), or varnish (Chapter IV., Paragraph 58).

## Optional and Home Projects Employing Similar Principles.

## PANTRY SHELVES.

1. The plan of shelf construction presented in this lesson is very suitable for the construction of shelves in the pantry. The length and spacing of the shelves should be determined by local conditions.

## HARDWARE CABINET.

2. For small hardware, such as nails, screws and sundries, a very simple but serviceable cabinet may be prepared by constructing a series of shelves on the plan given in this lesson. For the sake of economy, discarded cigar boxes could be used for drawers, the shelves being conveniently spaced to suit them.

# SLED

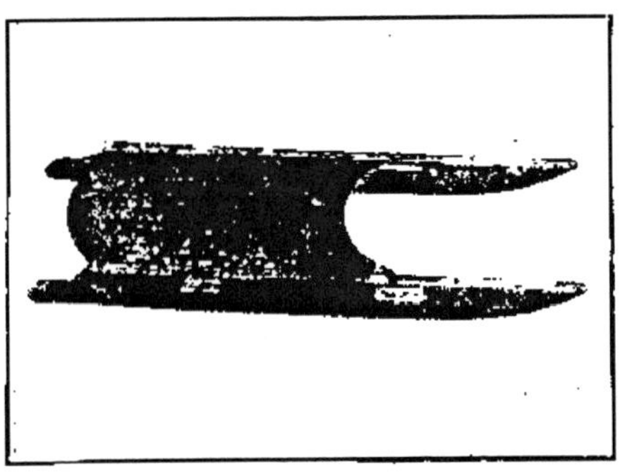

MATERIALS.

Poplar (Chap. III., Par. 42)

2 pcs. ¾"x3¾"x36" S 2 S
Runners.

2 pcs. 1"x2"x11½" S 2 S
Cross braces.

1 pc. ⅜"x9½"x22" S 2 S
Top.

4-6d finishing nails.

1 dozen 1¼" brads.

2 pcs. 5/16"x40" soft iron rod or 2 pcs. ¾"x40" strap iron for soles.

INTRODUCTORY STATEMENT.

The sled represents one of the earliest used and simplest methods of hauling. Wherever there is snow the sled is used in a great many ways. Perhaps its most important use is in the lumber regions, where it provides an easy means of hauling immense loads of logs. The sled also furnishes a great means of sport and it has a number of modifications, such as skees, toboggans and the common hand sled, with which every boy is familiar.

**References:**


Library of Work and Play, Foster.

Scientific American Boy at School, A. Russel Bond.

A Back Yard Toboggan Slide, The Boy Craftsman, Hall. Lathrop, Lee & Shepard, Boston.

Winter Sports, Library of Work and Play, Miller. Doubleday, Page & Co., New York.

Boy's Book of Sports and Outdoor Life, Thompson. The Century Co., New York.

Ice Boats, Sleds and Toboggans, Scientific American Boy, Bond. Munn & Co., New York.

The Outdoor Handy Book for Playground, Beard. Chas. Scribner's Sons, New York.

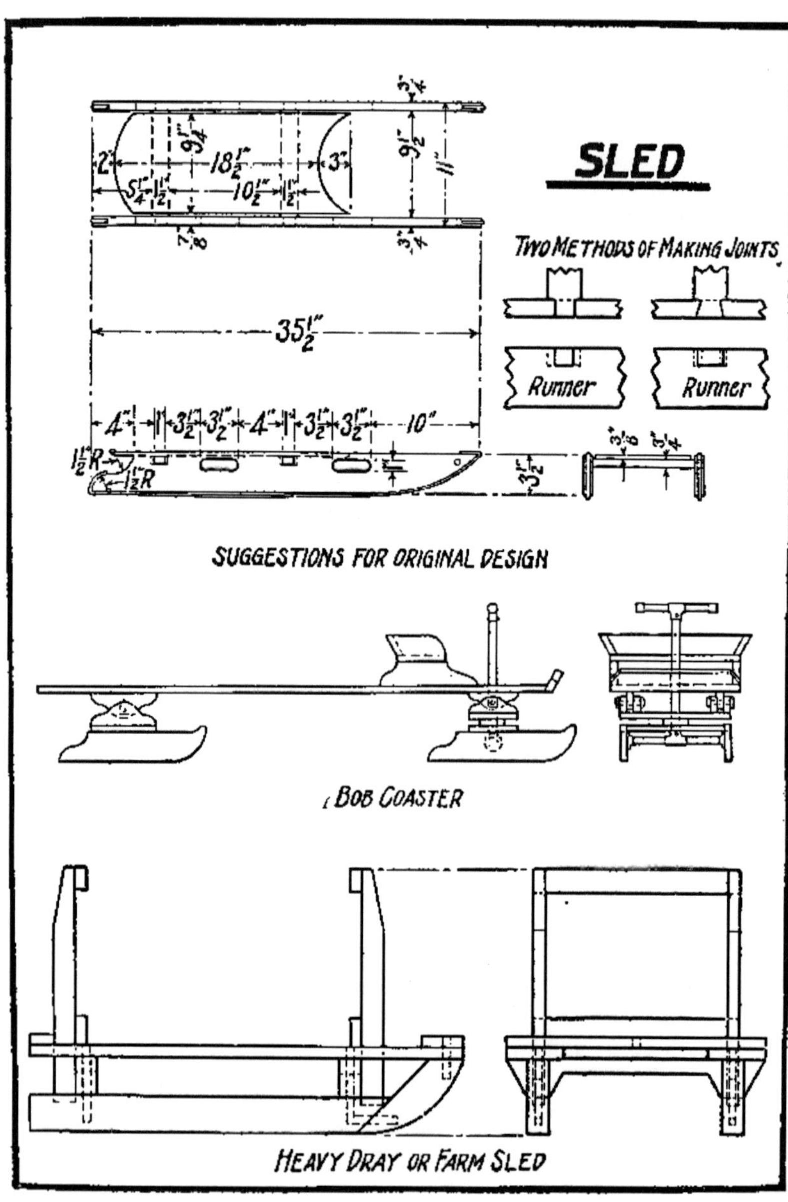
SLED
TWO METHODS OF MAKING JOINTS
Runner
Runner
SUGGESTIONS FOR ORIGINAL DESIGN
BOB COASTER
HEAVY DRAY OR FARM SLED

# SLED SPECIFICATIONS

## RUNNERS.

As this material is furnished S 2 S, it will not be necessary for you to replane it. Select the best surface of one piece and mark it the working face (Chapter II., Paragraph 2). Plane one edge perfectly straight for a working edge (Chapter II., Paragraph 4). Gauge the width of the runners (Chapter II., Paragraphs 6 or 7). Plane to the gauge line. Lay out the shape of the front and of the rear curves; with the coping or compass saw saw just outside these lines. Smooth the edges with a block plane and wood file; make the edges perfectly square. In like manner make the second runner.

Lay out the mortises (Chapter IV., Paragraph 67) for the cross braces. These mortises should be laid out on both surfaces of each runner so you may chisel part way from one side, and the remainder from the other side. Be very careful not to get the mortises too wide; the thickness of the cross braces must fill them snugly. Lay out the holes for the hand holds. To make the hand holes, bore two holes with the 7/8" or 1" bit the proper distance apart to make the hole the desired length; with the compass saw saw from one hole to the other, and smooth with the wood file.

## THE CROSS BRACES.

Square the stock for one of the cross braces (Chapter II., Paragraphs 2, 3 and 4). Lay out the tenon (Chapter V., Paragraph 67) the exact size of the mortise which you have cut in the runner. Form the tenon by sawing just outside the gauge line (Chapter II., Paragraph 14); make a tenon on each end. Prepare the second brace in the same manner as the first. Be sure the braces are exactly the same length between shoulders.

## THE TOP.

The top is to be made of one wide board, although it may be made of strips if preferred. If furnished S 2 S, it will not be necessary to resurface this piece of material. Plane one edge perfectly straight and square (Chapter II., Paragraph 2). With the pencil and ruler, gauge the width (Chapter II., Paragraph 7); plane to the gauge line. Lay out the desired curves for the two ends. Saw them out with the coping or compass saw, and smooth the edges with the wood file.

## ASSEMBLING.

Assemble the sled by driving the cross braces into the mortises, and fastening each with a nail driven through the top edge of the runner into the tenon. Space the top properly on the cross braces, and with small nails, nail down through the top into each cross brace. Space the nails uniformly (Chapter II., Paragraph 21).

## THE SOLES.

The soles of this sled are to be made of round iron rods. Flat soles are sometimes used, but the round soles are preferable if carefully put on. With a gouge or chisel, slightly groove the rear, and also the front curved portion of each runner. You should also groove the top edge of each runner where the short turn of the iron lies. Bend the rods the desired shape; this can be done by a little careful work with a hammer and vise. When the rods are the desired shape they will be held in position by the grooves which you have just cut in the runners. NOTE: Flat strap iron may be used for the soles, if you prefer; it should be fastened with screws. Bore a ⅜″ hole in the front of each runner to fasten the rope. Sometimes a round cross rail is put in the front of a sled at this place. It is usually undesirable in a coasting sled, but if you care for it, it may be put in at the time the sled is assembled by having it prepared and the holes bored.

## FINISHING.

Paint or stain the sled the desired color. This will add to its beauty (Chapter IV., Paragraph 52). As a sled is exposed to considerable moisture, paint is the most serviceable finish. However, a good oil stain will be satisfactory. An enamel paint will give a beautiful and lasting finish.

### Optional and Home Projects Employing Similar Principles.

## BOB COASTER.

1. The bob coaster shown in the first suggestion affords an opportunity of employing the sled principle in a very elaborate project. However, there is none of the construction that is particularly difficult. The steering device should be made of iron pipe. It may be necessary to have this part of the work made at a plumber's shop. The rest of the project will be very clear from the drawing.

# SAWHORSE

MATERIALS.

Beech (Chap. III., Par. 32) or any hard wood.

| | | |
|---|---|---|
| 1 pc. | 1½"x3¾"x36½" Saddle. | S 2 S |
| 4 pcs. | ⅞"x3¾"x25" Legs. | S 2 S |
| 2 pcs. | ⅞"x5½"x 9" Braces. | S 2 S |

24-1½" No. 10 F. H. B. screws

## INTRODUCTORY STATEMENT.

The sawhorse, sometimes called a trestle bench, is used to hold material in a convenient position for sawing or for assembling work. In handling long boards, usually two trestles of the same height are used. They should be perfectly rigid so as to hold the material solid while the work is being done.

The sawhorse shown in this lesson is a convenient size for shop use. By observing the picture you will note that there is a little notch block fastened on the sawhorse near one end; this is to serve as a substitute for a vise when you wish to do planing. If you do not have a work bench at home you can easily make a sawhorse like this and thus be able to do a great many pieces of work about your home. If properly cared for it should be serviceable for many years.

---

**References:**

The Young Mechanic, John Lukin. G. P. Putnam's Sons, New York.
The Jack of All Trades, D. C. Beard. Chas. Scribner's Sons.
Practical Forestry, Fuller.

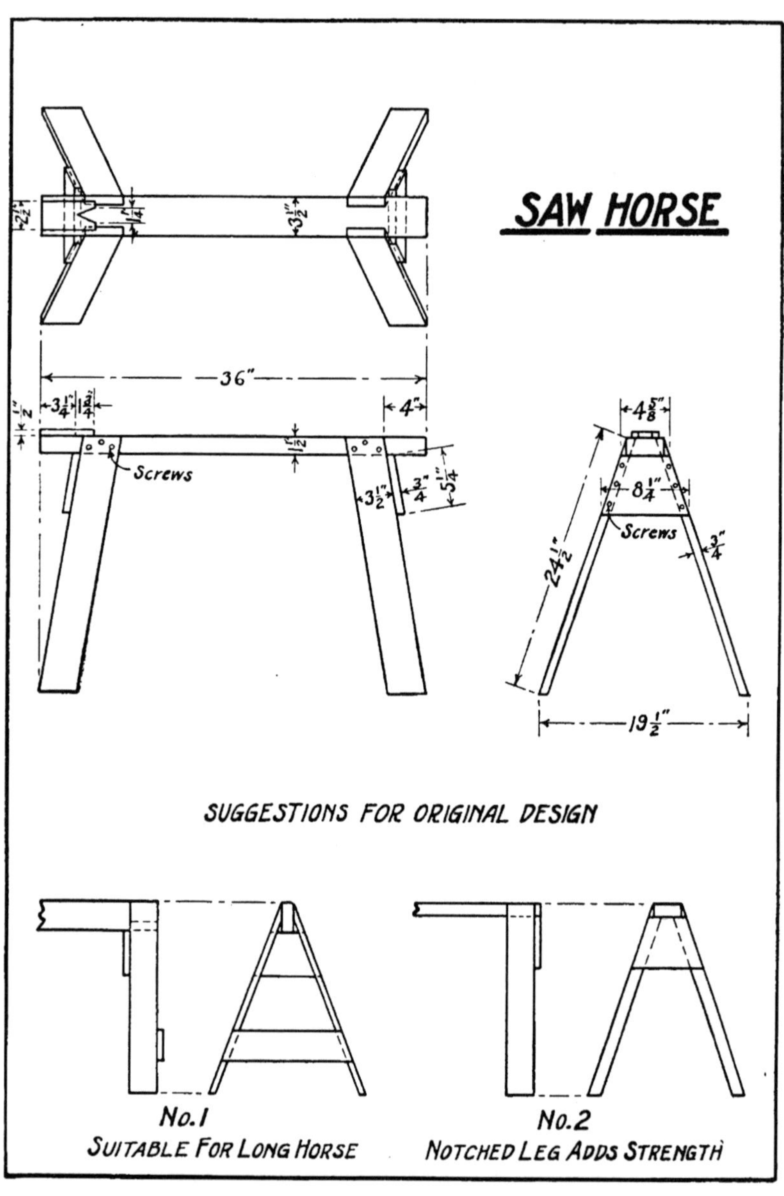
SAW HORSE
36"
4"
Screws
Screws
19 1/2"
24 1/2"
SUGGESTIONS FOR ORIGINAL DESIGN
No.1
SUITABLE FOR LONG HORSE
No.2
NOTCHED LEG ADDS STRENGTH

# SAW HORSE SPECIFICATIONS

## THE SADDLE.

As this material is furnished S 2 S, it will not be necessary to resurface it. Select the best surface, and mark it the working face (Chapter II., Paragraph 2). Plane one edge perfectly square Chapter II., Paragraph 4). Gauge the width (Chapter II., Paragraphs 6 or 7) and plane to the gauge line. Square one end (Chapter II., Paragraph 5). Measure, and cut the length. The gains to receive the legs should not be laid out until after the legs have been made.

## THE LEGS.

If the material is furnished S 2 S it will not be necessary to resurface the legs. Plane one edge perfectly square for a working edge (Chapter II., Paragraph 4). Gauge the width (Chapter II., Paragraph 6); plane to the gauge line. Cut the length about 25" long (this will give a chance to recut the legs after the work is assembled).

## CUTTING GAINS IN THE SADDLE.

The gains are to be cut in the saddle to receive the legs. These should be cut so the legs will fit them perfectly. Hold one leg at the proper slant (this is a matter for your judgment, after a study of the drawing) and set the T-bevel. With the T-bevel lay out the gains on the saddle. Gauge the depth of the gain on the top face of the saddle. Notice that on the bottom face of the saddle the gains lose their depth and come just to the lower edge of the material. Saw to these lines, and with a sharp chisel carefully cut away the wood. In like manner prepare all the gains.

## ASSEMBLING THE LEGS AND SADDLE.

Fasten the legs in place by means of screws. The holes in the legs should be large enough to receive the body of the screws freely, but not loosely. Countersink the holes so the heads of the screws will come level with the surface.

## THE BRACES.

Prepare the stock for the braces the proper width (Chapter II., Paragraphs 2, 3, 4). Spread one pair of legs to their proper position, and be sure that both legs stand at exactly the same angle with the saddle. Hold a piece of the brace material in position, and mark its shape by running a lead pencil along the outside of each leg. With the T-bevel, test these two lines to make sure they are the same angle; if they are not exactly the same, make them so, and set the T-bevel. Saw out the two braces, making them exactly alike. Bore holes for the screws (Chapter II., Paragraph 9).

In fastening the braces in position, regulate the angle of the legs so they exactly fit the braces. NOTE: With a keen block plane, plane the ends of the braces until they are exactly even with the outside of the legs. There may be some little variation. Also saw off the top of the legs exactly even with the top of the saddle, and finish with a block plane. Set the saw horse on a level floor, and with a pair of compasses, or with a ruler and lead pencil, mark a line parallel with the floor entirely around each leg; saw off the bottom of the legs to this line.

## NOTCH BLOCK.

The notched block on the top of the saw horse is not necessary for sawing purposes, but is quite convenient for holding small pieces of material for planing and other tool operations.

For shop work saw horses are often used in pairs. However, the one horse will give very good satisfaction for small work because the saddle is wide.

## FINISHING.

With a sharp scraper (Chapter II., Paragraph 16), or sandpaper, remove all pencil and tool marks from the work, and finish with a coat of shellac (Chapter II., Paragraph 57).

## Optional and Home Projects Employing Similar Principles.

## TABLE TRESTLE.

1. The plan of making a trestle, as shown in Suggestion No. 1, will be very suitable as a support for a portable table. The height may be determined by individual needs. A pair of such trestles, with a wide board top, will afford a convenient portable table for picnics, lawn parties or outdoor home canning work.

NOTE: There is almost no limit to the application of this trestle principle. It may be used in the construction of temporary stages and platforms, movable laboratory equipment, and many other purposes about the home and school.

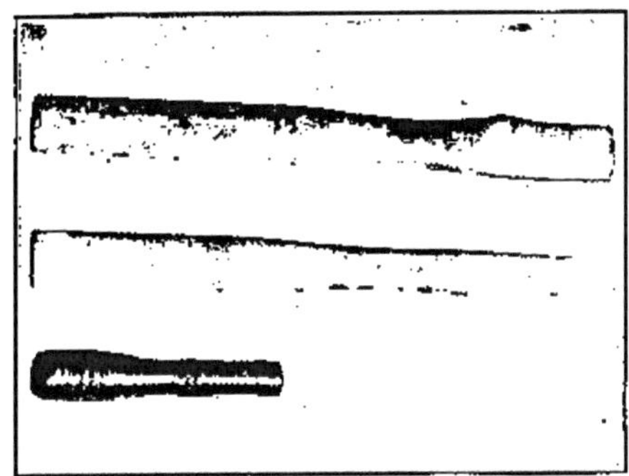

# HATCHET AND HAMMER HANDLES

MATERIALS.

Hickory (Chap. III., Par. 39).

1 pc. 1⅛" x 1¾" x 14½" rough (split).

## INTRODUCTORY STATEMENT.

Everybody is more or less familiar with the use of a hammer, for there is possibly no one tool which is so generally employed in all kinds of work. The handle is usually the first part of the hammer to wear out or break, and while a new handle can be purchased at a very reasonable price, yet it is quite convenient for a boy to be able to make a hammer handle. Most hammer handles are broken by carelessness or abuse; this is not likely to occur if one has had the experience of making a few handles.

Hammer handles should be made of clear, straight-grained hickory, and if the material is properly selected a hand-shaved handle is usually far superior to the machine-made handles which are on the market.

---

**References:**

U. S. Farmer's Bulletin No. 347, The Repair of Farm Equipment.
The Lathe and Its Uses, Stories of Industries. G. P. Putnam's Sons.
The Repair of Farm Equipment, Scientific Am., June 5, 1909.
Farm Conveniences. Orange-Judd Co., New York.

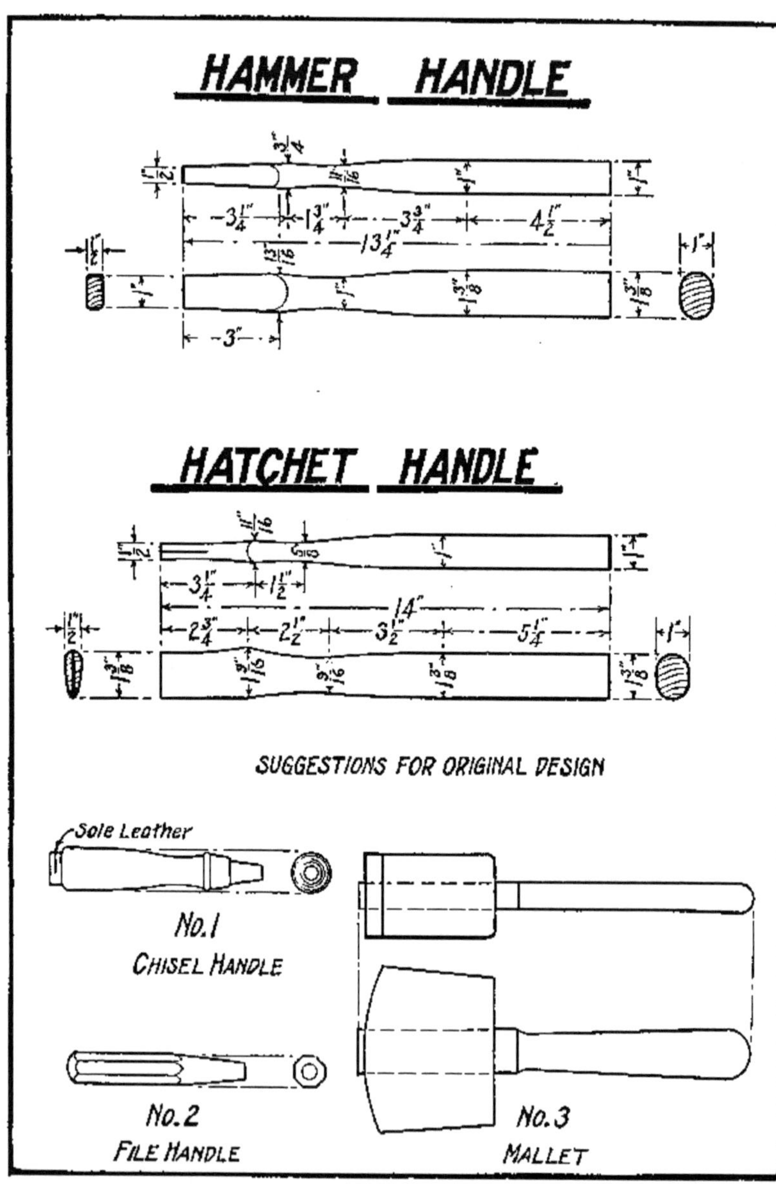
HAMMER HANDLE
HATCHET HANDLE
SUGGESTIONS FOR ORIGINAL DESIGN
Sole Leather
No. 1
CHISEL HANDLE
No. 2
FILE HANDLE
No. 3
MALLET

# HATCHET AND HAMMER HANDLE SPECIFICATIONS

The material for your hammer, or hatchet handle, is rough on all sides, because it is split out of the log. The purpose in furnishing split material is that you may get your handle perfectly straight grained. The hammer handle cannot be laid out with a marking gauge and try-square in the same way that you lay out most pieces of work, because the completed handle does not have straight and parallel edges. If you have a drawing knife in the shop, it will be found the most convenient tool with which to do most of the cutting.

It would be well to square this stock to the largest size shown in the drawing (Chapter II., Paragraphs 1, 2, 3, 4). In any kind of shaved work you must be very careful not to cut against the grain, or the wood will tear and be very rough. This is particularly true in making a handle. After you get the stock squared, so it is thick enough for the thickest dimension of the drawing, and wide enough for the widest place, you should then block it out with the drawing knife or plane, or pocket knife, by cutting away the corners and making it approach the shape of the handle. You must be very careful not to cut it too small at any point, or to allow any of the shavings to cut in too deeply by following the grain.

Making the final shape of the handle is largely a matter of judgment, and you will show your skill by shaving out the handle to the desired shape, and bringing it to the dimensions at all of the points shown in the drawing.

## FINISHING.

After you have made the shape of the handle, and have it almost the desired dimensions, it should be finished with a sharp steel scraper (Chapter II., Paragraph 16); it may be scraped with a pocket knife, or a piece of glass. The purpose of the scraping is to remove all marks made by the cutting tools, and to make the surface perfectly smooth all over. In the scraping process it may be necessary to scrape part way from one direction, and the remainder from the other direction, to avoid tearing the grain. The final smoothing should be done with fine sandpaper, sandpapering the direction of the grain. After it is completed give it a good coating of linseed oil.

## FITTING THE HANDLE INTO THE HAMMER OR HATCHET.

The handle should be carefully shaved, and fitted into the eye of the hammer or hatchet, whichever it may be. In shaving the handle, make it fit the eye snugly at all points, taper it sufficiently so that it will reach through the eye and extend a little on the other side. After it has been well fitted, and driven in perfectly tight, examine it carefully to be sure that the hammer or hatchet hangs properly on the handle. Then either split or saw the end of the handle which extends, and drive in hard wood wedges to hold it securely in position. Saw the handle off even with the tool, and finish smoothly with a wood file. The other end of the handle may be sawed and slightly rounded, and smoothed with the wood file and sandpaper. When the handle is entirely finished, it should have a final coating of linseed oil. An occasional coat of linseed oil on hammer handles will cause them to wear smoothly.

**Optional and Home Projects Employing Similar Principles.**

### MATTOCK OR PICK HANDLE.

1. The principle of the shaved handle can be applied to a great number of tools about the shop, home or farm. The mattock or pick handle is almost identical with the hammer handle, except in size.

### CHISEL OR FILE HANDLE.

2. A very excellent chisel or file handle may be hand-shaved. The size and detail of shape are largely matters of personal taste.

### HOE OR RAKE HANDLE.

3. The hoe or rake handle differs from the other handle problem but little, except in length.

# SUGGESTIONS FOR COMMUNITY RESEARCH.

No. 1. Are there any mills of any kind run by water power anywhere in your community? Make inquiry and find out some of the advantages and disadvantages connected with the use of water power.

No. 2. What kind of flowers should be selected for a window flower box? What kind of dirt would you select and how would you prepare it for a window flower box?

No. 3. Visit a shop or hardware store and examine a patent miter box. What advantage does this miter box have over the wood miter box which you made in the shop? How does it compare with your handmade box in price?

No. 4. Examine the picture frames in your home and see if you can tell of what kind of wood they are made. How are the joints made?

No. 5. Visit a carpenter's or cabinet-maker's shop and ask the man in charge to show you the different kinds of planes which he uses. You may be able to find some of the old-fashioned wood stock planes in your community. By inquiry from some of the carpenters, find out what advantages modern all-steel planes have over the old-fashioned wooden planes.

No. 6. For what practical purposes have you seen sleds used in your neighborhood? Which will run more easily on snow, a sled or a wagon? Discuss this matter with some of the teamsters in your community and get their opinions.

No. 7. Make a very careful search about your home to see how many articles you can find which are made of hickory; examine each one carefully and explain why hickory is selected for that particular purpose. Do you know of any objections to the use of hickory for frame material in a house?

No. 8. At what season of the year should shade trees be trimmed? From the study of the references and inquiries which you may make of practical men, what do you think would be the result of trimming shade trees very closely during the hot, dry summer months?

No. 9. Examine the ironing board used in your home to see whether it folds easily. If you find any faults in its construction, remedy them.

No. 10. Visit an art store or gallery and study the pictures; note the kind of frames used on the different pictures. Ask the person in charge to explain why different types of frames are used on certain pictures.

## REVIEW QUESTIONS AND PROBLEMS.

1. Why is it necessary to square the stock before attempting to lay out work which is made up of circles or curves?

2. In assembling with screws, how large should the hole in the first piece of material be?

3. What are the important principles to be observed in making a rectangular box?

4. How do you lay out the angle in making a miter box?

5. What are some of the advantages in the use of corrugated nails?

6. Name and explain the construction of three pieces of work which could be assembled satisfactorily with corrugated nails.

7. How deep should the gains be cut in setting a hinge?

8. How can you adjust a screen door hook that is either too tight or too loose?

9. In building shelves, what is the advantage of the gained, or housed, joint?

10. Why will a sled with round soles coast more readily than one with flat soles?

11. Why should the saddle of a long trestle be turned edgewise?

12. What is the advantage of a notched block on a saw horse?

13. Why is a shaved hammer or hatchet handle stronger and better than one turned by machinery?

14. How many board feet of material in the Sleeve Board? What is the cost of the material (including the screws)?

15. Counting your time at 12½ cents per hour, what is the work on your Sleeve Board worth?

16. Count your time and material and estimate the value of each article made in this section.

17. If you should repeat any project which you have already made, how much time do you think you could save without slighting the work? Why is this true?

18. If you should undertake to make a dozen of any one lesson, would it require twelve times as long as to make one? Why?

19. How would you manage your work if you had the task of making six window screens all just alike? What are the advantages in doing it as you suggest? Why would you not make one complete before cutting the stock for any of the others?

20. Why can a factory, which is making articles by the thousand, produce them much cheaper than a man who simply makes one or two by hand?

## REVIEW QUESTIONS AND PROBLEMS (Concluded).

21. At what angle do you cut the pieces in making a picture frame or window screen?

22. How many paddles are necessary on a water wheel? Why?

23. Why should the inside of a flower box be painted?

24. How many board feet of material required to make the book shelves?

25. What would be the difference in expense of oak and pine in the material for the book shelves?

26. Are hatchet and hammer handles made exactly the same shape? Can you explain the difference?

27. What is the advantage in making a dish cloth rack so it will fold?

28. How much time was required to make the dish cloth rack? What was the cost of the material?

29. Can you explain why some articles are rather expensive even though they do not contain much material?

30. What two things must be considered in figuring the cost of a completed article?

# INTRODUCTION TO SECTION IV

THIS section presents a number of modifications and developments of the elementary tool processes and principles set forth in the earlier sections. Students who have successfully accomplished the work of the first half of this book, or its equivalent, are sufficiently grounded in the fundamentals of shop work to be able to exercise considerable judgment not only in the choice of projects to be undertaken, but also in incorporating original ideas and personal tastes in the designs.

The projects of this section are so varied in nature and function, as well as in amount and expense of materials, that there should be no difficulty in appealing to the immediate interest of every member of any class. While the projects do not all present the same mechanical principles, yet they deal with forms of construction which the students should be capable of handling.

Some students will desire to make some of the smaller projects, which give an opportunity for artistic expression. The candlestick, vase and hand mirror are particularly suitable for practice along this line. A study of the references given under these lessons will guide to the proper conception of motive and design. Other students of a more practical turn of mind may be interested in making projects which will be useful about the home or farm; such lessons will, of course, necessitate a little more expense on account of the amount of material used, but when the value of the finished article is considered the making of usable projects is quite economical.

No attempt is made in this section to introduce principles of cabinet construction; however, the simple box type is employed in some of the projects and the fundamental principles of making opposite sides exactly equal and of assembling parts perfectly square should be carefully impressed.

In practical drawing work students should be able to make a simple sketch and to prepare regular three-view drawings of projects to be undertaken in the shop.

Before leaving this section all students should appreciate the value of keeping their tools in good order and should be able to sharpen the edge tools, such as chisels and plane blades, with considerable skill.

# WASH BENCH

MATERIALS.

Cypress (Chap. III., Par. 46) or any soft wood.

1 pc. 7/8"x13½"x35½" S2S Top.

2 pcs. 7/8"x11¾"x18½" S2S Legs.

2 pcs. 7/8"x4"x34" S2S Skirt boards.

2½ doz. 8d finishing nails.

INTRODUCTORY STATEMENT.

Although washing machines are quite generally used, the washtub has a place in home laundry work, and for that reason it is necessary to provide some sort of bench for it.

The wash bench shown in this lesson is a convenient size to accommodate one tub and leave some room at the side for other purposes. The slot in the top of the bench is to serve as a hand hold, enabling one to move it from place to place with the use of one hand. The height of the bench is largely a matter of choice with the person who is to use it. The general plan of this bench is the same as should be used in constructing a substantial bench for other purposes. The length, height and width can be changed to suit the purpose for which the bench is intended.

**References:**

U. S. Bulletin No. 607, The Farm Kitchen As a Workshop.
With the Men Who Do Things, A. Russel Bond.
U. S. Bureau of Forestry, Bulletins No. 22, 30, 36.
The Story of Lumber, Bassett. The Penn Pub. Co., Philadelphia.

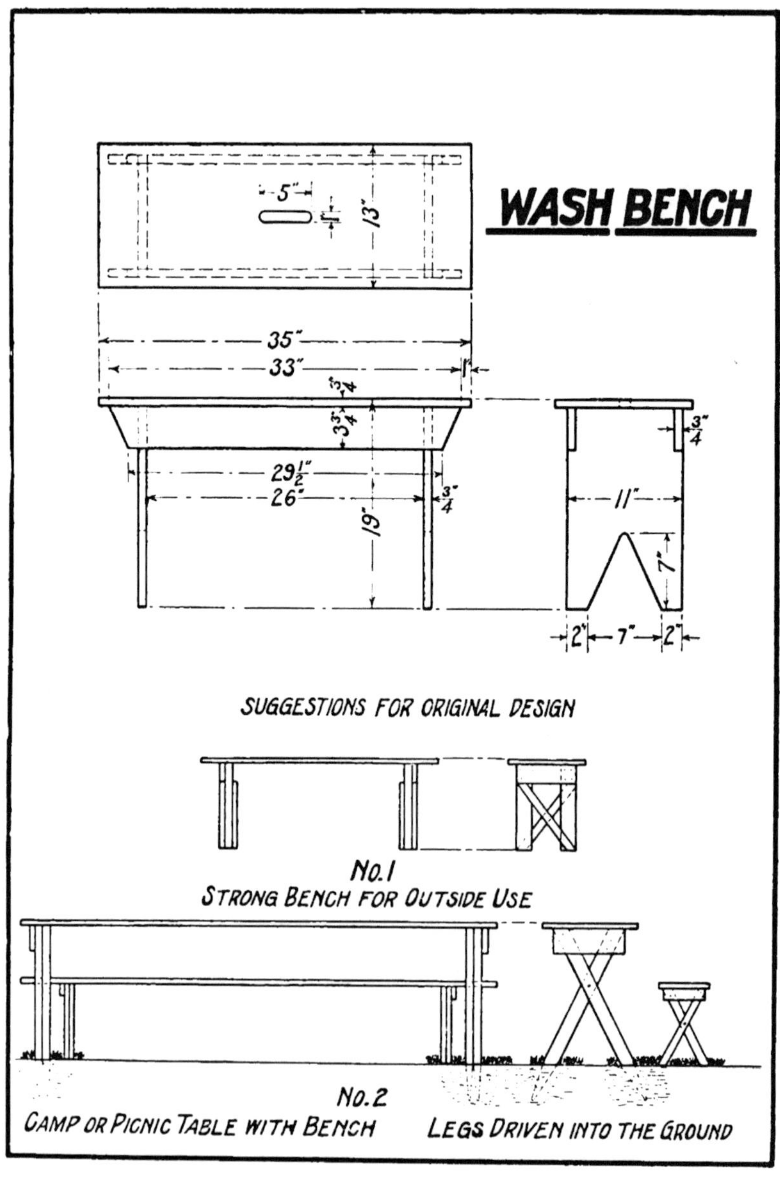
WASH BENCH
5"
1"
13"
35"
33"
1"
3/4
3 3/4
29 1/2"
26"
3/4
19"
3/4
11"
7"
2"
7"
2"
SUGGESTIONS FOR ORIGINAL DESIGN
No. 1
STRONG BENCH FOR OUTSIDE USE
No. 2
CAMP OR PICNIC TABLE WITH BENCH
LEGS DRIVEN INTO THE GROUND

# WASH BENCH SPECIFICATIONS

## THE LEGS.

As this material is furnished S 2 S, it will not be necessary to resurface it. Select the best side for the working face (Chapter II., Paragraph 2). Prepare a working edge (Chapter II., Paragraph 4). Prepare a working end (Chapter II., Paragraph 5). Lay out the shape and dimension of one of the legs as given in the drawing. Carefully cut this leg to these lines. Be sure that all edges are planed perfectly straight and square. In like manner lay out, and make the second leg. Do not cut the gains in the top ends of the legs to receive the skirt board until after the skirt board has been prepared.

## THE SKIRT BOARD.

Square the stock for the skirt board (Chapter II., Paragraphs 1, 2, 3 and 4). Lay out and cut the skirt board the desired shape and dimension as given in the drawing. In like manner prepare the second skirt board. Notice that the gains in the top ends of the legs are to be cut just wide enough and deep enough to receive the skirt board.

You may lay out these gains, making them just that size. The depth of the gains may be laid out with the marking gauge by setting it to the thickness of the skirt board. Saw out these gains, using the back saw to saw down to the gauge line, and the rip saw to rip them down. Prepare all four gains in the same manner.

## THE TOP.

Select the best surface for the working face (Chapter II., Paragraph 2) ; prepare a working edge (Chapter II., Paragraph 4) ; prepare a working end (Chapter II., Paragraph 5). Lay out and make this the size indicated in the drawing. If inconvenient to get a board wide enough to make the top in one piece, two or more pieces may be used by joining them with dowels (Chapter V., Paragraph 72). By using battens on the under side, the top may be made of strips with uniform cracks left between them.

The hole in the top of the bench will afford a place for the hand in picking it up. This will make it possible to handle the bench easily with one hand. Lay out and cut this hole. You may easily do this by boring two 1-inch holes the correct distance apart, and sawing out between them with a compass saw (Chapter II., Paragraph 9).

## ASSEMBLING.

The bench is to be assembled with nails. The skirt boards are to be nailed in position on to the legs. This might be done first. With the steel square, test carefully to make sure that the legs stand exactly at right angles to the edge of the skirt board. Nail both skirt boards securely in position, carefully testing all angles to see that they are square. The top is to be nailed down through into the skirt board, and into the ends of the legs. See that the top is evenly divided, letting it extend the same distance on each end, and on each edge. Nail it in position, being very careful not to bruise it with the hammer (Chapter II., Paragraph 21). In any kind of work where the heads are to show, nails should be uniformly spaced.

## FINISHING.

With a sharp steel scraper remove all pencil and tool marks. The nails may be set and puttied, if so desired. As this bench is to be used for laundry purposes, it will no doubt often be wet, and for that reason will need a coating of paint to protect it against the moisture (Chapter IV., Paragraph 52). If you are not supplied with paint, it might be given a coating of oil stain (Chapter IV., Paragraph 54). This will serve the purpose very well. A coating of shellac might be added; it will help to harden the surface, thus making it more durable (Chapter IV., Paragraph 57).

### Optional and Home Projects Employing Similar Principles.

## OUTDOOR STATIONARY BENCH.

1. The principles of bench construction can be applied in an unlimited number of ways for practical purposes. Suggestion No. 1 shows a very serviceable plan for the construction of a strong outdoor bench for any kind of general service about the barn or dairy.

## PICNIC BENCH.

2. It is often necessary to construct a bench and table for camping, picnic or lawn festival purposes. The idea given in the suggestion will be found very practicable. It represents a very easy and economical plan, for the stakes are simply driven into the ground; thus the bench does not require much material in the way of braces.

# NAIL OR SCREW TRAY

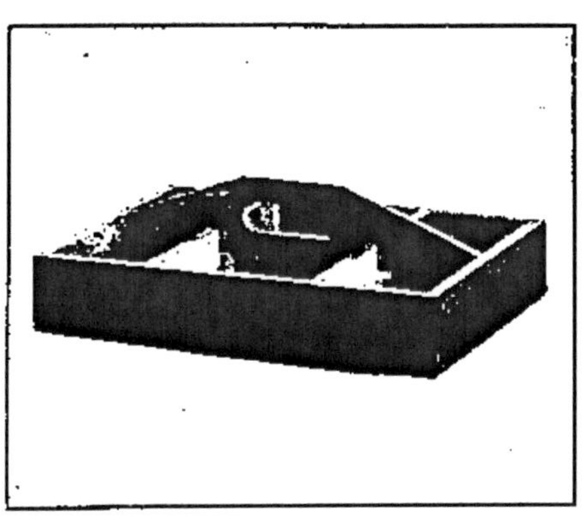

MATERIALS.

Poplar (Chap. III., Par. 42) or any soft wood.

2 pcs. ½"x5¾"x16" S 2 S Bottom.

2 pcs. ½"x3¼"x16½" S 2 S Sides.

2 pcs. ½"x3¼"x11½" S 2 S Ends.

1 pc. ½"x5"x16" S 2 S Middle partition.

4 pcs. ½"x3"x 5½" S 2 S Partitions.

2½ doz. 1½" Brads.

## INTRODUCTORY STATEMENT.

Nails and screws of various sizes are almost constantly in demand for odd jobs about the home and the farm. For this reason every home should be provided with some sort of convenient place to keep a few nails and screws for emergencies. It is not uncommon to find a large box containing a promiscuous lot of all sizes of nails, screws and other small hardware usually quite rusty and dirty. This method of caring for those things render them almost worthless for good workmanship.

The purpose of this lesson is to present a means of keeping nails and screws handy for use and also making it possible to have them classified and kept in separate bins. The tray may be divided into as many compartments as desirable. It is well to have one tray for nails and a separate one for screws.

**References:**

Nails and Screws, How We Are Housed, Carpenter. American Book Co.

Nail Making, Stories of Industries, Chase and Clow. Educational Pub. Co.

Every Man His Own Mechanic, Barnard. Fredrick A. Stokes Co., New York.

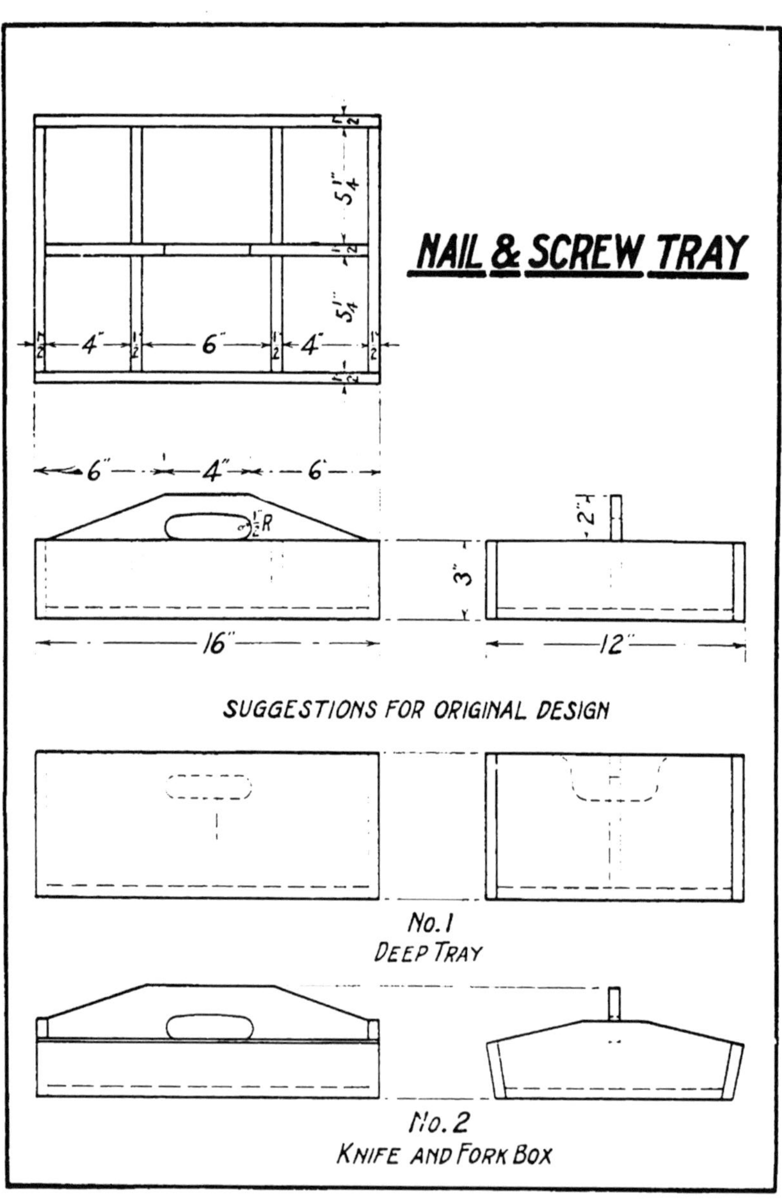
NAIL & SCREW TRAY
4"
6"
4"
5 1/4"
1/2
6"
4"
6"
1/2 R
2"
3"
16"
12"
SUGGESTIONS FOR ORIGINAL DESIGN
No. 1
DEEP TRAY
No. 2
KNIFE AND FORK BOX

# NAIL OR SCREW TRAY SPECIFICATIONS

As this material is furnished S 2 S, it will not be necessary for you to resurface it.

## THE SIDES.

Select the best surface of one of the side pieces for a working face (Chapter II., Paragraph 2). Square this stock (Chapter II., Paragraphs 4, 5), and lay out the side the size and shape shown in the drawing. Carefully cut this piece, and plane all the edges perfectly straight and square. In like manner prepare the opposite side. Compare the two sides to make sure they are exactly the same width and length.

## THE ENDS.

Square the stock for one of the ends (Chapter II., Paragraphs 2, 3, 4, 5). Lay out and cut one end the size and shape shown in the drawing. In like manner square the other end. Make sure that the opposite ends are exactly the same length and width.

## THE HANDLE PARTITION.

The main central partition is also to serve for the handle, so it must be laid out wide enough to extend sufficiently above the side pieces to form the handle, as shown in the drawing. Square this piece of stock (Chapter II., Paragraphs 2, 3, 4, 5). Lay out and make it the shape and dimensions shown in the drawing. (If you care to, you may modify the design for the handle).

## THE BOTTOM.

The bottom may be made of two pieces of material, in which case the joint should come exactly under the central partition. This will prevent the joint from showing from the top side of the work when it is completed; it should, however, be carefully done. Square the stock (Chapter II., Paragraphs 2, 3, 4, 5) ; lay out and execute the dimensions shown in the drawing.

## THE PARTITIONS.

Square the stock (Chapter II., Paragraphs 2, 3, 4, 5) for the partitions. Plane the material the right width; the lengths of these partitions may be cut after the rest of the box is assembled. This will give you a chance to measure the length of each partition, and make it fit perfectly, even if there happens to be a little variation.

## ASSEMBLING.

The box is to be assembled with brads (Chapter II., Paragraph 21). Nail the end pieces on to the ends of the bottom piece. Make sure that they are exactly even at the outside edges so that when the side pieces come on, they will strike the bottom piece and also the ends. If they are not exactly even, plane them so. Nail the side pieces in position, making sure they are perfectly square with the ends. Test frequently with the try-square in assembling the work. Nail the handle partition in position, and test with the try-square to make sure it stands perpendicularly.

In cutting the short partitions, make them just long enough to fit snugly between the handle partition and the sides. Do not try to force them or they will spread the box out of shape. These partitions are to be fastened in position by nailing through the bottom and sides. The first two may be nailed through the handle partition; the last two will be difficult to nail, although a small brad may be toe-nailed in the top edge of each, if desirable (Chapter II., Paragraph 22).

## FINISHING.

With a keen block plane go over the outside of your work and plane off any joints that may be uneven. Finish with sandpaper (Chapter II., Paragraph 17). Stain this piece of work any desirable color (Chapter IV., Paragraph 54). If the wood is left unstained, it will soon become soiled, and will not be neat in appearance. Finish with shellac (Chapter IV., Paragraph 57).

### Optional and Home Projects Employing Similar Principles.

## KNIFE AND FORK BOX.

1. By leaving out the cross partitions, and changing the general design slightly to suit personal taste, a very convenient knife and fork box may be constructed on this plan.

## SEWING TRAY.

2. The principles set forth in this tray lesson may be employed in making sewing trays, particularly adapted to the needs of school classes. By leaving out all the partitions, and changing the size of the tray as local needs might demand, a very satisfactory receptacle for sewing materials may be provided.

# CANDLE-STICK

MATERIALS.

Oak, quartered (Chap. III., Par. 29 and 51).

1 pc. 7/8"x4¾"x4¾" S 2 S Base.
1 pc. 1½"x1½"x4¾" S 4 S Upright.
1 pc. 3/8"x1½"x4" S 2 S Handle.
1 pc. 3/8"x2"x2" S 2 S Top.
1-1½" No. 10 F. H. B. screw.
6-¾" No. 17 Brads.

## INTRODUCTORY STATEMENT.

In these days of modern means of lighting, gas and electricity have completely supplanted the old-time use of the candle. This old-fashioned way of lighting a home entirely by tallow candles and of doing all our reading by such a light would now seem impossible, and while we never expect to return to this plan of equipment, yet the candle-stick is a very popular and unique bit of decoration in a modern home because of its historic interest.

The candle-stick presented in this lesson is the plain mission style; it is intended to present simplicity of design. It will be found quite appropriate for a Christmas or birthday present.

**References:**

The Chemical History of a Candle, Michael Farraday. Harper & Bros., Pub.
The Candlestick, Design and Construction in Wood, Noyes. Manual Arts Press.
The Application of Ornament, Lewis F. Day.
Design in Theory and Practice, Ernest A. Batchelder.
Copper Work, Augustus Rose. Atkinson, Mentzer & Co., Chicago.

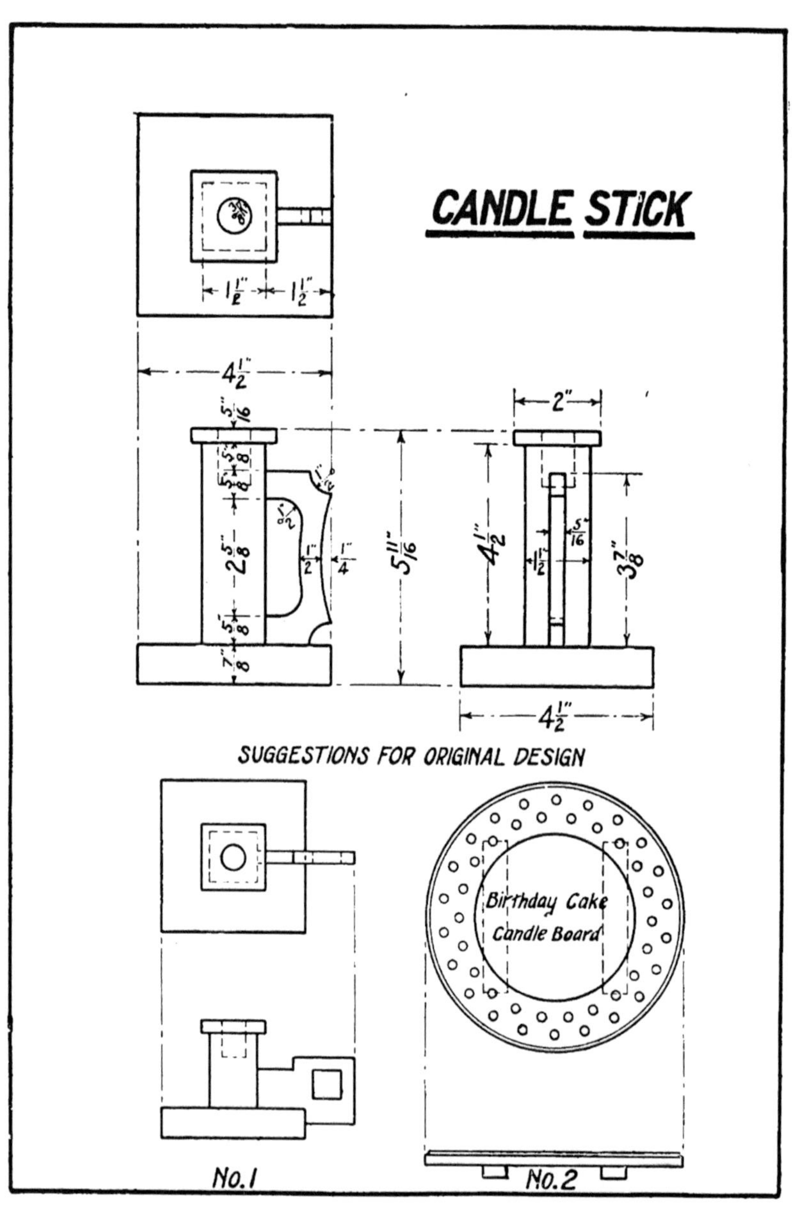
CANDLE STICK
SUGGESTIONS FOR ORIGINAL DESIGN
Birthday Cake
Candle Board
No. 1
No. 2

# CANDLE STICK SPECIFICATIONS

## THE BASE.

Even though this material is furnished S 2 S it should be carefully surfaced either with a very keen plane, or with the steel scraper (Chapter II., Paragraph 16). In selecting the face side of this class of material, select the side which has the most beautiful grain appearance. Square the stock for the base (Chapter II., Paragraphs 2, 3, 4, 5). Lay out and execute the dimensions of the base as indicated in the drawing. Make sure that all edges are perfectly straight and square and that the base is absolutely square when completed. All edges must be smooth. On the end grain you will find this just a little difficult; it will require a very sharp block plane, and much careful work. Be sure you do not splinter out the edges as you plane the end (Chapter II., Paragraph 5).

## THE UPRIGHT.

Although this piece of material is furnished S 2 S you should carefully resurface every face of it with a steel scraper (Chapter II., Paragraph 16). The corners must be left perfectly distinct and sharp. This is a straight line design, and if you should round the corners of the upright, it would destroy the design of your candle stick. Cut the upright the desired length. If you have a miter box you will find it convenient for making this square cut. If not, be sure to square it on all sides with the try-square and cut carefully to the line.

## THE TOP.

Boring the hole in this top piece is a very delicate operation. If you have a Forstner bit, it can be used for this purpose. If not, an ordinary bit, if very sharp, will do the work satisfactorily, if you will be very careful not to bore too rapidly. You can take further precautions to prevent splitting by laying this small piece on a scrap block of the same width, then tightening the two slightly in your vise. Do not attempt to bore this hole entirely through from one side (Chapter II., Paragraph 9). After the hole is bored, lay out and cut the material the size given in the drawing. Finish the edges carefully with a wood file, or a block plane and sandpaper. Make sure that all edges are perfectly square, and that the corners are sharp and distinct.

## THE HANDLE.

Square the stock for the handle (Chapter II., Paragraphs 2, 3, 4). Lay out the shape of the handle as shown in the drawing, or any other design which you may desire. Whatever design you use should have well-defined lines to correspond with the general idea of the design of the candle stick. With the coping, or compass saw, saw out the shape of the handle. Carefully finish with the wood file and sandpaper, leaving all edges distinct and square.

## ASSEMBLING.

This piece of work is to be assembled with screws and brads. Fasten the upright to the base by a large screw up through the bottom of the base. Bore the hole in the base large enough for the screw to pass through freely (Chapter II., Paragraph 9). Make sure this hole is bored exactly in the center of the base. You can locate this center by drawing pencil lines across the bottom from one corner to the other. Countersink this hole freely so the screw will go slightly below the level of the baseboard. Also be sure that the upright stands perfectly square when it is in position. Fasten the top to the upright with four small brads in the corners. Make sure that it projects equally on all sides of the upright.

The handle is to be fastened to the base and upright with brads; holes should be made for the brads (with a very fine brad awl) entirely through this piece of material, for it is very delicate. You will have to use a fine-pointed nail-set to finish driving these brads.

## FINISHING.

The finishing on this piece of work is very important; it must therefore be done with great care. Stain it the desired color (Chapter IV., Paragraph 54); finish with shellac (Chapter IV., Paragraph 57) or wax (Chapter IV., Paragraph 56).

## Optional and Home Projects Employing Similar Principles.

## VASE.

The vase shown in the photograph will be found a very interesting companion piece for this candle stick. You should make a working drawing of your own for this piece of work. It will be suitable for dry flowers, or to contain a small, glass vase of water for a bouquet of fresh flowers.

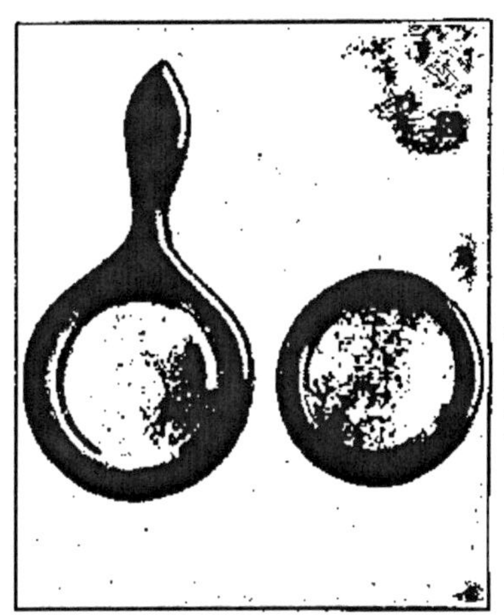

# HAND MIRROR

MATERIALS.

Mahogany (Chap. III., Par. 50),
Walnut (Chap. III., Par. 44),
Cherry (Chap. III., Par. 34),
Gum (Chap. III., Par. 37).

1 pc. ¾"x6¼"x11" S 2 S
1-5" D bevel plate mirror.
1 pc. rattan ⅛"x16".

INTRODUCTORY STATEMENT.

A small mirror is a convenient article for the dressing table or the traveling bag. While there are innumerable kinds of hand mirrors on the market, yet a hand-made one will be very much appreciated because of its special personal interest.

This mirror should be made from one of the finer cabinet woods, such as mahogany, gum, cherry or walnut. It must be carefully executed so as to be free from all tool marks and must have a fine finish or it will not be appropriate for the purpose intended. This piece of work well done will make an especially attractive gift.

---

**References:**

Glass Manufacture, Walter Rosenhain. D. Van Nostand Co.
The Making of Plate Glass, Pittsburgh Plate Glass Co., Pittsburgh, Pa.
A Visit to a Glass Factory, How the World Is Housed, Carpenter. American Book Co.
Silvering Glass, C. C. Baly. Scientific Am. Sup., January 11, 1908.
Mirrors, Young Folks' Cyclopedia of Common Things, Champlin. Henry Holt & Co.
Materials Used in Silvering Glass. Scientific Am. Sup., February 11, 1905.

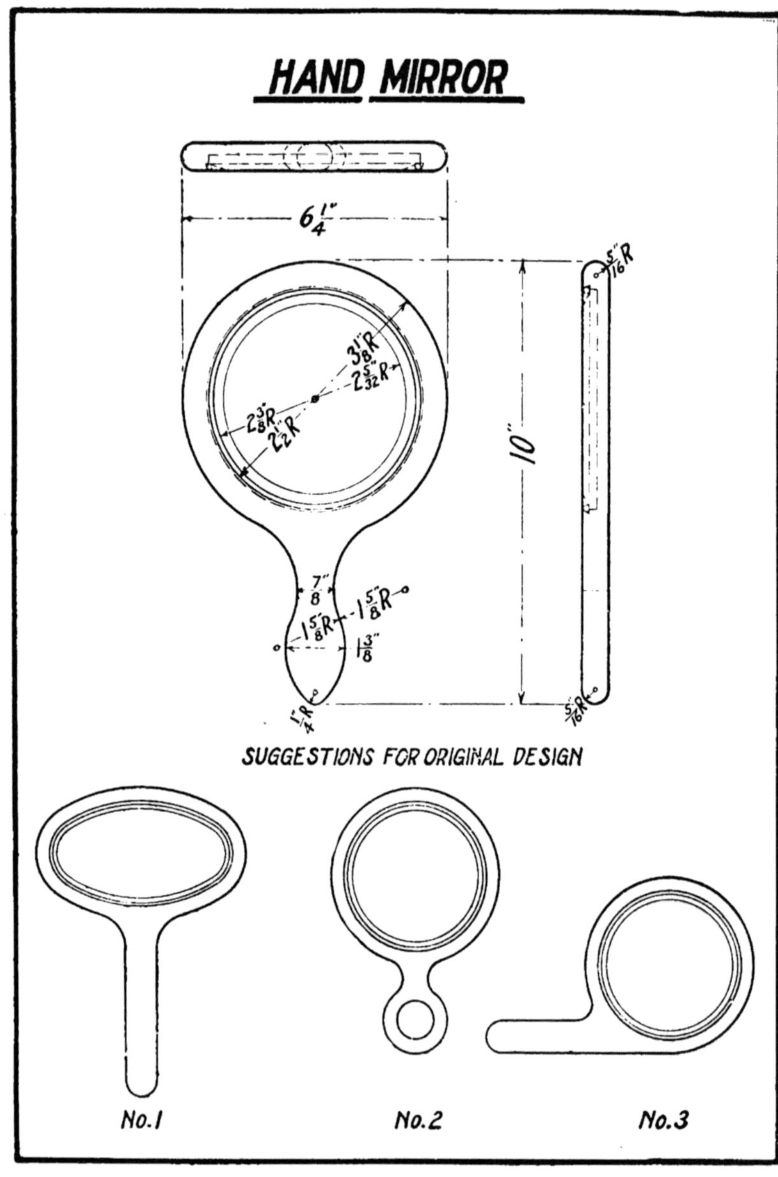
HAND MIRROR
6 1/4"
10"
5/16 R
3 1/8 R
2 5/32 R
2 3/8 R
2 1/2 R
7/8"
1 5/8 R
1 5/8 R
1 3/8"
1/4" R
5/16 R
SUGGESTIONS FOR ORIGINAL DESIGN
No.1
No.2
No.3

# HAND MIRROR SPECIFICATIONS

Since this piece of material must be completely surfaced as one of the last operations, it will not be necessary to resurface it now. Prepare a working edge (Chapter II., Paragraph 4) and a working end (Chapter II., Paragraph 5). Make all measurements from the working edge and working end, and lay out the entire shape of the mirror.

With your compasses lay out the opening which is to be cut to receive the mirror plate. (It would be well to measure the mirror which you are to use to make sure that it is exactly the size shown in the drawing). This opening for the mirror plate should be cut as the first operation. If you have an expansive bit, this hole can be easily cut with it. If you do not have one, lay out the circle very carefully with the compasses, and with a sharp-pointed knife trace this compass mark, cutting it as deeply as you can conveniently; then with a sharp chisel cut away the wood in the central part up to this line. *This will have to be done with extreme care*, or you will chip out the edge beyond the compass line and completely spoil the appearance of the work. Continue cutting this compass line deeper and deeper as you cut away the material in the central part, until you have reached the desired depth. By studying the drawing you will notice that this line should be cut back at an angle to receive the small piece of rattan which holds the mirror in position.

After you have cut the opening the required depth and shape to receive the mirror, saw out the other curves with a compass or coping saw. You should be careful to have the edges perfectly square. As all of these edges are to be rounded, the first operation would be to chamfer them equally all the way round. To do this, gauge on all surfaces and all edges, using the pencil and finger (Chapter II., Paragraph 8). This chamfering can be most satisfactorily done with a sharp sloyd knife or pocket knife. This whittling, however, must be done with great care, or you will split out beyond the gauge line and mar your work. After the chamfering has been completed, you should go entirely around the work again, cutting away the remaining corners of the chamfer. This causes the edge to approach the rounded shape. After as much work has been done with the pocket knife as convenient, the wood file should be used to complete the rounding. All edges should be made perfectly round and smooth. This portion of the work cannot be hurried and must be carefully completed, after which all edges should be sandpapered. The plan used in sandpapering a cylinder (Chapter II., Paragraph 15) could be successfully used. All tool marks, rough places and irregularities must be removed.

## FASTENING THE MIRROR IN POSITION.

Cut a piece of blotting paper, or any other soft paper, the exact size of the mirror; lay it in the bottom of the opening before putting in the mirror; this will prevent the mirror from becoming scratched. Press the mirror firmly in position, and cut the piece of rattan long enough, so that when it is laid around the outside edge of the mirror in position, it will fit perfectly tight. A little glue should be placed in the joint which is to receive the rattan; it should then be pressed closely in position. The work should be left undisturbed for several hours for the glue to harden. Use but little glue or it will ooze out and mar the surface of the work; if any glue gets on the surface, it should be removed before it hardens.

## FINISHING.

After all tool marks have been removed, and the work has been made absolutely smooth, it should be finished with shellac. As this piece of work is made of fine cabinet wood, it possibly will not be desirable to stain it. The French polish will be a very suitable finsh (Chapter IV., Paragraph 57). In rubbing the work with sandpaper or pumice stone and oil, be very careful not to rub the glass, for these materials will scratch it. Do not leave this piece of work until a beautiful polish is made.

## Optional and Home Projects Employing Similar Principles.

### ROUND MIRROR.

1. A round mirror, as shown in the illustration at the opening of this lesson, will be found very convenient as a part of a traveling bag equipment.

### ELLIPTICAL MIRROR.

2. An elliptical mirror may be made using the plan given in this lesson. The ellipse may be laid out after the manner suggested in supplementary problem P in the chapter on mechanical drawing.

# FLOWER POT STAND

MATERIALS.

Yellow Pine (Chap. III., Par. 48) or any soft wood.

2 pcs. 7/8"x5 1/4"x35" S 2 S Shelves.
1 pc. 7/8"x5 1/4"x44" S 2 S Top.
2 pcs. 7/8"x4 1/2"x36" S 2 S Legs.
3 pcs. 7/8"x4 1/2"x35 1/2" S 2 S Back shelf.
2 pcs. 7/8"x4 1/2"x24" S 2 S Legs.
2 pcs. 7/8"x3"x5 1/2" S 2 S Brackets.
2 pcs. 7/8"x2 1/2"x3" S 2 S Brackets.
5 dozen 6d finishing nails.
4 small castors.
8-1/2" corrugated nails.

## INTRODUCTORY STATEMENT.

Many homes are made more cheerful and beautiful by keeping a few pots of growing plants and flowers. Unless some special way is provided to care for them there is considerable inconvenience connected with the task.

The purpose of this flower pot stand is to provide a substantial and satisfactory stand upon which the flower pots may be placed where there will be no danger of their being knocked over. It will also give the flowers a chance to be seen and to be moved about conveniently.

This stand can be made any size to suit the room and the purpose for which it is intended. A very large stand would be suitable for outdoor or porch use, while a smaller and more neatly made one would be required for inside service. If the stand is placed on castors it will be found a great convenience in moving it from place to place for the purpose of sweeping or accommodating the plants to the sunlight.

---

**References:**

U. S. Bulletin No. 113, Experimental Gardens and Grounds.
Garden Making, Bailey. The Macmillan Co., publishers.
How to Know Wild Flowers, W. S. Dana. Chas. Scribner's Sons.
Plants, J. M. Coulter. Appleton Pub. Co., New York.

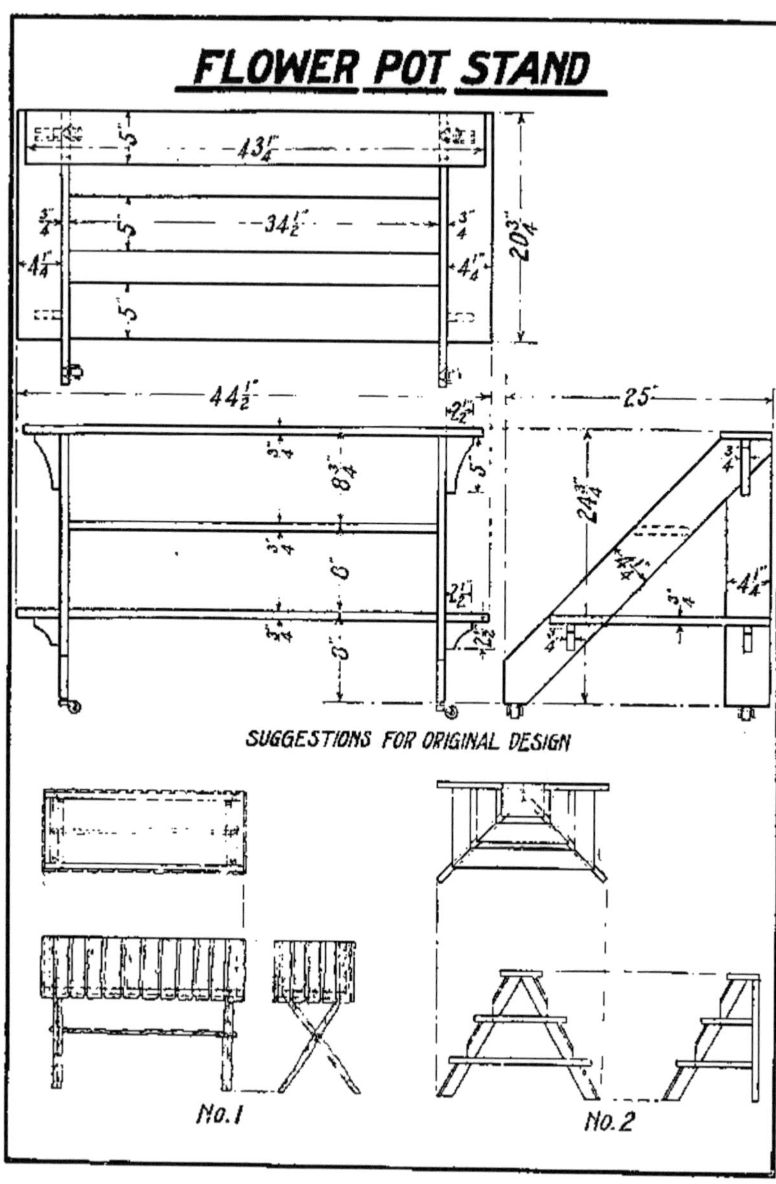
FLOWER POT STAND
SUGGESTIONS FOR ORIGINAL DESIGN
No. 1
No. 2

# FLOWER POT STAND SPECIFICATIONS

## THE LEGS.

As this material is furnished S 2 S it will not be necessary for you to plane the surface. Select the best side for a working face (Chapter II., Paragraph 2). Prepare a working edge (Chapter II., Paragraph 4). This angle for the legs is known as the half pitch cut (Chapter V., Paragraph 75). This cut should be laid out as explained in Chapter II., Paragraph 24. Cut all the legs the dimensions shown in the drawing.

## THE SHELVES.

It will not be necessary to resurface this material. Prepare a working edge (Chapter II., Paragraph 4) and a squared end (Chapter II., Paragraph 5). Cut the material the width and length shown in the drawing. Make sure all the shelves are exactly the same length.

## THE TOP.

The top shelf should be long enough to project at each end, as shown in the drawing. Since the ends of the top piece will be exposed, they should be block planed (Chapter II., Paragraph 5), and finished with sandpaper.

The side shelves should also have the ends block planed and sandpapered.

## THE BRACKETS.

Lay out one of the larger brackets the desired shape. (If you wish you may make an original design.) With the coping or compass saw, saw it out and with the wood file or block plane make all edges perfectly straight and square. Be sure that the angle of the bracket is a perfect right angle; test it with the square. Using this as a pattern, lay out and cut the other large bracket exactly like it.

In similar manner design and make the required number of small brackets.

## ASSEMBLING.

The front legs are to be joined to the rear legs with corrugated nails (Chapter II., Paragraph 23).

The shelves are to be fastened in position by nailing through the legs at each end of the shelf. Lay out and place the shelves carefully so they will stand parallel; nail them in position (Chapter II., Paragraph 21). The top is to be nailed down through into the legs. The side shelves may be toe-nailed (Chapter II., Paragraph 22).

Test with the square to make sure that all angles are perfect, then nail the brackets in position. If properly made and nailed, these brackets will brace the stand securely.

Bore the holes for the castors. The castors need not be put on until after the finishing is done; if they are put on before, care must be exercised not to get any stain on them.

## FINISHING.

With a sharp steel scraper remove all pencil or tool marks and make sure that the surface is perfectly smooth. The nails may be driven slightly below the surface with a nail set. The holes can be filled with putty. Stain the desired color (Chapter IV., Paragraph 54). Finish with one or two coats of shellac (Chapter IV., Paragraph 57) or a coat of varnish (Chapter IV., Paragraph 58). NOTE: If the flower pot stand is to be used out of doors, one or two coats of paint (Chapter IV., Paragraph 52) will be preferable to the shellac or varnish, although a good coating of oil stain would stand considerable outside wear.

**Optional and Home Projects Employing Similar Principles.**

## RUSTIC FLOWER POT STAND.

1. A rustic flower pot stand is particularly suitable for the porch or lawn. Suggestion No. 1 presents an idea for a combination stand and flower box. This idea may be modified in a great many ways which will suggest themselves when the work is undertaken.

## PYRAMID STAND.

2. The shape of a flower pot stand may be modified to suit one's personal taste. In suggestion No. 2 the idea of arranging the flowers in a pyramid is presented.

# BIRD HOUSE

MATERIALS.

Basswood (Chap. III., Par. 31) or any soft wood.

1 pc. ¾"x8"x14½" S 2 S Bottom.

2 pcs. ⅝"x5½"x10½" S 2 S Sides.

2 pcs. ⅝"x6"x8" S 2 S Ends.

1 pc. ¾"x3¼" dowel rod.

1 pc. ¼"x15" dowel rod.

2½ dozen 1½" brads.

1 pc. galv. iron 12"x14". Roof. ½ doz. ¾" No. 6 R. H. screws.

## INTRODUCTORY STATEMENT.

Most people enjoy the presence of song birds, but many people do not realize what a great benefit they are to the production of farm and fruit crops. The Government and various societies are spending considerable time in an effort to educate the public to a proper appreciation of bird life. The days of the thoughtless killing of song birds have gone by and now no boy can claim to be a manly fellow if he insists upon being destructive to bird life.

This bird house will provide a safe place for the shelter of desirable birds and their nests. When completed it should be mounted upon a pole or on some building where it will attract the birds.

---

**References:**


U. S. Bulletin No. 609, Bird Houses.
Song Birds and Water Fowls, Parkhurst. Chas. Scribner's Sons, Pub.
Bird Portraits, Ernest Thompson Seton. Ginn & Co.
What I Have Done With Birds, Gene Stratton Porter. Bobbs-Merrill Co.
A Watcher in the Woods, Dallas Sharp. Century Pub. Co.
U. S. Agricultural Bulletin No. 133, Birds as Weed Destroyers.
U. S. Agricultural Bulletin No. 630, Some Common Birds in Their Relation to Agriculture.
Our Native Birds, Lange. Macmillan Co., publishers.
Bird Life, Frank Chapman. Appleton Pub. Co., New York.
The Bird, Its Form and Function, C. W. Beebe. Holt Co., New York.
U. S. Bulletin No. 493, The Relation of Sparrows to Agriculture.
Bird Neighbors, Blanchan. Book Supply Co., Chicago.
Handbook of Birds, Frank Chapman. Book Supply Co., Chicago.

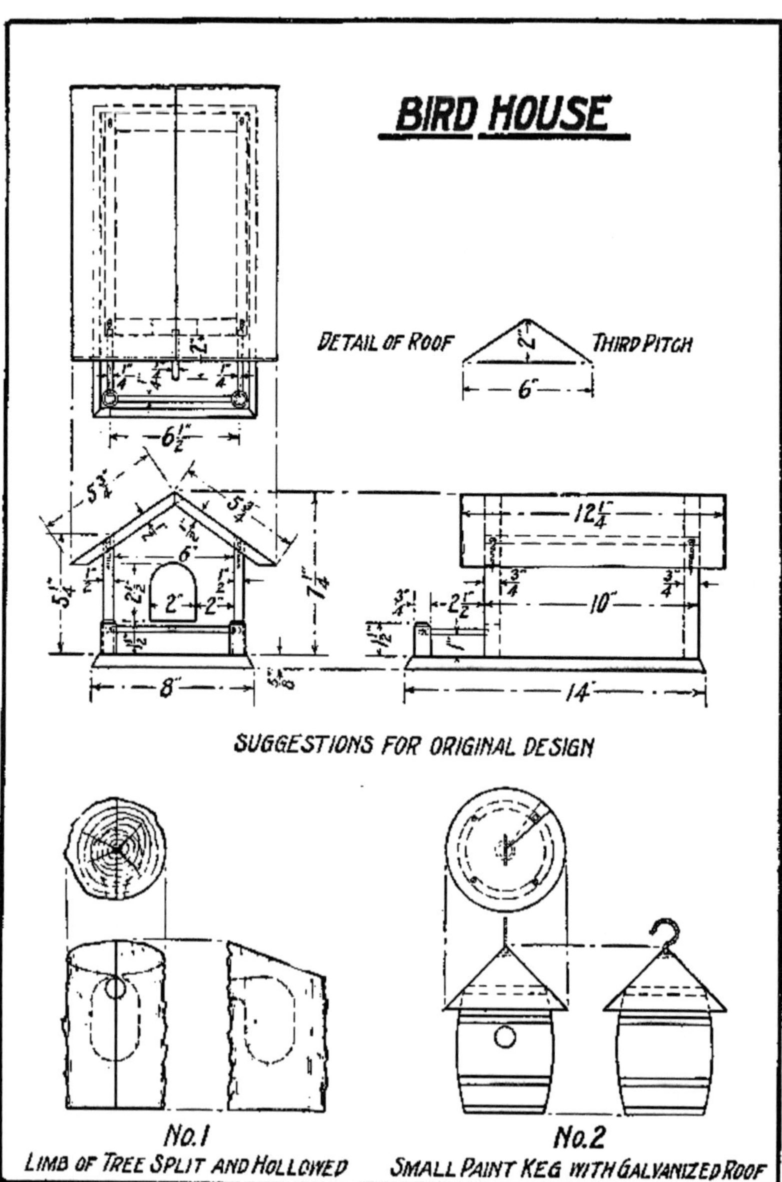
BIRD HOUSE
DETAIL OF ROOF
THIRD PITCH
SUGGESTIONS FOR ORIGINAL DESIGN
No.1
LIMB OF TREE SPLIT AND HOLLOWED
No.2
SMALL PAINT KEG WITH GALVANIZED ROOF

# BIRD HOUSE SPECIFICATIONS

## THE BOTTOM.

As this material is furnished S 2 S it will not be necessary for you to resurface it. Plane a working edge (Chapter II., Paragraph 4) and a working end (Chapter II., Paragraph 5). Lay out and cut the material the size shown in the drawing. Lay out the chamfer (Chapter II., Paragraph 8) and plane to the gauge line.

## THE SIDES.

It will not be necessary for you to resurface this material. Prepare a working edge (Chapter II., Paragraph 4) and a working end (Chapter II., Paragraph 5). Lay out and cut the material the size indicated in the drawing. NOTE: If you prefer, you need not bevel the top edge of the board to receive the roof until after it is assembled. Prepare the two sides exactly the same length, and make sure they are perfectly square.

## THE ENDS.

Square the stock (Chapter II., Paragraphs 2, 3, 4, 5). Cut the ends the exact shape and size shown in the drawing, making sure that the edges are perfectly straight, and that the ends are absolutely square. The detailed drawing of the roof construction will show you that this roof is to be third pitch (Chapter V., Paragraph 76, also Chapter II., Paragraph 25). Lay out and cut the two ends the required pitch. Test the two ends to make sure they are exactly the same shape and size.

The size of the door in the bird house is considered an important matter if you are building your house for any special kind of bird. (A study of the references given will furnish you some valuable information on this subject.) Lay out and cut the door.

## ASSEMBLING.

Assemble by nailing the side pieces on to the end pieces, as shown in the drawing. Test to make sure that the angles are perfectly square and that the edges are all even at the bottom. Carefully plane the side pieces to the same bevel as the gable ends. This will make sure that the roof will fit perfectly on the sides. Be sure the house is perfectly square, then fasten the bottom in position by nailing through into the side and end pieces.

## ROOF.

The roof is to be made of tin or galvanized sheet iron. This will be a rectangular piece of tin large enough to make the two sides and long enough to turn down on each end to form the finish, as indicated in the drawing. If you do not have tinner's snips in your shop, this piece of sheet iron may be cut with an old pair of shears.

Fasten the roof in position with four small screws, as shown in the drawing; the use of screws will make it possible to remove the roof, when the bird house should be cleaned out for the new season.

## PERCH PINS.

The perch pins are to be of dowels fastened to the house by inserting them in small holes. The corner posts are fastened in position by screws put through from the bottom.

## FINISHING.

This house will be exposed to sun and rain, and it should therefore be well painted (Chapter IV., Paragraph 52). If you have no paint, oil stain may be used. The roof may be painted or left, as desired. When completed the house should be put up on a building, on a tall pole or in a tree.

### Optional and Home Projects Employing Similar Principles.

## RUSTIC BIRD HOUSE.

1. By splitting an old limb of a tree and hollowing out the inside and re-assembling it, a very attractive rustic bird house can be made.

## KEG BIRD HOUSE.

2. In suggestion No. 2 you will find the drawing for a very easily constructed bird house. It is made of a small paint keg, with a piece of galvanized iron arranged in conical shape for a roof.

## DOLL HOUSE.

3. The principle of construction of the small house, set forth in this lesson, may readily be employed in the making of a doll house suitable for primary or kindergarten work. The size of the house may be governed by the material available. One side or end should be movable so the interior may be seen when desired. Other modifications of these principles will suggest themselves during the progress of the work.

# WAGON JACK

MATERIALS.

Beech (Chap. III., Par. 32) or any hard wood.

1 pc. 1¾"x3¾"x16½" Base.
2 pcs. ⅞"x3¾"x25" Sides.
1 pc. ⅞"x3¼"x30" Lever.
3-⅜"x3" carriage bolts
3-⅜" washers.
1 pc. soft iron rod 5/16"x4 ft.
1 pc. ¾" strap iron 12" long.
4-¾" No. 8 F. H. B. screws.

INTRODUCTORY STATEMENT.

The necessity of keeping a wagon, buggy or other vehicle constantly greased demands that some sort of handy jack should be in the tool shed or barn. There are a great many patent lifting jacks on the market, but not every barn is supplied with such equipment.

This wagon jack can be made of scrap material, and usually odd bolts can be found in the tool shed, and thus all of the material may be provided without any expense. If possible it should be made of some kind of hard wood, although almost any straight-grained lumber will do. It should be painted or well oiled with linseed oil.

**References:**

Handy Farm Devices and How to Make Them, Cableigh. Manual Arts Press, Peoria, Ill.
Agricultural Apparatus and How It Is Made, Soils and Fertilizers, Quear.
Life on the Farm, Shepard. Book Supply Co., Chicago.
Making the Farm Pay, Bousfield. Book Supply Co., Chicago.
The Young Farmer, Hunt. Book Supply Co., Chicago.

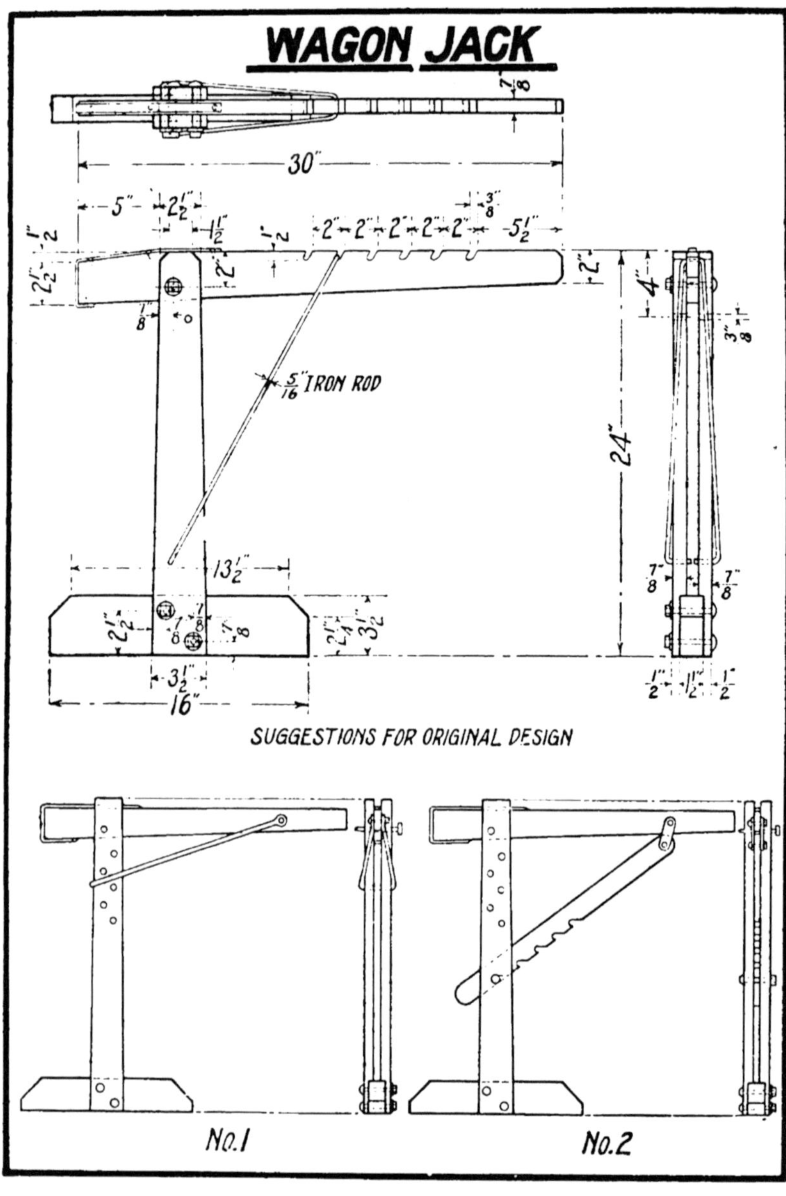
WAGON JACK
30"
5"
$2\frac{1}{2}$"
$1\frac{1}{2}$"
2" 2" 2" 2" 2"
$\frac{3}{8}$"
$5\frac{1}{2}$"
$\frac{5}{16}$" IRON ROD
24"
4"
$13\frac{1}{2}$"
$3\frac{1}{2}$"
16"
SUGGESTIONS FOR ORIGINAL DESIGN
No.1
No.2

# WAGON JACK SPECIFICATIONS

## THE BASE.

As this piece of material is furnished S 2 S it will not be necessary for you to resurface it. Select the best surface for the working face (Chapter II., Paragraph 2); prepare a working edge (Chapter II., Paragraph 4); prepare a working end (Chapter II., Paragraph 5). Lay out and execute the dimensions of this piece as shown in the drawing. Make sure that the edges are all perfectly square, and that the corners are chamfered at a regular half-pitch cut. This can be done with a miter box, if you care to, or you may set the T-bevel to the half-pitch cut (Chapter II., Paragraph 24) and use it in laying out; and cut with a back saw.

## THE SIDE PIECES.

Square the stock for the side pieces (Chapter II., Paragraphs 2, 3, 4, 5). Lay out and make the two side pieces the dimensions shown in the drawing. Notice that these pieces are to be shouldered on to the base piece leaving ½" thickness at the bottom. This sort of joint will afford great strength against a downward pressure, for it will relieve the bolts of considerable strain. Lay out these joints with the marking gauge and saw them down just as you would saw a tenon (Chapter II., Paragraph 14).

## THE LEVER.

Square the stock of the lever (Chapter II., Paragraphs 2, 3, 4, 5); lay out and execute the dimensions of the lever as shown in the drawing. In forming the notches in the top part of the lever, it would be well to bore holes equally spaced at the proper distance from the edge, and then saw into these holes, thus forming the notches. The piece of strap iron on the front of the lever is to protect it from wear. You can drill the holes in the strap iron with an ordinary drill bit used in a brace. Countersink the holes with an ordinary rose countersink.

## ASSEMBLING.

The two side pieces are to be fastened to the base with bolts, as indicated in the drawing. It might be well to put the two side braces in position, and fasten them with two or three small brads, making sure that the joints fit snugly on the top edge of the base. Then bore for the bolts through all three of the pieces at once, testing with the try-square to make sure that you are boring perpendicularly (Chapter II., Paragraph 11). Do not bore entirely through from one side (Chapter II., Paragraph 9).

Drive the bolts in position, place a washer on each, and run the nuts on perfectly tight.

The hole for the lever bolt might be bored in like manner by clamping the lever in position between the two side pieces. This can be done by putting them in the vise. When you are attempting to bore through all these pieces of material at one operation, care must be exercised to bore the hole perpendicularly (Chapter II., Paragraph 11).

### THE IRON ROD.

The rod may be bent by fastening it in the vise at about 1″ from the end, carefully bending it over. A few careful blows with the hammer will help to form a perfect right angle. In like manner another short crook must be bent on the other end. Measure to find the middle of the rod and make the middle bend. By carefully working with this rod you will be able to adjust it so it will fit perfectly.

### FINISHING.

When the wagon jack is completed, with a sharp steel scraper (Chapter II., Paragraph 16), or wood file and sandpaper, remove all pencil or tool marks, and give it one or two coats of linseed oil. This will make it wear smooth, and will protect it against moisture. It may be painted if desired (Chapter IV., Paragraph 52).

## Optional and Home Projects Employing Similar Principles.

### FRICTIONAL WAGON JACK.

1. Suggestion No. 1 shows a very convenient form of wagon jack which has the advantage of catching at any point, for the rod holds by friction, rather than by a notch as is usually the case. The portion of the rod which does the holding should be mashed slightly so as to present a flat surface and edge. It may require a little experimenting to get it shaped to hold satisfactorily.

### NOTCHED-BRACE WAGON JACK.

2. Suggestion No. 2 shows still another method of providing the wagon jack with a means of holding in position. This notched brace is attached to the lever by means of two small pieces of strap iron, one on either side, as shown in the drawing.

# SEED TESTER

MATERIALS.

Yellow Pine (Chap. III., Par. 48) or any soft wood.

2 pcs. ⅞"x4"x37" S 2 S Sides.
2 pcs. ⅞"x4"x16" S 2 S Ends.
9 pcs. ⅞"x4"x15" S 2 S Bottom.
6 pcs. ⅞"x3½"x18" S 2 S Legs.
2 pcs. ⅞"x3½"x4'8" S 2 S Rear standards.
1 pc. ⅞"x3½"x38" S 2 S Stretcher.
10 pcs. ⅞"x2"x36" S 2 S Corn racks.
3 pcs. ¾"x ¾"x36" S 4 S Inside strips.
100-10d common nails.
9 dozen 6d finishing nails.

INTRODUCTORY STATEMENT.

Before men thoroughly understood the reproduction of plants from seeds, it was thought that any kernel of corn which appeared to be of good size and shape would be satisfactory for seed purposes. It has been proven that while we may be able to judge most of the qualities of a kernel of corn by examining it, we cannot always definitely tell about its vitality.

**References:**

Testing Seed Corn; The Book of Corn, Myrick. Orange-Judd Co.
U. S. Farmer's Bulletin No. 111, Farmer's Interest in Good Seed.
U. S. Farmer's Bulletin No. 415, Seed Corn.
U. S. Farmer's Bulletin No. 400, Profitable Corn-Planting Method.
Minnesota College of Agriculture, Bulletin No. 24, Seed Testing.
Development of the Corn Plant, J. R. Steward, Muncie, Ind.
U. S. Bulletin No. 414, Corn Cultivation.
U. S. Bulletin No. 253, Germination of Seed Corn.

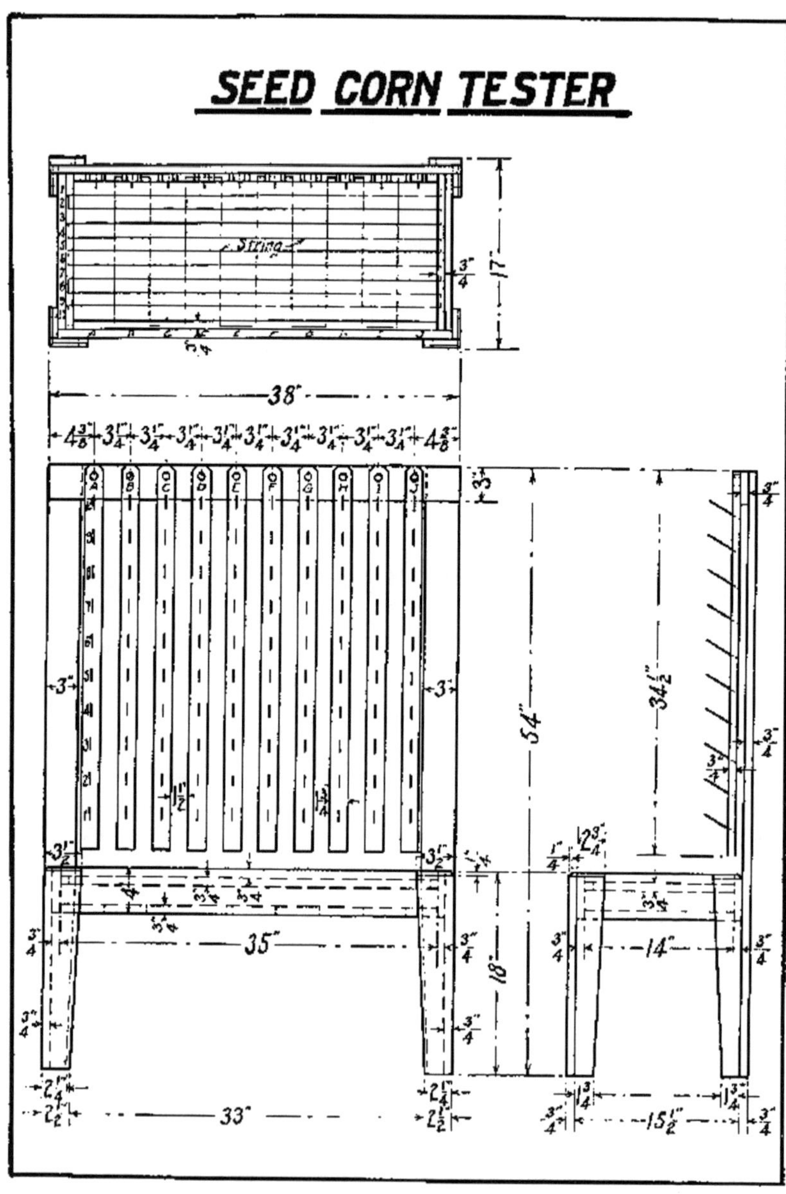
SEED CORN TESTER
String
17"
38"
54"
35"
33"
18"
14"
15½"
34½"

# SEED CORN TESTER SPECIFICATIONS

## THE SIDE PIECES.

Plane one edge of each of the side pieces perfectly straight and square (Chapter II., Paragraph 4). Prepare a working end (Chapter II., Paragraph 5). Lay out the dimensions of the side pieces and cut them, making sure that the opposite sides are exactly the same length and width. In like manner square the stock and prepare the two end pieces.

## THE BOTTOM.

The bottom is to be made up of narrow strips, and as the box is to hold moist dirt or sand, it will not be well to fit the joints too closely, as they must have room to swell. It will not be necessary to joint the edges of the strips which are to form the bottom. Nail together the two sides and the two ends, forming the frame. Cut the pieces for the bottom just long enough to fit snugly inside the frame. Put in a sufficient number of strips to make a solid bottom. Nail through the side pieces into the ends of the bottom pieces.

## THE LEGS.

Square the stock (Chapter II., Paragraphs 2, 3, 4, 5). Lay out, and make pieces the dimensions for the legs, as shown in the drawing. Notice that the two rear legs extend above the box to form a rack on which to hang the seed corn racks. Fasten the legs in position by nailing through them into the box, and by nailing the edges together, "pig trough" fashion.

## THE CORN RACK.

The corn rack consists of strips through which 10d nails are driven at an angle; each nail to support one ear of corn. This provides room for 100 ears, thus making it possible to test at least one bushel of corn at one time.

Prepare the ten strips and insert the nails as shown in the drawing. It will probably be necessary to bore for the nails to avoid splitting the strips. The boring should be done at a definite angle (Chapter II., Paragraph 12).

## INSIDE LEVELING STRIP.

On the inside of the tray you are to nail leveling strips which will receive the brads for the dividing string. Nail these strips in position as shown by dotted lines in the drawing. Drive small brads into the top edges of these strips to receive the string which divides the tray into equal spaces, as shown in the drawing.

## FINISHING.

It is not necessary for the seed corn rack to be given a coat of any sort of finishing material. However, it will be much more durable if well painted (Chapter IV., Paragraph 52).

## THE USE OF THE SEED CORN TESTER.

The seed corn tester is used to make a germinating test of seed corn. The tray of the tester should be filled with fine sand; level with the top of the strips. The strings should be stretched, as shown in the drawing. Choice corn should be selected, two kernels taken from near the butt of the ear, two from near the middle of the ear, and two from near the tip of the ear. These six kernels should be planted in a row in one of the little divisions of the tester marked out by the string. This ear should then be hung on the strip on the nail which corresponds in number to the division in which the kernels are planted. In like manner the entire corn tester should be filled; it should be kept in a warm place, and the sand moistened frequently for a few days until the kernels sprout, and send the little corn plants above the surface. You can then tell the exact vitality of each ear by noticing the sprouts put forth by the kernel taken from that ear. Sometimes it will be found that the kernels near the butt will grow well, while those in the middle of the ear will grow only moderately well, and those near the tip very poorly. In this case the ear should be discarded, or only the butt portion used for seed. Only ears of strong vitality should be used for seed.

After the seed corn tester has been used to test out the corn for the spring planting the tray may be filled with dirt and used to raise tomato, cabbage or other plants for early spring planting.

### Optional and Home Projects Employing Similar Principles.

## SAND TABLE.

1. A sand table for the use of primary classes may be prepared in the same manner in which the tray of the seed corn tester is made. It may be made as wide and long as local needs may demand.

## SOIL BINS.

2. In connection with the work in agriculture, some sort of storage bin is required in caring for the samples of soil which must be kept on hand. By making the legs very much longer, several bins may be installed, one above the other.

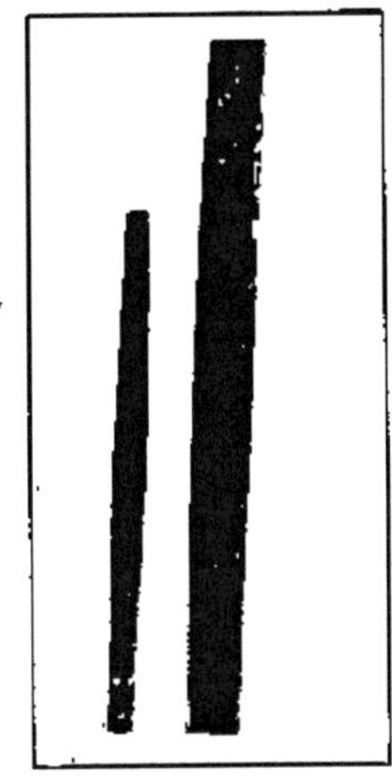

# EVENER AND SINGLETREE

## MATERIALS.

Hickory (Chap. III., Par. 39) or Straight-grained Oak (Chap. III., Par. 29).

Singletree—
1 pc. 2″x2¾″x35″ rough or S 2 S

Evener—
1 pc. 2⅛″x4¾″x48″ rough or S 2 S

## INTRODUCTORY STATEMENT.

Singletrees are in constant use both in cities and on the farm or wherever any kind of team work is being done. Singletrees are frequently broken, and although they can be purchased on the market, yet since they are so simple in construction it is well for a boy to be able to make them.

The best material for this purpose is clear, straight hickory; a good quality of ash or oak may be used.

One great advantage in a farmer boy's being able to handle tools comes from the fact that he can spend his odd hours or rainy days in making things which will save him considerable expense.

**References:**


Modern Blacksmithing and Wagon Making, Holmstrom. Fredrick Drake Co., Chicago.
Farm Buildings, H. V. Van Holst. The National Builder, Chicago, Ill.
The Gasoline Engine on the Farm, Putnam. Norman Henly Pub. Co., New York.
Electric Light for the Farm. Schneider, Spon & Chamberlain, New York.
Home Water Works, Lynde. Sturgis & Walton, New York.
Suggestions for Home Blacksmithing, Library of Work and Play, Sleffel. Doubleday, Page & Co.

## DOUBLETREE OR EVENER

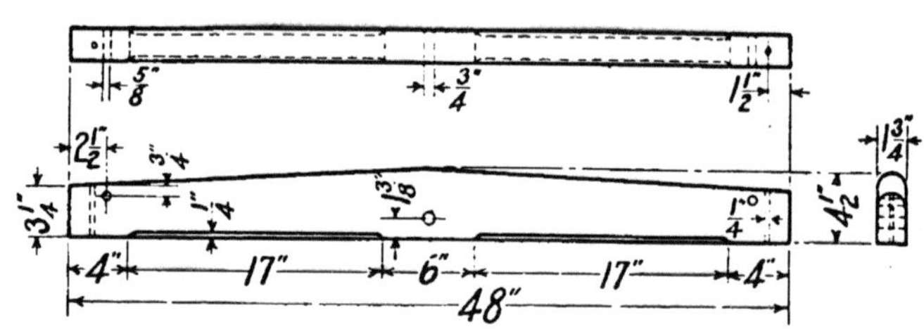


## SINGLETREE

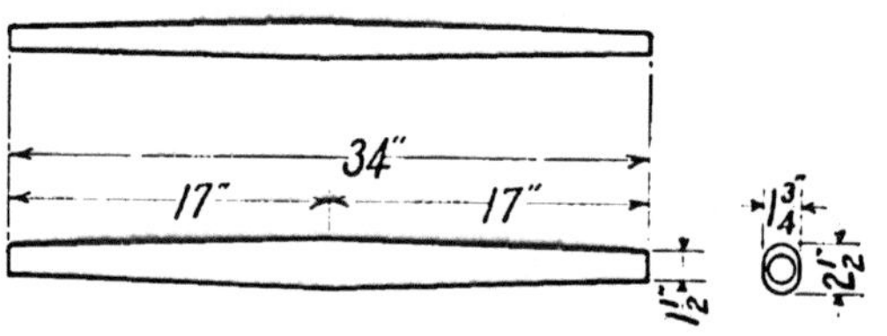


SUGGESTIONS FOR ORIGINAL DESIGN

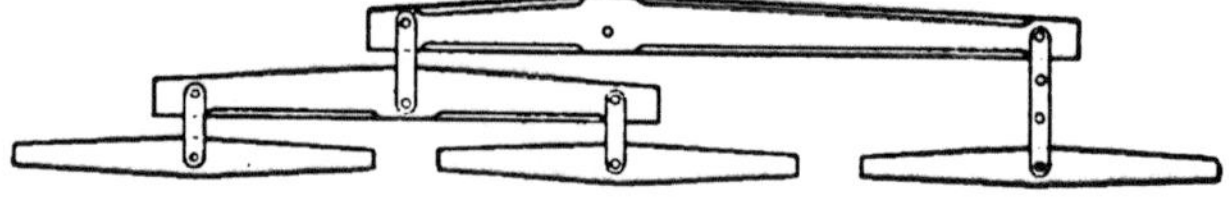

THREE HORSE EVENER

# DOUBLE TREE OR EVENER SPECIFICATIONS

Plane one surface of the material perfectly smooth and mark it the working face (Chapter II., Paragraph 2). Plane one edge perfectly straight and square for the working edge (Chapter II., Paragraph 4). Square one end (Chapter II., Paragraph 5). Gauge the width which the evener must be at the widest point (Chapter II., Paragraph 6 or 7); measure and cut the desired length. Lay out the width at each end; measure carefully and locate the middle; with a lead pencil square a line across the working face at this point.

You will notice from the drawing that the front side of the evener is to be perfectly straight, with the corners chamfered, while the rear side is to be tapered, or rounded, just as you may see fit. Lay out these lines for the taper on the rear side, saw them out with the rip saw, and finish with the plane; round this edge slightly, as shown in the drawing.

On the front side lay out the chamfer (Chapter II., Paragraph 8). This chamfer may be cut with the drawing knife (if you have none use a pocket knife and complete it with a small plane). Locate and bore the holes as shown in the drawing (Chapter II., Paragraph 9).

## FINISHING.

With a sharp steel scraper remove all pencil marks and rough places; finish with one or two coats of linseed oil.

# SINGLETREE.

Although the singletree does not have any perfectly straight surfaces it will be well to prepare a working face and working edge from which to lay out dimensions (Chapter II., Paragraphs 1, 2, 3, 4). Lay out the tapered shape of the singletree, and saw it out with the rip saw. With the drawing knife or plane chamfer the corners, and plane the singletree to the proper shape.

## FINISHING.

With the wood file or sharp steel scraper remove all tool marks. It may be smoothed with sandpaper (Chapter II., Paragraph 16). When all tool marks have been removed, finish with one or two coats of linseed oil.

### Optional and Home Projects Employing Similar Principles.

## THREE-HORSE EVENER.

1. In the Suggestions for Original Design the idea of a three-horse evener is presented. The evener is very similar in construction to the doubletree presented in the lesson. The principal difference is that the hole for the king-pin is bored at one-third the distance from the end, thus giving the single horse sufficient leverage to equal the team.

## NECK YOKE.

2. The problem of making a neck yoke is very similar to that of shaving and shaping the form of a singletree. Of course the length and shape of this project will not be the same but the principles of construction are almost identical.

# FARM GATE

## MATERIALS.

Yellow Pine (Chap. III., Par. 48).

7 pcs. 7/8"x4"x12' S 2 S — 2 pcs. 7/8"x4½"x12' S 2 S

5 dozen 8d common nails. — 6 pcs. 7/8"x4"x 5' S 2 S

28-¼"x2¾" carriage bolts, with washers and nuts.

## INTRODUCTORY STATEMENT.

In visiting farms throughout the country it is not uncommon to find the large gates in bad repair. Many a farmer has been dragging or carrying a gate open and shut for several years when a few minutes' work would so repair the gate as to cause it to swing freely on its hinges.

The purpose of this lesson is to show how a large gate can be constructed so as to have the greatest strength and the longest endurance. The size of the gate is determined by the opening for which it is intended, but the principle of the construction, such as the bracing and bolting, should not be neglected.

**References:**

U. S. Bulletin No. 126, Practical Suggestions for Farm Buildings.
Concrete Fence Posts. Atlas Portland Cement Co., Chicago.
Concrete for the Farmer. Universal Portland Cement Co., Chicago.
Studies in Concrete, in Soils and Fertilizers, Quear, Muncie, Ind.
Ideas for the Handy Farmer. Scientific Am., May 29, 1909.
Stables and Outbuildings. Country Life in America, April, 1906.
Gates, Fences and Bridges. Orange-Judd Co., New York.
Farm Conveniences. Orange-Judd Co., New York.

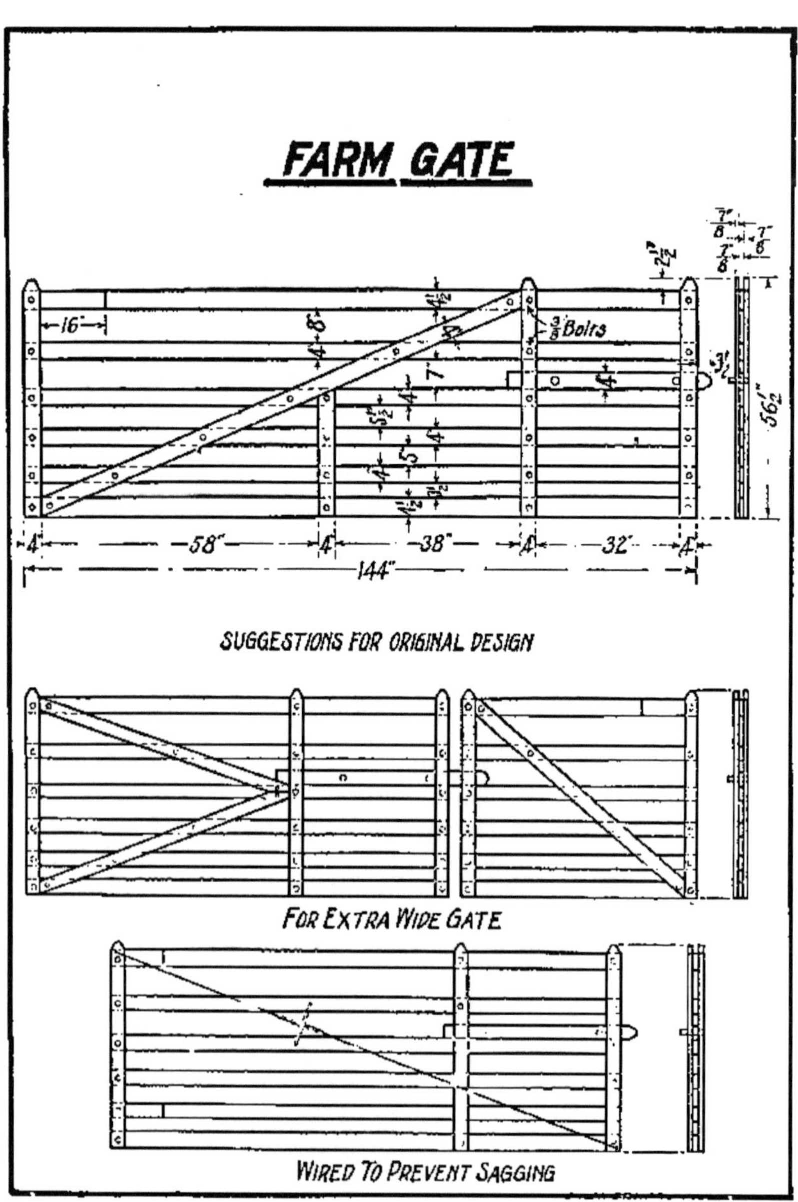
FARM GATE
16"
4"
8"
$4\frac{1}{2}$"
10"
7"
4"
$5\frac{1}{2}$"
4"
5"
4"
4"
$3\frac{1}{2}$"
$1\frac{1}{2}$"
4"
$3\frac{1}{2}$"
$\frac{3}{8}$ Bolts
$2\frac{1}{2}$"
$\frac{7}{8}$"
$\frac{7}{8}$"
$\frac{7}{8}$"
$56\frac{1}{2}$"
4"
58"
4"
38"
4"
32"
4"
144"
SUGGESTIONS FOR ORIGINAL DESIGN
FOR EXTRA WIDE GATE
WIRED TO PREVENT SAGGING

# FARM GATE SPECIFICATIONS

In making a farm gate it is not customary to use absolutely first-class and clear material. Sound material, although it may have some knots, is very satisfactory. It is not good economy to use strictly clear selected stock for a gate.

## THE SLATS.

On the drawing, it will be noticed that the bottom and top slats are 4½" wide, while all the others are only 4" wide. These slats are a little wider than the others in order to give greater strength to the strip which must withstand the most strain.

Plane the edges of all the slats perfectly straight and square (Chapter II., Paragraph 4); cut the slats the proper length.

## THE UPRIGHTS.

Cut the six upright pieces exactly the same length; plane their edges; shape their tops.

## ASSEMBLING.

If you do not have a long pair of saw horses on which to build your gate, you may lay the material flat on the floor very satisfactorily. On the upright pieces, lay out the spacing of the strips. Although this work is to be assembled with bolts, you will find it convenient to assemble it by driving one nail through the upright into each slat. The nails must *not* be driven near the centers where the bolts are to be, or they will interfere with the boring. When all of the slats and the uprights have been properly assembled, make sure the gate is perfectly square; test in several places with the long steel square; measure the length and cut the braces. These braces should be made to fit very accurately.

NOTE: They are to be bolted through each slat. Sometimes braces are housed; that is, notches or footings, as they are sometimes called, are cut in the uprights to receive the ends of the braces.

If you care to make your gate for some particular opening at home, measure the opening, and change the dimensions of this drawing to suit your need.

## BORING.

In boring for the bolts it will be well to bore until the point of the bit begins to show through on the opposite side of all the holes;

then turn the gate, and complete the boring from the opposite side (Chapter II., Paragraph 9). Another plan of boring the holes which might be used would be to have a scrap piece of material on the opposite side to prevent splintering (Chapter II., Paragraph 9). Insert a bolt in each hole, put on the washers, run the nuts on very tight. Prepare the latch slide as shown in the drawing.

## FINISHING.

The gate should be given one or two coats of paint (Chapter IV., Paragraph 52).

## Optional and Home Projects Employing Similar Principles.

### EXTRA WIDE GATE.

1. It is sometimes desirable to provide a very wide gate. This is most satisfactorily done by the use of a double gate, as shown in the suggestions. This suggestion also presents another method of bracing which is very satisfactory. In hanging the double gate a short post extending only a few inches above the ground should be set in such a position that when the gates are closed one or both of them may be hooked to it at the bottom.

### WIRING A GATE.

2. It is not uncommon to find a gate cheaply and poorly made without a brace. Such a gate can be very much improved by having a wire put on it, as indicated in the drawing. This wire is a complete loop extending from the top of the hinge side to the lower front side of the gate. A small iron rod, or bolt, is used to twist the wire, as indicated in the drawing; the wire tightens as it is twisted, and thus raises the front side of the gate. A gate so repaired will give good service for a long time.

## SUGGESTIONS FOR COMMUNITY RESEARCH.

No. 1. How many different sizes and kinds of nails can you find used about your home or farm? You will find it interesting to collect one of each and acquaint yourself with these sizes. Learn to identify as many nails as possible by sight. You will be surprised to see how many people are unable to tell the number of a nail by looking at it.

No. 2. See if you can find any of the old-fashioned iron cut nails about your home. Possibly by tearing up a chest or box which was made many years ago you will be able to find some of them. See if you can find out why cut nails have gone out of use and why the wire nails have taken their place. What advantages have modern wire nails? What is the price per pound of 2d, 8d and 16d nails at your local hardware store?

No. 3. Make inquiries of some of the older people of your community and find out how their homes were lighted years ago. See if you can find an old-fashioned candlestick, candle mould or grease lamp anywhere in your community. Find out how the old handmade candles were made. If you can find any of these old-fashioned articles in the community, it would be interesting to take them to school for general discussion.

No. 4. Are growing plants and pot flowers considered healthful in a living room? Get the opinion of your parents on this subject; see what you can find out by the study of the references given in this text.

No. 5. How many different birds of your community can you recognize by sight? How many can you recognize by hearing their songs? Are the people of your community friends to the birds? Inquire from a number of people and make a list of the benefits which they recognize as coming from the birds. You will be surprised to learn what an incorrect impression a great many people have regarding birds.

No. 6. Study as many as possible of the references given and make a list of all of the birds which are beneficial to us. Make another list of the ones considered harmful.

No. 7. For what purpose have you seen a wagon jack used? On most machinery greasing or oiling is done without removing the wheels. Why is it necessary to remove a wagon or buggy wheel to grease it?

No. 8. What is the attitude of the farmers in your community on the question of testing their seed corn? How do you think it could be proven that it pays to test seed corn?

## REVIEW QUESTIONS AND PROBLEMS.

1. In building a bench, what is the purpose of the Skirt Boards? Do you know of any other article on which Skirt Boards could be used in similar manner?

2. What are the essential principles in making a Nail Tray? What changes would be desirable in constructing it for knives and forks?

3. What points should be given special attention in a piece of work like the Candlestick, Vase or Hand Mirror?

4. What is the purpose of the brackets in the Flower Pot Stand?

5. Name three other articles in which some form of brackets may be used.

6. What is the advantage of a metal roof on a bird house?

7. Name three or four kinds of wood which would be suitable for a wagon jack.

8. Name three kinds of wood which would not be suitable for a wagon jack. Why are they unfit for this purpose?

9. How many board feet of material are required to make the Seedcorn Tester?

10. What kind of material would you select for an Evener or Singletree? What are the qualities of wood required for these articles?

11. How many feet of material are required to make the Farm Gate?

12. Figuring the cost of the material plus the cost of labor, for how much must your Farm Gate be sold to make a profit of 50 cents?

13. Why should the bottom and the top slats of a Farm Gate be especially strong?

14. What would be the size of the smallest single board from which the Wash Bench could be made? The size and shape of the scraps after cutting to avoid waste?

15. Suggest two articles, either of which could be made from these scrap pieces.

16. What kind of wood would you select for a Hand Mirror? Why?

17. What was the most difficult process found in making the Hand Mirror?

18. What kind of joints are used in making the Flower Pot Stand?

## REVIEW QUESTIONS AND PROBLEMS (Concluded).

19. If by testing your seed corn you find that one-third of it is useless as seed, in what ways have you profited by knowing this?

20. What points should be considered in deciding the sort of finish to use on an article?

21. What method would you use in fastening a bird house on the top of a pole?

22. Name and explain all of the different joints which you have used thus far.

23. What points should be given special attention in working out original designs in any piece of work?

24. Why should a drawing be made before attempting to lay out any piece of work?

25. Name and explain all the laying out tools which you have used thus far.

26. How many different cutting tools have you used?

# INTRODUCTION TO SECTION V

THE work of this section offers wide opportunity for the exercise of the originality of each student. If the tool processes already set forth have been duly mastered, and if the work of design and drawing has had proper attention, students should have a fund of experience and judgment from which to derive ideas for modifications of the work to suit individual taste.

The projects vary very much in difficulty in order to provide for the speedy and adept students as well as for the less capable ones. This latitude can, of course, be carried a great deal farther by introducing more or less difficult features in connection with each project as the needs of a particular student may require.

This section is so designed as to make possible a general review of practically all the principles previously set forth. The all-important principle of squaring stock is, of course, brought out in every lesson; this must not be neglected simply because the work has passed its elementary stage. The mortise and tenon joint is introduced in its simplest applications; it may be modified and developed as individual needs may suggest.

By giving a little thought to the selection of projects from this section it will be possible to present a sequential review of many of the most important processes and principles of elementary bench work. The simple butt joint, miter, half-lap, mortise and tenon, dowel, and tongue and groove are all found in their most common application in this section.

Students should not be allowed to leave this section until they have acquired considerable skill with all the more common tools and until they are thoroughly grounded in the idea that there can be no such method as "cut and try" in good work.

# SHOE-POLISHING BOX

MATERIALS.

Cypress (Chap. III., Par 46) or any soft wood.

2 pcs. 7/8"x12"x13½" Legs.
1 pc. 7/8"x 9"x17½" Side.
1 pc. 7/8"x 6½"x17½" Side.
2 pcs. 7/8"x 7"x19" Top.
1 pc. 7/8"x3½"x17½" Drawer front.
2 pcs. 7/8"x 2¼"x12" Drawer sides.
2 pcs. ¼"(3-ply)x10"x15" Bottom and drawer bottom.
2 pcs. 3/8"x 3/8"x12" S 4 S Drawer carriers.
1 pc. 1½"x2¾"x10" Foot rest.
1 pc. 7/8"x2¼"x14"
1 pair 1½"x2½" brass butts.
1 ¾" drawer pull.
2½ dozen 8d finishing nails.
1 dozen 6d finishing nails.
2-1" No. 12 F. H. B. Screws.
2 pcs. ¾"x¾"x12" S 4 S Bottom cleats.
2 pcs. ¾"x¾"x15" S 4 S Bottom cleats.
2 dozen 1¼" brads.

INTRODUCTORY STATEMENT.

A shoe-polishing box is very convenient in caring for the shoe brushes, polishing materials and polishing cloths.

The box given in this lesson is large and strong and has several attractive features, and yet it is not difficult to construct. As it is not supposed to be a piece of living room furniture it is not designed in accordance with all the principles of regular cabinet work.

References:

How to Make a Hundred Useful Things for the Home, Bingham. The Century Co., New York.
Home Decoration, Chas. F. Warner. Doubleday, Page & Co., New York.
Forest Planting, Jarchow. Orange-Judd Co., New York.
Practical Forestry, Fuller. Orange-Judd Co., New York.

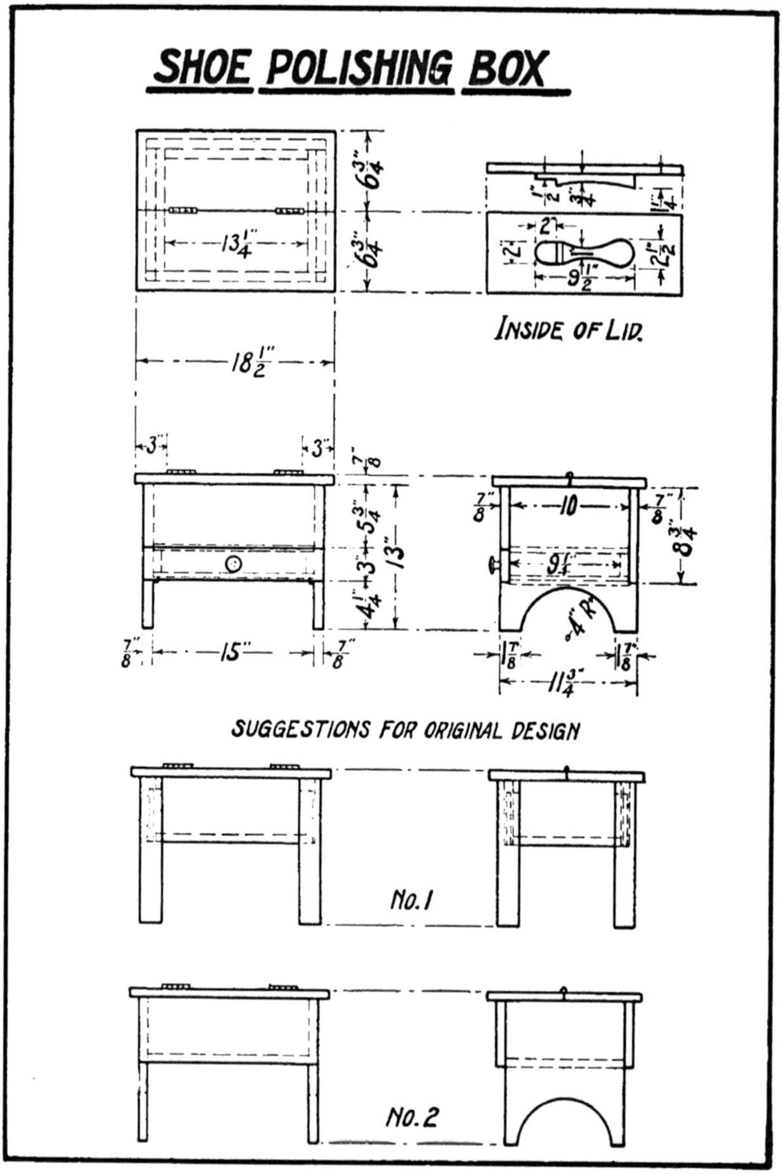

# SHOE POLISHING BOX

INSIDE OF LID.

SUGGESTIONS FOR ORIGINAL DESIGN

No. 1

No. 2

# SHOE POLISHING BOX SPECIFICATIONS

## THE ENDS.

Square the stock for one of the end pieces (Chapter II., Paragraphs 1-5). Lay out and make the end as shown in the drawing. With the wood file and block plane, carefully smooth all of the edges to make them perfectly square. In like manner prepare the second end piece. Make sure these two pieces are exactly the same size in every way. Always keep in mind that in any kind of rectangular box construction, opposite sides must be identical in size and shape.

## SIDES.

Notice that the front side is divided into two parts; the upper part furnishes the front of the box, while the lower portion provides the front of the drawer. The rear side of the shoe polishing box in one wide piece. Square the stock (Chapter II., Paragraphs 1, 2, 3, 4, 5), lay out and make these side pieces.

## THE TOP.

Square the stock (Chapter II., Paragraphs 1, 2, 3, 4, 5). Lay out and make the two pieces which are to form the top; be sure that they are perfectly square, and that the two edges which are to be hinged together fit perfectly.

## ASSEMBLING.

The side pieces are to be nailed on to the end pieces. Be sure to make them perfectly even on the outside. Use finishing nails and drive them carefully (Chapter II., Paragraph 21). The bottom of the shoe polishing box is to be made of one piece of 1/4" three-ply material. This bottom is to be fastened in position by small strips nailed on the inside of the ends and sides. It may be well to fasten these strips and the bottom in position before the top is put on. Fasten the stationary side of the top by nailing it down through the side pieces. Make sure it projects exactly the same at each end, and that it is parallel with the edge of the box. Hinge the other half on to this piece. Be very careful to cut neat gains in which to bed the hinges, so that the joint will be tight when the box is closed.

## FOOT PIECE.

Square the stock (Chapter II., Paragraphs 1, 2, 3, 4, 5) for the foot piece. Lay out and execute the shape of this piece of material. Much of this piece of work can be done with the drawing knife. Finish with the pocket knife and wood file. Fasten this piece in position with screws. It must not be fastened too near the outside edge, or it will strike the edge of the box when it is being closed.

## THE DRAWER.

Plane out the drawer sides and the back piece, making sure they are exactly the same width. Assemble with nails and test with the try-square to make sure that it is perfectly square. Nail a three-ply bottom on to this drawer frame. Turn the box upside down and nail the drawer carriers in position. Do not nail the drawer carriers too tight, or the drawer will not work well.

## FINISHING.

With a sharp block plane smooth any joints which may not be perfectly even. With a steel scraper (Chapter II., Paragraph 16), remove all pencil and tool marks. Set all nails slightly below the surface; putty the holes; smooth with fine sandpaper (Chapter II., Paragraph 17). Stain the desired color (Chapter IV., Paragraph 54); finish with shellac (Chapter IV., Paragraph 57) or varnish (Chapter IV., Paragraph 58). When the finish is dry, add the drawer knob.

## Optional and Home Projects Employing Similar Principles.

### MORTISED AND TENONED SHOE POLISHING BOX.

1. Suggestion No. 1 gives a plan of construction which will make a very excellent shoe polishing box. This is a much more difficult design but is worth while because of the excellent cabinet principles involved.

### SIMPLE SHOE POLISHING BOX.

2. Suggestion No. 2 shows a very simple plan for the construction of a shoe polishing box. It is assembled with plain butt joints. This plan of simple box construction is correct in every detail, and at the same time has no particular difficulties.

### MEASURING CRATE.

3. The principle of plain box construction can be applied in innumerable ways. A very practical problem is found in working out proper dimensions, and making a peck, half-bushel or bushel crate.

# TABOURET

## MATERIALS.

Oak (Chap. III., Par. 29), plain or quartered.

| | | | |
|---|---|---|---|
| 4 pcs. | 1½"x1½"x18". | S 4 S | Legs. |
| 2 pcs. | ⅞"x6 "x11" | S 2 S | Shelf. |
| 2 pcs. | ⅞"x6½"x13" | S 2 S | Top. |
| 1 pc. | ½" dowel 24" long. | | |

## INTRODUCTORY STATEMENT.

A tabouret is a very useful article as a stand for a flower pot, vase or any other ornament. There are a great many styles of tabouret construction, many of which are equally good; the size, shape and general design are largely matters of personal taste.

In working out a design for your tabouret be sure it is sufficiently substantial for the purpose for which it is intended. Do not undertake a form of construction which is too difficult for you; a simple design well made is much better than a difficult one poorly constructed.

The staining and polishing should be made to correspond with the furniture of the room in which it is to be used. In any piece of household furniture the finish is a very important part of the work and should be given considerable time and attention.

References:

The Tabouret, Noyes, Construction and Design. Manual Arts Press, Peoria, Ill.
Part One, Mission Furniture, Windsor. Popular Mechanics Co., Chicago.
Furniture Repairing, Taylor. Book Supply Co., Chicago.

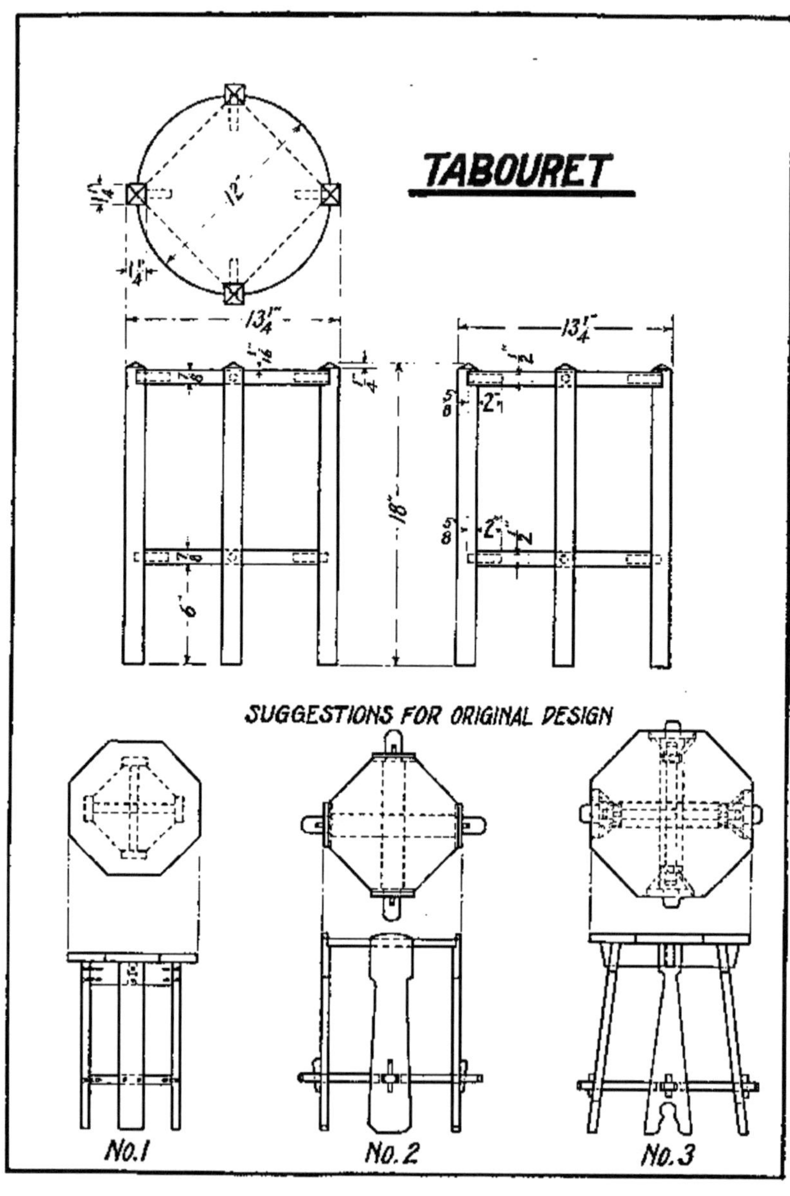
TABOURET
SUGGESTIONS FOR ORIGINAL DESIGN
No.1
No.2
No.3

# TABOURET SPECIFICATIONS

## THE TOP.

This top is to be made of two pieces with the edges glued and doweled together. It is inconvenient to get a board wide enough to make this in one piece; furthermore, a glued up top is much better because it does not warp so badly. In gluing up the top, you should arrange the boards so as to match the grain as nearly as possible. Plane the edges which are to come together until they fit perfectly (Chapter II., Paragraph 4). Lay them on your bench top, and test to make sure that the joint will be perfect. Lay out and bore for the dowels (Chapter V., Paragraph 72; Chapter II., Paragraphs 13 and 18). Clamp securely, and leave the glued joint at least twelve hours to harden.

## THE SHELF.

The shelf board is to be glued up in the same manner as the top. Prepare this piece so the glue joint can harden at the same time with the top.

## THE LEGS.

Although the legs are furnished S 4 S, you should go over them with a sharp plane set to take a very thin shaving to make them perfectly square and smooth. Finish with a steel scraper (Chapter II., Paragraph 16). Lay out and cut the length of the legs as shown in the drawing (the legs may be cut in a miter box if you have one which you can set at the desired angle). Shape the top end of the legs very carefully; if you have no miter box, this may be done with a back saw and finished with a wood file.

## SHAPING THE TOP.

When the glue is thoroughly dry, with the compasses lay out the circular top. Saw this out with a compass saw or turning saw. With a wood file carefully square the edge all the way around. This must be perfectly done, for the edge of the material cannot be well finished unless all tool marks are removed.

Notice that the legs are to be gained into the top about half their thickness. Lay out these gains the exact width so as to receive the legs and make the joints fit snugly. Saw these gains the required depth; with a very sharp chisel cut out the wood, making each gain smooth and square. Fasten the legs in position with dowels as shown in the drawing.

## SHAPING THE SHELF.

The shelf is to be made perfectly square with the corners cut off where it fits against the legs. These joints are to be fastened with dowels.

## ASSEMBLING.

Assemble all joints with glue, and clamp securely. Clean off any surplus glue.

## FINISHING.

When the work is all assembled, give it a final cleaning with a sharp steel scraper (Chapter II., Paragraph 16) and sandpaper (Chapter II., Paragraph 17). Remove all pencil, tool marks or rough places. Stain the desired color (Chap. IV., Paragraph 54). This piece of work should have a good coat of filler (Chapter IV., Paragraph 55). Shellac may be substituted for the filler; it may then be given a French polish (Chapter IV., Paragraph 57), or varnish finish (Chapter IV., Paragraph 58).

**Optional and Home Projects Employing Similar Principles.**

## STRAIGHT TABOURET.

1. Suggestion No. 1 shows a very simple yet pleasing design for a straight tabouret.

## STRAIGHT-KEYED TABOURET.

2. The tabouret shown in suggestion No. 2 presents the idea of the keyed mortise and tenon construction. This is a very popular idea, the design of which may be modified to suit one's taste.

## TABOURET WITH SLANTING LEGS.

3. Suggestion No. 3 introduces the idea of slanting legs in tabouret construction. This feature makes the keyed mortise and tenon construction a little more difficult.

## STAND TABLE.

4. The idea of a four-legged round-top tabouret, presented in this lesson, with very little modifications, can be employed in making a very pleasing round top card or game table. The stock for the legs should be somewhat heavier than for the tabouret. Such a table should be about 28″ or 29″ high.

# FOOT STOOL

1 pc. tape to match 78″ long.
3 dozen tacks to match.
5 dozen carpet tacks, 8-oz.
4 castors.

MATERIALS.

Oak (Chap. III., Par. 29).

4 pcs. 1¾″x1¾″x10″ S 4 S Legs.
2 pcs. ¾″x1½″x15″ S 4 S Cross rails.
2 pcs. ¾″x1½″x12″ S 4 S Cross rails.

Any soft wood.

2 pcs. ⅞″x2″x15″ Top cross rails.
2 pcs. ⅞″x2″x12″ Top cross rails.
2 pcs. ⅞″x5″x14″ Top.
1 pc. upholstering material 17″x21″. Top cover.

## INTRODUCTORY STATEMENT.

A foot stool is one of the most useful and comfortable little articles of household furniture. Its variations in design are innumerable, ranging from the mere cushion or floor pillow to very heavy and elaborate cabinet work.

The stool given in this lesson is one of the standard ways of constructing a stool, seat or even a straight chair. You should therefore master its principles because you will employ them often in future work.

The upholstering presents a problem which is not particularly difficult, but calls for careful effort. On account of the great expense of leather, other upholstering materials have been devised which are much less expensive and yet very satisfactory, being both dust-proof and durable.

References:

Problems in Furniture Making, Crawshaw. Manual Arts Press, Peoria, Ill.
Mechanical Training for Common Schools, Allen.
A Boy's Workshop, Cragin.
Upholstering and Cabinet Making, Hodgson. Book Supply Co., Chicago.

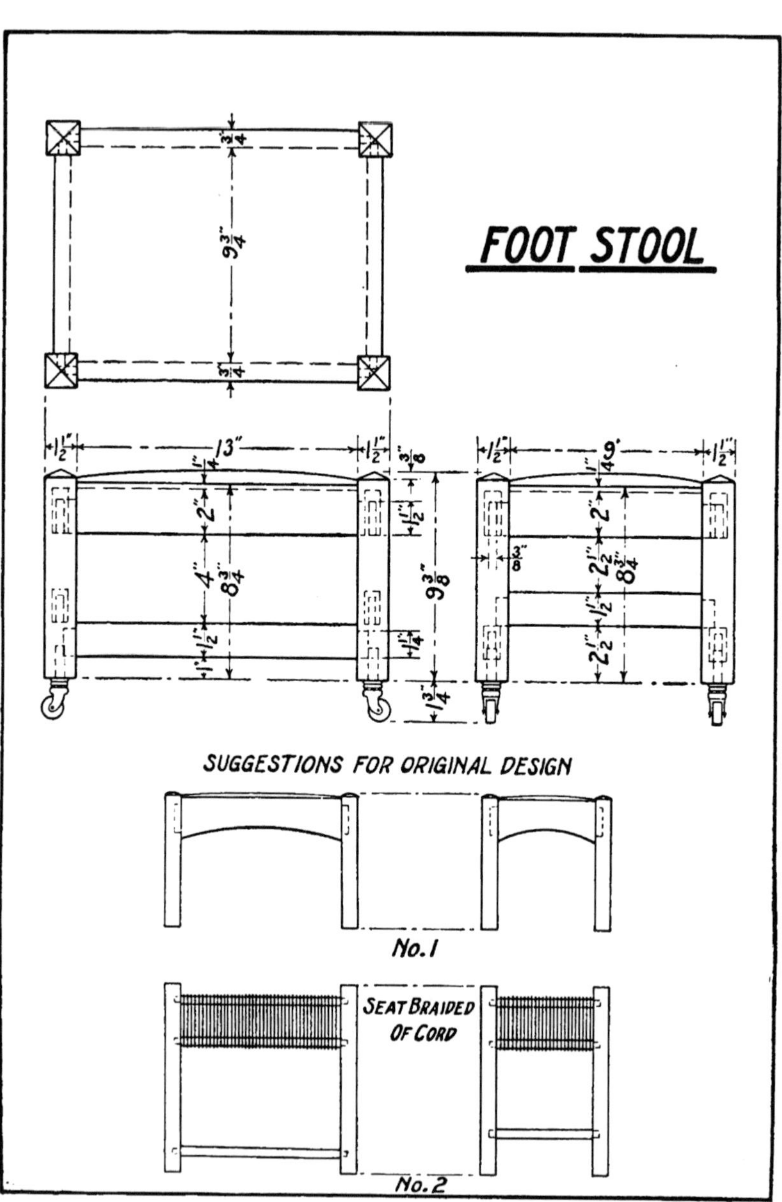
FOOT STOOL
SUGGESTIONS FOR ORIGINAL DESIGN
No. 1
SEAT BRAIDED OF CORD
No. 2

# FOOT STOOL SPECIFICATIONS

## LEGS.

Although the legs are furnished S 4 S, they will need to be planed slightly with a sharp plane set to take a very thin shaving, and finished with a sharp steel scraper (Chapter II., Paragraph 16). The ends of the legs might be cut in the miter box, and finished with a wood file. Be sure all the legs are cut exactly the same length. This piece of work is to be assembled with mortise and tenon joints (Chapter V., Paragraph 66). Measure and lay out the mortises as shown in the drawing. Examine the legs in pairs, and be sure that the mortises are all properly laid out before beginning to cut any of them, then cut them.

## THE BOTTOM CROSS RAILS.

The cross rails should be resurfaced and finished with a steel scraper (Chapter II., Paragraph 16). Lay out the tenons exactly to fit the mortises you have cut in the legs. Saw out the tenons (Chapter II., Paragraph 14). In laying out the lengths of the cross rails, be sure the opposite sides are exactly the same length.

## THE TOP CROSS RAILS.

In like manner cut the top cross rails of the soft wood material. You will notice that all of the relish is on the top side of the top rails; this is arranged in this manner to avoid cutting the mortises so close to the top ends of the leg. Make sure that these rails are exactly the same length between shoulders as the corresponding bottom rails.

## ASSEMBLING.

All joints are to be glued. Put the cross rails in their proper position and assemble one pair of legs; clamp them to make sure the joints fit closely. Test with the try-square to be sure they are perfectly square. In like manner assemble the other pair of legs. Glue the end rails in their proper positions, thus completing the assembling of the stool frame. Clamp securely. In any glued up piece of work of this kind, be very careful that it is in line in every direction; sight through to see that all the cross rails stand parallel.

## THE TOP.

The top is to be made of soft wood. It will not be necessary to surface it because it is to be covered with upholstering material. These pieces are to be nailed in position between the top cross rails.

Be sure that the stool is perfectly square when the top is nailed in position.

## FINISHING.

The finishing should be done before the upholstering is put on. With a sharp steel scraper and sandpaper remove all tool marks, pencil marks or rough places (Chapter II., Paragraph 16). Stain the work the desired color. As this is a piece of furniture, it should be very carefully finished. After staining the desired color (Chapter IV., Paragraph 54), add a coat of filler (Chapter IV., Paragraph 55); finish with shellac (Chapter IV., Paragraph 57), or varnish (Chapter IV., Paragraph 58).

## UPHOLSTERING.

After the finish is thoroughly dry, do the upholstering. A few layers of cotton batting should be used to give the rounded appearance, and to form the cushion before the upholstering material is put on. This batting should be evenly spread over the top of the stool. Carefully stretch the upholstering material, and tack it with carpet tacks on the under side of the top rail. Be very careful about cutting out around the corners to make it fit the legs neatly; tighten it evenly in every direction to avoid wrinkles. Trim with the tape and ornamental upholstering tacks as indicated in the photograph.

## Optional and Home Projects Employing Similar Principles.

### SIMPLE FOOT STOOL.

1. Suggestion No. 1 shows a plan of constructing a very simple mortised and tenoned foot stool. It may be upholstered, or have a hardwood top, as desired.

### BRAIDED TOP STOOL.

2. A very pleasing stool or seat can be easily constructed in accordance with suggestion No. 2. The top is to be braided of cord of some suitable quality.

### STRAIGHT CHAIR.

3. The principles set forth in the construction of this stool are very similar to those employed in the construction of a simple, straight chair. One pair of legs would have to be sufficiently long to extend above the seat, and provide the back. Other modifications should be worked out in your drawing before undertaking the work.

# FOLDING GAME TABLE

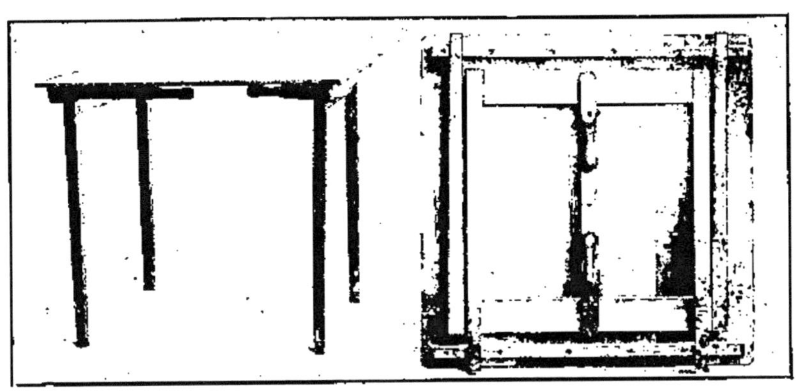

## MATERIALS.

Chestnut (Chap. III., Par. 35) or any soft wood.

Sufficient number of pieces to make ½"x31"x31" S 2 S Top.
2 pcs. ⅞"x2 "x30" Top braces.
4 pcs. 1⅜"x1⅜"x27" Legs.
2 pcs. 1⅜"x1⅜"x 9" Leg braces.
1 pc. 1⅜"x1⅜"x18" Center braces.
2 pcs. 1 "x3¼"x25" Cross braces.
12-1¾" No. 10 F. H. B. Screws.
3 pr. Hinges.
36-½" No. 6 F. H. B. Screws. 2-2½" No. 12 R. H. Blued Screws.
3-1¾" No. 12 F. H. B. Screws. 10-1¼" Brads.

## INTRODUCTORY STATEMENT.

The need of some sort of small, easily handled table quite frequently arises in connection with games or sewing work. A folding table which will occupy but little space when closed and can readily be moved from the house to the porch or lawn is a handy article of household furniture.

This table is sufficiently large to be quite serviceable, and while it cannot be expected that a folding table will be as rigid as one which is permanently built, yet if carefully constructed it will be reasonably solid.

---

References:

Home Furniture Making, G. A. Raeth. Fredrick Drake Co., Chicago.
Mission Furniture—Part III., Windsor. Popular Mechanics Co.

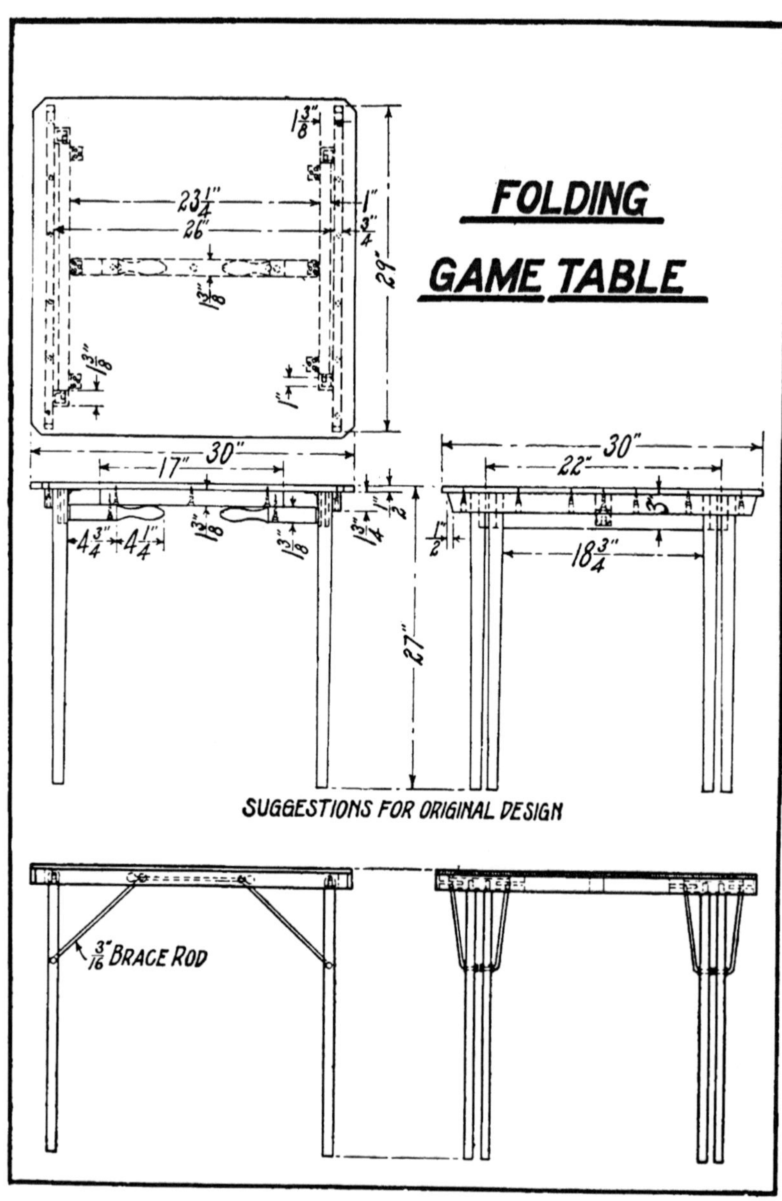
FOLDING
GAME TABLE
23 1/4"
26"
1"
3/4"
1 3/8"
29"
1 3/8"
1"
30"
17"
4 3/4"
4 1/4"
1 3/8"
1 3/8"
1 3/4"
1/2"
27"
30"
22"
1/2"
18 3/4"
SUGGESTIONS FOR ORIGINAL DESIGN
3/16" BRACE ROD

# FOLDING GAME TABLE SPECIFICATIONS

## THE TOP.

As the top is to be made of several pieces glued together, you should prepare it first in order that the glue may have plenty of time to dry. The edges of these boards must be perfectly fitted. These should be joined with dowels, but the dowels are sometimes omitted. However, the top will be very much stronger if the dowels are used. As this material is furnished S 2 S, and since it will be necessary to resurface it after it is glued, you will not need to resurface it now. Carefully plane the edges of all the pieces (Chap. II., Par. 4). Lay the pieces in position on your bench top and press them closely together to see whether all the joints fit perfectly. When they are properly fitted, lay out and bore for the dowels (Chap. II., Par. 18). Glue the top. Clamp it and leave it to dry for at least twelve hours. All surplus glue should be cleaned off before it hardens.

## THE SKIRT BOARDS.

The skirt boards serve as battens to hold the top perfectly straight. Square the stock for these pieces very carefully (Chap. II., Par. 2, 3, 4). Resurface them on all sides. Cut them the required length and shape at the ends. You will note from the drawing that the skirt boards are to be fastened with screws. You will also observe that these screws are buried in the edge of the skirt board about half its width. In spacing the screws arrange them so that none will strike the joints in the top. These holes must not be bored too deep or they will allow the screws to extend entirely through the top.

## THE LEGS.

Although the material for the legs is furnished S 4 S, you should test them carefully with a try-square and resurface them on all sides, making them perfectly square. (Chap. II., Par. 2, 3, 4.) Cut them the required length. The legs should be tapered slightly as indicated in the drawing. If desired, the corners may be chamfered (Chap. II., Par. 8). The legs are to be fastened with cross rails with mortise and tenon joint (Chap. V., Par. 66). The exact size of these mortises is not important. It is therefore not given on the drawing. It should be about ⅜″ or ½″. You might suit it to the size of the bit and chisel.

## THE CROSS RAILS.

The cross rails are to join the pair of legs firmly. Plane these pieces the exact width shown in the drawing. Form the tenons on the ends to fit the mortise in the legs. (Chap. II., Par. 14.) Notice that these cross rails are not the same length. One is made enough shorter than the other so that this pair of legs will fold between the opposite pair.

## ASSEMBLING.

Assemble the two pairs of legs by gluing the tenons in their proper mortise. When they are assembled they may be bored and pinned (Chap. V, Par. 66), or two small nails may be driven into each tenon.

The skirt board should be fastened to the top with glue and also with screws as already indicated.

Each pair of legs is to be attached to the top with three hinges, as shown in the drawing.

## CENTER BATTEN.

The center batten is for the purpose of receiving the two braces. It should be cut just long enough to fit between the two cross rails of the legs when the table is folded. It is fastened at the top with screws, as indicated in the drawing. It should also be glued.

## THE BRACES.

The purpose of the braces is to lock the legs in position when the table is standing. The study of the drawing will show that they pivot on the screws so as to turn and allow the table to fold. They also hold the legs in position when the table is folded. These braces should be very carefully made and adjusted, for much of the strength of the table depends on the accuracy with which they are placed. The two very long screws are to be used to attach these braces.

## FINISHING.

With a sharp steel scraper, remove all tool marks and other rough places from the surface of the table. Smooth with fine sandpaper (Chapter II., Paragraph 17). Stain it the desired color (Chapter IV., Paragraph 54); finish with shellac (Chapter IV., Paragraph 57) or varnish (Chapter IV., Paragraph 58).

### Optional and Home Projects Employing Similar Principles.

## SEWING TABLE.

1. A sewing table for home use may be made on the same plan as this folding game table. It would be desirable to make it considerably longer, and perhaps use a little heavier stock in constructing the legs.

## PAPER HANGER'S TABLE.

2. The principle of a folding table is practically employed in making a paper hanger's pasting table. Such a table is usually about 18″ wide and about 8 feet long. Each pair of legs should have cross braces, and there should be some means of bracing and fastening it rigid when in use.

# STEPLADDER

MATERIALS.

Yellow Pine (Chap. III., Par. 48) or any soft wood.

2 pcs. 7/8"x4 5/8"x5' 2" S 2 S Sides.
4 pcs. 7/8"x5 1/2"x16 1/2" S 2 S Steps.
1 pc. 7/8"x7"x17" S 2 S Top.
2 pcs. 7/8"x1 3/4"x5' S 2 S Legs.
1 pc. 7/8"x2 1/4"x15" S 2 S Top strips.
2 pcs. 3/8"x1 1/2"x3' 4" S 2 S Leg brace.
2 pcs. 3/8"x1 1/2"x15" S 2 S Leg brace.
1 pair 1 1/4"x3" hinges with screws.
4 dozen 6d finishing nails.
3 dozen 1 1/4" brads.
1-1/2" screw eye.

INTRODUCTORY STATEMENT.

One of the handiest articles about the home, particularly in housecleaning and fruit season, is the stepladder.

This stepladder is so designed as to present the greatest possible strength and the most serviceable features. While it is not unduly heavy, yet it is sufficiently strong to stand many years of hard use. The top step is made wide enough to provide a satisfactory place to set a basin of water or a paint bucket.

The method of attaching the legs with hinges affords strength which can hardly be provided by any other means. In the suggestions you will see some other ideas for ladder construction, but they are not so substantial as those given in the working drawing.

---

References:

Seven Hundred Things for Boys to Do. Popular Mechanics Co., Chicago.
Modern Carpentry and Joinery, Hodgson.
The Handy Man's Book, Hasluck. Book Supply Co., Chicago.

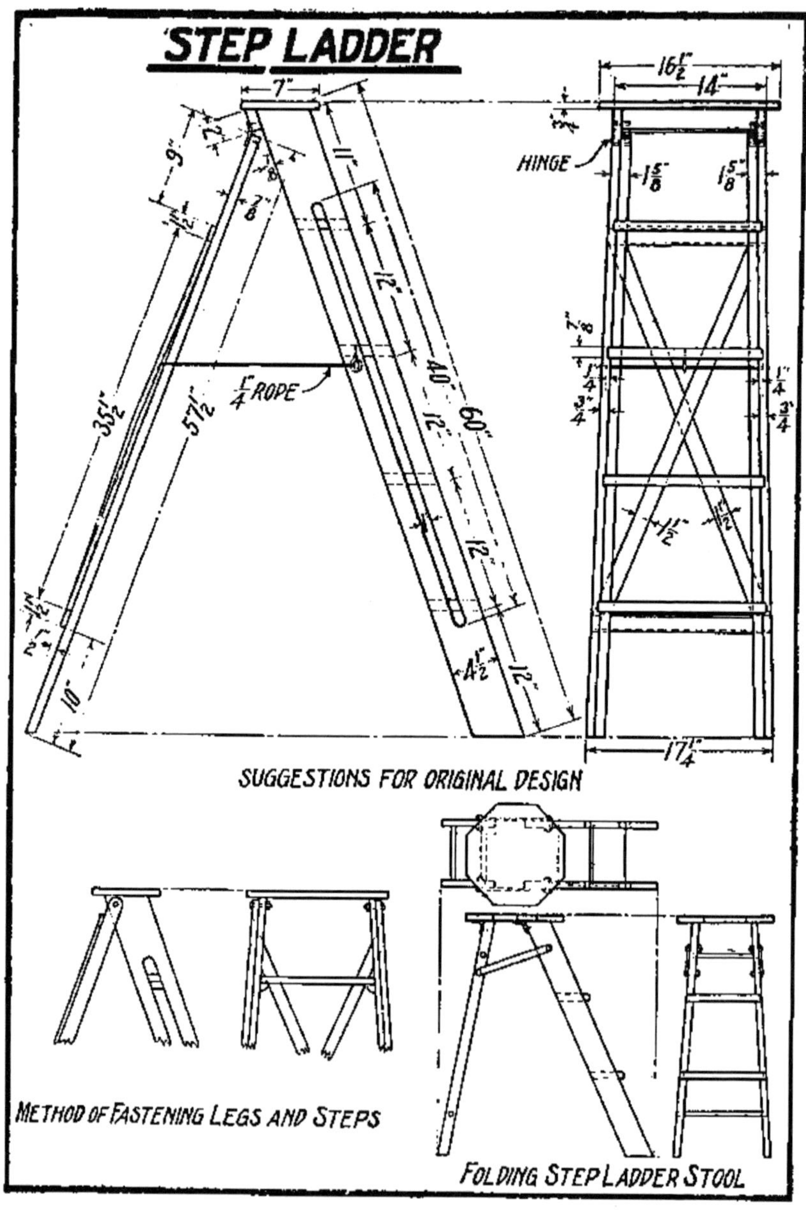
STEP LADDER
HINGE
ROPE
SUGGESTIONS FOR ORIGINAL DESIGN
METHOD OF FASTENING LEGS AND STEPS
FOLDING STEP LADDER STOOL

# STEPLADDER SPECIFICATIONS

## THE SIDES.

Square the stock for the side pieces (Chapter II., Paragraphs 2, 3 and 4); lay out and cut them the dimensions shown in the drawing. Make sure that the two side pieces are exactly the same size. (The opening cut in each side piece makes the stepladder somewhat lighter without making it any weaker; it also improves the appearance of the ladder). Lay out the spaces for the gains. Notice that the steps are to stand level when the ladder is open. It will be well to set the T-bevel to this angle and use it in laying out these gains. Be sure not to lay out the gains any wider than the thickness of the step material or the joints will not fit snugly. Lay out and cut these gains (Chapter V., Paragraph 61).

## THE STEPS.

Plane the edges of the steps to the angle shown in the drawing. You should use the T-bevel again as you did in making the gains. Cut the top step the correct size; cut the bottom step the correct length. You will notice that the stepladder is a little narrower at the top than at the bottom. For this reason the steps are not all the same length, and in order to get the length of each, you should assemble the work as follows: Nail the top and the bottom steps in their respective positions. Make sure that the sides are perfectly straight and measure the length of each of the other steps separately. The steps are to be fastened in position by nailing through the side pieces. Use finishing nails and set them slightly below the surface.

## THE LEGS.

Square the stock (Chapter II., Paragraphs 2, 3 and 4). Make the legs the dimensions shown in the drawing. Notice that the legs are attached to the stepladder with two hinges, and that the hinges are planted on a cross rail which is nailed to the side pieces, and also down through the top. This makes a very strong piece of construction. Prepare this piece and nail it firmly in position. Hinge the legs in position with screws, making them exactly even with the outside of the side pieces.

With the ladder in a closed position, and the legs exactly even with the side pieces their full length, you can nail the cross braces on to the legs. Be sure that the cross braces are straight; fit all the joints accurately. This will not only add to the appearance, but to the strength of your ladder. The ladder is to be kept from spreading when in use by a small rope fastened to a screw eye, as indicated in the drawing.

## FINISHING.

With a sharp plane set to take a very thin shaving, go over the edges of the steps, if necessary, and plane them down to the exact width of the side pieces. Plane any other joints which may not be absolutely even. Smooth with sandpaper, putty the nail holes; stain it the desired color (Chapter IV., Paragraph 54); add a coat or two of shellac (Chapter IV., Paragraph 57). If the stepladder is to be used mostly out of doors, it would be well to give it a coat of paint (Chapter IV., Paragraph 52).

**Optional and Home Projects Employing Similar Principles.**

## STEPLADDER WITH BOLTED LEGS.

1. A stepladder may have the legs attached with two small bolts, as shown in the suggestions. This is an easy method of construction, but not so substantial as the method presented in the lesson.

## STEPLADDER STOOL.

2. A handy folding stool, which will also serve the purpose of a short stepladder, can be easily made in accordance with the idea presented in the suggestions.

# AUTOMOBILE CREEPER

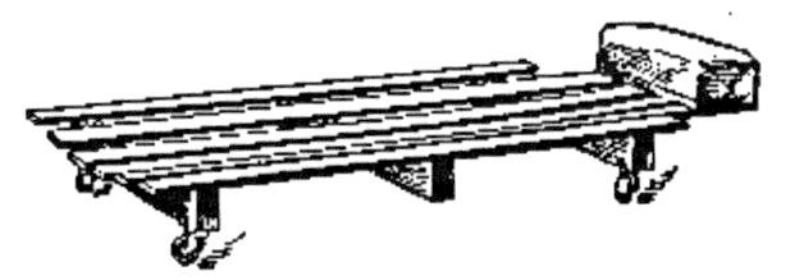

## MATERIALS.

Oak (Chap. III., Par. 29).

| | |
|---|---|
| 4 pcs. ⅜"x1⅞"x38" | Slats, hard wood. |
| 2 pcs. ⅜"x1⅞"x30" | Slats, hard wood. |
| 3 pcs. ⅞"x2"x16" | Cross pieces, hard wood. |
| 1 pc. ⅞"x4"x10" | Head piece, soft wood. |
| 4 dozen 6d box nails. | 30" gimp. |
| 1½ dozen 8-oz. tacks. | 12 uph. nails. |
| 1 set castors. | Enameled muslin, 10"x15". |
| 4-3/16"x1¼" stove bolts. | 8 screws, ¾" No. 8. |

## INTRODUCTORY STATEMENT.

People who have had any experience with automobiles know that it is sometimes necessary to get under the car to do some sort of cleaning, adjusting or repair work. This is always an inconvenient and unpleasant task, not only because it is uncomfortable, but because it soils one's clothes so badly.

This "automobile creeper" furnishes a very handy solution to the problem of providing a way to get under a car easily and quickly with least damage to the clothing.

It is not the intention to make this a piece of cabinet construction, but nevertheless it should be accurately laid out and carefully executed. Because a piece of work is to be used at the barn or garage is no reason why it may be incorrectly or carelessly constructed.

**References:**

Automobile Handbook, Elliott Brookes. Fredrick Drake Co., Chicago.
Automobile Catechism and Repair Manual, Swingle. Fredrick Drake Co., Chicago.
Care and Operation of Automobiles, Hall. Am. Tech. Society, Chicago.
The Gasoline Automobile, Longheed and Hall. Am. Tech. Society, Chicago.

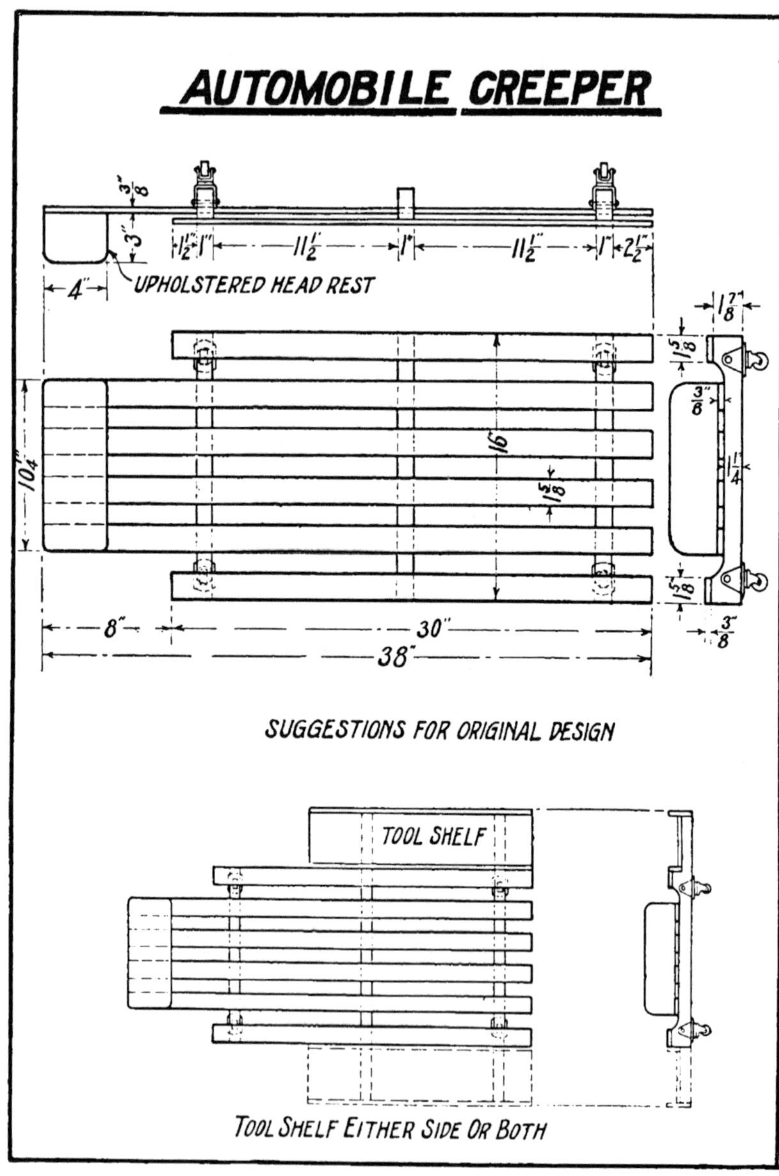
AUTOMOBILE CREEPER
UPHOLSTERED HEAD REST
SUGGESTIONS FOR ORIGINAL DESIGN
TOOL SHELF
TOOL SHELF EITHER SIDE OR BOTH

# AUTOMOBILE CREEPER SPECIFICATIONS

## BOTTOM CROSS PIECES.

Square the stock for the bottom cross pieces (Chapter II., Paragraphs 2, 3 and 4). From the end view you will notice that these pieces are to be curved out on the top edge to receive the slats. Cut them the required length; lay out one and saw it out with a compass saw; smooth with a wood file; use this one for a pattern, lay out and make the others just like it.

## THE SLATS.

Square the stock (Chapter II., Paragraphs 2, 3 and 4) and make the slats the dimensions shown in the drawing.

## THE HEAD REST.

The head rest is to have a solid wood base upholstered with enameled muslin. Plane out this wood block for the base a little less than the dimensions shown in the drawing. Upholster it neatly, covering it with enameled muslin; it may be padded with excelsior or cotton batting, whichever is most convenient. Trim with gimp and upholstering nails.

## ASSEMBLING.

Space the bottom cross braces properly, nail the slats in position; make sure they are square with the cross braces.

Fasten the upholstered head rest in position with screws or nails from the bottom side of the slat into the wood base of the rest.

Attach the castors to the bottom cross rails, as shown in the drawing. These castors are to be fastened with stove bolts.

## FINISHING.

Finish with a coat of good oil stain (Chapter IV., Paragraph 54). A good coat of shellac or hard varnish will keep the stain from rubbing off.

## Optional and Home Projects Employing Similar Principles.

### AUTOMOBILE CREEPER WITH TOOL SHELF.

1. In the suggestions will be found an idea for adding a shelf for the purpose of holding tools. This shelf may be added on either side of the creeper; if desired two shelves may be used, one on each side.

# SHOP TOOL CASE

MATERIALS.

Yellow Pine (Chap. III., Par. 48) or any soft wood.

3 pcs. 7/8"x10"x36½" S 2 S
Side and partition.

2 pcs. 7/8"x10"x48½" S 2 S
Bottom and top.

3 pcs. 3/8"x1¾"x35" S 2 S
Casing strips.

1 pc. 3/8"x 1¾"x48½" S 2 S
Top casing.

2 pcs. 7/8"x9"x24" S 2 S
Shelves.

1 pc. 7/8"x1½"x48" S 2 S
Rabbet strips.

30 pcs. 3/8"x4"x36" S 2 S
Beaded ceiling, back and doors.

4 pcs. 7/8"x2½"x22" S 2 S
Door battens.

2 pcs. 7/8"x1¾"x33" S 2 S
Door braces.

2 prs. T hinges 2½" with screws.

2 spring catches.

6 dozen 6d finishing nails.

12 dozen 2d lath nails.

## INTRODUCTORY STATEMENT.

In the shop, barn, garage or tool shed it is very convenient to have some sort of tool case on the wall. This plan of caring for tools not only keeps them in good condition, but also saves room.

This shop tool case is very simple in construction; it may be built of almost any dimensions you may desire. It would be well for you to measure the space which you have for a tool case and then build your case the proper size to fit the space.

This case illustrates the principle of making a simple batten door; you will also notice a brace extending from one batten to the other; this is to prevent sagging. If you have any sagging doors about your home buildings you should straighten them and put in braces as illustrated in this lesson.

---

References:

A Boy's Workshop. David Williams Co., New York.
Jobbing Work for the Carpenter, Crussell. David Williams Co., N. Y.
Saw Filing, Grimshaw. Book Supply Co., Chicago.
Hand Saws—Their Use and Abuse, Hodgson. Book Sup. Co., Chicago.

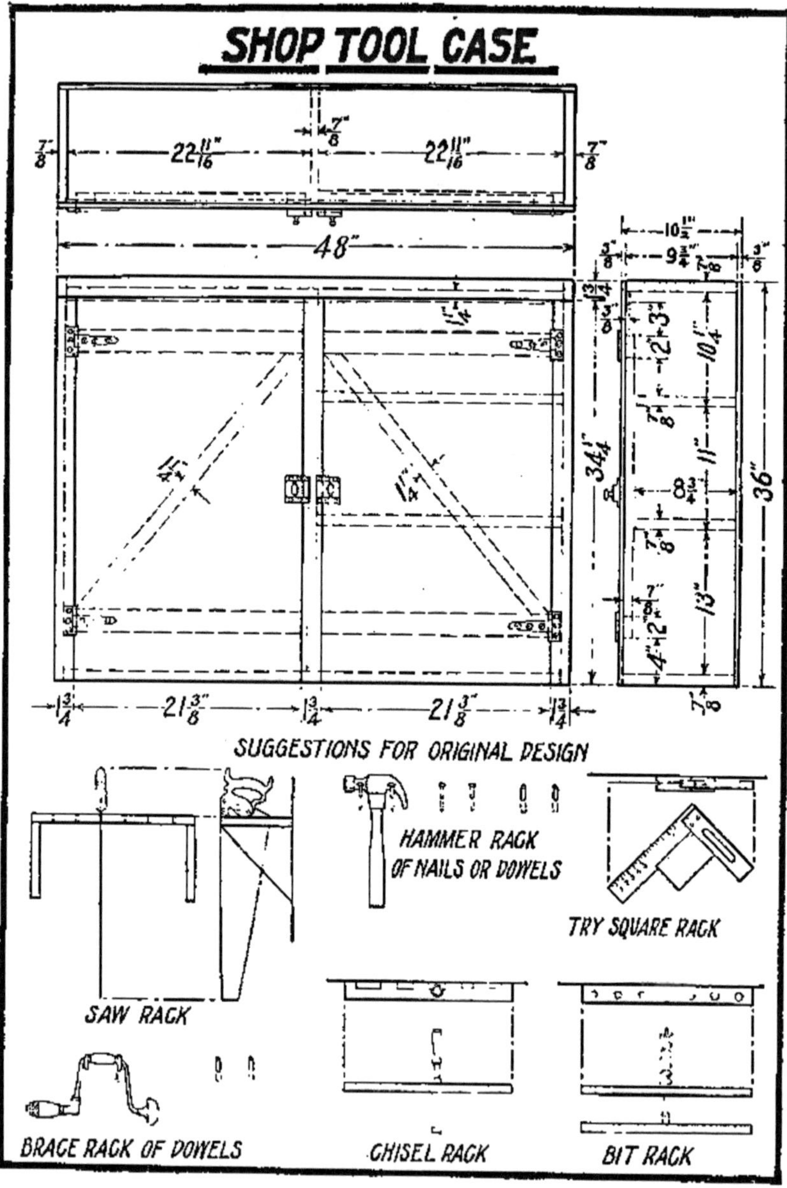
SHOP TOOL CASE
48"
SUGGESTIONS FOR ORIGINAL DESIGN
SAW RACK
HAMMER RACK
OF NAILS OR DOWELS
TRY SQUARE RACK
BRACE RACK OF DOWELS
CHISEL RACK
BIT RACK

# SHOP TOOL CASE SPECIFICATIONS

## THE SIDES.

A study of the drawing will show you that the shop tool case is made very much like a box; it is then cased in front and doors are hung to the casing.

Square the stock (Chapter II., Paragraphs 2, 3, 4 and 5) and prepare the side pieces the dimensions shown in the drawing. If you are making this case to fit some particular place, you should follow the sizes of your own drawing. Be sure that the two sides are exactly the same size in every way. Square the stock (Chapter II., Paragraphs 2, 3, 4 and 5).

## TOP AND BOTTOM.

Prepare the top and bottom the dimensions given in the drawing. These two pieces must be made exactly the same size.

## ASSEMBLING.

Nail this framework together with plain butt joints (Chapter V., Paragraph 60) and test with a large steel square to make sure it is perfectly square. You might nail a brace temporarily across the front edge to hold it perfectly square while you turn it over on the tressels, and put on the back of beaded ceiling. The case must be kept perfectly square while the back is being put on, for if it is crooked it will remain in that shape when completed. The middle partition should be cut exactly the same length as the outside pieces, less the thickness of the top and bottom, and nailed in position through the bottom and the top.

## THE SHELVES.

Square the stock (Chapter II., Paragraphs 2, 3, 4 and 5); prepare the shelves the dimensions shown in the drawing. (If you prefer these shelves may be put in with a gained joint (Chapter V., Paragraph 61) or they may be made adjustable by inserting screw eyes or screws into the side pieces to support them). You will note in the drawing that only one side is equipped with shelves. The other side may be similarly equipped, if desired.

## THE CASING.

Square the stock (Chapter II., Paragraphs 3, 4 and 5); prepare the casing the proper dimensions. Nail this casing in position, making it exactly even with the outside of the case all around.

## THE DOORS.

The doors are to be made of beaded ceiling nailed on cross strips called battens. Prepare these battens the proper size. Also prepare the brace strips which are to extend diagonally between the battens. Plane off the groove from the edge of the first piece of beaded ceiling (this will give it a firm edge to receive the hinges). Make sure that the battens stand perfectly square when the first strip is nailed into position; keep the work square as the ceiling strips are added. The doors, when completed, may be re-sawed at bottom and top to fit the opening perfectly. Fasten them in position with T-hinges, as shown in the drawing. The doors should be provided with spring catches, or a lock, if desirable. Add the rabbet or bumper strip, against which the doors close at the top.

## FINISHING.

When the work is completed go over it with a sharp plane and smooth any joints that may not be perfect. Set the nails a little below the surface of the wood and fill the holes with putty. Finish with paint (Chapter IV., Paragraph 52) or stain (Chapter IV., Paragraph 54). NOTE: In the suggestions will be found a number of ideas for tool racks for shop tool cases. By following these suggestions you should be able to work out a great many other convenient racks and hangers which you may fasten in your tool case or on the doors in such shape as you find desirable and convenient for your particular set of tools.

### Optional and Home Projects Employing Similar Principles.

## SEWING CABINET.

1. A sewing cabinet particularly adapted for school use may be made on a plan very similar to the shop tool case. Each student should be provided with a tray or box in which to keep all sewing materials. A cabinet of this kind fitted with shelves to accommodate the size and number of the trays will be a valuable piece of equipment.

## DRAWING BOARD CABINET.

2. A very serviceable cabinet, for the protection of drawing boards in the mechanical drawing department, can be easily constructed on the principles given in this lesson. The cabinet should be made deep enough to receive the full width of the boards when standing on end.

# WORK BENCH

MATERIALS.

Maple (Chap. III., Par. 41).

1 pc. hard wood 1½"x12"x 50" Top.
1 pc. hard wood ⅞"x8½"x 50" Tool trough.
1 pc. hard wood ⅞"x5½"x 50" Back brace.
1 pc. hard wood ⅞"x1¼"x 50" Tool rack.
4 pcs. hard wood 1½"x3½" x21" Top and base pieces.
4 pcs. hard wood 1½"x3½"x24" Legs.
2 pcs. hard wood 1½"x6"x31" Stretchers.
1 pc. hard wood 1½"x3½"x32" Vise jaw.
1 pc. hard wood 1½"x6"x29" Vise jaw.
1 pc. soft wood ⅞"x3½"x12½"
16-⅜"x6" square head bolts with washers and nuts.
9-2½" No. 16 F. H. B. screws.
12-1½" No. 10 F. H. B. screws.
1 steel vise screw ¾" with nut, complete.
6-8d finishing nails.
4-1" No. 12 F. H. B. Screws.

INTRODUCTORY STATEMENT.

In every home there are so many odd jobs to be done that it is worth while to have some sort of work bench. The material required for the construction of an excellent bench is not expensive, and if properly used it would soon save you enough to pay for it.

A work bench should be absolutely solid and rigid so it will not shake when you are attempting to do careful work.

The bench shown in this lesson is so constructed as to be strong and solid; the bolted joints can be tightened from time to time if necessary; the wide stretchers between the pairs of legs are held by two bolts at each end and are thus made absolutely rigid.

---

**References:**

Handy Man's Work Shop and Laboratory, A. Russel Bond.
U. S. Bureau of Forestry, Bulletins Nos. 97, 117, 130, 138, 145.
Handbook in Woodwork and Carpentry, King. American Book Co.
Manual of Carpentry and Joinery, Riley.

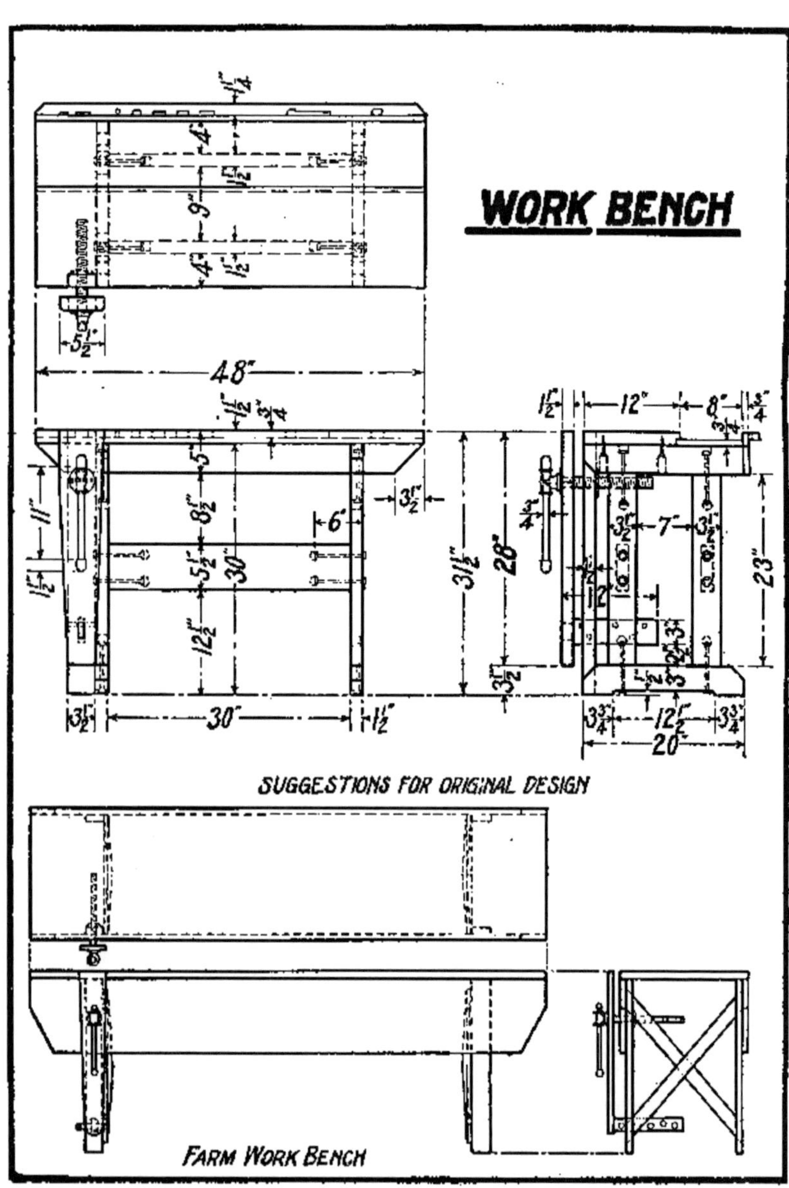
WORK BENCH
SUGGESTIONS FOR ORIGINAL DESIGN
FARM WORK BENCH

# WORK BENCH SPECIFICATIONS

## THE TOP.

The heavy portion of the top of the work bench may be one wide board or it may be made of several pieces glued together, depending upon the manner in which your stock is furnished. Prepare the top the dimensions shown in the drawing. Notice that it is to be rabbeted to receive the board which forms the tool trough. If you do not have a rabbeting plane, this may be done with the grooving side of a matching plane, and finished with a sharp chisel. Prepare the board for the tool trough, as shown in the drawing.

## THE LEGS.

Square the stock (Chapter II., Paragraphs 2, 3, 4 and 5) for the legs. Cut the four legs, making sure they are all the same length. Any variations will make your bench unlevel.

## THE BASE PIECES.

Prepare the two base pieces as shown in the drawing; make sure that they are perfectly square so the legs will rest upon them with a good joint. In like manner prepare the two top cross braces.

## STRETCHERS.

Square the stock (Chapter II., Paragraphs 2, 3, 4 and 5); cut the two stretchers (the braces between the two pairs of legs) as shown in the drawing.

## ASSEMBLING.

As this bench is to be assembled with draw bolts, you will have considerable boring to do. This is a very particular process, therefore you must do it carefully. Notice that the legs are fastened into the bottom and top pieces with bolts, and that the bolt heads are sunk into the top brace about an inch. You should therefore bore into the places with a bit large enough to allow the bolt head to enter. Then finish the boring with a bit the right size for the body of the bolts. It will require a socket wrench to tighten the bolts when their heads are below the surface. If you cannot secure a socket wrench, you may be able to tighten them by using a nail set, and driving the nuts which are in the holes. In boring for all these bolts be sure that you hold the bit perpendicularly (Chapter II., Paragraph 11). In the stretchers the holes for the nuts do not go entirely through. This gives the bench a little neater appearance than if those holes showed on the front side of the stretcher. Assemble the frame of the bench and tighten all the nuts securely. NOTE: The top is held in position with large screws put through from the bottom side of the cross brace of the legs. These screws are sunk in the wood in order to make them reach.

## THE VISE.

This bench may be equipped with an iron vise if you care to purchase one. You can readily make the wooden vise shown in the drawing, and you will find it a very satisfactory one. It is held in position by large screws fastened into the bench top, and into the leg braces.

## TOOL RACK.

The tool rack on the rear of the bench may be prepared for whatever tools you desire it to hold.

## FINISHING.

When the bench is completed, with a sharp steel scraper remove all lead pencil marks and rough places; give it a good coat of linseed oil or shellac (Chapter IV., Paragraph 57).

## Optional and Home Projects Employing Similar Principles.

## FARM WORK BENCH.

1. For general purpose work about the farm a long bench is often required. The idea shown in the suggestions will be very suitable, yet inexpensive, for the construction of such a bench. A very valuable feature may be added by purchasing a small machinist's vise, and attaching it to the rear end of this bench. Such a vise will be found very useful in a great many odd jobs about the farm.

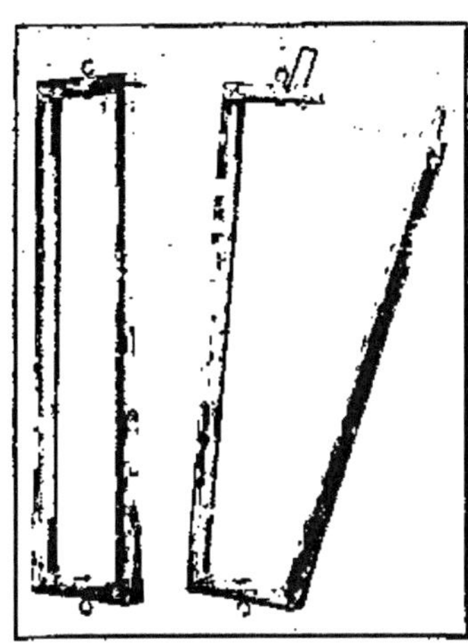

# STANCHION

## MATERIALS.

Beech (Chap. III., Par. 32) or any hard wood.

2 pcs. 1⅛"x2½"x10½" S 2 S Ends.
2 pcs. 1⅛"x2½"x49" S 2 S Sides.
2 pcs. chain 12".
1 pc. small anchor chain 14".
2 angle irons with screws.
2 eye bolts 5/16"x1¾".
1 pc. 5/16" soft iron rod 16" long.
1 strap hinge, 2½" pin measure, with screws.
2-¾" staples.

## INTRODUCTORY STATEMENT.

In studying the various problems of dairying it has been found a great benefit not only to improve the sanitary conditions, but also to provide for humane treatment of the stock. The stanchion has been worked out as a solution to the problem of tying the cows securely and at the same time giving them all possible freedom.

The stanchion given in this lesson has been so designed as to present both strength and convenience; it is to be held in position by chains fastened at the top and bottom. This will make it possible for the cow to raise and lower her head or to turn from side to side and still not be able to pull back from her position.

---

**References:**

U. S. Farmer's Bulletin No. 106, Breeds of Dairy Cattle.
U. S. Farmer's Bulletin No. 143, Beef and Dairy Cattle.
U. S. Farmer's Bulletin No. 55, The Dairy Herd, Its Function and Management.
U. S. Farmer's Bulletin No. 42, Facts About Milk.
U. S. Farmer's Bulletin No. 74, Milk as Food.
U. S. Farmer's Bulletin No. 29, Souring and Other Changes in Milk.
U. S. Farmer's Bulletin No. 413, Care of Milk and Its Uses in the Home.
U. S. Farmer's Bulletin No. 457, Production of Sanitary Milk.
Building the Dairy Barn, James. James Manufacturing Co., Ft. Atkinson, Wis.
Barn Plans and Outbuildings, Shawver. David Williams Co., New York.
Twentieth Century Practical Barn Plans, Radford. David Williams Co., New York.

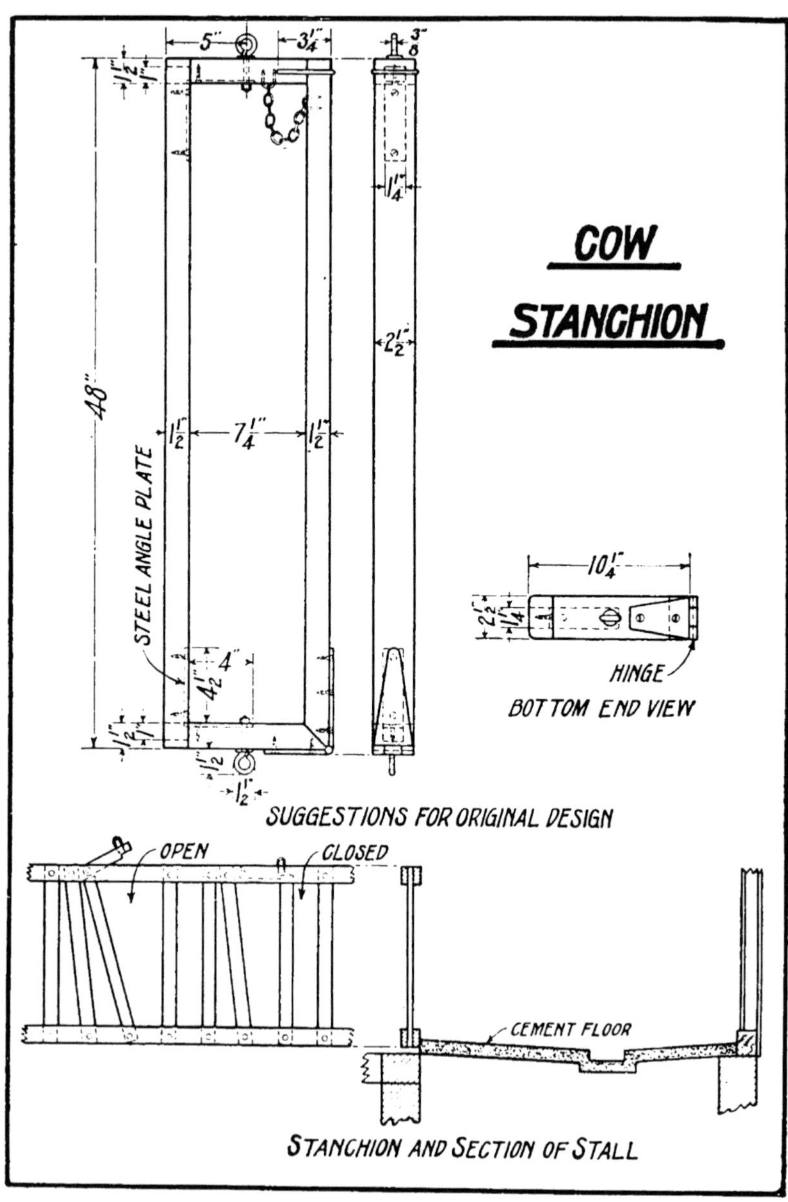


SUGGESTIONS FOR ORIGINAL DESIGN

STANCHION AND SECTION OF STALL

# COW STANCHION SPECIFICATIONS

## SIDE RAILS.

Square the stock for the side rails (Chapter II., Paragraphs 2, 3 and 4); your stock will probably be furnished in two pieces, each long enough to make one side rail and an end rail. By squaring each piece its full length you will thus prepare the sides and ends at one operation.

Cut the side rails the lengths shown in the drawing. NOTE: Notice that the end rails are to join one side rail with mortise and tenon joints; the other side rail is movable, being attached to the bottom rail with a hinge. Lay out and cut the mortises in the first side rail (Chapter V., Paragraph 66). Cut the second side rail, as shown in the drawing.

## THE END RAILS.

As the stock has already been squared, cut the pieces the required length; lay out and cut a tenon at one end of each (Chapter II., Paragraph 14). Cut the other end of each, as shown in the drawing.

## ASSEMBLING.

Assemble the mortise and tenon joints (they may be draw bored and pinned if desired (Chapter V., Paragraph 66). These corners are to be reinforced with angle irons. These angle irons are to be bedded into the wood until they are level with the surface. Lay them out carefully (be sure to calculate the length of each gain properly); with a sharp chisel cut the gains into which the irons are to fit; fasten the irons with screws.

Fasten the second side rail into position with a strong hinge.

## THE EYE BOLT.

Each eye bolt should have a washer on the outside; none will be required on the inside, for the bolt goes through the angle iron, thus helping to hold it rigid. Each eye bolt should be supplied with a few inches of chain by which the stanchion is to be hung when in use.

## THE FASTENING.

The fastening consists of a movable loop of iron rod which can be raised and lowered as needed to hold the hinged side rail.

## THE ANCHOR CHAIN.

The small anchor chain should be fastened with staples; its purpose is to keep the hinged side rail from falling when the stanchion is open.

## FINISHING.

This piece of work does not require a fine finish. However, if given a good coat of linseed oil it will be protected against moisture. The oil will also cause the wood to wear smooth.

**Optional and Home Projects Employing Similar Principles.**

## STATIONARY STANCHION.

1. A stationary cow stanchion may be easily provided, as shown in the suggestions; the movable side of the stanchion consists merely of a slat pivoted on a bolt. The stanchion is held closed by a pivoted block at the top, as shown in the drawing. The stationary stanchion is not as satisfactory as the movable stanchion presented in this lesson.

## CHICKEN YARD GATE.

2. The principles involved in the construction of the cow stanchion may be employed in making any kind of strong rectangular frame, such as would be needed in building a gate for a chicken park or garden. This frame should be assembled with mortise and tenon construction, and it would be well to have the joints reinforced with angle irons in exactly the same manner as the cow stanchion. In constructing the gate it will be desirable to use a diagonal brace. The entire framework could be covered with pickets or poultry net, as might be desired.

# CHICKEN BROODER

MATERIALS.

Cypress (Chap. III., Par. 46) or any soft wood.

| | | | |
|---|---|---|---|
| 8 pcs. | 7/8"x 6½"x20" | S 2 S | Sides and roof. |
| 7 pcs. | 7/8"x 4½"x25" | S 2 S | Back, back door and roof. |
| 3 pcs. | 7/8"x 6½"x25" | S 2 S | Bottom. |
| 2 pcs. | 7/8"x 2"x18" | S 2 S | Bottom battens. |
| 2 pcs. | 7/8"x 6"x25" | S 2 S | Front. |
| 2 pcs. | 7/8"x 7"x12" | S 2 S | Front. |
| 1 pc. | 7/8"x10"x30" | S 2 S | Roof. |
| 4 pcs. | 3/8"x 1¾"x20" | S 2 S | Roof strips. |
| 2 pcs. | 7/8"x 2"x12" | S 2 S | Roof door battens. |
| 2 pcs. | 7/8"x2"x18" | S 2 S | Front door step. |
| 7 pcs. | 7/8"x 2"x 4' | S 2 S | Runway. |
| 6 pcs. | 7/8"x 2"x25" | S 2 S | Runway and door. |

1 gross small staples.
1 pc. fly screen 12"x18".
3 pair screen door hinges.
1 pair tight pin butts.
3 screen door knobs.

10 ft. 12" poultry net.
1 yard 24" poultry net.
6 doz. 6d fin. nails.
6 doz. 8d fin. nails.
1 doz. ½" corrugated nails.

**References:**

U. S. Bulletin No. 41, Fowls, Care and Feeding.
U. S. Bulletin No. 51, Standard Varieties of Chickens.
U. S. Bulletin No. 141, Poultry Raising on the Farm.
U. S. Bulletin No. 287, Poultry Management.
U. S. Bulletin No. 182, Poultry as Food.
U. S. Bulletin No. 236, Incubators.
The Practical Poultry Keeper, Lewis Wright. Cassel & Co., Publishers.
Minnesota Bulletin No. 8, Poultry Houses.
Poultry Houses, Foster. Doubleday, Page & Co., New York.
Poultry Architecture, Fiske. Orange-Judd Co., New York.

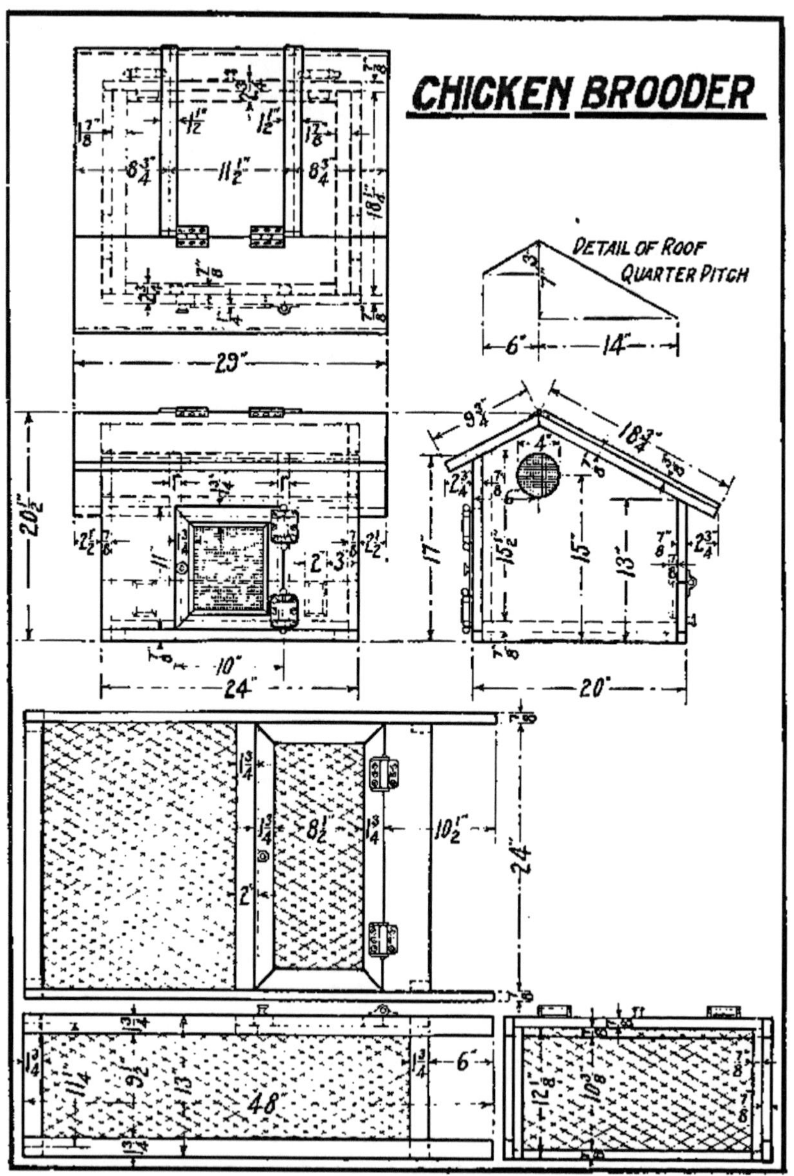
CHICKEN BROODER
DETAIL OF ROOF
QUARTER PITCH

# THE CHICKEN BROODER SPECIFICATIONS

## THE BOTTOM.

This little house is to be built very much like a plain box. Notice that the bottom is provided with battens. This is for the purpose of holding it up off the ground slightly, and also to protect the bottom from warping. The bottom may be made of any number of boards; it will not be necessary to join their edges. Nail the bottom boards on the battens, then cut the bottom the size shown in the drawing.

## THE ENDS.

The ends must be made of several boards. They may be cut the proper length and toe-nailed together (Chapter II., Paragraph 22), or they may be fastened with corrugated nails (Chapter II., Paragraph 23). Make these two ends, then lay out and cut the gables third-pitch (Chapter II., Paragraph 25). Be sure the two ends are exactly the same size in every way. With the compasses lay out the ventilator holes. Bore a hole to start and saw them out with the compass saw.

## FRONT AND BACK.

Prepare the front and back sides. They may be made of several boards nailed together.

## THE ROOF.

If possible the front portion of the roof should be one wide board; the rear portion, which receives the door, may be made up of several pieces, provided small strips are tacked over the cracks in the same manner in which the door cracks are protected. The door is fastened in position by hinges at the top, as shown in the drawing.

## THE REAR DOOR.

The rear door is for the purpose of cleaning out the house. It is not expected to be used to put in chickens; this is to be done at the top door. Notice that this small door also has battens to keep it from warping.

## THE FRONT DOOR.

The front door is a mitered frame (Chapter V., Paragraph 64) assembled with corrugated nails (Chapter II., Paragraph 23). It is covered with screen wire and trimmed with small binding strips. The ventilator holes should also be covered with screen wire. This makes the house rat proof.

## THE RUNWAY.

The frame of the runway is made up of strips fastened with plain butt joints (Chapter V., Paragraph 60). In cutting the material for this runway care should be exercised to cut opposite sides the same length so it will be square when completed. The door of the runway is a mitered frame construction, the same as the front door to the house; it is also fastened with corrugated nails (Chapter II., Paragraph 23). The entire runway should be covered with poultry net, 1″ mesh. The door to the runway and both doors to the house should be hung with screen door hinges. This will insure their holding shut without any fastenings and will also allow them to stand open when desired.

## ASSEMBLING.

Assemble the bottom ends and sides with plain butt joints (Chapter V., Paragraph 60). Nail all the joints securely, testing frequently with the try-square to make sure that all angles are right angles.

## FINISHING.

As this work is to be exposed to the weather, it should be finished with one or two coats of paint (Chapter IV., Paragraph 52). In this lesson no suggestions are offered for original designs; there are, however, a great many ideas which will no doubt occur to you in the construction of this piece of work. The size, shape of the house and the runway may be made to suit your needs.

### Optional and Home Projects Employing Similar Principles.

## HALF-BARREL CHICKEN BROODER.

1. An inexpensive and easily constructed chicken brooder may be made by sawing a sugar barrel into two equal parts. The hoops should be driven on very tightly and nailed securely before the sawing is begun. This will make sure that the two parts will hold their cylindrical shape. The door is provided by sawing out a notch, or by sawing off one stave a few inches shorter than the others.

## DOG KENNEL.

2. By changing a few of the features of the chicken house, and making the house considerably larger, a very satisfactory dog kennel may be provided.

## SUGGESTIONS FOR COMMUNITY RESEARCH.

No. 1. Examine the under side of a couch or an upholstered chair, or, if convenient, visit a place where upholstering work is done and find out how the springs are held in position. Why is leather, or some of the imitations of leather, more sanitary than the old-fashioned cloth coverings for upholstering work in the home?

No. 2. Examine the furniture in your home and see if you can tell of what kind of wood each piece is made. In making this examination do not scratch the front of the furniture, but examine hidden edges and the back parts where you can see the natural wood without destroying the finish.

No. 3. Is any of your furniture veneered? Of what kind of wood is the veneering made? To what kind of wood is it glued?

No. 4. What kind of tool case or other method of caring for the tools do you have in your home? Why should a tool case be kept perfectly dry? See if you can find out, by inquiry, where the rust comes from that gets on the metal parts of a machine or on tools which are exposed to the weather. What will be the final result if a piece of metal is continually left exposed to rust?

No. 5. What are the advantages in hitching a cow in a stanchion rather than with a halter or rope?

No. 6. Make inquiry in your community and find out what influences are most harmful to young chicks. How can these influences be overcome? Does the chicken brooder provided in this section solve any of those problems?

No. 7. What advantages can you see in painting a chicken brooder, window flower box or flower trellis?

No. 8. Is there any advantage besides appearance in keeping a house properly painted? Make inquiry from your father or other men who have had experience and find out whether they think it is really economical to neglect properly painting a house.

No. 9. Of what kind of wood are shingles made? Why is this particular kind of wood selected for the purpose? Inquire from some of the older men of the community and find out what sort of wood was used for the old-fashioned hand-split clapboards. Why did that kind of roof go out of use in your community?

No. 10. Find out how many trades or occupations are represented by patrons of your school. How many of them use some sort of hand tools in their work? Which trades are most promising for young men to enter? Why?

## REVIEW QUESTIONS AND PROBLEMS.

1. What likeness in construction did you notice in the shoe polishing box and the wash bench?

2. What were the principal points of difference between these two articles?

3. What do you consider the most difficult process in the construction of the tabouret?

4. How do you determine the color of stain and kind of finish to use on an article of household furniture?

5. What sort of material would you recommend for upholstering? Why?

6. What points must be given special attention in upholstering work?

7. What are the principal difficulties in planning and making a folding table?

8. Why should the steps of a stepladder be gained into the side pieces? By what other methods may they be fastened?

9. What is the advantage of attaching the stepladder legs with hinges rather than small bolts?

10. What is meant by ball-bearing castors? Explain why they are the most satisfactory.

11. What points must be given careful attention in making a batten door?

12. How would you design and construct a tool rack for chisels?

13. What is the purpose of the wide stretchers between the legs of the work bench?

14. Why are draw bolts better than lag bolts in constructing a work bench?

15. What sort of wood would you select for a work bench? Why? Name two other kinds which would be suitable.

16. What is the purpose of the angle irons in the cow stanchion?

17. Name two or three articles in which angle irons might be used to reinforce the joints.

## REVIEW QUESTIONS AND PROBLEMS (Concluded).

18. Would white pine or bass wood be suitable for a cow stanchion? Why? Name four kinds of timber that would be suitable.

19. Name and explain at least three important problems that must be considered in designing a chicken brooder.

20. Why are screen door hinges particularly suitable for a chicken brooder door?

21. Why should a chicken brooder have a floor?

22. Estimate the number of board feet in each article in this section; find out local prices per hundred and figure the cost of lumber for each.

23. Figure the cost of the labor, counting your time at 12½ or 15 cents per hour, on each article which you have made in this section.

24. Add the cost of labor to the cost of material (do not forget to include the cost of hardware and sundries) and estimate the value of each article which you have made.

25. Make a list and classify all the tools which you have used thus far? Which are laying out, and which are cutting tools?

26. Make a list of all the different kinds of timber which you have used thus far. Describe each and tell all you can about its nature and properties.

27. Which tool have you found the most difficult to keep sharp?

28. What kind of oil should be used on an oil stone? Is linseed oil suitable for this purpose?

# INTRODUCTION TO SECTION VI

THIS section is intended only for students who have had sufficient training in bench work to enable them to understand working drawings, to originate simple designs with some taste and judgment and to handle the principal tools with such skill as to avoid wasting material. The matter of preparing the stock, of laying out and executing ordinary processes should furnish no difficulty.

Throughout this section no references will be made to the detail of simple processes in the supplement; students who have not mastered those elementary principles should continue their work in an earlier section of the text.

The projects set forth in this section deal with cabinet principles in an elementary way, employing them in a widely varying list of ideas, in order to appeal to the taste of all students. Some of these lessons afford an opportunity to develop a high degree of skill in the art of wood finishing, and while it is sometimes a little difficult to provide satisfactory conditions to do fine varnishing work, yet the results will be very gratifying if such arrangements can be made.

In as much as the articles presented in this section will become a part of the student's home equipment and should last an indefinite number of years, each student should be urgently advised to use only the very best of carefully dried cabinet lumber. While the quartered oak is a little more expensive than plain oak, yet its advantages, in the way of beauty and permanency of the work, make it much to be preferred.

# PORCH SWING

MATERIALS.

Oak (Chap. III., Par. 29).

14 pcs. 3/8"x1 7/8"x3' 6" Slats.
7 pcs. 3/8"x1 7/8"x3' 8" Slats.
8 pcs. 3/8"x1 7/8"x 8" Arm slats.
6 pcs. 7/8"x3"x 24" Arm and curved back pieces.
2 pcs. 7/8"x1 1/4"x 17" Upper arm pieces.
2 pcs. 7/8"x2"x 17" Lower arm pieces.
4 pcs. 1-1/16"x2"x 11" Arm supports.
2 pcs. 1 1/8"x2 1/4"x4' 3" Sills.
4 pcs. 7/8"x2"x 22" Bottom supports.
1 Set chains.
36-6d fin. nails.
4-1 1/2" No. 10 screws, oval head.
15 dozen 1 1/4" No. 16 oval-headed hobnails.
2 dozen 3/4" No. 17 wire brads.
18-1/2" corrugated nails.
4 eye bolts.
2 ceiling hooks.
2 No. 5 screw eyes.
6-1/4"x2 1/2" carriage bolts.
2-1/4"x3 1/2" carriage bolts.

INTRODUCTORY STATEMENT.

In planning a porch swing one of the most important features is that it shall be comfortable; it should also be attractive and so constructed as to be durable.

The design given in this lesson has been used by one of the largest swing manufacturing concerns in the country for a number of years and it has proven to be correct in every detail. You will observe that the sills are especially heavy and that the swing is so hung as to throw the weight upon these sills.

---

**References:**

Outdoor Furniture, Good Housekeeping Magazine, June, 1914.
Simple Rustic Work, Louis Sucad. Harper's Bazaar, May, 1912.
Garden Furniture, The Craftsman Magazine, June, 1913.

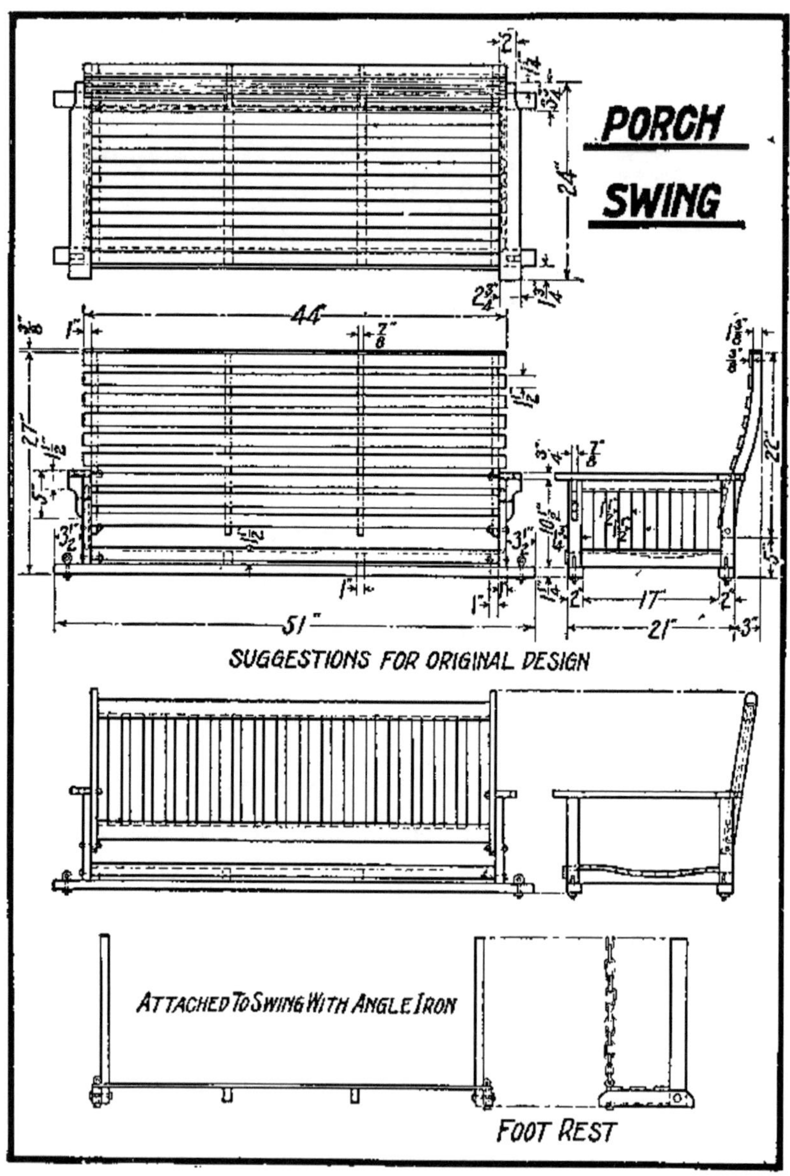
PORCH
SWING
SUGGESTIONS FOR ORIGINAL DESIGN
ATTACHED TO SWING WITH ANGLE IRON
FOOT REST

# PORCH SWING SPECIFICATIONS

## THE SILLS.

Plane the sills perfectly square and smooth and cut them the length shown in the drawing.

## THE BOTTOM.

Cut the four bottom supports the proper length. You will notice, from the dotted lines shown in the end view, that the supports are to be curved on the top side. Lay out this curve freehand and cut it out with the drawing knife. Do not curve these pieces too deeply, or it will weaken them. Nail these bottom supports upon the sills in their proper position. These pieces are to be covered with slats, placed side by side, making a solid bottom.

## THE ARMS.

Notice that the bottom and top arm rails are to be plowed to receive the slats. This can be done with the grooving side of your matching plane. If the plane does not cut the opening wide enough, you might lay it out with the marking gauge, and cut it wider with the chisel. Cut the arms the desired length, and assemble them with corrugated nails. Space the slats properly, and fasten with nails at the bottom and top in the cross rails.

## THE BACK.

Notice that the back pieces are curved. This is to give them the proper shape to make a comfortable seat. Lay out these curves free-hand, and cut out one of the pieces. Use this one for a pattern; cut the others exactly like it. Assemble by nailing the slats in position. Observe that these slats are not put closely together, as in the bottom, but they are spread as shown in the drawing.

## ASSEMBLING.

The arms are to be fastened to the bottom by means of bolts. The back is fastened in position by means of bolts through the arms. The arms are nailed through into the bottom supports, and are also bolted to the back.

Lay out the brackets free-hand and saw them out with a compass saw. These brackets are to be fastened in position under the arms with screws. Insert the eye bolts in the ends of the sills.

The swing is to be hung with the chain fastened through the screw eyes. The small anchor chain is fastened to the back to prevent tipping over.

## FINISHING.

When the swing is all assembled, go over and examine it carefully to see that there are no rough places or nails extending. Make sure that it is perfectly smooth all over and give it a coating of stain. You must use a good grade of stain, as it is exposed to the weather; it must have a good quality of oil stain which will neither rub off nor fade.

In the Suggestions there are some ideas for a swing of a little easier construction; however, you will note that this swing would not be so comfortable on account of the back being perfectly straight. The suggestion for a foot rest is a very excellent one. This foot rest can be attached to any swing; it is to be fastened to the front sill by means of two heavy angle irons.

## Optional and Home Projects Employing Similar Principles.

### PORCH CHAIR.

1. The plan of construction used in this porch swing can be very readily modified, so as to provide an excellent porch chair. The back and seat need not be changed, except in length. Some plan should be devised to provide suitable legs securely braced.

### PORCH ROCKER.

2. The porch chair may be easily converted into a porch rocker with the addition of suitable rockers.

### LAWN SEAT.

3. A lawn seat may be constructed on a plan almost identical with the porch swing. Rustic seats are especially suitable for lawns and parks. The general idea for such a seat may be gathered from the principles and proportions presented in this lesson.

# JARDINIERE STAND

## MATERIALS.

Oak (Chap. III., Par. 29), plain or quartered.

2 pcs. 7/8"x4¼"x35" S 2 S Uprights.
2 pcs. 7/8"x2¾"x35" S 2 S Uprights.
4 pcs. 7/8"x6¾"x14" S 2 S Sub. base and top.
4 pcs. 7/8"x3"x3" S 2 S Base blocks.
2 pcs. 7/8"x8¾"x9½" S 2 S Base and sub top.
2 dozen 6d finishing nails.
16-1¼" No. 10 F. H. B. screws.
1 pc. ¼"x12" dowel rod.

## INTRODUCTORY STATEMENT.

This stand is intended to be used as a piece of room or porch furniture. It should therefore be constructed with great care, for its value depends very largely upon the neatness and beauty of its workmanship. It will serve as a suitable receptacle for a flower pot, vase or small piece of statuary.

In working out your design, you will find the straight line effects are most satisfactory; attempts at elaborate design or scroll effects are likely to have a cheap appearance. In designing any piece of cabinet work you should consider the style of furniture of the room in which it is to be used.

References:

The Wood Finisher, Maire.
The Up-to-Date Hardwood Finisher, Hodgson. Fredrick Drake Co., Chicago.
Woodworking for Schools on Scientific Lines, Bailey and Pollitt. Manual Arts Press, Peoria, Ill.

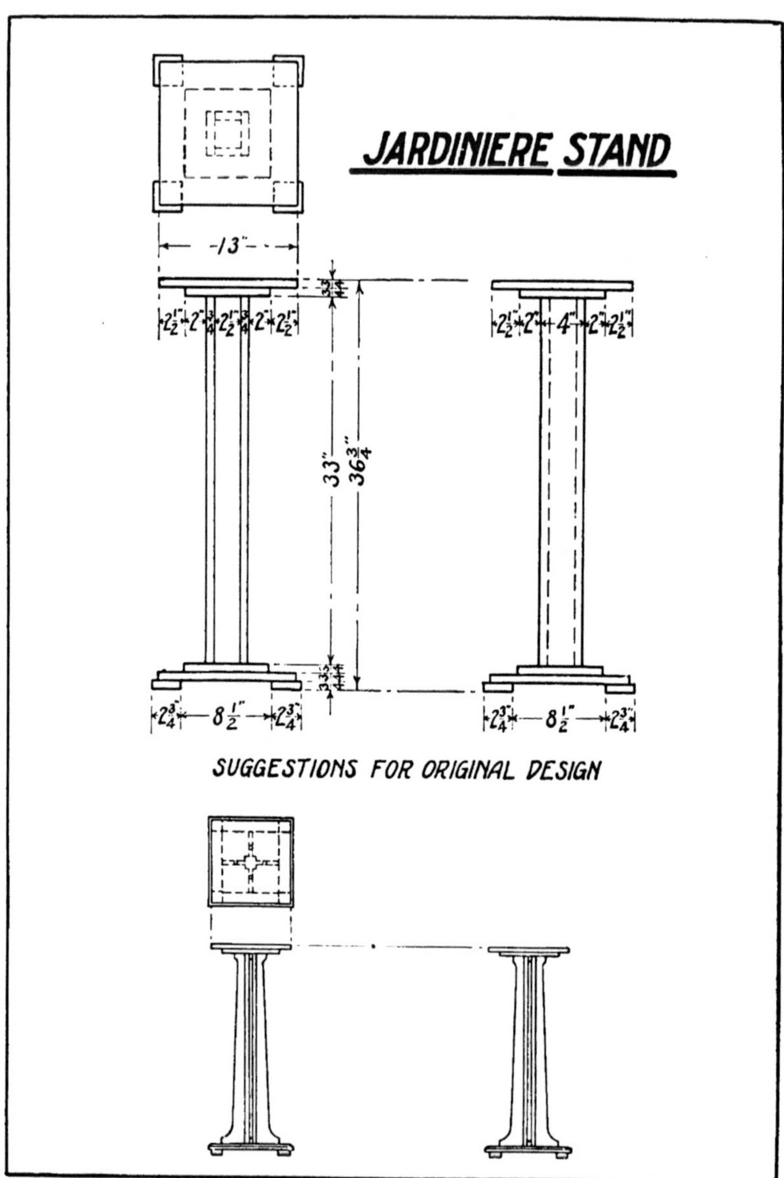
JARDINIERE STAND
13"
33"
36 3/4"
2 1/2"
2"
3/4
2 1/2"
3/4
2"
2 1/2"
4"
2 3/4"
8 1/2"
2 3/4"
SUGGESTIONS FOR ORIGINAL DESIGN

# JARDINIERE STAND SPECIFICATIONS

## THE BASE AND SUB-BASE.

As this sub-base calls for a very wide board, it will be necessary for you to join two boards with dowels. Cut the sub-base the exact size shown in the drawing, and make sure all the edges are perfectly straight and square.

Where the end grain of wood is exposed in cabinet work, it should be very carefully finished. Do this with the block plane and finish with fine sandpaper. The small corner blocks under the sub-base must be perfectly straight and project evenly on all sides.

Prepare the base; it may also be necessary to glue up this piece. Be sure it is perfectly square when finished.

## THE UPRIGHT.

The upright is to be a boxed column, made up of four boards glued together. The edges must be perfectly straight and square, so the joints may be perfect. NOTE: It would be a very excellent plan to join these corners with miter joints, if you are skillful and patient enough to do it well. Fasten the column together with glue (small finishing nails may be added, if necessary).

## THE TOP AND SUB-TOP.

The top is to be made up of two pieces joined with dowels. Be sure this piece is perfectly square when completed.

## FINISHING.

When the work is completely assembled, with a sharp steel scraper smooth all surfaces perfectly. With a fine-pointed nail set, set the nails slightly below the surface. NOTE: These holes may be filled with putty made the same color as the stain you expect to use, or with a little glue and wood dust made by the sandpapering. Sandpaper carefully; as this is a straight line design, it would not be in harmony with itself if any of the corners were rounded or marred in any way. Stain it the desired color. It should be given a coat of filler, and finished with shellac, or varnish. NOTE: This will be an excellent piece of work on which to practice the rub varnish finish, because all its surfaces are broad and flat, and there are no complicated parts to offer unusual difficulties.

## Optional and Home Projects Employing Similar Principles.

### PEDESTAL.

1. The general idea for the construction of a pedestal, as shown in the Suggestion, is a very popular one. It admits of a great many variations in design. As a rule the graceful straight line effects will be found most pleasing in elementary work.

### HALL TREE.

2. The principle of constructing a base to support a tall, slender upright is employed in making a hall tree. As a rule the central upright is a solid piece of material from 1½″ to 2½″ square. The box construction of upright, as shown in this lesson, may be used if desired.

# TOOL CHEST

MATERIALS.

Redwood (Chap. III., Par. 49) or any soft wood.

4 pcs. 7/8"x 9½"x35" S 2 S Top and bottom.
2 pcs. 7/8"x10¼"x35" S 2 S Sides.
2 pcs. 7/8"x10¼"x18" S 2 S Ends.
2 pcs. 7/8"x 4"x36" Bottom trim.
2 pcs. 7/8"x4"x21" Bottom trim.
4 pcs. 7/8"x2"x36" Lid and top trim.
4 pcs. 7/8"x2"x21" Lid and top trim.
2 pcs. ½"x¾"x17" Till support.
1 pc. ½"x 5¾"x32" Till bottom.
3 pcs. ½"x3¾"x32" Till sides, ends and partitions.
1 pair hinges, with screws. 1 mortise lock.
8 chest corners, with screws. 8 doz. 6d finishing nails.
1 pair handles. 4 doz. 1½" brads.

INTRODUCTORY STATEMENT.

A good strong box is necessary in moving tools from one place to another; for convenience such a box should be fitted with handles. For this purpose there is nothing better than the old-fashioned tool chest. It will also furnish an excellent place to store extra tools which are not in every day use.

The tool box given in this lesson is built on the plan which for many years has been recognized as the standard tool chest design. There are a great many different styles of handy tool chests prepared particularly for different kinds of tools; you will find it interesting to work out a plan which will be fitted to your need.

References:

Saws in the Filing Room. Atkins Saw Co., Indianapolis, Ind.
How to Sharpen Tools. Pike Manufacturing Co., Pike, N. H.
The Story of Carborundum as a Sharpening Material. Carborundum Co., Niagara Falls.
Carpentry, Townsend. American School of Correspondence, Chicago, Ill.

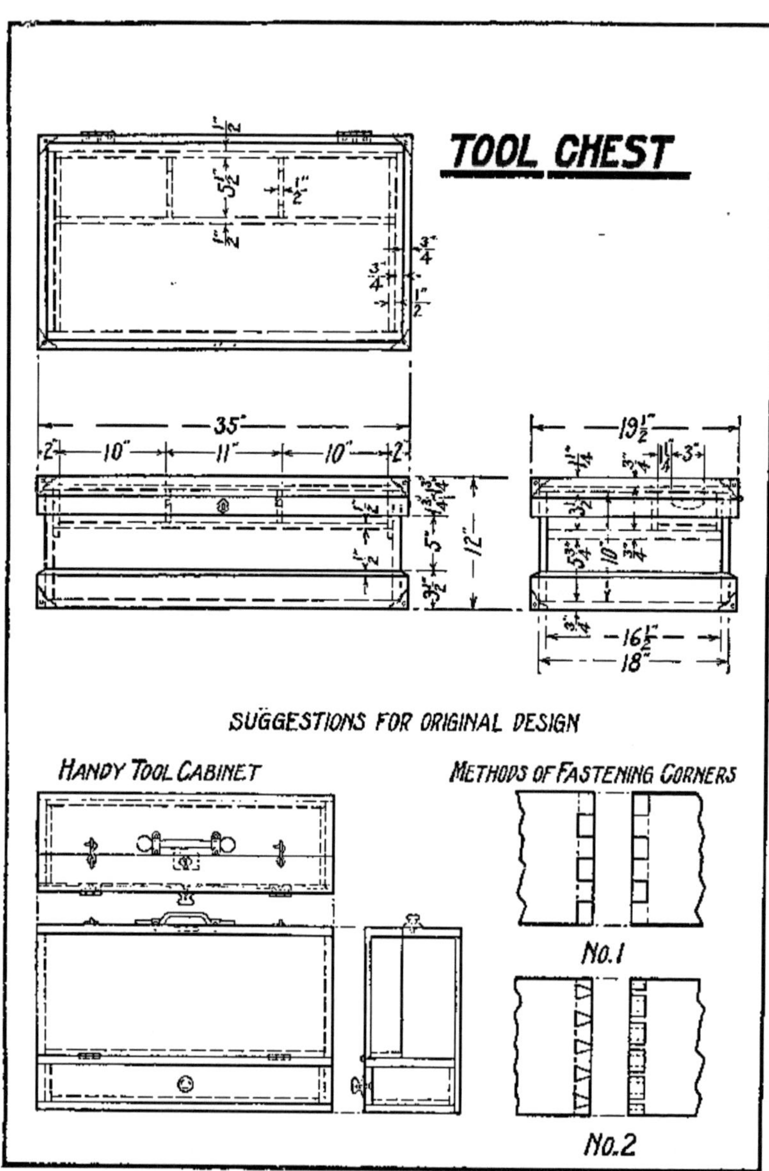
TOOL CHEST
35"
2" 10" 11" 10" 2"
12"
5"
19½"
16½"
18"
SUGGESTIONS FOR ORIGINAL DESIGN
HANDY TOOL CABINET
METHODS OF FASTENING CORNERS
No.1
No.2

# TOOL CHEST SPECIFICATIONS

## THE SIDES.

Square the stock; lay out, and make the sides the dimensions shown in the drawing. Be sure these sides are exactly the same width and length. They must also be perfectly square on all corners, or your box will not be square when assembled.

## THE ENDS.

Square the stock; lay out, and make the ends the exact size shown in the drawing. Be sure these ends are exactly square and the same size.

## THE BOTTOM.

It will be necessary to make the bottom out of two or more pieces. These pieces should be joined with a tongue and groove joint made with the matching plane, or they may be joined with dowels if you prefer this method.

## ASSEMBLING.

Join with a plain butt joint. (If you care to take the trouble, you may use the dovetail method shown in the suggestions). Nail through the sides into the ends, making the outside corners exactly even. Test with a large steel square, and hold the framework perfectly square while you nail on the bottom. The bottom is to be nailed down through into the sides and edges. Make the bottom even on all edges. If it is not exactly even, plane it so.

## THE TOP.

Prepare the wide board for the top either by matching or doweling, as you did the bottom.

## THE BINDING STRIP.

The binding strips should be planed perfectly straight and square, the width shown in the drawing. They are to be joined with mitered joints. Cut them in the miter box, or lay them out the half-pitch cut and set the T-bevel. The length of each piece must be measured separately, taking the measure from the place where it is to be fastened; in this way you can be accurate. Fasten the trim to the lid, make it exactly even on the top. The top trim on the body of the box is put a little below the edge, thus forming a rabbet to receive the lid. The base trim should be mitered around the box in a similar manner. The trim is to be nailed through the box from the outside. (If you desire, screws may be put in from the inside of the box into the trim. In this case the screws should be countersunk so as to be even with the surface).

### THE TILL.

The till is a small box on the inside of the chest. Notice that it rests on strips tacked on the inside of each end. This till should be provided with openings for hand holds.

### HINGING THE LID.

Fasten the lid to the box with hinges. It may be necessary to refit it slightly in order that it may work easily after the hinges are in position. Test it, and plane wherever necessary to make it work easily. Cut the mortise and set the lock.

### FINISHING.

With a sharp block plane, or sharp steel scraper, remove any pencil, tool marks, or rough places in the work. Be sure that all the surfaces are perfectly clean. Smooth with fine sandpaper; stain the desired color; finish with shellac or varnish. When the coating is dry, fasten the brass corners in position.

In the Suggestions for Original Design you will find a drawing showing a handy tool cabinet to be carried from place to place.

## Optional and Home Projects Employing Similar Principles.

### BOY'S TRUNK CHEST.

1. The plan of construction given in this lesson may be employed in building a strong box, or trunk chest, which a boy may find quite serviceable in his room.

### CAMP CHEST.

2. On camping trips there is a demand for a strong box which will answer the purpose of a shipping crate, and will also serve in camp as a cupboard. This plan of construction will be found quite satisfactory. It would probably be necessary to make such a chest considerably larger, and equip it with a number of divisions which would answer as shelves while it was serving the purpose of a camp cupboard.

# PIANO BENCH

MATERIALS.

Oak (Chap. III., Par. 29), plain or quartered.

2 pcs. 1⅛"x8"x36½" S 2 S Top.

2 pcs. ⅞"x3¼"x35" S 2 S Side rails.

2 pcs. ⅞"x3¼"x14" S 2 S End rails.

4 pcs. 1¾"x1¾"x16" S 4 S Legs.

3 pcs. 2½"x3¼"x17" S 4 S Base pieces and angle blocks.

1 pc. 1¼"x4¼"x32" S 2 S Stretcher.

2 pcs. ½"x½"x35" S 4 S Trim.

2 pcs. ½"x½"x16" S 4 S Trim.

1 pc. ½" dowel 12" long.

1 dozen 1¼" brads.

2 dozen 6d finishing nails.

3 dozen 1½" No. 10 F. H. B. screws.

## INTRODUCTORY STATEMENT.

In recent years the piano bench has almost entirely taken the place of the piano stool; the bench is preferred for several reasons, not only because it is more pleasing from the artistic standpoint, but also because it is more serviceable. The bench affords room for two people and is thus convenient for duet work or for teacher and pupil.

Benches are often so constructed as to furnish a receptacle for music; the one given in this lesson is not so designed, but if desirable you can easily make it in this way by adding a bottom and hinging the top.

The kind of wood and style of finish for a piano bench should correspond as far as possible with the piano case. This is a piece of work which calls for great care and skill in every detail, for no one would want to use a piano bench which showed evidence of poor workmanship.

---

**References:**

The Expert Wood Finisher, Kelly. The National Builder, Chicago.
Elements of Handicraft and Design. Benson.

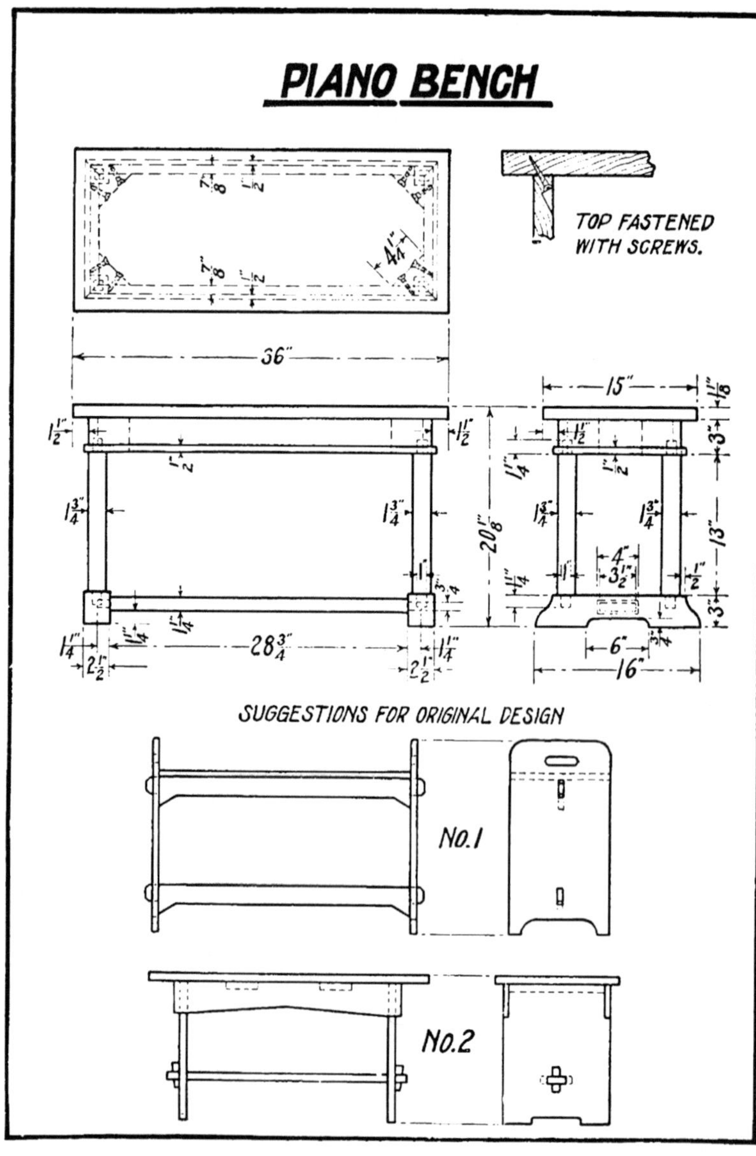
PIANO BENCH
TOP FASTENED WITH SCREWS.
36"
15"
28 3/4"
20 1/8"
13"
16"
6"
4"
3 1/2"
SUGGESTIONS FOR ORIGINAL DESIGN
NO.1
NO.2

# PIANO BENCH SPECIFICATIONS

## THE TOP.

As the top is to be made of two pieces glued together, you should prepare it first, in order that the glue may have ample time to dry. These edges must be perfectly fitted and joined with dowels.

## THE LEGS.

Although the legs are furnished S 4 S, you must go over them with a keen plane, and make them smooth and perfectly square; they must then be finished with a sharp steel scraper. Cut them the desired length, being careful to make allowance for the tenons; cut a tenon 1″ square on each end.

## THE RAILS.

Square the stock, and carefully plane the rails to the dimensions shown in the drawing. These rails are to be joined at the corners with mitered joints. They should be cut in the miter box. Be sure the opposite side and opposite ends are exactly the same length. All joints must fit perfectly. On a piece of work of this sort ill-fitting joints would render it absolutely worthless.

## CORNER BRACE BLOCKS.

These blocks are to be fastened on the inside of the railing with glue and wood screws. This operation must be carefully done to avoid spreading and damaging the joints at the corner. If this is carefully done, the framework will present a very solid corner into which the mortises are to be cut to receive the tenons of the legs. Lay out and cut these mortises.

## THE BASE PIECES.

Square the stock for the base pieces. Lay them out the desired shape, saw them out with the compass saw, and carefully finish with a wood file. This portion of the work must be accurately done, and edges must be left perfectly square and smooth. Lay out and cut the mortises for the legs; be sure to make them the same distance apart as the mortises in the top rail. Lay out and cut the mortise for the stretcher.

## THE STRETCHER.

Square the stock, lay out and make the stretcher according to the drawing. (Be careful to cut it long enough to allow for the tenon at each end). Lay out and make the tenon on each end to suit the corresponding mortises in the leg bases.

## ASSEMBLING.

Glue all of the tenons in their proper mortises; make sure that all angles are perfectly square; test frequently with the square. Clamp securely in such a way as to bind all joints. Remove all surplus glue.

Putting on the top might be left until the glue is thoroughly hardened and the clamps removed. Resurface the top and cut the shape and dimensions shown in the drawing. Make sure that all the edges are perfectly square. The top is to be fastened to the rails by screws from the under side, as shown in the drawing; make sure that it projects evenly on all sides; use enough screws to bind it firmly to the rail.

## THE TRIM.

The small trim strips are to be fastened to the lower edge of the rail. They are to be made even with the rail; however, if let down a very small fraction of an inch they will hide the leg joints. Miter these strips at the corners; fasten them in position with brads and glue.

## FINISHING.

With a sharp steel scraper refinish the entire surface of the piano bench. Remove all pencil and tool marks. Smooth with fine sandpaper. Give special attention to smoothing all places where end grain is exposed.

**Optional and Home Projects Employing Similar Principles.**

## OTTOMAN.

1. Suggestion No. 1 presents an idea of bench construction which is particularly suitable for an ottoman. It may be upholstered with leather, tapestry, or some other suitable material.

## CRAFTSMAN PIANO BENCH.

2. Suggestion No. 2 presents a general idea for a craftsman piano bench. A number of modifications are possible in a design of this sort. Care must be exercised to avoid rude and clumsy appearance in any of the craftsman or mission designs.

# MAGAZINE RACK

## MATERIALS.

Oak (Chap. III., Par. 29), plain or quartered.

4 pcs. 1¾"x1¾"x40" S 4 S Corner posts.
2 pcs. ⅞"x8¼"x30" S 2 S Top.
2 pcs. ⅞"x4½"x25" Rear cross rails.
4 pcs. ⅞"x4½"x12" Side cross rails.
5 pcs. ½"x4¼"x33" Panel strips.
6 pcs. ⅞"x6 "x25" Shelves.
1 pc. ¼" dowel 24" long.
7 1½" No. 10 F. H. B. screws.

## INTRODUCTORY STATEMENT.

This magazine rack is constructed on principles which would be suitable not only for a magazine or newspaper rack, but for a music cabinet or bookcase. It is very strong and substantial, being assembled with mortise and tenon joints throughout; of course this form of construction will call for very careful and accurate work.

If a closed cabinet is desired instead of the open rack, this plan can easily be modified by making the panels wide enough to fill the space between the corner posts. A panel door could be made to correspond with the remainder of the work and thus a completely closed-in cabinet would be provided.

In the suggestions for original design a very simple idea is presented. A rack made on this plan would be much less work, but it would be neither so artistic nor so substantial as the one presented in the regular lesson.

**References:**

Library Furniture, in Adventures in Home Making, Shackleton. John Lane Pub. Co., New York.
Furniture for the Craftsman, Paul D. Otter. David Williams Co., New York.

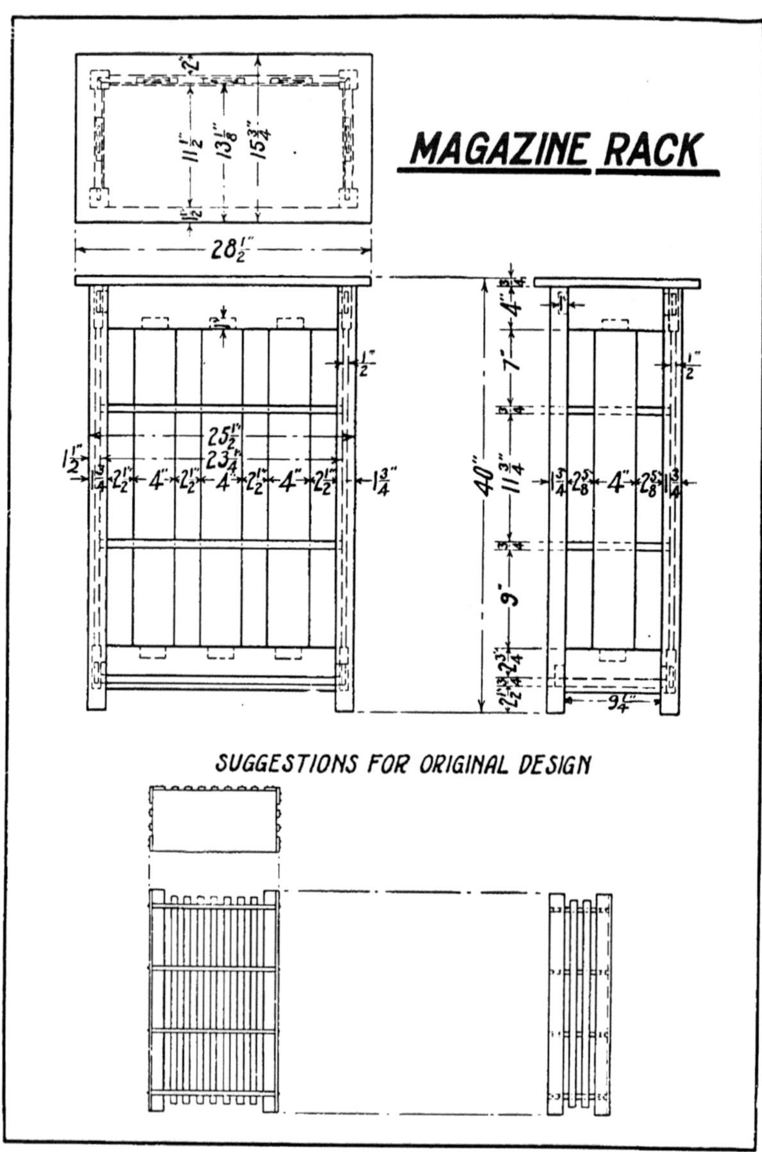
MAGAZINE RACK
SUGGESTIONS FOR ORIGINAL DESIGN

# MAGAZINE RACK SPECIFICATIONS

## THE CORNER POSTS.

Although these posts are furnished S 4 S, it will be necessary for you to resurface them with a keen plane, making sure that they are perfectly square. Finish with a sharp steel scraper. Cut them the required length; lay out and cut all mortises for the rails.

## THE TOP.

The top is to be made by gluing together two or more boards. These edges must be perfectly planed and joined with dowels. Clamp the boards securely; leave at least twelve hours for the glue to harden.

## THE CROSS RAILS.

Square the stock for the cross rails; lay out and make them the exact shape shown in the drawing. These rails are to be joined to the corner posts with mortise and tenon joints; in cutting the length be sure to allow for the tenons; lay out and cut all of the tenons to correspond with the mortises in the corner posts. Lay out and cut the mortises for the panel strips.

## THE PANEL STRIPS.

The panel strips are to be fastened into the bottom and top cross rails with mortise and tenon joints, so they will have to be prepared before the other work is assembled. Resurface these pieces and finish with a steel scraper. Make sure that the edges are perfectly square, and that they are all exactly the same size. You will have to exercise great care in cutting the length of the panel pieces so they will make good joints when the work is assembled. They must be long enough to fit snugly between the cross rails when they are assembled. Test them.

## THE BOTTOM AND SHELVES.

The bottom and shelves are to be formed by gluing up two or more boards with dowels, in the same manner in which you glued up the top. When the glue is thoroughly hardened remove the clamps, and surface these boards on both sides. Finish with a steel scraper and fine sandpaper.

## ASSEMBLING.

In assembling this work, assemble one side at a time. (Glue all mortises in tenon joints); test all angles frequently with the square. Place the bottom and top rails properly on one of the side panel pieces; then assemble with the two corner posts. In like manner assemble the other side. Glue the three panel pieces into the rear bottom and top rail, then glue these rails into their proper mortises. NOTE: If you are using the dowel method of fastening the shelves, they will have to be put in at this time. If not, they can be put in after the back is assembled. Clamp securely. If you do not have a sufficient number of clamps to clamp the entire work at one time, it would be well to clamp up one end section and allow the glue to harden, then clamp up another section, allowing it to harden before undertaking the back. The top may be fastened in position by screws put in on an angle on the inside of the side rail (as shown in the preceding lesson), or by short dowels in each post, extending almost through the top piece.

The shelves and bottom are to be fastened in place with small nails driven through the panel pieces; if desired, short dowels may be used in the corner posts.

## FINISHING.

When all the work is properly assembled go over it with a sharp steel scraper, making all surfaces perfectly smooth. Finish with very fine sandpaper. Stain the desired color (it should have a coat of filler; shellac may be substituted). Finish with shellac or varnish.

## Optional and Home Projects Employing Similar Principles.

### MUSIC CABINET.

1. With very slight modifications this magazine rack may be converted into a very excellent music cabinet. Instead of strips, it should be provided with tight panels. A door should be constructed of similar panel design.

### UMBRELLA STAND.

2. The plan of four corner posts with mortise and tenon cross rails may be effectively used in designing an umbrella stand.

### CRETONNE-COVERED CABINET.

3. A very pretty cabinet may be afforded by using this same plan of construction, and lining it on the inside with cretonne. Such a cabinet would be particularly suitable for a sewing room at home.

# TELEPHONE STAND AND STOOL

MATERIALS. Oak (Chap. III., Par. 29).

| Stand: | | | | Stool: | |
|---|---|---|---|---|---|
| 2 pcs. | ⅞"x9¼"x19" | S 2 S | Top. | 2 pcs. | ⅞"x6¼"x13" |
| 3 pcs. | ⅞"x4¾"x15" | S 2 S | Top rail. | 4 pcs. | ⅞"x2¾"x10" |
| 4 pcs. | 1½"x1½"x30" | S 4 S | Legs. | 4 pcs. | 1½"x1½"x18" |
| 3 pcs. | ½"x2¼"x15" | | Trim. | 3 pcs. | ¾"x2¼"x10" |
| 2 pcs. | ¾"x6½"x13" | | Shelf (soft wood). | | 1½ dozen 1½" No. |
| 1 pc. | ¾"x1½"x15" | | Front edge of shelf. | | 10 F. H. B. screws. |
| 3 pcs. | ¾"x2¾"x15" | | Lower cross rails and stretcher. | | |

## INTRODUCTORY STATEMENT.

It is often desirable to have the telephone on a stand rather than on the wall; in this case it is well to provide a stand and stool on purpose for the use of the 'phone.

The one given in this lesson is so planned that when the stool is not in use it hangs under the stand. In this position it is out of the way and still always ready for immediate use. The illustration shows two views, one with the stool in front of the stand ready for use and the other with the stool hanging in position.

---

References:

Modern American Telephony in All Its Branches, Smith. Fredrick Drake Co., Chicago.
Telephone Hand Book, Victor Laughter. Fredrick Drake Co., Chicago.
Drake's Telephone Hand Book, Moreton. Fredrick Drake Co., Chicago.
Wireless Telephone and Telegraph, Chas. Ashley. American Technical Society.

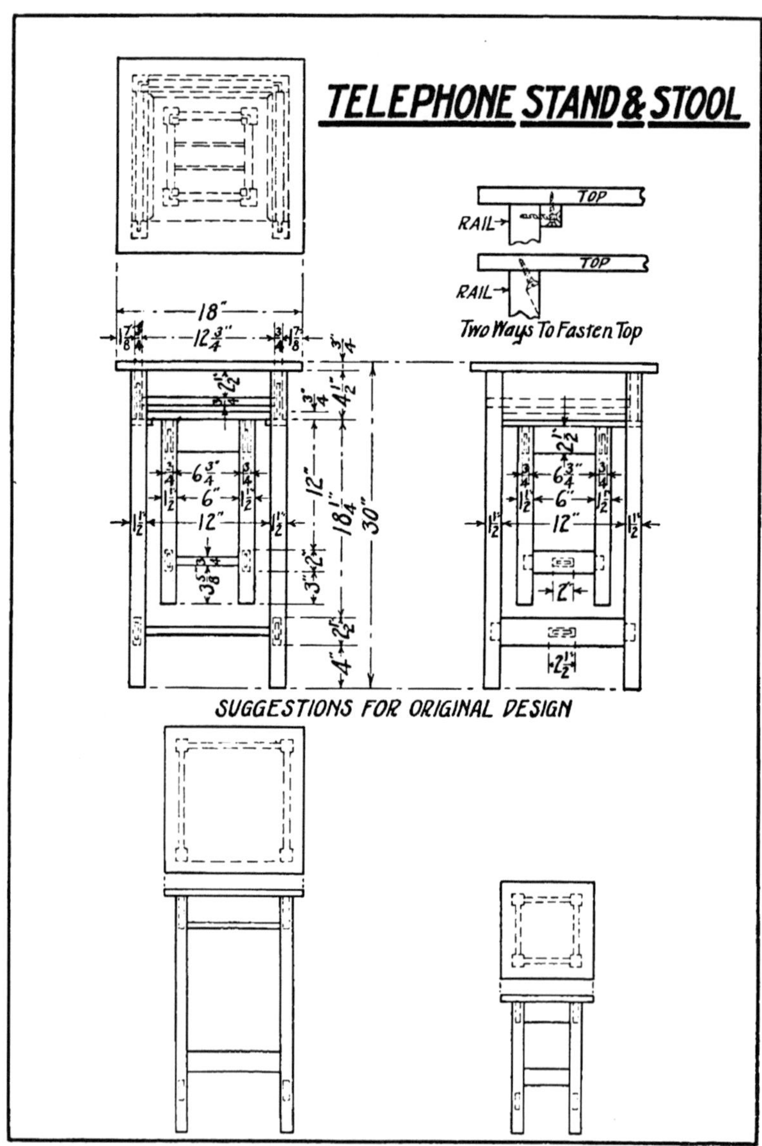
TELEPHONE STAND & STOOL
TOP
RAIL
TOP
RAIL
Two Ways To Fasten Top
18"
12 3/4"
30"
18 1/4"
12"
4 1/2"
SUGGESTIONS FOR ORIGINAL DESIGN

# TELEPHONE STAND AND STOOL SPECIFICATIONS

## THE STAND.

### TOP.

The top of this stand is to be made by gluing together two pieces. This must be done with a dowel joint. Clamp up the work securely, remove all surplus glue, and leave it at least twelve hours for the glue to harden.

### THE CORNER POSTS.

Although this material is furnished S 4 S, it will be necessary for you to resurface it, making it perfectly square. Finish with a sharp steel scraper. Cut the required lengths, lay out and cut the mortises to receive the rails.

### THE TOP RAILS.

Notice that there are top rails only on three sides; the front is left open to form a shelf.

The top rails are to be joined to the legs with mortise and tenon joints. Square the stock for the rails, and make them the width shown in the drawing. Cut the required length, allowing for tenons. Lay out and cut the tenons. Be sure that the lengths of the opposite side rails are the same between shoulders. Test each tenon in the mortise for which it is intended; they must fit snugly. The tenons must not bind sidewise, or they may split the posts.

### THE BOTTOM CROSS RAILS.

The bottom cross rails are to be joined to the corner posts with mortise and tenon joints. Square the stock, and make these pieces the dimensions given in the drawing. Lay out and make tenons. Test each tenon in its proper mortise.

### THE SHELF.

The shelf takes the place of a front cross rail. The shelf is made of soft material, but it should have a front edge of hardwood. It may be made by gluing up pieces, the same as you have glued up the top. Remove the clamps from the top, and surface it on both sides; cut it the size shown in the drawing.

### ASSEMBLING.

In work of this kind you will find it convenient to assemble one pair of legs at a time. Glue the joints, test with the square to make sure the legs stand perfectly square with the cross rail. Clamp securely and leave for the glue to harden. In like manner clamp the opposite pair of legs. When these two are well set, put in the back cross rail and the stretcher between the lower cross rails and assemble. The top is to be fastened in position with screws, either with strips or the angle screws. When the top is fastened securely in position, put in the shelf and fasten it by nailing through the side rails. Be very careful in the nailing process not to bruise the work. With a sharp-pointed nail set, drive the nails slightly below the surface of the wood.

### THE BINDING STRIP.

This small strip is tacked to the lower edge of the top rail around three sides of the stool, and thus forms a carrier to hold the stool, and also gives a sort of panel appearance to the top rail; it should fit the corner posts snugly.

## THE STOOL.

The stool is to be built almost exactly as the stand has been built, except that it has a top rail entirely around. Prepare each part and assemble the stool in a similar manner to which you have constructed the stand.

### FINISHING.

When both pieces of work have been properly assembled, go over them with a sharp steel scraper, and remove all pencil and tool marks. Be sure the corners are all sharp and distinct. Wherever the end grain is exposed it must have special attention to make it perfectly smooth. Stain the desired color, and finish with shellac or varnish.

**Optional and Home Projects Employing Similar Principles.**

### KITCHEN TABLE.

1. This plan of constructing a table, with the rails tenoned into the legs, has a great many applications in practical work. By using heavier legs, and changing the size of the top as desired, a very servicable kitchen table may be constructed.

### CHAFING DISH TABLE.

2. With very slight modifications this stand could be converted into a satisfactory chafing dish table. It should have a small cabinet in which to keep the chafing dish and utensils. This could be easily prepared by using a very wide skirting board with a shelf in the bottom; the cabinet should be provided with a dustproof door.

# MEDICINE OR SHAVING CABINET

MATERIALS.

Poplar (Chap. III., Par. 42) or any soft wood.

1 pc. 7/8"x5 1/2"x18" S 2 S Top.
2 pcs. 7/8"x4 3/4"x24" S 2 S Sides.
1 pc. 7/8"x4 3/4"x15" S 2 S Bottom.
1 pc. 7/8"x3 1/4"x15" S 2 S Apron.
2 pcs. 1/2"x3 3/4"x15" S 2 S Shelves.
1 pc. 1/4" (3-ply) x15"x20" S 2 S Back.
1 pc. 1/4" (3-ply) x10"x15" S 2 S Door panel.
2 pcs. 7/8"x3 1/4"x20" S 2 S Door side styles.
2 pcs. 7/8"x3 1/4"x14" S 2 S Door cross rails.
1 1/2 doz. 6d finishing nails.
2 doz. 1 1/4" brads.
8 screw eyes, No. 114.
1 pair 1 1/2" hinges.
1 small cupboard catch.

INTRODUCTORY STATEMENT.

In every home it is very important that some place be provided for the care of medicines and various home remedies; a small, neat cabinet with a close-fitting door is most suitable for this purpose.

There is no standard size for a medicine cabinet, for it is often desirable to make it to fit a certain space in the bathroom or wherever it is to be used. It would be well for you to measure your space at home and then make your cabinet to fit.

This lesson presents the principles of a mortised and tenoned door, and since this is such an important piece of construction, you should give it special attention. A door made of one wide board or with battens is not so good nor so neat for small cabinet work.

There are so many uses for various kinds of wall cabinets, such as shaving cabinets, china cabinets, built-in bookcases and the like that you should master these principles.

---

**References:**

Cabinet Work and Joinery, Hasluck.
Elementary Cabinet Work, F. H. Selden. Rand-McNally Co., Chicago, Ill.
Inside Finishing, King. American Book Co., Chicago, Ill.

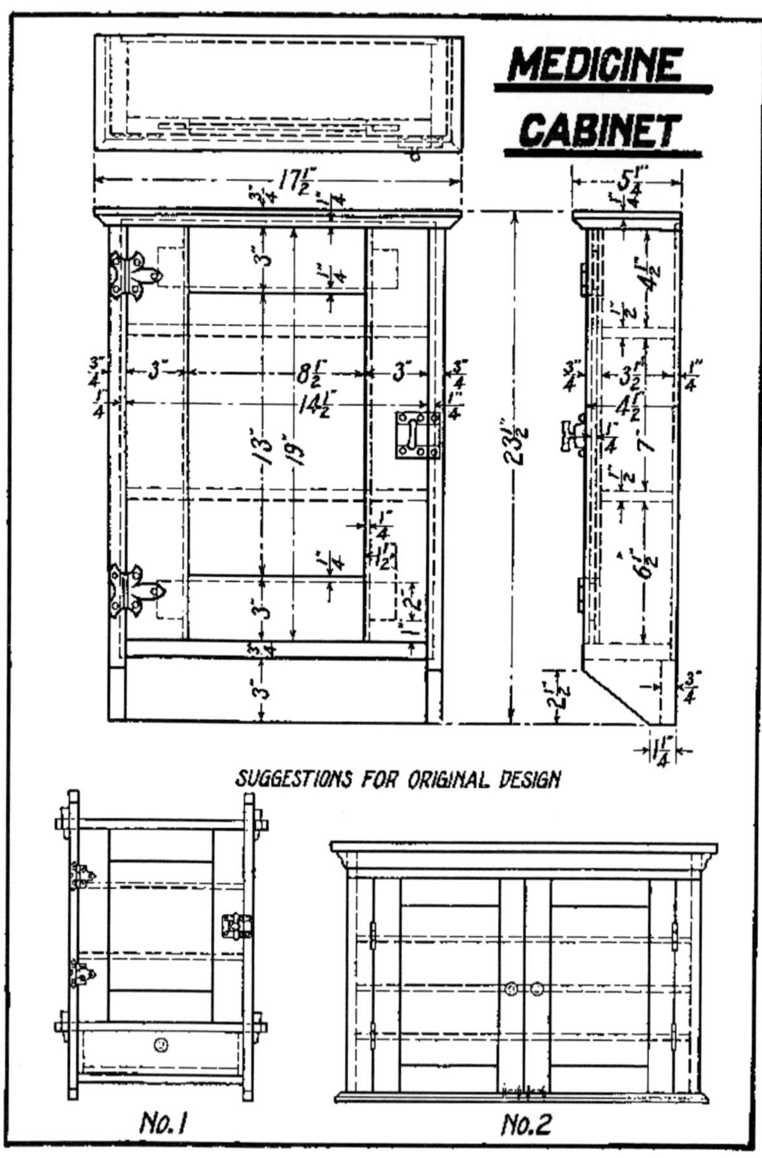
MEDICINE
CABINET
17½"
5¼"
23½"
14½"
8½"
13"
19"
SUGGESTIONS FOR ORIGINAL DESIGN
No. 1
No. 2

# MEDICINE OR SHAVING CABINET SPECIFICATIONS

## THE TOP.

Square the stock, lay out and make it the proper dimensions.

## THE SIDES.

Square the stock, lay out and make the side pieces the size shown in the drawing. Although the material is furnished S 2 S, these pieces should be carefully surfaced, and finished with a steel scraper.

## THE RABBET.

The side pieces and the top are to be rabbeted to receive the back. If you rabbet them with a plane this will cut away the material to the end of each piece, and when the work is assembled will leave holes, which will have to be neatly filled. If you desire, you can cut these rabbets only as far as required, by laying them out with a marking gauge, and carefully cutting them with a pocket knife, first scribing deeply on one gauge line, and then on the other until the rabbets are completely cut out.

## THE BOTTOM.

The bottom is to be made the width of the sides, less the thickness of the back. You will notice in the drawing that the back laps down upon the bottom. Square the stock and make this piece.

## THE BACK.

The back piece should be furnished in one board of three-ply material. You will notice that this is made up of three thin pieces glued together. The grain is reversed; this makes a very strong board. You need not cut it to size until the frame is assembled.

## THE BOTTOM SKIRT BOARD.

The bottom skirt board joins the side pieces with a plain butt joint. Square the stick and make the piece the required size.

## ASSEMBLING.

This work is to be assembled with nails driven through from the outside. These nails should be carefully set with a sharp-pointed nail set. Make sure that the cabinet is perfectly square in every way when the back is nailed in position.

## THE SHELVES.

The material for the shelves should be planed to the exact size shown in the drawing. You may make the shelves adjustable if you wish, allowing them to rest on small screw eyes.

## THE DOOR.

The door is to be put together with mortise and tenon joints, as indicated in the drawing. The door material is to be plowed or grooved to receive the panel, which is of 1/4", three-ply. This plan of making a door is a very excellent one; you should exercise great care and learn to do it well. Practically all doors for fine cabinets are made in just this manner. Study the drawing very carefully and execute each piece accurately. Assemble the door with glue. You should not glue the panel; it will be less likely to warp if left free to contract or expand with changes of temperature. Clamp the door, and allow it to stand at least twelve hours for the glue to harden. When it is thoroughly dry, with a sharp plane, plane all surfaces, and finish with a steel scraper and sandpaper. Plane the edges to make it exactly fit the cabinet. Put on the hinges and the spring catch.

## FINISHING.

Medicine cabinets are usually finished white. To do this give it two coats of white paint, allowing each to dry thoroughly, and if you desire to have a very beautiful finish, one or two coats of white enamel. If you prefer, you may stain it the desired color and finish with shellac or varnish. It is customary to finish both the inside and outside of a small cabinet like this. NOTE: If this is to be used for a shaving cabinet you will find it very convenient to have a mirror in the door panel.

**Optional and Home Projects Employing Similar Principles.**

## CHINA CABINET.

1. By enlarging this cabinet as one's needs may require, and providing it with glass doors, a china cabinet could be made.

## BOOK CASE.

2. The plan of the china cabinet will require but little modification in making a book case.

## SCHOOL LOCKERS.

3. Inexpensive school lockers may be constructed on the plan given in this lesson; the size and shape could be determined by local needs.

# CEDAR CHEST

## MATERIALS.

Red Cedar (Chap. III., Par. 45).

Sufficient number of pieces to make:

2 sides ¾"x11¼"x43" S 2 S
2 ends ¾"x11¼"x18" S 2 S
2 pcs. ¾"x17"x43" S 2 S Top and bottom.

2 pcs. ½"x1"x43" S 4 S Lid trim.
2 pcs. ½"x1"x18" S 4 S Lid trim.
4 pcs. 2¾"x3"x3" (Glued) S 4 S Legs.
5 pcs. sheet copper 2"x6" for trim.
34 tacks to match.
1 pr. hinges with screws.
5 doz. 1¼" brads.
5 pcs. ¼"x12" dowel.
4 castors.
1 pr. copper handles with screws.
1 doz. 1¼" No. 10 F. H. B. screws.

## INTRODUCTORY STATEMENT.

For a great many years cedar chests have been popular for storing furs, woolens, linens and other fine fabrics where they would be free from moths. Red cedar wood contains a peculiar, everlasting odor which seems to be very unpleasant to insects, at least they will not go about it. This unusual quality, connected with the fact that it will last indefinitely, has made it a very valuable wood.

Red cedar is rather a difficult material to work on account of the knots, however these knots do not lessen its value; in fact, when properly finished, they add to its beauty and fragrance.

---

References:

The Story of Red Cedar. Red Cedar Chest Co., Statesville, N. C.

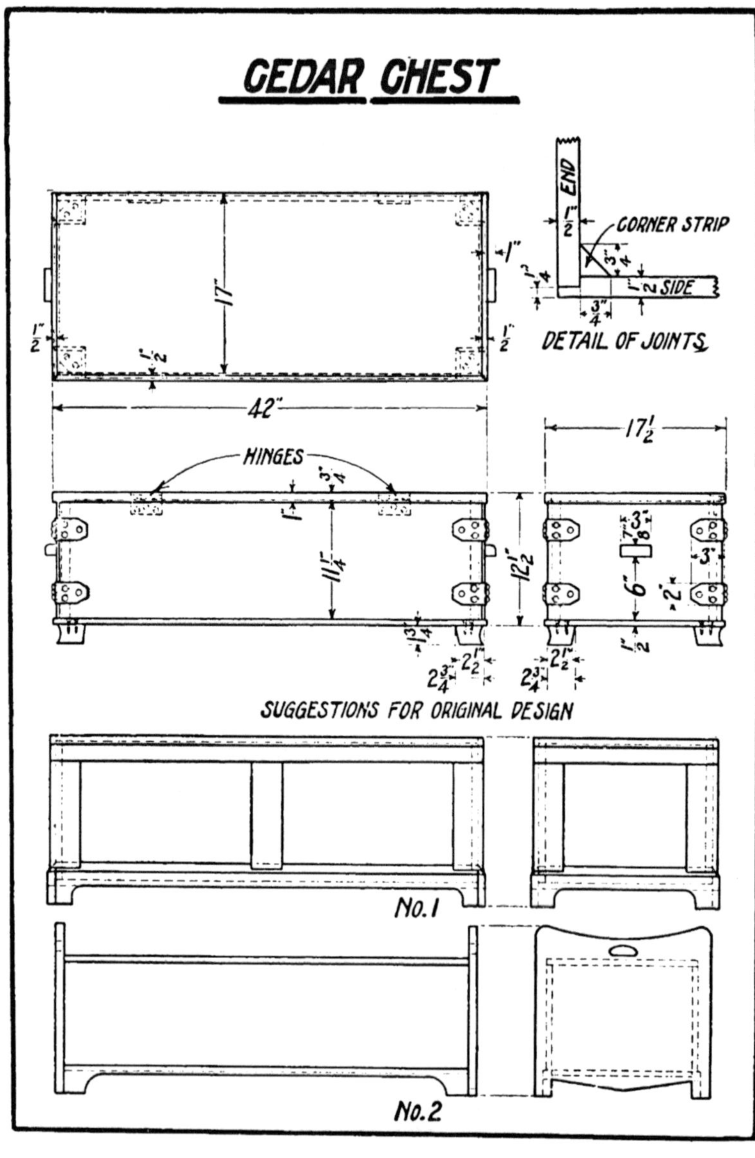
CEDAR CHEST
END
CORNER STRIP
SIDE
DETAIL OF JOINTS
17"
42"
17½
HINGES
11¼"
12½"
6"
SUGGESTIONS FOR ORIGINAL DESIGN
No.1
No.2

# CEDAR CHEST SPECIFICATIONS

## PREPARING THE STOCK.

As it is practically impossible to get wide boards of cedar, it will be necessary for you to glue up narrow boards in forming the bottom and top, and also the sides and ends. On account of the knots (a feature which adds beauty and value to the wood), you will find it rather difficult to plane. You must have your plane very keen, and make up your mind to be extremely patient. Square the edges and join them with dowels, making a board of sufficient width for the bottom. In like manner glue up material for the two sides, the two ends and the top. When the glue is thoroughly hardened, with a sharp smoothing plane resurface the boards. It will possibly not be necessary to plane them anywhere except on the joints; the remainder of the surfacing can be done with a sharp steel scraper.

## THE SIDES.

Lay out and cut the two sides the dimensions given in the drawing. Be sure they are absolutely square, and exactly the same length and width. Prepare the two ends, and compare to see that they are exactly the same size. You will notice that the side pieces are to be rabbeted to lap over on the ends (this sort of joint is not absolutely necessary; you may join them with a straight butt joint if you desire). The rabbet will not be difficult to make. It is to be laid out with a marking gauge, or a straight edge and sharp-pointed knife; it may be cut down with the back saw, and cut out to the gauge line with a chisel. All the corners are to be formed in the same manner.

## ASSEMBLING.

Assemble your box by nailing through the side pieces into the ends, using small finishing nails or brads. The bottom is to be nailed through into the sides and ends; see that it projects evenly on all sides and at both ends. Test frequently to make sure that the box is perfectly square when the bottom is nailed on.

The triangular strips are glued in each corner to reinforce the joints. They may also be bradded, but this must be very carefully done to avoid disturbing the joints. You should lay the box flat on the side, while driving small brads into the side pieces; then turn it on to the ends when you nail into the end pieces.

## THE LEGS.

The legs are to be made the desired shape, and fastened one

on each corner with screws from the inside through the bottom, as shown in the drawing.

### THE LID.

The lid is to be bound on both ends, and on the front edge with a narrow strip which extends a little below the lower edge of the lid, as shown in the drawing. This strip is to be joined at the corners with a mitered joint. It is fastened to the lid with brads driven straight through. Hinge the lid to the back edge of the box; make sure that it fits perfectly and works easily.

### THE HANDLES.

The handles are to be made the desired shape, and to be fastened with screws from the inside of the box.

### THE ORNAMENTAL TRIM.

The ornamental trim is of art copper; it may be cut any shape you desire. Some simple design, as shown in the drawing, will be found most pleasing.

### FINISHING.

With a very sharp steel scraper, remove all pencil or tool marks and make every surface perfectly smooth. Finish it with shellac or with rub varnish. Do not stain it, and do not use shellac or any kind of finish on the inside. Leave the natural wood exposed on the inside in order to get the full benefit of its fragrance.

## Optional and Home Projects Employing Similar Principles.

### COVERED BEDROOM CHEST.

**1.** A very much cheaper, and fairly satisfactory, chest may be provided where red cedar is too expensive. This chest may be made of any sort of wood. It should be well constructed, and may be neatly lined on the inside with imitation of cedar paper. On the outside it should be neatly covered with cretonne, denim or some other suitable material.

### WINDOW SEAT CHEST.

2. A chest built on the plan shown in Suggestion No. 2 will be found very suitable for a window seat. It may be upholstered or furnished with cushions. It should be finished to correspond with the furniture of the room in which it is to be used.

# WRITING DESK

## MATERIALS.

Oak (Chap. III., Par. 29).

4 pcs. 1½"x1½"x32" S 4 S Legs.
1 pc. ⅞"x5¾"x28" S 2 S Back rail.
1 pc. ⅞"x4"x28" S 2 S Front rail.
2 pcs. ⅞"x5¾"x20" S 2 S Side rail.
3 pcs. ¾"x6½"x28" S 2 S Bottom (soft wood).
1 pc. ⅞"x7"x32" S 2 S Top.
3 pcs. ⅞"x5¾"x32" S 2 S Lid.
1 pc. ½"x7"x32" S 2 S Back of paper holders.
4 pcs. ½"x2½"x7" Sides of paper holders.
4 pcs. ¼"x2½"x8½" Front of paper holders.
1 pc. ½"x3"x32" Base of paper holders.
2 pcs. ¾"x2½"x20" Bottom cross rails.
1 pc. ¾"x3¼"x28" Stretcher.
½ doz. 1½" No. 10 F. H. B. screws. 2 doz. 6d fin. nails.
1½ doz. ¾" No. 6 R. H. blue screws. 1 pc. ¼"x12" dowel rod.
1 pair hinges.

## INTRODUCTORY STATEMENT.

The writing desk or study table is one of the most useful articles of furniture found in a boy's room, and the fact that a boy has made his own table always adds considerable to its value.

This writing desk is so designed as to provide ample room inside to care for stationery and valuable papers. If desirable this space could be divided with partitions so as to classify papers more easily.

The mortise and tenon joints will require careful work, but when completed will be well worth all the effort. The principles set forth in this lesson are employed a great deal in all kinds of desk and table construction, so you should endeavor to master them.

---

**References:**

Part II, Mission Furniture, Windsor. Popular Mechanics Co., Chicago.

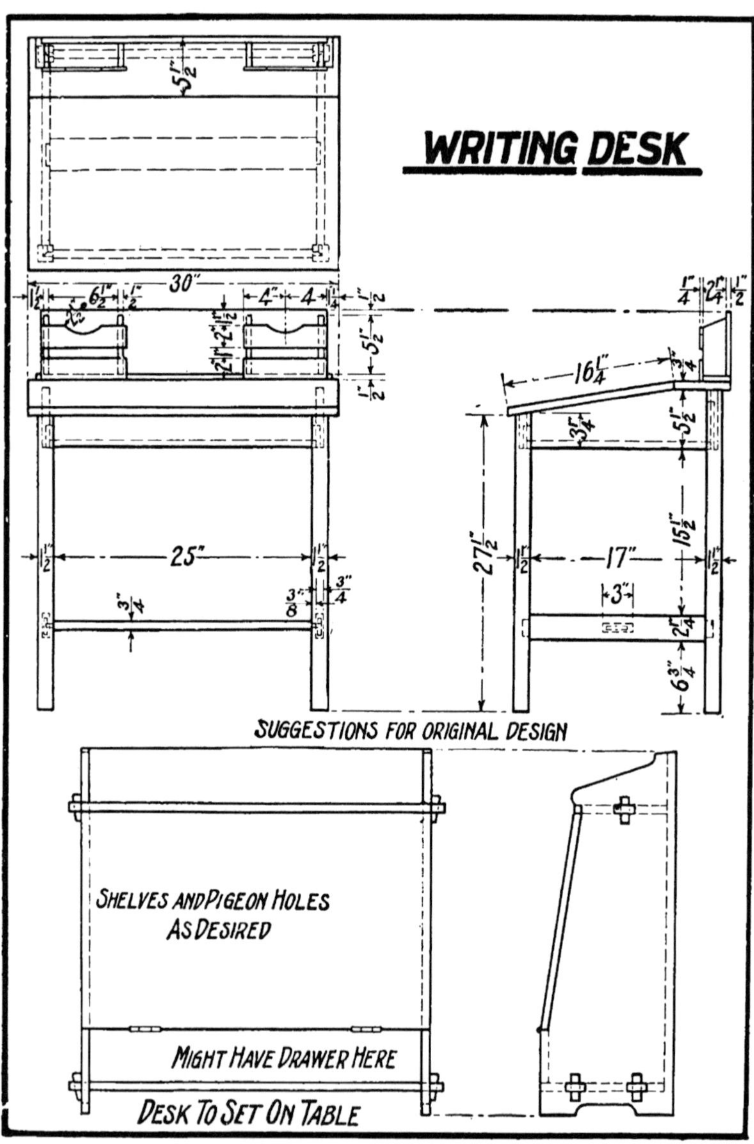
WRITING DESK
30"
25"
17"
27 1/2
16 1/4"
SUGGESTIONS FOR ORIGINAL DESIGN
SHELVES AND PIGEON HOLES
AS DESIRED
MIGHT HAVE DRAWER HERE
DESK TO SET ON TABLE

# WRITING DESK SPECIFICATIONS

## THE LEGS.

Although these legs are furnished S 4 S, it will be necessary for you to plane them with a very sharp plane, testing to make sure that they are perfectly square. Finish with a sharp steel scraper. In cutting the length of the legs note that the lid of the writing desk slants forward, and thus the front pair of legs is not so long as the rear pair. Observe that the lower edges of the side rail are perfectly square with the legs. These side rails are to join the legs with a mortise and tenon joint. If you will make the bottom end of the legs the working end, and make all measurements from these points, in locating the mortises, you will have no difficulty on account of the slant of the top. Lay out and cut the mortises.

## THE CROSS RAILS.

Square the stock and make the cross rails as indicated in the drawing. Notice that the back cross rail is the same width as the widest portion of the side cross rails (5½"). Form all tenons to fit their respective mortises.

Square the stock and make the lower cross rail. Cut the tenons, making sure that the distance between shoulders is the same as in the top cross rail.

## THE STRETCHER.

The stretcher is to join the lower cross rails with a mortise and tenon joint. Study the drawing carefully in getting the length of this piece. Notice that it will have to be longer than the top cross rail, because it does not stand between the legs, but is between the bottom cross rails.

## ASSEMBLING.

Assemble one side at a time. Glue all tenons in their places. Test to make sure that the legs and rails stand perfectly square. Clamp securely and allow the glue to harden. When you have assembled the right and left ends of the writing desk, put in the front and the rear rail and also the stretcher. Glue them in position and clamp them securely, making sure that all angles are perfectly square. (The plan of gluing and clamping a piece of work, part at a time, will usually insure satisfactory results.)

## THE TOP.

A portion of the top is perfectly level. This may be fastened with angle screws, or with blocks screwed on from the under side.

## THE LID.

This is to be made of two or more pieces glued and doweled together. In order that the lid may fit perfectly, it may be necessary to plane the top ends of the front leg and edges of the side rails. Do this very carefully, and lay the top in position to see that it fits properly. It will have to be beveled slightly at the top edge where it is to be hinged to the stationary portion of the top. The hinges must be gained into the wood, so as not to leave a crack at this joint.

## THE BACK AND LETTER POCKETS.

The back piece, which holds the letter pockets, is attached to a small base strip. The uprights and the main back piece are nailed through from the bottom of this base strip. This part may all be assembled independent of the remainder of the desk, and then fastened to the desk top with two screws in the bottom of each letter pocket; in this position the screws will not be seen.

## THE FINISHING.

When the work is all assembled, go over it with a sharp steel scraper and remove all pencil and tool marks; finish with fine sandpaper. Stain the desired color and finish with shellac or rub varnish.

**Optional and Home Projects Employing Similar Principles.**

## DRESSING TABLE.

1. By using this same plan of construction provided with a level top, and adding a wide central mirror, with a small mirror hinged on each side, a pleasing dressing table may be made.

## SERVING TABLE.

2. This plan of construction, with a very few modifications, will be suitable for a serving table.

# LIBRARY TABLE

MATERIALS.

Oak (Chap. III., Par. 29).

4 pcs. 1"x7¼"x49" S 2 S Top.

2 pcs. ⅞"x5¼"x48" S 2 S Top side rails.

2 pcs. ⅞"x5¼"x28" S 2 S Top end rails.

2 pcs. 1¾"x1¾"x26" S 4 S Leg cross rails.

| | | | |
|---|---|---|---|
| 1 pc. | 1"x8"x48" | S 2 S | Shelf. |
| 3 pcs. | ⅝"x4¼"x24" | S 2 S | Drawer sides and ends. |
| 2 pcs. | ⅞"x4½"x26" | S 2 S | Draw carrier supports. |
| 4 pcs. | 3½"x3½"x30" | S 4 S | Legs. |
| 2 pcs. | ⅝"x1½"x26" | S 4 S | Drawer carrier. |
| 8 pcs. | 1"x1"x5" | S 2 S | Corner blocks. |

1 pc. (3-ply) ¼"x15"x20" drawer bottom.
2 doz. 1½" No. 10 F. H. B. screws.
1 doz. 1½" brads.
1½" doz. 1¼" brads.
1 pc. 1¾"x1¾"x4" for knobs.
1 pc. ¼" dowel 27" long.

## INTRODUCTORY STATEMENT.

There is probably no one piece of furniture which is more popular than the library table; it has a function in every home and adds a touch of comfort and refinement which no other article can quite furnish.

The modern straight line design makes it possible to produce substantial and artistic effects in handmade furniture. The library table offers excellent opportunities to carry out these designs.

The design presented in this lesson will be found very pleasing in all its proportions and the construction has been worked out to avoid difficult and elaborate processes.

---

**References:**

The Practical Cabinet Maker and Furniture Designer, Hodgson. F. Drake Co., Chicago.
Windsor's Mission Furniture. Popular Mechanics Co., Chicago.

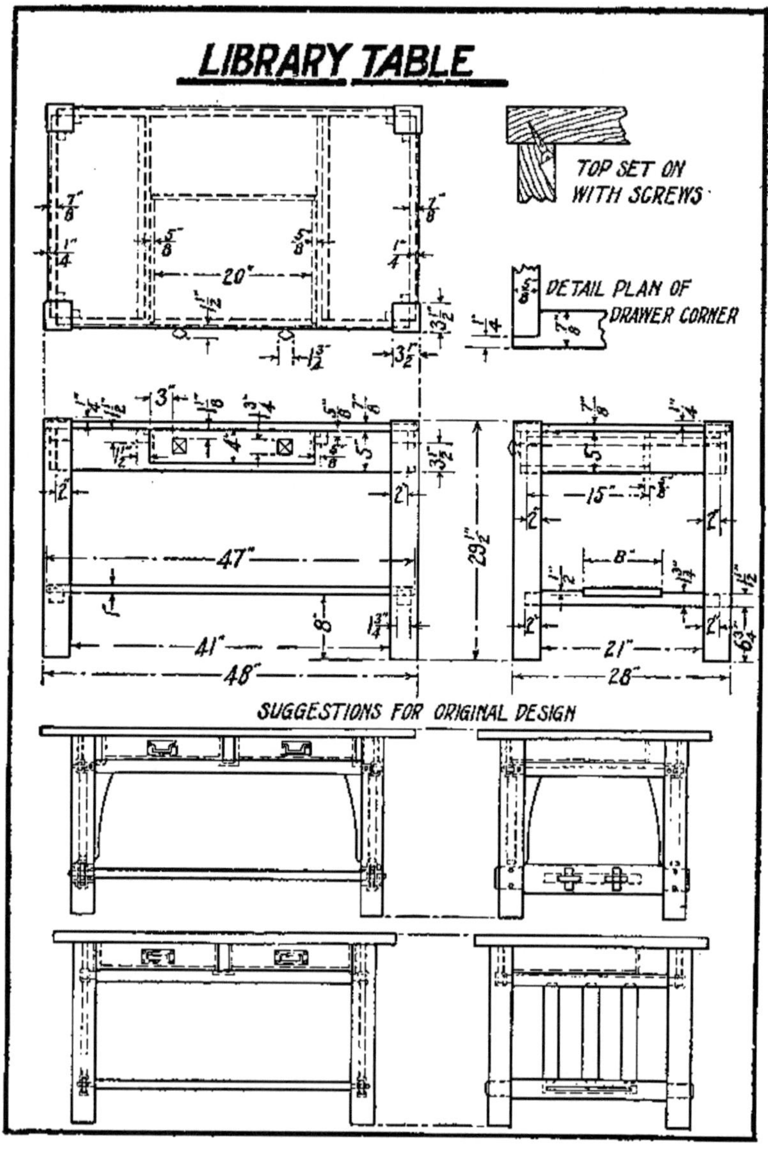
LIBRARY TABLE
TOP SET ON WITH SCREWS
DETAIL PLAN OF DRAWER CORNER
SUGGESTIONS FOR ORIGINAL DESIGN

# THE LIBRARY TABLE SPECIFICATIONS

## THE TOP.

The top is to be made by gluing together a number of pieces. This must be done with great care. Be sure that the edges are perfectly jointed. Assemble with dowels. Clamp securely and leave for at least twelve hours for the glue to harden.

## THE LEGS.

Although the legs are furnished S 4 S, it will be necessary to resurface them with a very sharp plane and finish with a sharp steel scraper. Lay out and cut the mortises as indicated in the drawing.

## THE TOP RAILS.

The top rails are to join the legs with mortise and tenon joints. Square the stock, lay out and make the rails. Form the tenons to fit the mortises in the legs. Be sure that the rails for opposite sides are exactly the same length between shoulders.

## LOWER CROSS RAILS.

The lower cross rails are to join the legs with mortise and tenon joints. Square the stock and cut these tenons to fit the mortises in the legs. Test each tenon in the mortise for which it is intended.

## ASSEMBLING.

Assemble one end at a time. Glue the tenons into the mortises, clamp securely, testing frequently with the square. It would be well to allow this section to harden before continuing the assembling. In like manner assemble the second end.

It will be noticed that the front cross rail has an opening cut for the drawer. This should be done before it is assembled. Complete the assembling of the frame by gluing the two cross rails in position and clamping.

## THE SHELF.

Square the stock and prepare the shelf, which is to serve as a stretcher, and brace the lower end of the legs. This shelf is set into the cross rails, and is fastened to them with screws from the lower side. Be sure that the legs stand perfectly square with the top rail when these screws are inserted.

## THE TOP.

Remove the clamps from the top and plane it perfectly smooth. Finishing the top is the most important part of this piece of work; it must be done perfectly. Use the steel scraper to make sure all plane marks, and rough places are removed. It will be observed that notches are cut in the corners to allow the legs to extend through slightly; this must be done with great care, for these joints will be exposed. The top ends of the legs should be rounded, or chamfered, and perfectly smoothed before the top is fastened on. When the top is perfectly fitted, it should be fastened in position with screws.

## THE DRAWER.

Prepare the drawer front so it will fit snugly into the opening left for the drawer. Rabbet the ends to receive the side rails, as shown in the detail in the drawing. Prepare the back and side rails. The side rails are to be plowed to receive the ¼" three-ply bottom.

## ASSEMBLING THE DRAWER.

The drawer should be assembled with nails. The side pieces, are to be nailed into the rabbet formed at each end of the drawer front. Test to make sure that it is perfectly square, when the bottom is nailed in.

## DRAWER CARRIER.

The drawer carriers are rabbeted strips nailed entirely across the lower side of the table top; small strips nailed on the sides of the drawer slide in these rabbets. Adjust these carriers so the drawer will work smoothly.

## THE KNOBS.

The knobs are to be made of wood, shaped to suit your taste.

## FINISHING.

When the work is entirely assembled, go over it with a sharp steel scraper and finish with very fine sandpaper. Stain it the desired color; give it a coat of filler, or shellac and finish with rub varnish.

### Optional and Home Projects Employing Similar Principles.

1. SCHOOL COOKING TABLE.
2. LABORATORY TABLE.
3. SEWING TABLE.

## SUGGESTIONS FOR COMMUNITY RESEARCH.

No. 1. Examine the methods of hanging porch swings in your community and see what advantages and disadvantages you observe in each.

No. 2. Examine the finish on the furniture in your home. Can you determine how it was made? Call at a local furniture store and ask the clerk to show you some waxed furniture and some that has a rub varnish finish. Ask him to explain the advantages of each.

No. 3. In designing any piece of furniture, the most important point to consider is, that it shall be useful for the purpose for which it is intended, and second that it shall be pleasing in appearance. Ask your local furniture dealer to show you the points of advantage in different styles of chairs, tables and other furniture. Examine the furniture in your home and see whether it is all well designed.

No. 4. What will be the result if a wide board is laid flat upon the ground and left for some time? Which way will it warp? You will find it interesting to experiment with a worthless board in this manner, noticing which way it warps; turn it over and note the results after a few days. This may help you to understand the action which often takes place if you stain or shellac only one side of a thin board.

No. 5. Perhaps you can find some piece of construction work about the school, or at home, in which the joints have opened slightly. What does this indicate regarding the condition of the lumber when the piece of work was constructed?

No. 6. Do you know of any batten doors about the buildings of your neighborhood? Examine these doors to see whether or not they are properly braced. What remedy can you suggest for a batten door that is beginning to sag? Have you tried it?

No. 7. For what purposes have you seen cedar wood used? Examine as many wood fence posts as you can find and see what sort of timber they are. Remove some of the dirt from around the post and scratch the post with your pocketknife to determine how deeply it has rotted. What kind of timber shows the greatest endurance? It may be necessary for you to inquire how long some of these posts have been in the ground.

## REVIEW QUESTIONS AND PROBLEMS.

1. Mention two or three points which should have careful consideration in designing a porch swing.

2. Name three kinds of wood which would be suitable for a porch swing.

3. What is meant by straight line designs in furniture?

4. Give two reasons why quartered oak is preferable to plain sawn oak for furniture construction.

5. Why is quartered oak more expensive than plain sawn oak?

6. About what per cent. would you have to add to the price of a plain oak piano bench to equal the price of the same bench made of quartered oak?

7. How is a fine varnish finish produced?

8. What are some of the advantages and disadvantages of a wax finish?

9. What are the important properties that make red cedar a very valuable wood?

10. For what purposes have you used three-ply material in your shop work? What advantages has it over a single board of equal thickness?

11. What kind of woods require a filler in producing a fine finish? Why is this true?

12. Estimate the number of board feet in each article which you have made from this section. Find out the price per hundred and figure the cost.

13. How could you tell what price to ask if you were offering a shop-made article for sale?

14. If by taking a course of training as a mechanic a boy can increase his wages from $7 to $12 per week, how much would his increase be for a year? If his course cost him $750, how long would it take for his increase in wages to repay the entire expense?

15. Suppose John and Harry are two boys of equal age, ability and opportunities; John quits school and goes to work at $8 per week; Harry continues in school and after four years of industrial training goes to work at $15 per week. After Harry has been at work ten years (John fourteen) how much has each earned? Suppose it cost Harry $200 per year to remain in school, after returning that money, how much has he profited over John? Which boy's future is most promising?

# SUPPLEMENT

# CHAPTER I

# MECHANICAL AND SHOP DRAWINGS

THE subject of drawing is very important in all lines of industrial work. A photograph, picture or perspective drawing shows how a thing will appear, but does not give dimensions nor show the detail of how it is made. A workman who is going to execute a piece of work in the shop must know the exact size and shape of every part. In order that the man who is designing the work may give correct ideas to him the science of mechanical drawing has been developed.

When you first look at a mechanical drawing it seems very complicated; it is not expected that you should be able to tell immediately just how it is constructed. It requires considerable thought and study to understand a mechanical drawing well enough to undertake the work. In fact, you must use your imagination a great deal, but after you have studied a few mechanical drawings they will soon become quite clear. There are just a few things which you need to know about the subject of drawing in order to interpret mechanical drawings correctly, because there are certain recognized and established ways of representing certain ideas. These established ways are called conventions and you should acquaint yourself with these conventions so you will understand exactly what they mean.

## HEAVY LINES.

Heavy, solid, black lines are used to denote edges of material which stand in plain view.

Very heavy lines are also used for border lines.

## DOTTED LINES.

In looking at an object there are of course a great many parts and lines which you are unable to see from any one view. In a picture these would not be presented at all, but in mechanical drawing the hidden parts are represented by dotted lines. At first they may have a tendency to confuse you just a little, but if you will remember that dotted lines always represent parts which lie back of the parts represented by the heavy line, you will soon learn to understand mechanical drawings.

## DIMENSIONS.

One of the most important things about a mechanical drawing is the fact that it gives dimensions, that is, it tells the exact size of every part. In order that you may understand perfectly the point from which the measurements are taken, broken lines are used with little arrow heads at each end to show you where the dimensions start and end. To illustrate, if you see a broken line with a figure 12″ somewhere in the line, that means that in the finished article it is 12 inches from the point represented by one arrow head to the other.

## CIRCLES.

Circles and curves are usually indicated in mechanical drawings by having the diameter (marked D) or the radius (marked R) given. The point where the compass should rest when the circle is drawn is also indicated. In measuring distances between circles the measurements are taken from the center of one to the center of the other.

## SCALE.

Mechanical drawings are usually drawn to some definite scale, because it is not often practical to make a drawing the same size as the object, unless the object is very small. By drawing to scale, we mean that the drawing is a certain fractional part of the size of the complete object. For illustration, 1″ is sometimes used to represent 1 ft. or ½″ or ¼″ for a foot. Of course, if the drawing is for some very large piece of construction, such as a house or a bridge, small fractions of an inch will be used to represent a foot; if the drawing deals with some smaller article, as a chair or footstool, 1″, 2″, 4″, or even 6″, may be used to represent a foot. It must be remembered, however, that the dimensions given on the drawings always refer to the sizes of the completed article and not to the size of the drawing.

## VIEWS.

In mechanical or shop drawing it is customary to give three views of the thing which is to be built, and of an ordinary piece of work the three views will be sufficient. However, if the thing is very complicated it may then be necessary to make more than the three views. But the three regular views, known as the *plan, front elevation and end elevation,* are the ones that are commonly presented. These are the regular views used throughout this text.

## PLAN.

The plan of an object simply shows how it would appear if looked down upon directly from above. Of course it would be impossible to get in a position where you could see all of an article exactly as shown in the plan, for the plan represents it as seen in parallel lines, that is, as though you were looking straight down upon every part at the same time. All parts which would be in view from this position are indicated by solid black lines in the drawing; of course there would be many underneath and hidden parts to be shown by dotted lines.

## FRONT ELEVATION.

By the front elevation we mean the representation of the article as seen from straight in front, when it is (sitting) on its natural base. The front elevation is seen at right angles to the plan; the hidden parts are represented in their proper positions by dotted lines.

## END ELEVATION.

By the end elevation we mean the appearance of the article from the right end, exactly at right angles to the plan and to the front elevation. Of course in the end elevation the black lines would represent the parts which would stand in plain view as seen from the end, and the dotted lines would represent the hidden or unseen parts in their proper positions. You will notice that this principle is true of each view. These three views of an object should be sufficient to enable one to form a clear idea of the full construction. Learn to study the drawings very carefully in order to get the desired information; this is exactly what every mechanic who works at any line of construction work must do. If you will provide yourself with the proper equipment and work out the following lessons in Mechanical Drawing you will then understand these principles pretty thoroughly. This is an important part of industrial work, for you should learn not only to read drawings, but to prepare simple working drawings for anything which you may desire to make. Throughout this book the photographs at the opening of each lesson will give you a clear idea of the appearance of the object presented and the working drawings will show you its exact construction.

## THE DRAWING OUTFIT.

The drawing outfit need not be expensive, but it should be good enough to enable you to do accurate work; you can make your own drawing board and T-square by following the instructions given in this text.

The following illustration shows rather a complete outfit, some of the articles may be omitted in your early work:

Figure 1.

## THE DRAWING INSTRUMENTS.

Drawing instruments are furnished at prices ranging from a few cents up to many dollars; your work will not demand a very expensive set, but it should contain at least the following tools of a very substantial quality. (*See Figure* 2.)

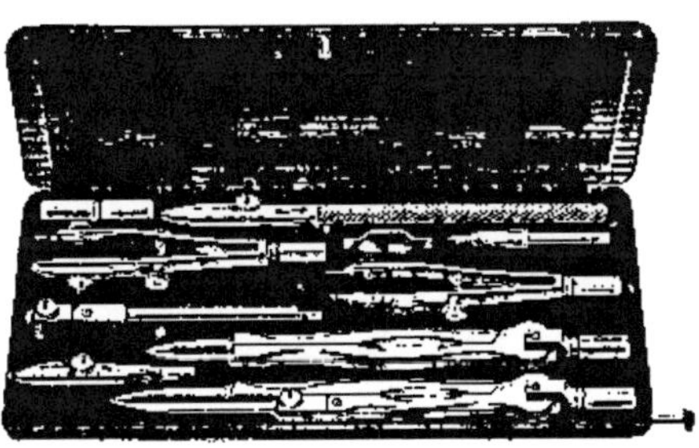

Figure 2.

One ruling pen.

One steel spring bow pencil.

One steel spring bow pen.

One plane divider.

Compasses with fixed needle point, pen and pencil points.

Box of leads.

The other instruments sometimes found in the drawing set are very convenient but not absolutely necessary for your early work.

## THE DRAWING BOARD.

A drawing board is simply a plain, smooth board with at least one absolutely straight edge. It should be made of some kind of soft wood which will easily receive the thumb tacks; either white pine or basswood is generally used.

The size is not material, although a board about sixteen or eighteen inches wide by twenty-two or twenty-four inches long will be found satisfactory for school use. (*See Figure* 3.)

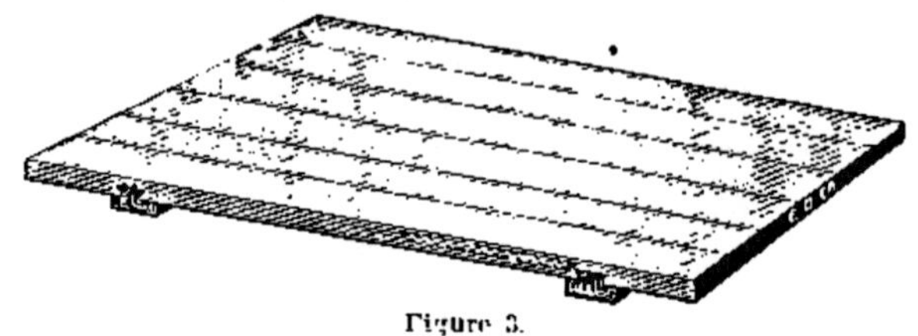

Figure 3.

## TRIANGLES.

You should have two triangles, one 8-inch 45-degree (*See Figure* 4) and one 8-inch 30x60-degree (*See Figure* 5). The triangles are to be used (resting on the top edge of the T-square, properly held) to draw all vertical and oblique lines. Triangles are made of various kinds of material, but the transparent ones will give best satisfaction.

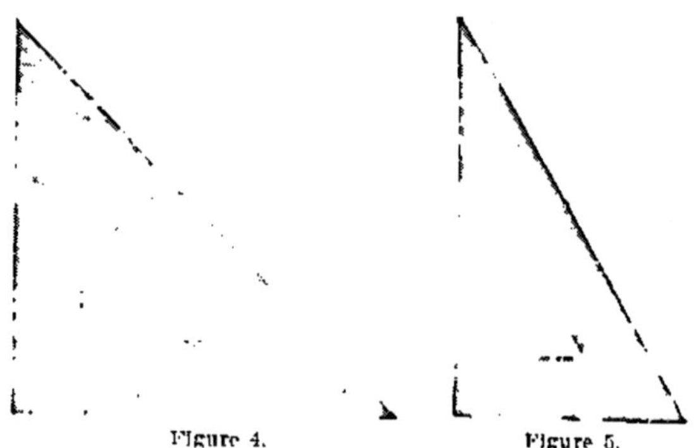

Figure 4. Figure 5.

## THE T-SQUARE.

The purpose of the T-square (which must have a perfectly straight blade) is to draw parallel horizontal lines; it should never be used to draw vertical lines. Its position is always against the lefthand edge of the board; it is not to be shifted about from one edge to another. The top edge of the square is to serve as a straight edge in ruling lines; the bottom edge is not to be used. (*See Figure* 6.)

Figure 6.

## RULER OR SCALE.

The ruler, or scale as it is usually called, is a triangular box-wood rule with the various fractional parts of an inch accurately marked. (*See Figure* 7.) An ordinary flat ruler may be used, but it is difficult to make absolutely accurate measurements with such a scale. You will observe that the inch marks do not continue to the extreme ends of the triangular scale; this is done to make sure that if the ends are damaged accurate measurements will not be hindered. The scale is to be used only in making measurements; it should never be used in ruling lines.

Figure 7.

## THE IRREGULAR CURVE.

Figure 8.

The irregular curve is used in drawing designs which employ curves that cannot be laid out with the compass. (*See Figure* 8.) It is not absolutely necessary, particularly in your early work, but it will be a great help in later work when you wish to lay out graceful designs.

## OTHER ARTICLES NEEDED.

One-half dozen thumb tacks with which to fasten the drawing paper to the board.

One rubber eraser.

One bottle of waterproof black drawing ink.

One penholder and fine pen-point.

Supply of drawing paper.

One drawing pencil. For this work you will need to use a very hard lead pencil; about No. 4H will be satisfactory. The pencil must be kept sharp; some draftsmen sharpen their pencils on both ends, making one point very slender and round while the other point is sharpened chisel shape; some prefer to have two pencils for this purpose. The round point is used in locating points and making measurements; the chisel point is used in drawing lines. You should have a small piece of fine sand-paper upon which to rub the pencil point in keeping it very keen.

## PRACTICE EXERCISE.

Cut your drawing paper to some convenient size; it is not material what size you use, but it would be well to decide upon the size you expect to make your plates or drawings and have them all uniform in size and shape; this will make your work neat and systematic, and will aid you considerably in taking care of the drawings when you have a number of them completed. The paper is to be fastened onto the drawing board with thumb tacks. To do this fasten one of the upper corners of the paper by pushing the thumb tack through it into the board, then hold the T-square with the head firmly against the lefthand edge of the drawing board and set the paper exactly straight with the upper edge of the T-square; insert thumb tacks at each corner to hold the paper perfectly smooth; push the tacks in such a position that the tendency is to tighten the paper without crimping it.

With your scale and round-pointed lead pencil lay out small dots one-half inch apart from bottom to top along the lefthand edge of your paper; hold the T-square in its proper position and rule a horizontal line across the paper through each of these points. These lines should be exactly parallel.

Lay out similar dots on the top line; hold your T-square in its proper position, and with one of your triangles resting exactly upon the upper edge of the T-square, rule a vertical line through each of these points. It will require a little care to hold the T-square and triangle in their proper positions while drawing vertical lines. In slipping the triangle from one point to another, be very careful not to allow the square to get out of position.

If these lines are properly drawn your paper will be laid out in half-inch squares; you might use the other edge of your triangles and draw oblique lines.

## MARGINAL OR BORDER LINES.

Drawing sheets are usually laid out with a very heavy line ruled around the edge, thus leaving a margin entirely around the drawing. You can decide about the width of your margins when you are determining the size and shape of your sheets.

## INKING.

After drawings are laid out with the lead pencil, they are inked to make them clear and permanent. The inking is done with the ruling pen, found in the set of drawing instruments. Do not dip this pen into the ink, but with your steel pen or the quill which is in the cork of the ink bottle put a little ink between the nibs of the ruling pen. The width of the line made by the ruling pen can be changed by loosening or tightening the small set-screw on the side of the pen. Always test the pen on a scrap of drawing paper or on the margin which is to be cut off of your drawing. Use the pen in much the same manner in which you used the pencil in ruling the lines; however, you must be careful not to allow ink to get on the edge of the triangle or T-square. The only way to become skillful at this process is by careful practice.

Be sure to clean your pen thoroughly before laying it away.

## LETTERING.

There is nothing which adds to the general appearance of a drawing so much as neat, attractive lettering. This does not mean that fancy and elaborate decorative lettering is advised, but that on all drawings the lettering should be clear and easily read; the style and spacing of letters should be uniform. The matter of slant is not important so long as it does not vary in the same drawing.

For all practical purposes lettering must be speedily as well as neatly done, so it is neeessary to develop skill in making letters freehand. Rule lines to guide you in the height of the letters, but train your eye and hand to space and execute the letters and figures without any further guide. Become familiar with some one form and style of letter and practice it until you can make that alphabet speedily and well. (*See Figure* 9.)

The following types are given to assist you in acquiring form; you should practice them over and over. You should frequently lay out and execute complete letter sheets the same size and style as your other drawing plates.

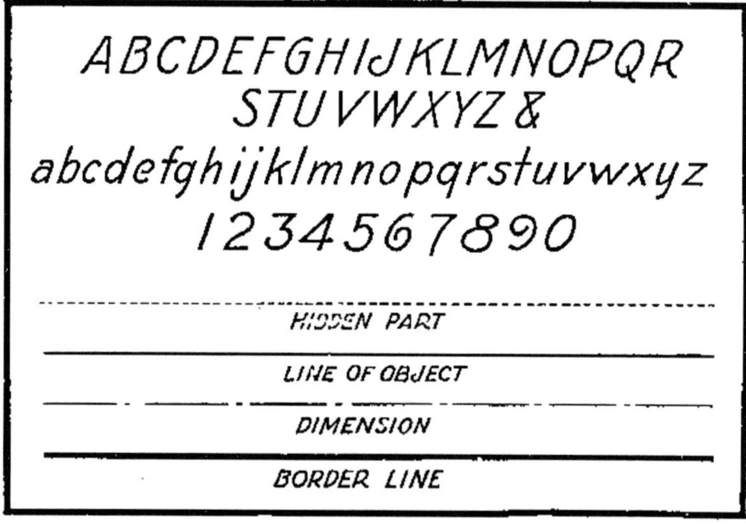


Figure 9.

## PROBLEMS IN CONSTRUCTION.

The following problems in construction will give you practice with the drawing instruments and will help you to understand some of the most important principles of mechanical drawing. The directions for the drawing are given in such a way as to allow you to think for yourself; the supplementary problems should also be worked out if time will permit, for they are intended to give further application of the principles set forth in the regular problems.

## WORKING DRAWINGS.

The matter of how working drawings are prepared for the shop is clearly explained in plate V. You should give this plate careful study, for it sets forth the principles upon which all the working drawings of this book are made.

For practice in this part of your drawing work use the shop projects, and after studying the drawings furnished, together with the suggestions, prepare working drawings of your own, employing original ideas as much as you can without violating any principles of construction. You will have to discuss these points with your teacher.

## PROBLEMS

(See Plate I., Page 299.)

**Problem No. 1—To Bi-Sect a Given Line.**

Let line AB be the given line. With a pencil compass set at a distance greater than one-half the length of line AB, using A as a center, draw an arc below and one above the line; using B as a center, with the same radius, draw arcs above and below the line, intersecting in points C and D respectively. Rule a line to connect points C and D. Point O, where this line intersects line AB, will be the point of bi-section (half way between points A and B).

In shop practice a line is usually bi-sected by measurements made with the scale, or dividers.

**Problem No. 2—To Erect a Line Perpendicular to a Given Line at a Given Point.**

Let AB be the given line and P a point within the line to which the perpendicular is to be erected. With the compasses set at any convenient radius, using P as a center, draw an arc cutting the line AB on each side of point P. Mark these points C and D respectively. With the compasses set at any radius somewhat greater than PD, using D as a center, draw an arc above the line AB; with the same radius, using C as a center, draw an arc intersecting the first arc. Rule a line E to P. This is the required perpendicular.

In shop practice this perpendicular would be erected by placing a triangle on the T-square and drawing the perpendicular line through the required point.

**Problem No. 3—From a Given Point Outside a Line to Drop a Perpendicular to the Line.**

Let AB be the given line and P the point outside the line. With the compasses set at any convenient radius, using P as a center, draw an arc cutting the line AB at points C and D. With the compass set at any convenient radius greater than one-half of CD, using D as a center, draw an arc above the line AB. Using C as a center, with the same radius, draw another arc, intersecting the first arc at point E. Rule a line passing through points P and E to the line AB. This will be the required perpendicular.

In shop practice this perpendicular would be drawn by the use of a triangle resting on the T-square.

**Problem No. 4—Through a Given Point to Draw a Line Parallel to a Given Line.**

Let AB be the given line and P the given point. With P as a center and the compasses set at any convenient radius great enough to cut the line AB, draw an arc cutting line AB at point Q. With Q as a center, and the same radius, draw an arc cutting the line AB at R (it will pass through the point P). Set the compasses with a radius equal to RP, using Q as a center, draw an arc cutting the first arc at point S. Rule a line through points P and S. This is the required line.

In shop practice this parallel line, if horizontal, would be drawn with the T-square; if vertical, with the triangle resting on the T-square.

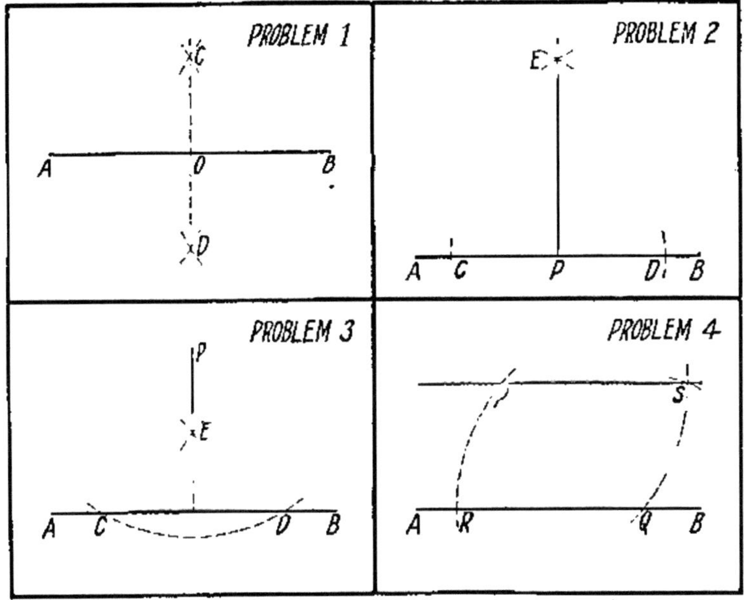


Plate I.

## SUPPLEMENTARY PROBLEMS.

**Problem A—To Erect a Perpendicular and the End of a Given Line.**

Draw a line AB. Assume a point P, any convenient position outside this line. With P as a center, and a radius equal the distance from P to B, draw a circle passing through B and cutting the line AB at the point C. Draw a line from C to P and extend it to intersect the circumference at F. Draw the line FB. This will be the required perpendicular at the end of the line.

In regular shop practice the perpendicular at the end of the line will be drawn with the triangle.

**Problem B—To Bi-Sect Any Given Arc.**

With the compasses draw any arc AB. Connect points A and B with a straight line. This straight line is called a chord. Bi-sect this chord with a perpendicular line (Problem 1). This perpendicular line will also bi-sect the arc.

**Problem C—(Test Problem).**

With your T-square draw a horizontal line AB. From any point P in this line erect a perpendicular with one of the triangles. Test the accuracy of this perpendicular by the method given in Problem 2.

**Problem D—(Test Problem).**

With your T-square draw two parallel horizontal lines and with your triangle draw two vertical parallel lines. Test both pairs of lines (Problem 4) to determine whether or not they are accurate.

**Problem No. 5—To Divide a Given Line Into Any Number of Equal Parts.**

Let AB be the given line, which, for illustration, we will divide into six equal parts. Draw the line AH at any convenient angle to line AB. Lay off six equal parts on line AH. This may be done by setting the dividers at any convenient distance and beginning at A mark off the required number of parts. Letter these points C, D, E, F, G, H; from H draw the line HB. From the other points in line AH draw lines parallel to line HB, cutting line AB; letter the points of intersection M, L, K, J, I. These lines will divide AB into the required six equal parts.

In shop practice these parallel lines would be drawn by the use of triangles.

**Problem No. 6—To Bi-Sect Any Angle.**

Let ABC be the given angle. With B as a center, at any convenient radius draw an arc cutting AB and CB and letter these points D and E respectively. With any convenient radius greater than one-half of DE, using D as a center, draw an arc. With the same radius, using E as a center, draw an arc intersecting the first. Letter this point of intersection F. Draw a line connecting points F and B. This is the required bi-section; that is, it divides the angle into two equal parts.

**Problem No. 7—To Construct a Triangle Having Its Three Sides Given.**

Let lines AB, CD and EF, respectively, be the given sides with which to construct a triangle. Draw a line OP equal to the line AB. Set the compasses to a radius equal to CD; using point P as a center, draw an arc above the line OP. Set the compasses to a radius equal the line EF. Using the point O as a center, describe an arc, cutting the first arc at point Q. Connect point Q to points O and P. This will be the required triangle.

**Problem No. 8—To Transfer An Angle.**

Let ABC be the given angle. Draw any line EF. On the given angle, using B as a center, and any radius, draw an arc cutting the sides of the angle at M and N. With the same radius, using E as a center, draw an indefinite arc, cutting the line EF at P. Now on the given angle set the compasses to a radius equal NM. Using P as a center, draw an arc cutting the first indefinite arc at point Q. Draw the line ED through the point Q. DEF will be the required transferred angle.

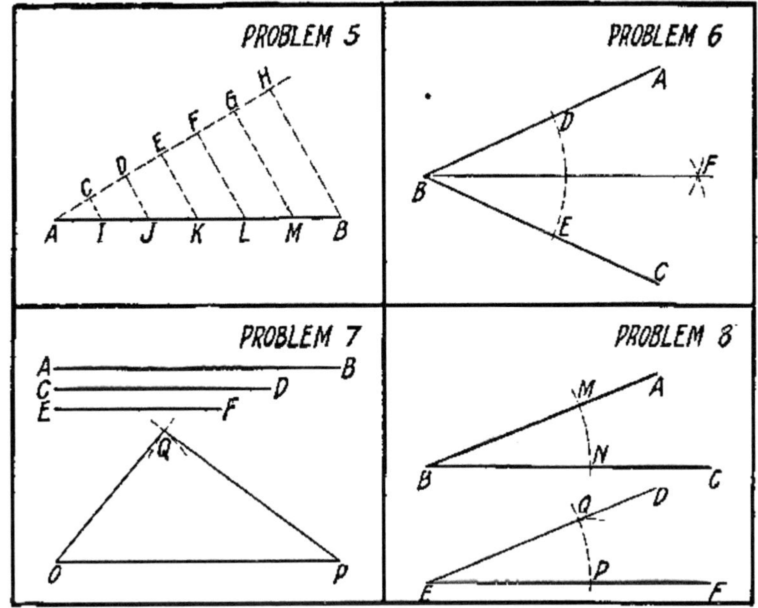


Plate II.

## SUPPLEMENTARY PROBLEMS.

**Problem E—A Circle Contains 360 Degrees.**

Draw any circle and with a T-square draw a horizontal diameter passing through point O, the center. At point O draw a vertical diameter. These four angles will be right angles. How many degrees will each contain?

**Problem F—Draw a Right Angle (With the T-Square and Triangle).**

Bi-sect this angle by method in Problem 6. How many degrees in each of the small angles? This angle is called a half-pitch cut (Chapter II, Par. 24. Chapter V, Par. 75).

**Problem G—Draw a Circle With Point O as the Center.**

Around point O how many 30-degree angles can be constructed? Draw them. How many 45-degree angles? Draw another circle and divide it into 45-degree angles.

**Problem H—Draw an Equilateral Triangle, One Side Being Given.**

Draw the line AB the length of the given side. With the compasses set to the radius AB, using A as a center, draw an arc. With the same radius, using B as the center, draw an arc intersecting the first arc. Letter this point of intersection C. Join C with A and with B. This will be the desired equilateral triangle.

**Problem No. 9—To Construct a Triangle Having Given One Side and the Two Adjacent Angles.**

Let line AB be the given side, angle CDE and FHG the two adjacent angles. Draw line XY equal to AB. Using X for the vertex, draw the angle KXL equal to the angle CDE. Using Y for the vertex, draw the angle MYN equal the angle FHG (this should be done by the method of transferring angles already given). Produce the sides of the angles thus constructed until they meet at point Z. ZXY will be the required triangle.

**Problem No. 10—To Inscribe a Circle in a Given Triangle.**

Let ABC be the given triangle. In order to inscribe the circle it will be necessary to find the center. To do this bi-sect any two angles (by the process already learned). Bi-sect the angle ABC with the line HB. Bi-sect the angle ACB with the line GC. These bi-sectors will intersect at the point K. Using K as a center and a radius equal to the perpendicular distance to any side of the triangle, draw the required inscribed circle.

**Problem No. 11—To Circumscribe a Circle About a Given Triangle, Or to Describe An Arc Or Circumference Through Three Given Points Not in the Same Straight Line.**

Let ABC be the vertices of the triangle (three points not in a straight line). Bi-sect any two sides of the triangle (by the process already learned). Side AB will be bi-sected by the line FG; side BC by the line DE. Produce these perpendicular bi-sectors until they intersect at point K. Point K is the center of the required circle. Using K as a center, with a radius equal to the distance AK, draw the required circle through A, B and C.

**Problem No. 12—To Construct an Equilateral Triangle Having the Altitude Given.**

Let line AB be the given altitude. Through the extremities of this line draw parallel lines, CD and GH perpendicular to line AB. With A as a center, and any convenient radius, draw the semi-circle CD. With C and D as centers, using the same radius, draw arcs, cutting the semi-circle at points E and F, respectively. Draw AE and AF; produce them to cut the line GH. AGH is the required equilateral triangle.

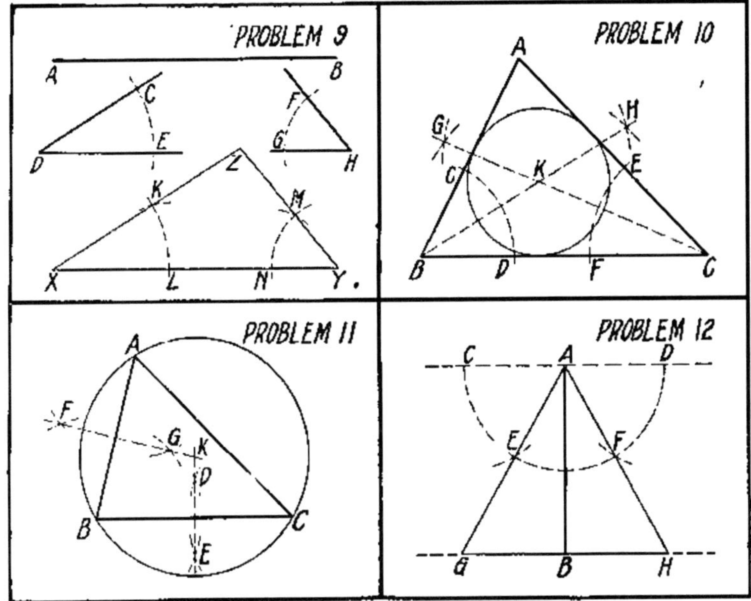


Plate III.

## SUPPLEMENTARY PROBLEMS.

**Problem I—The Sum of the Three Angles of Any Triangle Is Equal to 180 Degrees (the Total Angles on One Side of a Straight Line), Having Two Angles Given, to Find the Third Angle of Any Triangle.**

Let MNO be one of the angles, QRS the second, to find the third angle of the triangle; draw a straight line AB. At any point P in this line transfer the angle MNO, making the vertex fall on P. Let the line AP form one side of the angle. In like manner transfer the angle QRS, letting the vertex R fall on point P; letting PB form one side of the angle. The remaining angle would be the required angle.

**Problem J—To Construct a Triangle Having Two Sides and the Included Angle Given.**

Let MN and PQ be the two sides, and RST the given angle. Draw the line AB equal to the side PQ; transfer the angle RST making its vertex on point B. Prolong the side of the angle the length of the side MN, mark this point C; connect C with A. This will be the required triangle.

**Problem K—**

(Test problem in actual measurement). To find the largest circle that can be drawn in an equilateral triangle with one side given.

Draw the equilateral triangle of given size (Problem 7); inscribe the circle (Problem 10). Measure the diameter with the scale.

**Problem L—To Inscribe a Square in a Given Circle.**

In the given circle draw two diameters at right angles to each other (T square and triangles). Connect the points where these diameters cut the circumference; this rectangle will be the required square.

By drawing and actual measurements find the largest square that can be cut from a circular board 9 inches in diameter.

**Problem 13—To Inscribe a Regular Hexagon in a Given Circle.**

With A as a center, draw any circle. With the T-square draw the diameter of the given circle, cutting the circumference in points F and C. With the compasses set to the same radius with which the circle was drawn, using C as a center, draw arcs B and D above and below the diameter, respectively. With F as the center, and the same radius, draw arcs G and E. Connect these six points with straight lines, thus forming the required hexagon.

**Problem 14—To Construct an Octagon in a Given Square.**

Let ABCD be the given square. Draw the diagonals AD and BC intersecting at point E. With the compasses set to a radius equal to DE (one-half the diagonal), using D as a center, draw an arc intersecting the square at points G and F. Using B as a center, and the same radius, draw an arc intersecting the square at points H and I; using A as a center, draw an arc intersecting at J and K. Using C as a center, draw an arc intersecting at L and M. Draw lines from M to I, from G to J, from H to L and K to F, thus forming the required octagon.

**Problem No. 15—To Draw an Ellipse When the Two Axes (Diameters) Are Given.**

Draw the major axis AC; draw the minor axis BD perpendicular to AC at its middle point. Make BO equal to OD. With O as the center and a radius equal to OC, draw the circle A, E, F, G, P, C. With O as a center and a radius equal to OB, draw the circle IKNRT. Draw a number of radii from O, cutting both the circumferences. These radii may be drawn with the use of the 60 and 45-degree triangles. From the point where these radii intersect the inner circle draw horizontal lines (with the T-square). From the point where these radii intersect the larger circle draw vertical lines (with the triangle). Where these vertical and horizontal lines intersect will be points in the required ellipse. Locate a number of such points. Usually about four or five will be sufficient in each quarter of the circle. Draw a freehand curve touching all these points.

**Problem 16—To Construct an Ellipse With the Use of a Trammel.**

Draw the major and the minor axis as explained in Problem 15, letting AC be the major axis and BD the minor axis. Prepare a strip of cardboard, or paper, having a straight edge, and mark off EG equal to one-half the major axis and FG equal to one-half the minor axis. Place this slip of paper in a number of positions, keeping point E on the minor axis and F on the major axis. Point G will thus locate a number of points in the desired ellipse. Connect these points by means of a freehand curve.

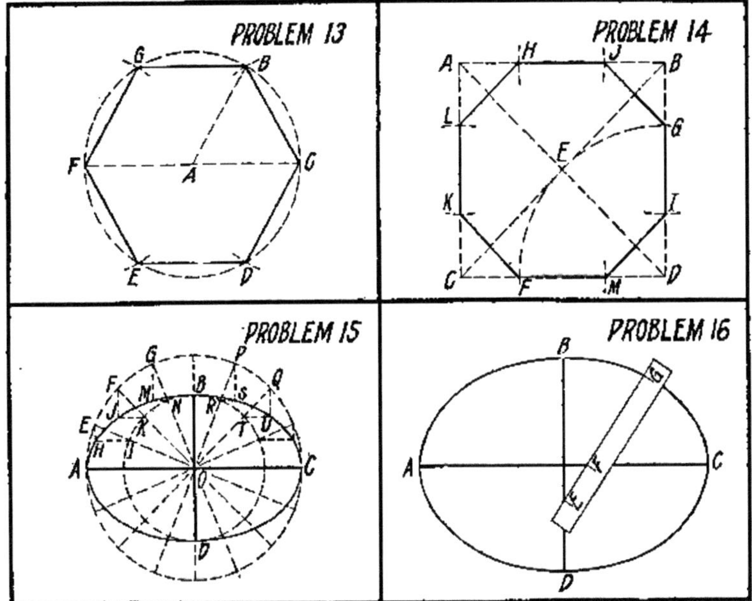


Plate IV.

Problem M—

## SUPPLEMENTARY PROBLEMS.

To draw a line tangent to a circle at a given point on the circumference.

With O as a center and any radius draw a circle; let P be the given point on the circumference. Join point P with the center O; through point P draw a line AP perpendicular to OP. This is the required tangent.

Problem N—

To draw angles of given number of degrees by use of the triangles.

Draw a semi-circle and by using the 45-degree and the 30-degree triangles divide it into angles of 15 degrees. Use your triangles in various combinations and draw as many different angles as you can.

Problem O—

Draw a right angle triangle with the altitude equal to the base; this forms what is known as a half-pitch angle, or cut-in rafter or brace construction (Chapter II, Paragraph 24, and Chapter V, Paragraph 75).

Draw a right angle triangle with the altitude equal to two-thirds of the base; this forms the third pitch cut (Chapter II, Paragraph 25, and Chapter V, Paragraph 76).

Draw a right angle triangle with the altitude equal to one-half of the base; this forms the quarter-pitch cut (Chapter II, Paragraph 26, and Chapter V, Paragraph 77).

Problem P—

Shop method of drawing an ellipse (with a string) when the two diameters are given.

Draw the longer diameter AB, at its middle point O draw the shorter diameter CD perpendicular to AB; make OC equal to OD. (The lines must cross at the middle point in each.)

With the compasses set to a radius equal to OA, using C as a center, draw arcs cutting AB in points X and Y.

Drive a small brad in point X, and another in point Y, another might be temporarily driven in point C; tie a string around the three brads; remove the brad from point C, insert the point of a lead pencil and swing it around, thus drawing the required ellipse.

# EXPLANATION OF PROJECTION DRAWING.

You have already been told that in shop drawings we use three views, the plan which represents the appearance of the object as seen from above; the front elevation, its appearance as seen from straight in front; and the end elevation, as seen from the right end.

At first it may seem a little difficult to understand these views. A careful study of Plate V will make the matter clear. In the upper half of this plate you will see a perspective drawing of a bracket shelf, represented as though it were surrounded by a glass box. On the top side, marked plan, you will see a drawing representing the portion of the bracket shelf which would appear on this piece of glass, if the parts directly below were projected upon it; the dotted lines represent the underneath parts. On the front side, marked front elevation, you will see a representation of the front of the bracket shelf projected. On the end, marked end elevation, there is a representation of the end of the bracket shelf projected.

If the top portion of the imaginary glass box should be raised, as though it were hinged on the line AB, and the end portion were opened as though it were hinged on the line BD, the three drawings would stand in the positions shown on the lower half of this plate. This explains how the three regular views of any article are made, and just how they should be arranged on the paper.

If the left end of an article is entirely different to the right, another end elevation would be given showing the detail of the left end. If the second end is not shown it is always understood to be identical with the end elevation which is shown.

For further practice in mechanical drawing, you should make practical application of all of the principles which you have learned, by constructing regular three-view drawings of the articles which you are to make in the shop. Further problems dealing with the subject of shop drawings are not given here, because any of the lessons presented throughout the text may be used as models and types, for development of as many plates dealing with shop problems as the time of the class and the inclination of the teacher may direct.

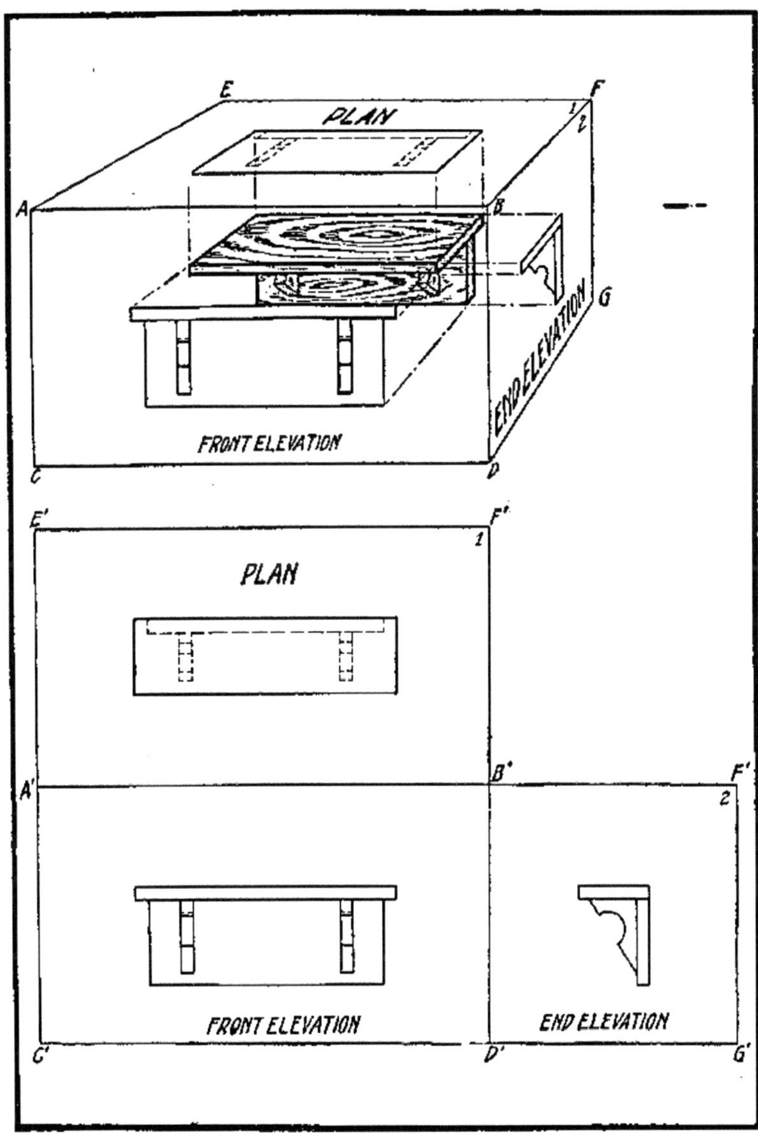
E
F
PLAN
1
2
A
B
G
END ELEVATION
FRONT ELEVATION
C
D
E'
F'
1
PLAN
A'
B'
F'
2
FRONT ELEVATION
END ELEVATION
C'
D'
G'

Plate V.

# CHAPTER II

# TOOL PROCESSES

## SQUARING STOCK.

**Paragraph 1.** In undertaking any piece of work the very first thing to do is to square the stock, that is, prepare a *working face*, a *working edge* and a *working end,* from which measurements are to be taken.

## PREPARING A WORKING FACE.

**Paragraph 2.** A *working face* is to be planed perfectly smooth and straight. This process is called surfacing. To do this, fasten the board in the tail vise on your bench. See that your plane is sharp and properly adjusted. (*Chapter* VI.) Start your cut with the plane in the position shown in Figure 11. Notice that the left hand rests firmly upon the knob of the plane, where some pressure must be used to keep the sole of the plane level with the surface of board. With the right hand push the plane forward, causing it to take a thin, even shaving as it comes to the position shown in Figure 12. In this position the plane sole is resting flat on the surface of the board. The plane should continue in a forward motion until the shaving has been taken the full length of the board, then the plane will be in the position shown in Figure 13. In this position the downward pressure should be on the right hand so that the sole

Figure 11.

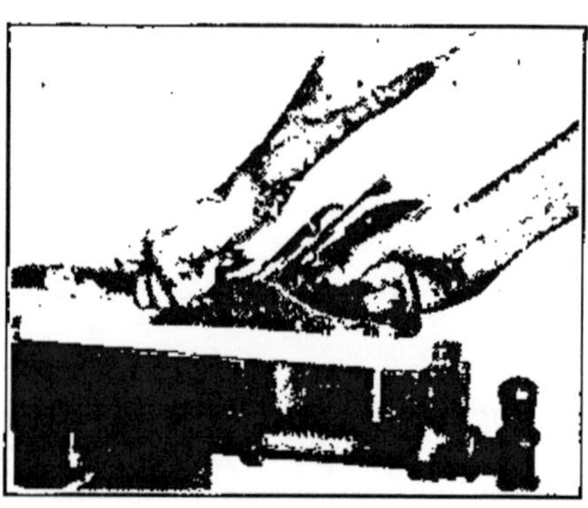

Figure 12.

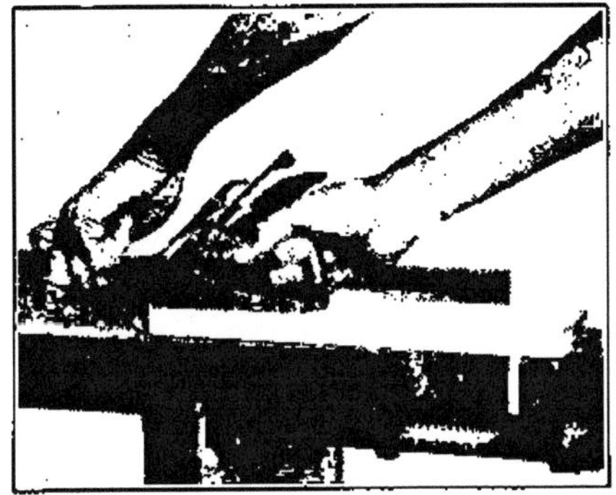

Figure 13.

of the plane will continue to lie level with the surface of the board. If the forward end of the plane is allowed to tilt downward at the finish of the stroke, a thicker shaving will be taken off at the end, thus causing the board to be unlevel. In surfacing a wide board it will be necessary for the plane to pass over several times in order to smooth the entire surface.

## TESTING THE SURFACE WITH A SQUARE.

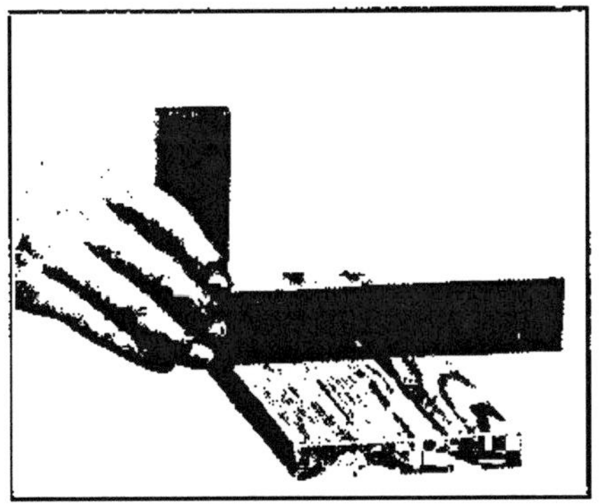

Figure 14.

**Paragraph 3.** With your try-square blade (which is perfectly straight) held in the position shown in Figure 14, you may test the surface to make sure that it is even. Push the square along the entire surface of the board carefully, watching to see that it fits closely upon the surface all the way across and that light cannot shine under it at any point. When the edge of the square blade will touch every point on the surface of the board as it passes, the *working face* is prepared. Mark this face with the letter "X," for you will want to refer to it from time to time in handling this piece of material.

## PREPARING A WORKING EDGE.

**Paragraph** 4. After the *working face* is completed the next step in squaring stock is to prepare a *working edge.* This is done by planing one edge at a perfect right angle to the working face. To do this place the material in the vise with the edge up, as indicated in Figure 15; with the long plane (a jack-plane or a jointer) plane the edge the entire length of the board. In starting and finishing the cut at each end be careful to hold the plane so it will be level with the edge of the board, as already shown in Figures 11 and 13. In planing a working edge be careful to hold your plane exactly level, that is, it must not be tilted to either side. Let the entire sole of the plane rest on the edge of the board. Test the edge with the try-square, as shown in Figure 16, holding the handle of the try-square firmly against the working face. Be sure to turn your work toward the light so you can determine accurately whether the square exactly fits the edge. In testing with the square, some mechanics prefer to hold the material on the level with the eye, as shown in Figure 17. In this position one can see whether light shines under the square blade at any point as it is being pushed along. Push the square from one end to the other so as to test the edge of the material its entire length. If it does not perfectly fit the square, plane down the high edge until it does.

Figure 15.

Figure 16.

Figure 17.

Also test the edges by sight, as shown in Figure 17, making sure that it is perfectly straight as well as square. You should train your eye so you will be able to determine accurately when an edge is straight, ability to judge lines, angles and measurements by sight is a great advantage to a mechanic. You may also test it with a long steel square, as shown in Figure 18. The edge of the large steel square is a perfect straight line, it can therefore be used to test the accuracy of your planing. When you have made sure that the edge is perfectly straight and square with the working face its entire length, mark this the working edge. This is indicated with two short parallel lines (||).

Figure 18.

## PREPARING A WORKING END.

**Paragraph 5.** After you have prepared a working face and a working edge, the next step in squaring stock is to prepare a *working end.* To do this means to make one end of the material perfectly square with the working face and also with the working edge. If the end of your material has been sawed reasonably square you may be able to plane it perfectly square by the use of the block plane. If not, you will have to saw it first. To do this, square a line across the working face, holding the handle of the try-square firmly

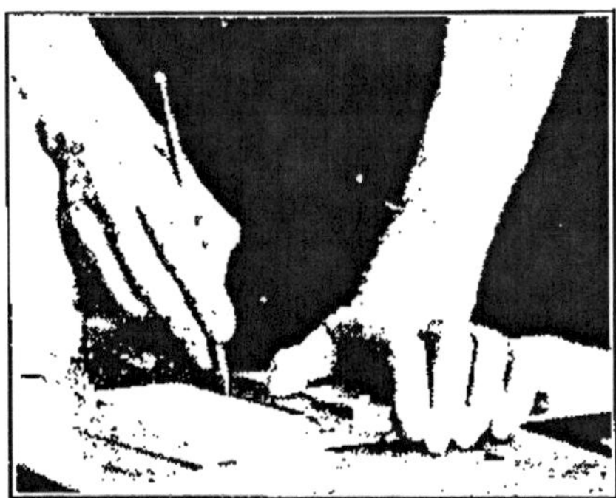

Figure 19.

against the *working edge,* as shown in Figure 19.

Then hold the try-square handle firmly against the *working face* and square this line across the working edge, as shown in Figure 20. With the back saw carefully saw it just outside this line. This may be done by holding the material on the bench hook, as shown in Figure 21. With the block plane smooth this end until it is perfectly square. Fasten the material in the vise with the end extending only a few inches above the bench top; handle your block plane as shown in Figure 22. Do not attempt to push the plane entirely across the board; if you do you will find that the material is damaged by splinters being torn out. Plane only part way across from one edge and then plane from the other edge. In preparing a working end, test with the try-square frequently to be sure that it is exactly square with both the working face and the working edge.

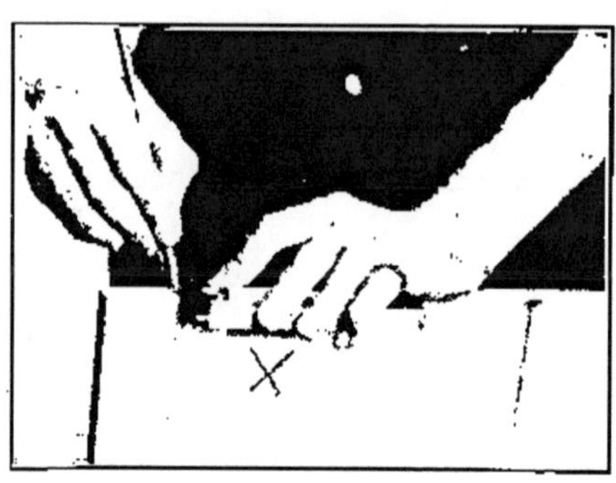

Figure 20.

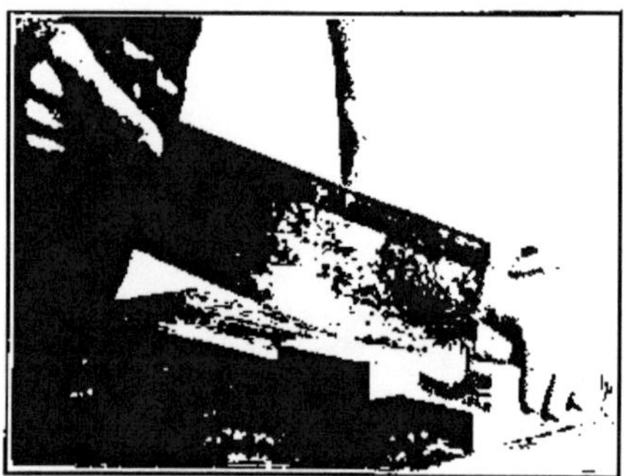

Figure 21.

Figure 22.

## GAUGING LINES WITH THE MARKING GAUGE.

Paragraph 6. The *marking gauge* is used to draw lines parallel with the working edge. By the use of the thumbscrew the marking gauge can be set to gauge lines at any distance from the working edge. To set the marking gauge use the ruler and measure from the head of the gauge over to the marking point, then tighten the thumbscrew. When the gauge is set to the desired distance, the line should be drawn by *pushing* the marking gauge the length of the material, carefully holding the head of the gauge firmly against the working edge, as shown in Figure 23. Note that the gauge should be tilted from you somewhat so the point will not enter the wood too deeply. A mechanic does not attempt to pull a marking gauge, because in so doing it is almost impossible to hold the head firmly against the working edge.

Figure 23.

## GAUGING LINES WITH LEAD PENCIL AND RULER.

Paragraph 7. It is sometimes more desirable to gauge a line with a lead pencil and ruler than with the marking gauge. With the left hand hold the ruler at the desired distance from the end, that is, if you wish to gauge a line 1½" from the working edge, with the thumb and finger hold the ruler at that distance. Then as the finger drags against the working edge it will serve as the head of the marking gauge (shown in Figure 24)., and keep the pencil at exactly the same distance from the edge. The pencil should be held firmly against the end of the ruler, then by sliding the ruler the length of the material, with the finger held firmly against the working edge, the line will be drawn parallel with the working edge. The motion may be either toward or from you, as you choose.

Figure 24.

## GAUGING LINES WITH LEAD PENCIL AND FINGERS.

**Paragraph 8.** It is sometimes quite convenient to gauge lines without the use of a ruler or marking gauge, but simply by the use of the pencil and fingers. This is particularly true in gauging lines which are a short distance from the working edge, as in laying out a chamfer. To do this hold the pencil and material as shown in Figure 25, allowing the second finger to drag against the working edge of the material, serving the same purpose as the head of the marking gauge, while the thumb and forefinger hold the pencil rather rigidly, thus causing it to make a line equally distant from the working edge as it is being drawn along on the material. In this process the pencil may be either pushed or pulled. It requires a little practice to be able to do this skillfully, but when the skill is once acquired it is a great convenience.

Figure 25.

## BORING ENTIRELY THROUGH MATERIAL.

**Paragraph 9.** In boring a hole through a piece of material which is likely to have both sides subject to view, it is necessary to take some precaution to prevent the bit from splintering the wood when it comes through the board. This splintering can be avoided by placing a scrap of material back of the board and boring through the board into the scrap, as shown in Figure 26. Another plan is to bore almost through from the face side, and just as the point of the bit begins to show on the opposite side, remove the bit and start on the opposite side, making sure that the bit point starts exactly in the tiny hole which it has formed while boring from the other side.

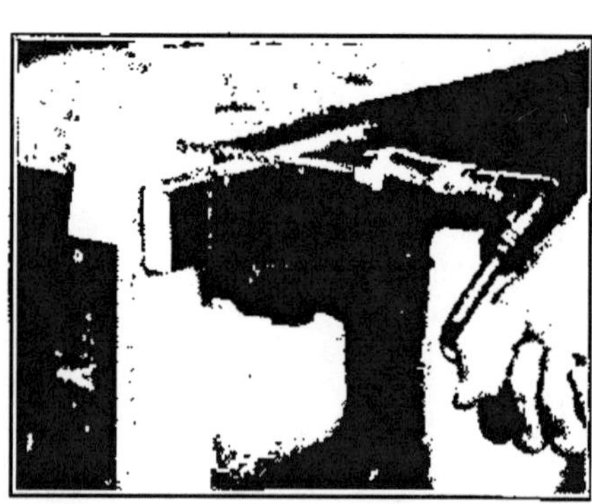

Figure 26.

## BORING TO DEPTH.

**Paragraph 10.** In boring for mortises, and sometimes in other lines of work, it is necessary to bore holes to a given depth. This is a little difficult unless you have some way of measuring, for it is inconvenient to remove the bit and measure the depth of the hole. Sometimes the shop is provided with a bit gauge, which can be attached to the bit and adjusted to allow the bit to bore any desired depth. If you do not have a bit gauge, a very satisfactory substitute can be formed by boring a hole through any scrap block, then sawing it off to the length which will leave the bit protruding as far as you want the depth of the hole to be. Then leave the block on the bit while the boring is done (*See Figure* 27), and you will not be required to pay any attention to the depth, simply bore until the block strikes the face of the material.

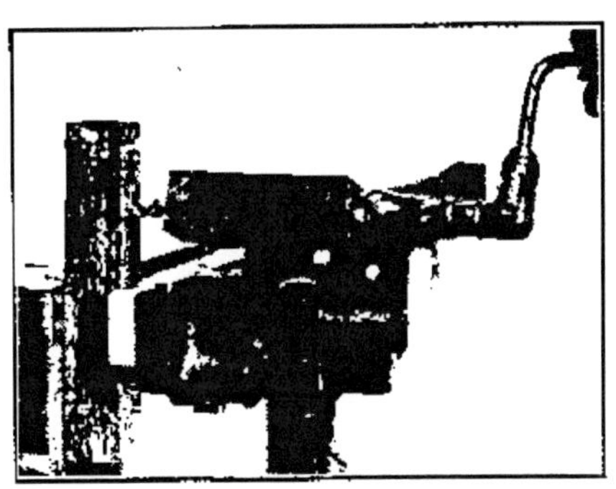

Figure 27.

## BORING PERPENDICULARLY.

Figure 28.

**Paragraph 11.** It is quite frequently necessary to bore holes perpendicularly into a piece of material. To do this it is necessary to hold the bit constantly at a right angle to the material in every direction. To be sure that you are doing so, it is well to have the try-square handy, and when you start the bit, test the position by holding the try-square as shown in Figure 28. You should also test frequently with the try-square while boring the hole.

## BORING AT A GIVEN ANGLE.

Figure 29.

Paragraph 12. It is sometimes necessary to bore holes at a definite angle. To do this determine the desired angle and set the T bevel. In starting the bit hold the properly set T bevel in such a position, as shown in Figure 29, so the bit will stand exactly parallel with the blade of the T bevel. Keep the T bevel handy so that you can test frequently during the boring and thus keep the angle constant. It is hardly safe to depend upon the eye in particular work if you are attempting to bore at an angle.

## BORING FOR DOWELS.

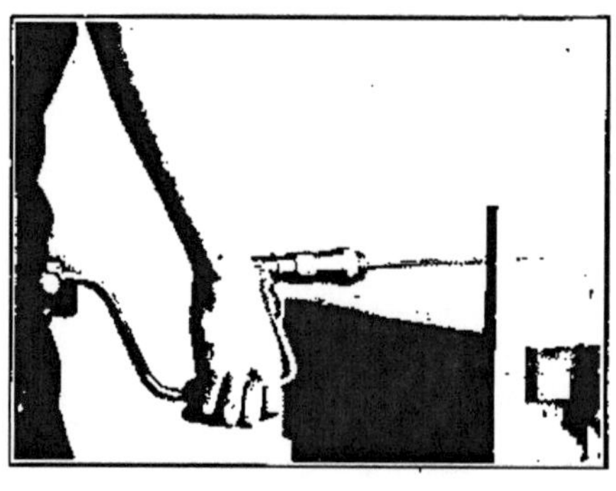

Figure 30.

Paragraph 13. In boring in the edge of material for dowels, it is well to square a line across the surface of the board as a guide to determine when the bit is held exactly perpendicular to the working edge. The material should be fastened in the vise as nearly straight up and down as possible and at a convenient height for the boring, as shown in Figure 30. The brace should be held so that it will be perfectly firm and so the bit will constantly stand in a straight line with the line which is squared on the working face of the material. Of course it is necessary to watch carefully to hold the bit in line in the other direction so it will not run out sidewise on the board.

NOTE: Another very good way of testing to make sure the boring is being done perpendicularly is to use the try-square as shown in Paragraph 11. It should be held with the handle against the edge of the board, the blade will then indicate the proper position for the bit.

## SAWING A TENON.

**Paragraph 14.** In forming tenons for mortise and tenon joints, the tenon should be sawed to the gauge line, as shown in Figure 31. The material should be fastened in the vise at an angle; this will make it more convenient for starting the saw. In sawing wide tenons it is sometimes convenient to saw part way from one edge, and then reverse and saw from the other edge, thus enabling one to follow the lines more accurately. Sometimes the back saw is used for this purpose, but the large saw is more desirable for larger work.

Figure 31.

## SANDPAPERING A CYLINDER.

**Paragraph 15.** In shop work it is sometimes necessary to make a cylinder without the use of a turning lathe. This is done with a plane and sandpaper. After all plane marks have been removed as nearly as possible with a wood file, then the cylinder is ready for sandpapering. To sandpaper a cylinder, fasten it in the vise so that it extends beyond the end of the bench, as shown in figure 32, then with a long piece of sandpaper cut in a strip of any convenient width, sandpaper the cylinder, making it perfectly round. The sandpaper should be grasped near the ends and then pulled back and forth over the cylinder very much like a belt would move around a wheel. By turning the cylinder frequently and continuing this process on all sides it can be made almost perfectly round.

Figure 32.

## THE USE OF A STEEL SCRAPER.

**Paragraph 16.** The purpose of the steel scraper is to finish and to produce a fine surface on the board by removing all tool marks and other blemishes. It is practically impossible to finish the surface of a board with a plane without leaving plane marks; for this reason a very sharp scraper must be used as the final cutting tool. The steel scraper should be used as shown in Figure 33. Notice that the scraper is held between the thumb and finger in such a way as to throw it in a small curve. This has a tendency to raise the corners and prevent their marring the work. Sometimes a scraper is so made as to fit into an iron frame which is equipped with handles; this sort of cabinet scraper enables one to work much faster than with a small hand scraper, shown in the illustration. In the shop where considerable resurfacing is to be done, such a scraper should be provided.

Figure 33.

The scraper should be kept very sharp. The cutting edge should be as nearly straight as possible, with the exception of the corners being slightly rounded to prevent scratching. The scraper may be sharpened with a file; the angle at which it is to be sharpened varies and is not of vital importance. After filing the scraper some men use the tang of the file or some other smooth piece of steel and rub it along the sharp edge of the scraper to turn the edge out slightly; this makes it cut more readily. You will have to experiment with this tool in order to sharpen it so it will do good work. The scraper should always be used in the direction of the grain, never across the grain, and it should be used to finish all surfaces of cabinet or other fine work.

NOTE: As a rule beginning students are inclined to neglect the use of the scraper, thinking that they can produce a satisfactory surface with a plane and sandpaper. In order to avoid this mistake you should learn to use the scraper early in your work, and practice it until you appreciate what an important tool it is when you are expecting to do fine work. Of course its value depends largely upon its being kept properly sharpened.

## SANDPAPERING A SURFACE.

**Paragraph 17.** In *sandpapering a surface,* the purpose is to make it absolutely smooth. Sandpapering should not be begun until the surface has been made as smooth as possible with a plane or a scraper. Sandpaper must not be used to remove the roughness left from the saw nor any other imperfection in the work. This must be removed by a cutting tool. A piece of fine sandpaper should be wrapped around a block, as shown in Figure 34, then the block should be grasped firmly with the thumb and fingers, holding the sandpaper in position, while the block is pushed back and forth in the direction of the grain. (*See Figure* 34.) The sandpapering block should never be pushed across the grain. If sandpaper is used crosswise of the grain it will leave ugly marks which can scarcely be removed. So, as a rule, you should adopt the motto of *"never sandpaper across the grain."* Beginning students are inclined to rely upon sandpaper too much. Fine workmen use sandpaper only for the final finish on the piece of material. They make the cutting tools do most of the work which a beginner attempts to do with sandpaper.

Figure 34.

Sandpaper is made in a great many grades or degrees of fineness, ranging from 00, which will probably be the finest you will require, to No. 3. No. 1 will probably be about the roughest you will need. Most of your work will be done with No. 0. Many students waste sandpaper by throwing it away when it is still valuable. You should not take a new piece of sandpaper until the old one is entirely worn out. In fact, a piece of sandpaper does better work after it has made several strokes across the board, because its first roughness is then worn down and it is smooth enough to leave a fine finish on the board. Worn sandpaper should be saved in the shop, for it is useful in polishing tools, where sharp sandpaper would be too rough and would scratch them.

NOTE: Somewhere in the shop there should be a box into which the partly worn sandpaper should be thrown; it would not only be handy for use, but would save expense.

## LAYING OUT FOR DOWELS.

Paragraph 18. It is very necessary that the laying out for dowel boring should be absolutely correct, otherwise the two edges will not join perfectly when the assembling is attempted. The edges to be joined with dowels should be carefully gauged with the marking gauge. After determining the distance apart which the holes are to be, a line should be squared across both boards at one operation in the manner shown in Figure 35. To do this, fasten the two pieces in the vise with their gauged edges even. With the try-square and lead pencil square lines entirely across both edges. In boring the holes be sure that the bit point starts exactly where the pencil line crosses the gauge line. The boring should be done as indicated in Figure 30 in this chapter.

Figure 35.

## LAYING OUT AND PLANING A CHAMFER.

Paragraph 19. The *chamfer* is a very important feature in a great many lines of mechanical work. You should learn to make a chamfer accurately. To do this a chamfer must be carefully gauged. This gauging should be done with a lead pencil and ruler or with a lead pencil and finger, as already shown in Figure 25, if you are able to do this accurately. After the gauging is done the board should be clamped in the vise and planed to the gauge lines. In planing the end grain the block plane will be found most convenient, although if you have no block plane the larger plane may be successfully used if you do it carefully. Planing with a block plane is shown in Figure 36. Notice that the plane is held at an angle, but that it is pushed straight across the board (not an upward motion). Thus

Figure 36.

it makes what is called a "shirring cut." This causes the plane to cut smoothly. The fingers on the left hand rest against the board as the plane slides along, and thus enable one to hold it at a constant angle. If the block plane is pushed entirely across the board in cutting the chamfer, care must be exercised not to tear out splinters of the farther edge of the board. This splintering process can usually be avoided by chamfering the ends first and making the side chamfer later, or by planing part way across from one edge and the remainder from the opposite edge. When a chamfer is well formed its edges should be sharp and straight, and should not have a rounded appearance.

## THE USE OF THE BENCH HOOK.

**Paragraph 20.** The bench hook is used in holding small pieces of material while they are being sawed, as already shown in Figure 21, Paragraph 5. Place the bench hook in such a position that one block rests against the edge of the bench. This will cause the other block to stand in a convenient position to receive the material to be sawed. Place the material against the block and grasp the bench hook with the left hand, with the palm of the hand resting on the material to be cut. The sawing should be done close to the block on the bench hook, thus when the cut is finished it will saw into the exposed portion of the bench hook and prevent splintering the material on the opposite side. The bench hook should also be used for chiseling purposes so as to avoid abusing the bench top.

## DRIVING NAILS OR BRADS WITH A HAMMER.

Figure 37.

**Paragraph 21.** In *driving nails* or brads, the hammer handle should be grasped in about the position indicated in Figure 37. A mistake frequently made is that of holding the hammer handle too close to the head of the hammer. With this sort of hold it is impossible to strike an accurate blow. Another error is in taking hold of the handle too close to the end. This also makes it impossible to be accurate. The position shown in the cut is the most desirable for ordinary work; you should cultivate the habit of holding a hammer handle in about this position. Notice that the handle is held just high enough that when the nail is driven level with the wood, the hammer handle will stand almost level. If you hold the hammer handle too high or too low the face of the hammer will not strike the nail head squarely and will either bend the nail or slip off the head and bruise the wood. The position for the left hand shows how the material should be held in place until the nails fasten it. In nailing any sort of fine work you should exercise great care not to miss the nail nor to strike it after it is driven level with the wood.

## TOE-NAILING.

Paragraph 22. The process of toe-nailing is quite frequently used, particularly in rough construction work, where one piece of material joins another with a butt joint. This process does not occur very frequently in shop work, however you should be familiar with it, for it is often used in general repair work. One piece of material should be made to fit perfectly against the other piece with a straight butt joint, and should be held in position while the nails are driven at an angle, as shown in Figure 38. If you are working with very hard wood, it is sometimes necessary to use a bradawl and make a small hole in which to start the nail.

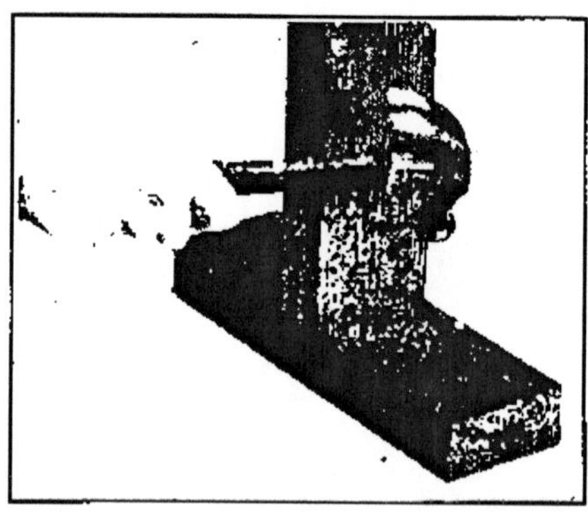

Figure 38.

In fine work, where you should be particular not to bruise the material with your hammer, it is necessary to finish driving your nail with a nail set. The illustration shows one nail which has been driven and set; a second one ready for the set, and a third one in the process of driving. This one, which is only partly driven, will give you an idea of the angle at which the nail should be driven.

In house construction the studding are toe-nailed to the wall-plate, as illustrated in this cut.

## THE USE OF CORRUGATED NAILS.

**Paragraph 23.** It is sometimes necessary to join two pieces of material with a straight butt joint where toe-nailing would not be satisfactory, or, at least, inconvenient. For this purpose the corrugated nail has been devised. A corrugated nail is simply a wavy piece of sheet steel sharpened at one end. These nails vary in length and width. Figure 39 shows an illustration of these nails and how they are used. The two pieces of material are brought together in a perfectly fitting butt joint, then the nail is driven across the joint standing practically at right angles to the line of the joint.

Figure 39.

The illustration shows a mitered joint fastened with two corrugated nails, one entirely driven and the other in the process of driving; it also shows the square joint being made in a similar way. By driving two or three corrugated nails into such a joint a very strong piece of work can be made. Sometimes two nails are driven from one side, the work is then turned over and two or three are driven from the other side; this is done only where great strength is required. You will notice that the corrugated nails show even when they are entirely driven; for this reason they are not used in fine work, unless the joint is of such a nature that the nail can be driven from the wrong side. They are used considerably in the making of window screens and in various lines of cheap construction which do not demand a cabinet finish. The great advantage of the corrugated nail is strength and speed in construction.

## LAYING OUT HALF-PITCH RAFTER OR BRACE CUT.

**Paragraph 24.** In laying out the half-pitch cut (Chapter V, Paragraph 75) use the large steel square, as shown in Figure 40. Lay the square on the working face of the material in such a way that the same figure on the blade and on the tongue are exactly even with the working edge of the material. Note: One side of a carpenter's square is 24 inches long—this arm is called the *blade;* the other arm is usually 16 inches long and is spoken of as the *tongue.* For illustration, if you take figure 12″ on the blade of the square and make it exactly even with the working edge, also make figure 12″ on the tongue of the square exactly even with the working edge. When the square is in this position you can mark along either the tongue or the blade and the angle will be exactly 45 degrees or the regular half-pitch cut. It does not matter what figures you use, but be sure you use the same figure on the blade and tongue, 4 and 4, 6 and 6, or any two numbers will give exactly the same angle.

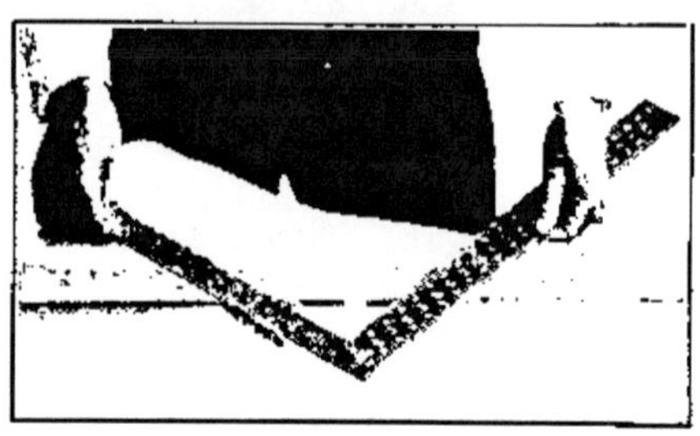

Figure 40.

## LAYING OUT THE THIRD-PITCH BRACE OR RAFTER CUT

**Paragraph 25.** In laying out a third-pitch brace or rafter cut (Chapter V., Paragraph 76), lay the steel square on the working face of the material in such a position that the figure on the tongue is equal to one-third of twice the figure on the blade. (*See Figure* 41.) For illustration, if on the blade you have the figure 12″, on the tongue you should have the figure 8″ (8 being one-third of twice 12, which is 24). By marking along the blade of the square you could lay out the lower end, or foot, of a third-pitch rafter. By marking along the tongue of the square you could lay out the top cut.

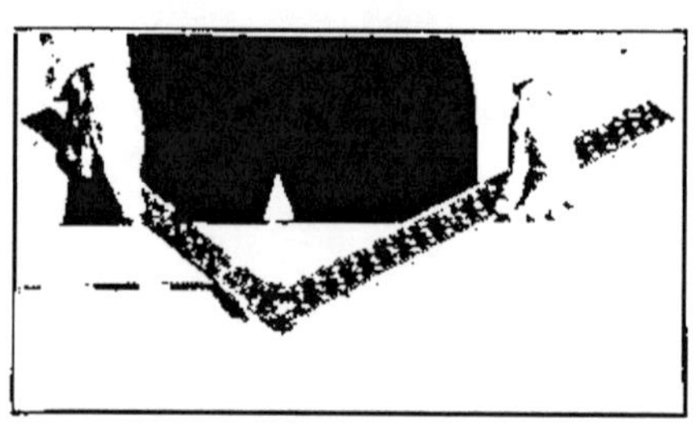

Figure 41.

## LAYING OUT THE QUARTER-PITCH BRACE OR RAFTER CUT.

**Paragraph 26.** In laying out a quarter-pitch cut (Chapter V., Paragraph 77), lay the steel square on the working face of the material in such a position that the number of inches indicated on the blade will be twice the number on the tongue, and make these figures exactly even with the working edge. (*See Figure* 42.) For illustration, if on the blade you make the number 8" even with the working edge, on the tongue make the number 4" even with the working edge. Then by marking along the blade of the square you will lay out the angle of the foot, or lower end of the quarter pitch rafter or brace. By marking along the tongue of the square you could lay out the angle for the top cut.

Figure 42.

## READING AND WRITING DIMENSIONS OF LUMBER.

**Paragraph 27.** In stating the dimensions of lumber, the thickness is always given first, then width, and last, length. Instead of writing out the word inches, the sign—two dots (written ")—is generally used, and for feet, one dot (written '). Instead of writing the word "by," as in the expression 2" by 4", the sign x is used, and it should be written 2"x4". Thus, in describing a piece of material which is ½-inch thick, 3 inches wide and 23 inches long, it will be written ½"x3"x23". The expression would be read, ½-inch, by 3 inches, by 23 inches. This rule of giving first thickness, then width and then length is universal in all lines of woodwork; always name dimensions in this order.

## LUMBER MEASURE.

**Paragraph 28.** In measuring the distance from one city to another we use the mile as the unit. In measuring grain we speak of so many bushels. Coal is measured by the ton. We are all, more or less, familiar with these various units of measure. In measuring lumber the *board foot* is used as the unit. So you should become familiar with the board foot. In speaking of the price of lumber, it is generally given at so much per thousand, or so much per hundred board feet. A board foot means a piece of material an inch thick, 12 inches wide and 12 inches long. The surface of a board foot would be one square foot, that is, it would measure 12″ each way. Of course we do not buy lumber cut in units of this size, so it is necessary for us to learn how to figure the number of board feet in any irregular-shaped piece of material. To do this you might think of how many board feet a piece of material would make if cut up into pieces the size of the unit. If you had a block of wood 2″ thick, 12″ wide and 12″ long, you can easily see that it could be ripped into two board feet. If it were 3″ thick it would make three; if it were 4″ or 5″ thick it would make four or five board feet, etc. It is also easy to see that a board 1″ thick and 12″ wide would contain as many board feet as it is feet long. If it were 10 ft. long it would of course contain ten board feet.

If the material is more than one inch thick, the thickness is always considered in figuring the board feet. If it is less than one inch it is considered an inch thick; this means that if you are buying material which is more than one inch thick, you are charged extra for it, but if it is less than one inch you do not usually get any reduction on that account. This may not seem quite fair when you are buying material, but as much of the thin lumber is made by planing down one-inch boards, you must pay for the material wasted in the planing, therefore you are charged for material one inch thick.

There are several ways to think of the problem in figuring the number of board feet in any piece of material, but they all get the same results.

A simple rule which is practical and easy is to multiply the thickness by the width by the length, *all being expressed in inches,* and divide by 1x12x12, the dimensions of a board foot. This makes a simple problem in cancellation. With thickness times width times length (in inches) above the line, and 1x12x12 below the line, you could then complete your problem by the method of simple cancellation and the answer will be the number of board feet. For an illustration, if a piece of material is 2″x4″x 16′, we would write above the line 2x4x16x12 (notice that the 16 is feet, therefore we must multiply by 12 to reduce it to inches), and 1x12x12 below the line—

$$\frac{2\times\cancel{4}\times16\times\cancel{12}=32}{1\times\cancel{12}\times\underset{3}{\cancel{12}}=3}=10\tfrac{2}{3}\text{ feet.}$$

# CHAPTER III

# VARIETIES OF TIMBER

A GREAT many men have spent almost their entire lives studying the nature of timber and still find there are new things to learn. You cannot expect to master the subject during your study of this text. However, if you will study the various references given you will learn a great many interesting things about timber. Whenever you are handling any kind of lumber you should think that it was once a part of a living tree. A tree, like any other living thing, is a great mystery. It is hard indeed to explain just how it produces its timber, but if you will study the function of every part of the tree—the roots, bark, trunk, leaves, etc., you will gather some idea of how it acquires its properties. We all know that most plants, like the various grains, vegetables and flowers, grow up and produce their fruit and then decay. Such plants must grow again from the seed the following year, thus making no use at all of the old stalk of the year before. Now, just why certain plants continue year after year to build a strong body upon which to support their branches, leaves and fruit, is hard to explain; but the fact that tree plants do produce a magnificent body that can be sawed up into valuable timber is a characteristic which makes the forests of so much importance.

There are so many different kinds of trees that it would be almost impossible to make a list and offer a description of all of them. Our very best authorities on trees and timber say it is almost impossible to describe a tree so accurately that it can be recognized. However, there are a few characteristics with which you should become familiar, for they will guide you very much in an effort to distinguish the trees. While you may never be able to identify every single tree found in the forest, yet it will be worth while to you to identify the more common forest trees.

If you should walk on the streets in a strange city you would see a great many people whose names you would never be able to call, but if you understood race characteristics you would be able to tell when you met a strange man whether he was a negro or a white man, whether he belonged to the Japanese or the American race, or at least you could form a judgment as to the great class of people to which he belonged. This same general classification is true in the matter of trees; while you might not be able to give the individual name of every tree, you could probably tell to what general class or family it belonged.

Our American trees are usually classified in two general classes. Those that shed their leaves every year (the deciduous trees) are called broad-leaved or hardwood trees; those that do not shed their leaves but remain green are called evergreen or softwood trees. The terms hard and soft wood are misleading, because the timber of some of the so-called hardwood trees is really very much softer than the timber of some of the so-called softwood trees. When we use the term hard or soft wood we should keep in mind the fact we do not mean hard or soft for tool operations, but that it refers to the general classification of those that do or do not shed their leaves.

The beauty of our forests is due mostly to the hardwood trees, which take on so many different colors and hues at different seasons of the year. We are all familiar with the beautiful green which is first seen in the spring and summer, then we know how the leaves change into red, yellow and gold, thus producing such beautiful effects before they drop off in the fall.

Of the hardwood trees the most important are the oak, walnut, elm, hickory, maple, beech, basswood, hackberry and sycamore. Of the evergreens, or softwoods, the most familiar are the pine, fir, hemlock and cedar. There are, of course, a great many more in each of these classes, but the ones enumerated are the most commonly found and best known. You will find it very interesting to study the trees of your own community and list them into the two general classes of hard and soft wood. You should study the general characteristics of the different kinds of trees, and when a tree is once pointed out to you, acquaint yourself with its characteristics so you will be able to recognize trees of that kind when you see them again. Many people who are not very familiar with standing trees are able to recognize timber when it is sawed and planed. It will be well for you to study not only the standing timber of your community, but also the different kinds of lumber as you handle them in the shop or at home.

Standing trees are identified by their general size and shape, by the appearance of the bark, color and shape of the leaves and the shape and position of the branches, and possibly most of all by the kind of flowers, fruit or nuts which the tree may bear. Some kinds of trees have such features that they may be easily and quickly recognized. The shellbark hickory is known for its rough, loose bark. The beech tree can be unmistakably identified by its smooth bark. The elm is known for the graceful curves of its long branches. Other kinds of trees have peculiarities of their own.

Men who handle material in the shops must recognize the different kinds of wood without seeing the leaves, bark and the standing trees. In identifying timber in this way it is necessary to consider other features rather than those which can be studied in the forest. If you are unable to see the trees, then you must identify the wood from its color, weight, odor, nature of grain, etc.

Some woods are extremely dark, while other woods are very white. Ebony (which is an imported wood) is very black—almost jet black, while basswood is a very light-colored wood. Black walnut is one of the darkest-colored woods which grows throughout the United States. Of course there are a great many shades of colors in wood, ranging from the dark walnut to wood as light as basswood or holly.

Weight is also a feature which is of considerable importance in identifying wood. Some woods are very heavy; hickory and white oak are the heaviest native timbers. White pine and basswood are very light in weight. When you attempt to acquaint yourself with any kind of wood, consider carefully the weight. Of course, it would be impossible to state accurately how much a given size of any kind of wood should weigh, because this depends very largely upon the amount of moisture it may contain, yet judging from weight you will be able to identify timber pretty accurately.

The odor of the wood is often an important factor in enabling one to identify it. Nearly all of the soft woods have a very distinct fragrance which is quite familiar, for it smells considerably like tu:pentine, although of course not so strong and disagreeable. Various cedars are noted for their odors. The red cedar, of which chests are made, is very valuable because of its peculiar and lasting fragrance. You should always notice whether or not wood has a peculiar odor if you are trying to identify it. It will not take you long to become familiar with the odor of black walnut, pine, oak, basswood, and some of the other more common woods. However, it is impossible to describe these odors sufficiently to enable you to identify them; you must learn them by experience.

The shape and feature of the grain is also of great assistance in enabling one to identify wood. The broad, prominent figure in the grain of yellow pine is quite familiar to every one who has ever handled that kind of wood. Oaks also have a very peculiar grain which is easily recognized. It is the attractive display and beauty of the grain which gives value to most of our cabinet woods. In some woods grain figure is not an important characteristic; basswood and white pine do not usually have distinct grain effects.

The very nature of the wood fiber and its strength also serve as a pronounced guide in identification. Some woods have very open pores. This is particularly true of chestnut. Other woods are very close grained, as may be seen by examining a piece of hickory or hard maple. Some woods are very flexible, and can be bent repeatedly without cracking. The elm, hickory and mulberry show this quality. Other woods are very brittle and will snap in two on slight bending. Some woods have a high power of resisting tool process and are planed and sawed with great difficulty, while still other woods are easily cut. Any boy who has had experience whittling with a jackknife knows that white pine or basswood will whittle more readily than a piece of hard maple, hickory or oak. You can oftentimes identify a piece of wood by attempting to whittle it. All of these various characteristics must be carefully studied when you are attempting to identify any piece of wood. It is not a matter of guessing, but a matter of judgment. Whenever you are using any kind of material in the shop you should assure yourself that you know what sort of wood it is. If you are unable to identify it, make inquiry until you find its name and then study its characteristics until you are sure you will recognize that same kind of wood when you see it again.

You will find it an excellent plan to save a small specimen of each kind of wood (no more than an inch wide, a quarter of an inch thick and an inch or two long, would serve very conveniently). The name of the wood might be written on the specimen. It could then be kept as a standard with which to compare and identify woods. Of course, in making up a set of specimens you should make sure that the one which you select is true to the type and not discolored or unusual in any way. The United States Government has taken the pains to prepare a set of samples of the different kinds of timber of commerce growing throughout the United States. Practical information regarding this matter can be had by addressing the Department of Forestry Service, Washington, D. C.

# THE HARD WOOD OR BROAD-LEAVED TREES

## OAK.

**Paragraph 29.** The most important hardwood trees are the oaks. The oaks have been called the "Royal Family" of American woods. This reputation has been given this class of trees on account of their broad application, their unusual durability, their great strength and unequalled beauty. Oak wood can be used for all kinds of constructive work, almost regardless of conditions. It has been performing satisfactory service for more than 2,000 years, so mechanics feel that oak has passed the experimental stage. A few years ago, when practically all constructive work was of wood, the important timbers, such as sills, beams and all foundation work, were made almost entirely of oak. This wood was selected because of its strength and durability. There is no other wood so broad in its application. This is true not only on account of its great adaptability, but because it grows in almost every part of the United States. The tree reaches a very large size, which makes it suitable for most any kind of heavy construction work.

On account of its attractive beauty, as well as its durability, oak has become the leading cabinet wood, and because of the great demand for choice oak in cabinet construction it has almost gone out of use for ordinary rough building work.

## THE OAK FAMILY.

The oak family is usually divided into two broad classes. They are known as the "White Oak Family" and the "Red Oak Family." The Government recognizes more than forty different species of oaks growing in the United States and they all belong to one of these two general families. The white oak, which is the most important of the oaks, is often spoken of as "the king" of hard woods. It is the standard timber of commerce; it is usually taken as the standard in measuring the strength of any other timber. Much of the beautiful quartered-oak which we see in fine cabinet work is white oak. While it is true that there are so many different classes and kinds of oak, they are all alike in one respect—that is, all oak trees bear acorns. That is about the only single characteristic that is pointed out as common to all oak trees.

The broad class of oaks, known as the "White Oak Family" (there are probably twenty-five different kinds of oak in this family), all produce their acorns in one year.

The red oaks require two years to produce acorns. This is the most important distinguishing feature between these two great families, although they can usually be told by the leaves. All trees belonging to the white oak family are recognized by their round-lobed leaves, the type of which is shown in Figure 43. The red oaks are known for the sharp-pointed lobes of their leaves, as shown in Figure 44. This is a family likeness which is found in practically all of the trees of the red oak family. These two characteristics will enable you to determine whether an oak tree belongs to the white or red oak family. On account of there being so many different kinds of oak and because they have so many different local names, you will probably not be able to recognize any great number of them and give them a specific name, although you should be able to determine whether or not a tree is an oak and to which one of the general families it belongs. The following table is a classification of oaks which is generally accepted as correct:

Figure 43.

Figure 44.

THE WHITE OAKS.

(Acorns ripen in one year.)

White oak,
Valley oak,
Brewer oak,
Sadler oak,
Pacific post oak,
Gambel oak,
Post oak,
Chapman oak,
Bur oak,
Overcup oak,
Swamp white oak,
Cow oak,
Chestnut oak,
Chinquapin oak,
Dwarf chinquapin oak,
Durand oak,
Rocky Mountain oak,
California blue oak,
Engelmann oak,
Rocky Mountain blue oak,
Arizona white oak,
Toumey oak,
Netleaf oak,
California scrub oak,
Live oak,
Emory oak.

THE RED OAKS.

(Acorns ripen in two years.)

Red oak,
Pin oak,
Georgia oak,
Texan oak,
Scarlet oak,
Yellow oak,
California black oak,
Turkey oak,
Spanish oak,
Blackjack oak,
Water oak,
Willow oak,
Laurel oak,
Bluejack oak,
Shingle oak,
White leaf oak,
Highland oak,
Myrtle oak,
California live oak,
Canyon live oak,
Woolly oak,
Price oak,
Morehus oak,
Tanbark oak,
Barren oak.

Although the oak timber throughout this country has been cut in great abundance, and has been wasted to a very large extent in clearing up the ground for agriculture, there is still an abundance of oak in almost every part of the United States, and the Government is taking steps to conserve our present standing timber. Lumbermen are also beginning to realize that every portion of the tree should be used, and thus waste is not going on as rapidly as in years gone by.

The use of veneer is also doing much to save the supply of oak. The veneer is merely a very thin layer of fine cabinet wood glued on the surface of some cheaper material. This gives the finished board the appearance of solid cabinet wood, but allows the cheaper wood to be substituted for the bulk of the work. Veneering is prepared in several ways. Some is rotary cut; that means that the log is turned over on a lathe and the veneering cut in large, thin sheets, very much as you would unroll paper. Another method is sawing. Some of the finest grade veneers are sliced with a very thin, sharp knife. A great deal of oak is used in making various veneers. You will find it interesting to examine some of your furniture at home to determine whether it is solid oak or merely overlaid with veneer.

While the oaks are the most important of all hardwoods, it must not be thought that the other woods deserve no consideration. There are a great many other excellent hardwoods growing in this country, and we should acquaint ourselves with some of the most important ones.

## ASH.

**Paragraph 30.** There are a great many different kinds of ash called by various names, such as black ash, blue, white, red, green, prickly and water ash. They are all very similar in general appearance and characteristics. Ash is very hard and strong. It is also a very heavy wood. It is stiff, white and tough, splits readily and shrinks moderately and takes on a good polish. It is used quite extensively in the manufacture of agricultural implements, also in building, particularly in the construction of floors. In carpentry work it is sometimes used for inside finish, stairbuilding and panel work. Ash is used in shipbuilding, construction of wagons, carriages and cars. Much ash is also used for the making of tool handles and in hoop factories. Many people are unable to distinguish ash from oak, although by making a careful study of the grain you will be able to recognize the difference.

## BASSWOOD.

**Paragraph 31.** Basswood is sometimes called American linden, lin, bee or lime tree. Basswood is very important among the timbers of commerce because it is still plentiful and very cheap. The wood is very light both in weight and color and is also soft and lends itself easily to tool processes. While it is not a strong wood, it is rather stiff, is of a fine texture and holds its shape well, although it shrinks considerably in drying. Basswood is used very much in various lines of carpentering, in the manufacture of furniture and in almost all kinds of woodenware. Because it is soft and easy to cut, it is convenient for carved work and for toy construction. It is used in car and carriage bodies. The basswood tree grows rather large, therefore the boards can be obtained in broad widths. The tree grows in almost all the eastern portions of the United States. The so-called "white basswood" is a variety of basswood found most abundant in the Allegheny region. The tree does not grow to a very large size, but the wood is beautiful, clear and almost white in color.

## BEECH.

**Paragraph 32.** The beech tree is pretty generally known by its smooth bark of gray color. Practically everyone is familiar with the small, triangular nuts which the beech tree bears. Beech is a very strong wood and was once used for house construction, although it is now used principally in lathe work, in the construction of handles, certain parts of furniture and plane stocks. Beech wood is heavy, stiff and hard and has rather a coarse texture. It is very light brown in color with a pronounced figure of the grain, which, when once learned, can be easily recognized. Beech is not durable when exposed to the weather, shrinks and checks badly in drying, but when it is thoroughly dry it holds its shape well and takes on a beautiful polish.

## BIRCH.

**Paragraph 33.** The United States produces several varieties of birch trees, although it is hardly worth while to attempt to distinguish between them. The birch is easily recognized by its smooth bark. The outer bark cracks open and rolls back, leaving the inner bark of almost ivory appearance. It is this feature which makes it easily recognized. Every schoolboy knows that birch bark was valuable to the Indians in the construction of canoes. Wood of the birch tree is all of a fine texture, almost white in color and very hard. It is a beautiful wood and takes on a finish which causes it to resemble cherry somewhat, yet it is not so rich in color. When once thoroughly dried it holds its form well, although it shrinks badly during the drying process. Birch wood does not stand exposure to weather; for that reason it is used mostly for inside work, such as finishing lumber or cabinet work. It is recently gaining an important place in woodturning; shoe lasts, wagon hubs, and shoe pegs are usually made of birch. Considerable birch is used in the various lines of woodcarving. Birch is frequently used as an imitation for mahogany, and if properly treated a very excellent imitation can be effected because of the similarity in grain and general appearance.

## CHERRY.

**Paragraph 34.** Cherry was once a rather plentiful wood, but it is now becoming very scarce, and for that reason so expensive that it is not in very general use. Our cherry lumber comes from what is commonly known as wild cherry trees. These trees produce a small black fruit with rather a bitter taste. In most parts of the country the larger cherry trees have been cut, and only the small trees can be found, and they are usually rather rare. The wood of the cherry tree is rather a reddish-brown in color; it is heavy, hard and strong and of a beautiful grain texture. Cherry holds its shape almost perfectly and takes a magnificent finish; for this reason it is very valuable for cabinet purposes, although its scarcity no longer permits its being used in larger pieces of furniture. It has been quite popular for inside finish, particularly in moulded and carved work.

## CHESTNUT.

**Paragraph 35.** Chestnut wood is not a very valuable cabinet wood. It is light in weight, has very open pores, is rather soft and does not possess very great strength. It shrinks very badly and checks considerably in drying; however, when thoroughly dry it holds its shape reasonably well. Chestnut is durable even when exposed to the weather. By people who are not thoroughly familiar with timber it is sometimes mistaken for oak, although it does not compare with oak in beauty or in value. The standing chestnut tree can be recognized by its long leaves and also by the familiar nuts which it bears. Chestnuts are known throughout all parts of the country.

## ELM.

**Paragraph 36.** Perhaps the most popular of all shade trees is the elm. This is true because of its size and the great beauty and grace of its branches. It is a very hardy tree and rather rapidly growing. Elm warps very badly and splits readily, but is one of the hardest and toughest woods when thoroughly dried. It is only moderately durable when exposed to weather conditions. It is capable of taking a high polish when completely dry. It is used principally in the construction of agricultural implements, boats, shipbuilding and also for the construction of cars and wagons. Because it bends so readily and is tough it is an excellent wood for the use of coopers. It is also used in the construction of cheap furniture. Sometimes elm is mistaken for oak, however there is little excuse for such an error, for the color and grain of the wood can be easily recognized if a little care is exercised. There are a number of different kinds of elms; their general characteristics are similar.

## GUM.

Paragraph 37. Sweet or red gum and the sour or black gum are the two kinds common to the United States. The most important is the sweet gum, which is perhaps more commonly known as red gum. It is sometimes spoken of as satin walnut. The wood is heavy and of a red brown color. It is very fine grained but not hard, although rather stiff and strong. Gum wood presents a great difficulty in shop work on account of its tendency to warp. It requires careful handling, but if properly cut and seasoned it holds its shape reasonably well. It takes a beautiful polish. Fine veneers are oftentimes cut from gum. It is also used considerably in the manufacture of furniture. On account of its beautifully marked grain it is sometimes used as a substitute for Circassian walnut.

## HACKBERRY.

Paragraph 38. Hackberry is a timber which grows in nearly all parts of the eastern United States and is usually a tree of medium size, but in some localities, particularly in the lower Mississippi valley, it grows to be a large-sized tree.

The wood is of a yellowish white color with moderately fine texture. It is hard and strong and quite tough. It takes a good polish and has a handsome appearance, although it has not been adapted to general use for furniture making.

## HICKORY.

Paragraph 39. For many years hickory has been one of the best known of all of our native timbers. The most familiar variety is the shell-bark hickory, so named from the tendency of the tree to shed its outside rough bark. The wood is very strong, heavy and hard and is probably the toughest wood that grows in this country. On account of its straight grain it splits straight and readily and this makes it of great importance in the making of shaved handles and certain parts of wagons and carriages. The wood of the hickory tree is almost white in color. It must be carefully dried to prevent shrinking and checking. It dries slowly because of its compact nature. Hickory does not stand well under exposure to weather conditions. It is very badly attacked by insects and will be rendered completely worthless by them if great care is not exercised.

## LOCUST.

**Paragraph 40.** There are several varieties of locust trees, but they are all very similar in their characteristics. They are known principally for their tough wood and coarse texture. They are very hard and strong and will stand exposure to weather conditions almost indefinitely; for this reason locust is the leading timber for fence posts. In recent years, in many parts of the United States, much has been done to raise locust trees for use as fence posts. The locust tree can be recognized by the beauty and grace of its foliage. At the period of its blossom the beauty and fragrance of its flowers render it unmistakable.

## MAPLE.

**Paragraph 41.** There are a number of different kinds of maple, known as the broad leaf maple, silver maple, red maple and sugar maple, sometimes called hard or rock maple. This is perhaps the most important maple of commerce. The wood is very hard, strong, stiff and tough and extremely fine in texture. In color it is a creamy white, sometimes having streaks of lightbrown, particularly in the heart. The grain is often quite wavy, from which is derived the beautiful effect called "bird's-eye" or curly maple. It shrinks moderately, works well and holds its shape. It wears smoothly without tearing up and will stand almost any amount of hard use. It does not, however, stand well under exposure to weather conditions, therefore it is used principally for inside work. It is our most valuable wood for floors, counter tops and other pieces of woodwork which must be subjected to hard wear. It is also used for finishing lumber in panels, stairways, ship and car construction. It is used a great deal for tool handles, piano framework and shoe lasts. It is almost always selected where an unusually hard wood of beauty and stability is required. Maple trees are quite popular as shade trees.

## POPLAR.

**Paragraph 42.** Poplar is sometimes known as whitewood or tulip, but in the lumber form is more often spoken of as yellow poplar. It was once one of our principal timbers of commerce. Only a few years ago large poplar trees were abundant and poplar boards could be had in almost any width. The wood is very soft and easily worked, has a fine texture, straight grain, light of weight, of a light-yellowish color, without a very pronounced grain. It checks but little in drying, does not warp badly and is one of the most durable woods for outside exposure. It has been abundantly used for weatherboarding of houses and other construction work where it is exposed to weather conditions. On account of the scarcity it is no longer used in larger construction work, but is used almost exclusively for paneling and in the making of drawers and other inside work in cabinet construction.

## SYCAMORE.

**Paragraph 43.** The sycamore tree is usually a familiar tree, known by its very large size, huge trunk and the striking feature of its white bark. This whiteness of bark is seen particularly in the upper branches. The wood of the sycamore tree is rather difficult to work because it is almost always cross-grained; it is very hard to split. It shrinks only moderately, but warps and checks considerably; however, when thoroughly dry, it holds its form well. Sycamore wood is only moderately hard and heavy, but rather tough and stiff; it was once used almost exclusively in the making of tobacco boxes. It is used in the making of drawers and bottoms of cabinet work. When sycamore is thoroughly dry and well finished it takes a magnificent polish, and for that reason is used considerably for inside finish.

## WALNUT.

**Paragraph 44.** Native walnut is divided into two general classes, black walnut and white walnut. The white walnut, or butternut, is of little importance among the timbers of commerce, but the black walnut is possibly our most valuable native cabinet wood. Black walnut once grew in abundance in almost all of the Mississippi basin, where the forests were practically filled with large and beautiful walnut trees. In the days of the early settlement of these regions the settlers felt that the logs had but little value and consequently piled and burned thousands of feet of this very valuable timber in order to clear the ground for agricultural purposes. Black walnut was also used very largely for fence rails, and much of it for firewood. On account of this great waste it is now almost entirely destroyed; what is left is used only for the finest of work, such as in gunstocks, tool handles and veneer for cabinet work. The name black walnut is derived from the color of the wood, for it is almost always very dark, at least a beautiful rich chocolate brown. The grain and figure of the wood are usually very pronounced. The most beautiful veneer comes from the cross-grained logs and knots. The wood shrinks but slightly in drying and does not warp badly and takes on a beautiful polish. The beauty of walnut seems to increase with age. On account of its scarcity it has almost entirely passed off the lumber market.

While there are a great many other kinds of hardwood trees which furnish more or less timber for commerce, the ones already enumerated are the most important because they are abundant and therefore the most common in general use. Most of the other hardwood trees belong to some of the families already mentioned.

# SOFT WOOD OR EVERGREEN TREES

In most parts of the United States the hardwood forests have been so nearly exhausted that much of the timber of commerce now consists of some of the evergreen trees.

## CEDAR.

**Paragraph 45.** There are a great many differenet kinds of cedar but they have certain characteristics which are pretty generally common. They are usually lightweight wood, soft and stiff and of rather fine texture. The wood seasons rapidly, shrinks and checks but little and is very durable even when exposed to weather conditions. Cedars are very valuable for shingles. They are also used abundantly for posts and ties. The two general classes of cedar are the white cedar and the red cedar. The red cedar is used principally in cabinet work for veneer. It is also used abundantly in the making of lead pencils, for which purpose alone many millions of feet are cut every year.

One of the most popular purposes for which red cedar has been used for many years is the building of chests in which to store furs, woolens and other fine fabrics. This wood contains a sort of fragrant oil which makes it proof against moths and all kinds of insects. The fact that this fragrance is apparently everlasting makes the wood very valuable for this purpose.

There is probably no wood that will outlast red cedar, and although there are specimens of cedar wood taken from work constructed more than three thousand years ago, they show no signs of decay. The Bible speaks of the "Cedars of Lebanon" from which Solomon's temple was constructed, and frequent references are made to the cedar as a type of permanence and wisdom. The famous cedar spoken of in the Bible is not the same as our native red cedar, but it is of the same family and the woods possess many of the same characteristics.

## CYPRESS.

Paragraph 46. Cypress is a wood that is very similar to the white cedar. It is a light wood of rather open pores. The boards can be had in great widths, because the trees grow very large. The wood is soft and lends itself easily to tool processes. It is used for various kinds of construction work which do not require great strength.

## HEMLOCK.

Paragraph 47. Hemlock is a wood of light reddish-green color, free from rosin pockets, but of very coarse fiber and usually cross-grained. Although very splintery and frequently defective on account of wind shakes, yet when sound it is a stiff and rather strong timber. It shrinks and warps badly and is not very durable, however it is used considerably for rough framing and for sheathing. The increasing cost of the better woods has forced hemlock into pretty general use for rough work in many localities.

## PINE.

Paragraph 48. There are so many kinds of pine, and the term is used so generally in speaking of all of them that it is almost impossible to give a clear idea of the nature of the wood without dividing it into separate classes.

There are two general classes of pines, the hard and the soft pines; the hard pines are also called yellow pine, while the soft pines are spoken of as the white pine.

## HARD PINE.

Hard pine wood is stiff and quite strong, very resinous, shrinks moderately, seasons rapidly, works well, but is not so durable as soft pine when exposed to weather conditions. It does not hold paint well but takes a fine varnish finish and for that reason is used quite extensively in cheaper grades of inside finish work.

While the term Hard Pine is used in the carpenter's trade to refer to any kind of pine other than white pine, yet there are about ten distinct varieties, of which only five are of any great importance to the building trade.

**The Long Leaf Southern Pine,** also known as Georgia pine, grows to a very large size, and furnishes a very hard and strong wood; it is one of the most agreeable to work and is therefore quite popular in construction work.

**The Short Leaf Southern Pine** is very much like the Loblolly pine. It grows in Missouri and Arkansas, and is also found in North Carolina and Texas.

**The Loblolly Pine** grows to a very large size; it is frequently confused with the long leaf pine, but its timber is coarser, lighter and softer. It is found in several of the southern states.

**Yellow Pine,** sometimes called Bull Pine, forms extensive forests in the Pacific and Rocky Mountain regions. The wood is very variable, with wide sap wood. Most of the hard pine of the west is of this variety.

**Norway Pine** is the northern hard pine; it grows in the northern states and Canada. This variety does not form forests but grows in small groves, usually with white pine; its timber is fine grained and of a very light color, it is largely sap wood and is not durable.

## SOFT PINE.

**Soft Pine,** white pine, pumpkin pine or sugar pine are names which are used in different localities in referring to the soft variety of pines.

White pine lumber is very valuable because of its many excellent features; it is of uniform texture, works easily without splitting, seasons well and shrinks but little, does not warp badly, holds paint well, and is very durable. White pine was once used considerably for all kinds of outside work, such as weatherboarding and shingles, but the advancing price has caused it to pass almost completely off the market of general building materials. It is now used only for finer construction work and for pattern making.

## REDWOOD.

**Paragraph 49.** Redwood is a very important member of the cedar family; it is famous for its magnificent size. It grows thickly along the coast in California. The wood is very light in weight and of a red color. It has great durability against weather conditions. It is being rapidly converted into lumber and used for weatherboarding and general construction work.

## MAHOGANY.

**Paragraph 50.** Although Mahogany is not a native wood and you may never have a chance to see a standing tree, or even a log of this kind, yet it is used so much in all kinds of fine furniture that you should know something about the nature of the timber.

There are several different varieties of Mahogany found in different countries, but the most commonly known Mahogany used in cabinet work grows in Central America. The trees do not grow in groups, but are found scattered throughout the tropical forests. They grow very large and tall and in certain seasons of the year can be distinguished by their fiery appearance above the other tree tops. Mahogany hunters, as the men are called, who go out and locate the trees, climb high in the other trees and look about over the forest until they can see the top of a mahogany tree in the distance. The difficult work of cutting a road through the dense undergrowth then begins and it is often quite a while before the tree is even reached. Cutting the logs and getting them out to a shipping point is another hard task, so there is little wonder that the lumber is expensive.

Mahogany is hard and serviceable, does not shrink nor warp to any noticeable degree, will hold its shape and form indefinitely, does not split nor check, is somewhat difficult to work because of the cross-grained nature, but will last indefinitely even under trying conditions. It is a close-grained wood, and usually has very marked and beautiful figures in the grain. This is the particular feature by which it is best known, and connected with the rich, dark red color makes it so familiar either in solid form or veneer in fine furniture, particularly piano cases.

## LUMBER AND METHODS OF SAWING.

**Paragraph 51.** While it is impossible to understand just how, and why, the tree plant produces a large and strong body, yet by careful study men have been able to find out much about how a tree grows. We cannot at this time make a full explanation of the tree and its manner of growing. The references regarding trees will help you to an understanding of these matters. We are concerned now in thinking of trees from the standpoint of lumber. In order that we may thoroughly understand the nature of lumber, we must remember that the tree grows by adding a layer of woody fiber to its trunk or stem every year. A tree grows very rapidly during the early spring, and continues its growth throughout the summer while the leaves are on. When the leaves have fallen off it indicates that the tree has practically ceased its growth for the season, and through the cold weather it does not add to its woody fiber as it does through the spring and summer. This will help you to understand how it is that a tree produces a ring of growth around its body every year. When the tree is cut down the end of the log shows a great number of rings, each ring representing the growth of one year. By counting these rings one can determine the approximate age of the tree.

It is important that we learn something about these rings because they have much to do with the nature of wood. When a log is sawed into boards these rings form the figure which we often speak of as the grain. In quarter sawed material there is another very beautiful kind of figure in the grain, which is caused by the rows of cells known as medullary rays. They extend from the heart to the bark of the tree.

## PLAIN SAWING.

The most common method of sawing logs into lumber is what is called plain sawing, or slash sawing. This is really a matter of slicing the log into the required sizes, as shown in the following illustration:

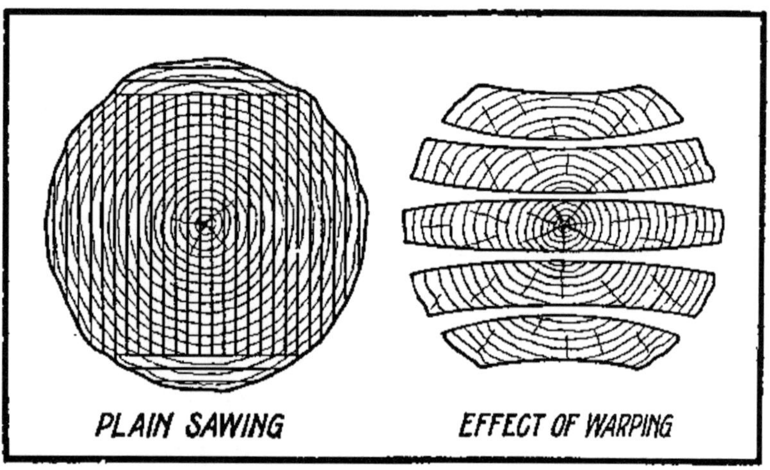


This is the most economical way of sawing logs, for it gives the greatest possible amount of lumber with the least waste. There are, however, some disadvantages in this method of sawing, particularly if the lumber is to be used for fine cabinet work. Plain sawed lumber usually warps very badly. If you are to understand why this is true, you will need to know something about the cause and effect of warping of lumber.

In a living tree there is always considerable moisture in the form of sap. When the tree is cut down the sap, of course, ceases to circulate, and the moisture in the log begins to evaporate. As the log dries, all of the concentric rings, representing the annual growths, become a little shorter and thus cause the log to crack. If it has been sawed into boards it will, of course, dry even more rapidly, causing the portion of the rings in each board to shorten considerably, and thus bend or warp the board, as shown in the illustration. You will observe that the edges of the board warp from the heart of the log, and you can readily understand why this is true if you will stop to consider the cause of the warping. You will notice that the plank in the central portion of the log does not bend, but the shortening of the rings causes it to become thinner on each edge.

## QUARTER SAWING.

In order to overcome this tendency to warp, another method of sawing has been devised. This method also adds great beauty to the appearance of the boards by exposing the medullary rays. This method is called quarter sawing. It takes its name partly from the fact that, in the process of sawing, the log is usually cut into quarters as the first operation. There are a number of different methods of quarter sawing, but they all have the same purpose in view, that of cutting the boards as nearly as possible in a direct line from the bark to the heart. The following illustration shows four different methods of quarter sawing:

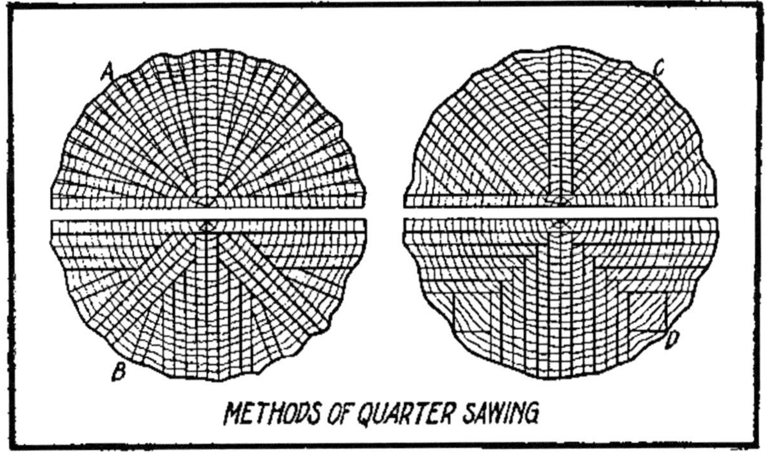

METHODS OF QUARTER SAWING

Figure A represents the method which makes each board perfectly quartered. By studying this illustration you will observe that this is a very wasteful method, because there are so many wedge-shaped pieces that cannot be used. The method shown in Section B produces fairly good results, but is not so perfect as shown in Figure A. This is also a wasteful method on account of the great number of small pieces left. The method shown in Section C produces very good quartered effect, although you will observe there are a good many boards which are not cut directly from the bark to the heart. This is one of the more common methods of producing quartered oak lumber. The irregular pieces left at the corners are usually cut into stock of some other character.

Illustration D represents still another method of quartering; it does not produce perfect effects and is rather troublesome to do.

You should keep in mind the fact that quartering is a *method of sawing,* and that it is in no way related to any particular kind of timber. Any sort of log can be quartered, although oak, which is our chief cabinet wood, is the most familiar. This is an excellent method of sawing any kind of wood which has an unusual tendency to warp. It would no doubt be in more common use if it were not for the fact that it necessitates some trouble and waste in handling the material.

## DRYING AND SHRINKAGE OF LUMBER.

As lumber changes its size and shape in giving up its moisture or sap, it must not be used in any sort of fine construction until it has been sufficiently dried to make sure that it will hold its shape when completed. In order to make sure that lumber is properly dried, or cured, as it is often called, great attention must be given to this matter. After coming from the sawmill, it is usually dried in the open air for a while. To do this the lumber is piled on strips in such a way that the air can circulate freely on all sides. Green material, fresh from the log, should be left piled in this way for a considerable time. To produce an excellent quality of cabinet material it is well to have the lumber air-dried for many months. It is then taken to a dry kiln, which is merely a room prepared for the purpose of continuing the drying process. Different methods of drying are used in different kilns. Steam is sometimes turned into the dry kiln, after which the steam is turned off, and dry air is introduced and the temperature is continually raised until it reaches as much as 175 and 180 degrees, where it is left for a number of days. A number of methods have been devised for the purpose of hastening the drying process. It is not desirable, however, to dry a board too rapidly, for there is danger of the outside surface becoming dry while the inner portion of the board still contains moisture which, upon drying, will cause the board to crack.

A point not generally understood by people who are inexperienced in handling lumber is the fact that a board may be properly kiln dried, and yet not remain so if it is improperly treated. If lumber is stored in a damp room it will absorb more or less moisture, and will become unfit for cabinet work. This makes it very necessary that any stock of material that you may have on hand for your manual training work should be kept in a room which is perfectly dry. A very excellent plan for the storage of cabinet lumber is to provide racks or hangers from the ceiling. This keeps it up where it will be out of the way, and at the same time free from moisture. You cannot hope to get good results, however perfect your material may be furnished, if you store it in a damp basement room. This tendency to absorb moisture from the atmsophere makes it necessary that any piece of cabinet construction should have its surface properly protected by being well finished, with filler, varnish or some other suitable protection, as explained in Chapter IV.

# CHAPTER IV

# WOOD FINISHING

## PAINTING.

**Paragraph 52.**

THERE are a great many different methods and processes of wood finishing, but they all have about the same purpose in view, that of bringing out and protecting the beauty of the wood. On any kind of woodwork which is exposed to outside weather conditions, some sort of paint is the common method of beautifying and preserving. A great many kinds of painting material have been used, and they are mixed in various ways to suit different special purposes, and while much of this is technical information, which belongs to the painters' trade, yet there are a few general rules regarding painting which can be easily understood. Wood exposed to the rain and snow, sunshine, wind and other weather conditions, if unprotected, will not last long. It absorbs moisture and swells, then shrinks when it is dried, and is constantly changing its shape and soon begins to decay. The purpose of the paint is to fill the tiny pores on the surface and provide a waterproof covering for the wood. Linseed oil and white lead have for many years been used as the principal ingredients of paint. Of course there are many other substances which have been added to change the color and the nature of the paint. Certain kinds of drying material and other secret preparations have been added, but the principal elements in the paint are still oil and lead.

Linseed oil is an oil pressed from the seeds of the flax plant; this oil is used either raw or boiled. The raw linseed oil is generally used in the first or prime coat on woodwork. The prime coat of paint is usually a thin coat, principally of oil, containing only a little lead; it should be evenly spread and well brushed into the pores of the wood.

It requires about three coats to do a first-class job of painting. The second coat contains considerably more lead and coloring material. The second coat should not be added until the first coat has become thoroughly dry. This coat should also be evenly spread. After the second coat has become thoroughly dry the third coat is usually added.

The third coat is often mixed with boiled oil, because this gives a little more gloss and a nicer appearance than the raw linseed oil. Sometimes a drier is added to the second and third coats of paints.

There are a great many kinds of excellent ready-mixed paints on the market, and for one who is not experienced and skilled in the mixing of paints it is much better to buy a ready-mixed paint and use it in accordance with the directions than to attempt home mixing.

## CABINET FINISHING.

**Paragraph 53.** We have just learned that paint is used principally on outside work or on things that are to be exposed to moisture and weather conditions. For cabinet work, all lines of furniture and inside work, other styles of finishing are used. Since paint covers the surface of the wood entirely, the natural beauty of the grain of the wood is lost, and for that reason paint is not used in furniture work. Other styles of finishing are used which will preserve and at the same time bring out the natural beauty of the wood.

It requires even more skill to produce a fine finish than it does to do painting. Many men spend their entire time and thought in wood finishing, so you must not expect to do beautiful work in a careless, thoughtless manner. If, however, you will give the matter your very best attention and be careful in every step, you will soon be able to produce some very beautiful finishes. In producing any sort of finish it is very necessary that you should consider the nature of wood. All wood is porous; that is to say, the surface presents a great many tiny pores, mouths or openings, which are ready to drink up anything which touches it. You have no doubt noticed when a little water, grease or ink is spilled on a bare board that the moisture is quickly absorbed and the board is stained. This is because the liquid enters the pores of the wood and carries whatever coloring matter it may contain into the surface of the wood. Men have taken advantage of this principle in all kinds of wood finishing, and you must thoroughly understand this in order to be able to produce a satisfactory finish. Before taking up the detail of the preparation of the finish, we must think about the condition of the wood before any of the finishing material is applied. Some people have the idea that the finish will cover up tool marks, rough places and other imperfections in the wood. This is not at all true, for any defect in the work will quite likely show more distinctly after the finish is put on than before, so it is absolutely necessary that the surface of the wood should be made as perfect as possible before any of the finishing material is added. To do this, broad surfaces should be carefully smoothed with a scraper, as explained in Chapter II, Paragraph 16. The surface should then be carefully sandpapered with a very fine sandpaper, perhaps 00, as explained in Chapter II, Paragraph 17. If there are any holes where nails have been set, or any other openings which must be covered, they should be filled with putty made the desirable color so as not to show. They can sometimes be filled with glue mixed with some of the wood dust which comes from the sandpapering. The matter of patching defects in the wood is quite a problem; it requires skill and practice to do it perfectly.

## GETTING THE DESIRED SHADE OF COLOR BY STAINING OR DYEING THE WOOD.

**Paragraph 51.** After the surface of the wood has been made perfectly smooth and absolutely all imperfections removed, the next thing to do is to decide upon the desirable color. If the natural color of the wood is wanted no staining nor dyeing will be required. There are a great many kinds of stains and dyes on the market, many of which are good while others are worse than worthless. The stains which are recommended to give satisfactory results with one coat, thus producing all of the steps of wood finishing, are not to be relied upon for satisfactory work.

Some wood dyes are mixed with water, some with alcohol, some with oil and turpentine. The *water dyes* are very cheap, but are not highly recommended because the water soaks into the wood and raises the grain very badly, leaving the surface very rough when it is dry. This is hard to overcome by inexperienced workmen.

The spirit dyes, as a rule, give rather satisfactory results, because they do not fade as badly as some of the other dyes. They penetrate the wood deeply, but, like the water dyes, they raise the grain considerably and cause the surface to be rough. It is also rather difficult to get an even, smooth color, for they are likely to leave blotches and spots in the stain.

The oil stains are very easy to use and can be handled by the inexperienced finisher with very satisfactory results. The oil stains do not penetrate so deeply and consequently do not raise the grain so badly. The oil stains are usually rubbed with a rag after being applied; this rubs off the surplus and allows the natural beauty of the grain to stand out in a very desirable way.

In mixing or preparing a stain of any sort you should first try it on a scrap of the same kind of wood upon which you expect to use it. Never test the stain on your piece of finished work. After the stain has become thoroughly dry, which may require several hours, examine the wood carefully and see that it is perfectly smooth. If the grain has been raised it may be necessary to go over it very lightly with sharp sandpaper, but you must be very careful not to sandpaper too hard or you will cut through the stain in places. If the article is not yet the desired color, another coating of stain may be added, but the desired color must be obtained before the next process of wood finishing is undertaken.

## FILLER.

**Paragraph 55.** We have already learned that the surface of a piece of wood is porous and that it is ready to absorb any sort of liquid which is applied. The stain which we have been discussing penetrates the wood through the pores and changes the color a little deeper than merely on the surface, but inasmuch as the stain is very thin, or as the painter would say, has "no body," it does not fill the pores of the wood, therefore even though the desirable color has been obtained on a piece of wood, the surface still presents innumerable open mouths ready to drink up any other liquid which at any time might touch it. The next step in our finishing process is to fill all of these tiny pores, and to do it without destroying the color or the beauty of the surface. A great many different kinds of filler have been devised, for different kinds of wood require different kinds of filler. Some wood has very large open pores—chestnut, for example—other wood is very close grained and has tiny pores, maple being a good example. Of course we would not expect that chestnut would require the same kind and quantity of filler material as maple. We must take into consideration the nature of the wood to be filled in order to determine the kind of filler to be used; the principles are so similar that it is not difficult to get a general idea of the process.

Wood filler is simply some sort of pasty material which can be made sufficiently thin to enter the pores. Then when the liquid dries the body, or substance of the paste remains in the pores and fills them up level with the surface. Various materials are used for this paste. In the cheaper fillers such material as starch is used, but in the better fillers a harder material, such as silex or ground stone, is employed. This is possibly the best filler, because the silex is composed of tiny crystals of stone which presents a great many sharp corners. If we could examine this filler with a microscope we could probably see that it is made up of innumerable crystals. The liquid of the filler would carry these crystals down into the tiny pores of the wood, then when the wood shrinks the crystals would be held fast because of their rough shape. This is the reason that ground stone makes such an excellent filler, because it makes the surface of the board so hard and solid that it is almost impossible for it to absorb any other liquid. Fillers are mixed with different sorts of material, sometimes oil and turpentine; sometimes a little alcohol or gasoline is used. The liquid is not a very important portion of the fillers because its principal purpose is to thin the filler so it will enter the pores of the wood. In your work you will find it best to use a good brand of ready-mixed filler and follow the directions for its use.

The filler should be applied with a stiff brush and it should be well rubbed. Since the filler is not to remain on the surface, you do not have to give any attention to avoiding brush marks. After the filler has stood for a few moments, or until it begins to lose its gloss, it is then time to rub it off with a piece of burlap or coarse cloth, rubbing first crosswise of the grain, to rub as much as possible into the wood, then afterward rub in the direction of the grain until all of the surplus is removed from the surface. A sharp stick should be used to remove the surplus filler from the corners and angles of your work. Always be sure that all of the filler on the surface is rubbed off before leaving a piece of work. If the filler is allowed to dry over night it will become hard and it will be almost impossible to remove it. After the filler has had time to become thoroughly hard, which usually requires several hours, you are then ready to take up the next step of your finishing process.

The work thus far (getting the desired color by staining or dyeing and stopping the pores by rubbing in the filler) might be called the foundation work of any sort of wood finish. No difference what sort of finish you desire, these steps should be carefully executed. After you have reached this place or completed the foundation work you should then decide what sort of finish you are going to make. There are three general classes which will be of interest to you: the *wax finish, varnish finish* and the *shellac polish*. Regardless of which you use, if you expect fine results the foundation work should be done as already explained.

## WAX FINISH.

Paragraph 56. The wax finish produces a soft, mellow luster which has but little gloss. It is a popular finish for hardwood floors, and particularly mission furniture. Wax finish is easily and cheaply applied and does not require any great skill. It can easily be renewed from time to time without much trouble. The wax used for this purpose is principally beeswax which has been melted in turpentine. Sometimes other ingredients are added, but these are the principal elements. The wax may be applied with a soft rag and should be rubbed evenly over the surface. While it does not require any great skill nor care, yet it should be evenly spread, and one should avoid leaving bits of the wax in the angles or corners of the work. After the wax is allowed to dry a few minutes it should be rubbed to a polish with another dry, clean cloth. If a little higher polish is desired a second coating of wax may be added and polished in similar manner.

Wax is sometimes applied immediately after the stain without the use of a filler. This will give only fairly good results and will not be durable for the reasons already explained regarding the open pores of the wood. If a first-class wax finish is desired it would be better to add one coat of shellac to the foundation coat. Allow this shellac to dry at least twenty-four hours, then sandpaper it perfectly smooth by adding a few drops of oil to a piece of well-worn sandpaper and carefully rubbing the surface. When the entire surface has been made perfectly smooth, then the wax should be applied, as already explained. One objection to a wax finish is the fact that it shows finger marks rather badly, and on work which is subjected to continual wear must be renewed occasionally in order to retain its beauty and luster, but the renewing is so easily done that the objection is not serious.

## SHELLAC FINISH.

**Paragraph 57.** The shellac finish is one of the hardest of all to produce. This is a finish which is known as the French polish. This should be undertaken only on small pieces of work where a very fine polish is desired and where there is ample time to give to the task. A fine French polish cannot be obtained in a few minutes. The foundation coat must be applied as already explained, then a good coat of shellac should be brushed on with a soft brush.

Shellac is a sort of resinous substance which is gathered from the bark of certain trees of India. This substance is dissolved in alcohol and then applied very much like varnish. The best grade of shellac is mixed with pure grain alcohol; this makes it rather expensive, so wood alcohol, which will do very satisfactorily for ordinary work, is usually substituted. Denatured alcohol is very frequently used, but it sometimes happens that denatured alcohol fails to dissolve the shellac because the substance used in the denaturing process will not dissolve shellac, and for that reason when it is added the shellac settles in the bottom in a sort of ropy substance and it is impossible to get satisfactory results with it. It is best to use wood alcohol unless you can buy a quality of denatured alcohol prepared on purpose for shellac work.

After the first coat of shellac is added it should be allowed at least twenty-four hours in which to dry and harden. By carefully examining the surface you will then find that it is somewhat rough. It should be made perfectly smooth before another coating of shellac is added. A few drops of linseed oil should be placed on a piece of sandpaper and then the shellaced surface should be carefully rubbed in the direction of the grain. The purpose of the oil is to prevent the rubbing from causing the shellac to become sticky. The linseed oil also helps somewhat in building up a polish. When the surface has been rubbed perfectly smooth, it is then time to begin the more difficult portion of building up the French polish.

A French polish is rubbed on with a rag. A "rubber" is made by twisting a piece of soft cloth into a wad and then covering it over with a small piece of cheesecloth about five or six inches square. The inside portion of this wad is saturated with the shellac, then by twisting it in the square of cheesecloth the shellac will be allowed to ooze through onto the surface of the work. The "rubber" is occasionally dipped into linseed oil and then rubbed over the surface of the wood in a circular motion. As the rubber is gripped the shellac oozes through and mixes with the linseed oil and a beautiful polish is built up. The rubber must be kept in constant motion while it is on the surface; if it is allowed to stand still it will stick and mar the polish very badly. The skill in this work is shown by being able to rub the surface to a perfect finish without leaving any uneven or marred spots. The rubber is opened from time to time and the inside portion is dipped into the shellac. Care must be exercised not to have too much shellac on the rubber or the work cannot be satisfactorily done. It will require several hours to rub even a small surface no more than a foot square to a beautiful rich polish.

A very excellent shellac finish is very often produced by applying the shellac with a brush and rubbing it down in the same fashion as a rub varnish. If you desire to do this instead of rubbing on with rag rubber, as explained, apply the second coat with a brush, allow it to dry about twenty-four hours and rub it down with sandpaper and oil in exactly the same way that the first coat was rubbed. Apply a third or even fourth or fifth coat, carefully rubbing down each coat before the next is added. In this way a complete smooth layer of shellac will be built on the surface of the board. For a final rubbing it is well to use ground pumice on a rag moistened with linseed oil. This is very much finer than sandpaper and will produce a more beautiful polish. By "spiriting off" with a piece of cheesecloth which has been *very slightly* moistened in alcohol, the surface may be rubbed to a magnificent gloss. This requires some skill, because if the rag with which the final rubbing or spiriting off, as it is sometimes called, is done is a little too moist with alcohol the entire surface will be destroyed. This final polishing rag must be so nearly dry that it will seem only the least bit moist when touched to the back of the hand. It will require a great deal of experimenting and patience to produce a satisfactory finish with shellac. It is well worth your while to attempt it; do not be satisfied until you get good results.

## VARNISH FINISH.

Paragraph 58. The varnish finish is one of the best known of all wood finishes. Some of the very cheapest furniture is treated with an inferior grade of varnish. The customary way of finishing inexpensive furniture is to brush on a thin coat of cheap varnish and allow it to dry and consider the job finished. Such a surface is always unsatisfactory for it is easily marred and does not present any great beauty. To prepare a satisfactory varnish finish, the foundation must be built up as has been previously explained. That is, the wood must be made a desired color with the stain or dye, and the filler must be applied so as to fill all the pores of the wood. Sometimes a cheaper grade of varnish is applied instead of the filler.

There are a great many kinds of varnish, some of which are very cheap and worthless and with which no amount of skill and painstaking would produce satisfactory work. They scratch easily and leave a white, dusty mark when scratched. You can always tell cheap varnish by scratching it with a piece of metal and noticing the white scratch and the dusty appearance. The finest grades of varnish do not leave such a scratch. The best varnish is made of copal gum which is imported. This gum is dissolved in turpentine. A good grade of varnish is expensive but will prove cheaper in the point of service than some of the less expensive varnishes. Varnish should be evenly and carefully spread with a soft brush and with a long smooth stroke. It should be thin enough to flow smoothly from the brush. Great care should be exercised not to allow the varnish to run down the corners nor to accumulate in the angles or low places of the work. Varnish can not be rebrushed after it begins to dry.

Varnishing should be done in a room which is clean and perfectly free from dust. The temperature should be about 75 to 80 degrees. Varnishing can not be done with satisfactory results in a cold room, neither should the varnish be allowed to chill until perfectly dry. You can not do satisfactory varnishing in your manual training shop where dusty work is being done. There should be a separate room free from dust and dirt and of even temperature if you expect to do varnishing. When the first coat of the varnish has had ample time to dry (which should be several days), then it can be rubbed down ready for the second coat. Varnish may feel dry to the touch after it has been on a few hours, but this does not mean that it is thoroughly dry. A second coating of varnish should not be added until the first coat is absolutely dry. This will require from four to seven days, depending upon the kind of varnish and drying conditions.

The first coat of the varnish should be rubbed smooth. This should be done with ground pumice stone and water. A rag should be dipped in water and then in the powdered stone, and rubbed on the surface of the varnish. If the varnish is satisfactory the water will not damage it. The rubber for this purpose is often made by taking a strip of cloth about an inch wide and rolling it up very much as a tape line would be rolled. A string is then tied around it and this pad is used for the rubbing purpose. Sometimes linseed oil is used as a rubbing liquid.

When the first coat has been rubbed smooth then the second coat should be applied. This coat is added in the same manner as the first coat, carefully brushing the varnish smooth and avoiding the possibility of its running or accumulating in the corners. The second coat should be given from five to seven days to dry, after which it should be rubbed down exactly the same as the first coat was rubbed. A third or fourth coat may be added if desirable, and each coat should be carefully rubbed. The final coat should be rubbed with the pumice stone and oil or water until it is perfectly smooth. If a high gloss is desired, such as is found on a piano or automobile bodies a finer rubbing material, such as rotten stone and water or oil, should be used. The careful rubbing with rotten stone will bring out a magnificent finish. You will observe that it takes considerable work to produce a beautiful varnish finish. One reason why so many people fail is because they are not willing to spend the time and the effort necessary. Sometimes varnish finish is left just as it comes from the brush without any rubbing. Possibly this is the varnish with which you are the most familiar. This leaves a sort of cheap-looking gloss on the surface and is not to be recommended for a fine piece of cabinet work.

If you will follow these directions you should in a little while be able to produce a surprisingly beautiful finish, but it will require thoughtful, painstaking efforts.

## CARE OF FINISHING MATERIALS.

**Paragraph 59.** One important point in producing a fine finish is to have the materials in good condition. No one can produce satisfactory finishes with dirty, stiff brushes, and finishing materials which have been exposed to dirt and dust. All finishing materials should be kept carefully closed. Bottles and cans of paint should always be closed as nearly air tight as possible when not in use. Brushes should be kept in some sort of liquid which would keep them soft. Shellac brushes may be cleaned in alcohol. Brushes may be kept in fairly good condition by keeping them in a can of water. It is not satisfactory to leave the brushes where they will dry and become hard, for they are thus not fit for use. When you are through using a brush and do not expect to use it soon again the best plan is to wash it in warm water and soap, then allow it to dry with the hairs straight, and it will be in good condition the next time it is needed.

All rub rags and papers which are covered with finishing materials should be gathered up and burned immediately after you are through with them. It is unsafe to throw dirty rub rags on the floor or in a corner somewhere and leave them. They are quite likely to take fire by what is called spontaneous combustion. So always gather and throw your rub rags into the stove or furnace or put them somewhere out of the way where they will not set fire to a building. This may seem like a small point but it is extremely important.

There should be some place in your manual training shop where you have a rack, table or safe for all staining materials. The staining and filling should be done at this staining table or staining rack. There should be separate places for all materials and they should always be kept in their proper places. A brush which is intended for one color should not be used in another color. The shellac brush should not be dipped into the stain. By having your staining and filling apparatus properly cared for you will be able to do this work without any difficulty.

# CHAPTER V

# THE PRINCIPAL JOINTS USED IN WOODWORK

## PLAIN BUTT JOINT.

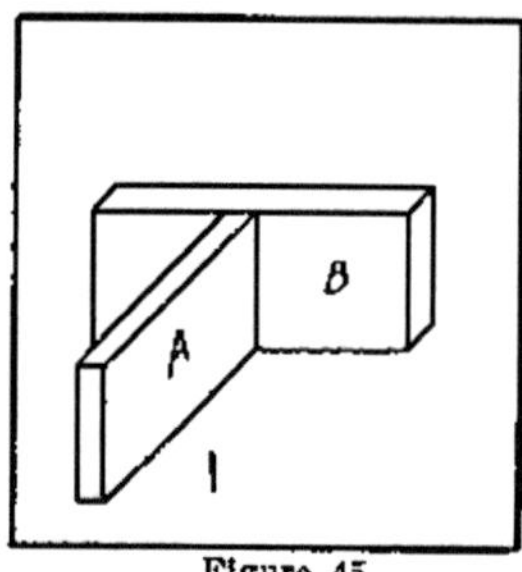


Figure 45.

Paragraph 60. The plain butt joint is the simplest and most frequently used joint found in woodwork. This joint consists of one piece of material sawed perfectly square and brought against the surface of another, to which it is fastened by means of nails or screws.

This joint is used in innumerable ways. It is employed in all kinds of cheap box construction, in the making of bins, trays and almost every project which belongs to the box type. The plain butt joint also occurs quite frequently in various parts of house framing and in bridge construction.

## GAINED OR HOUSED JOINT.

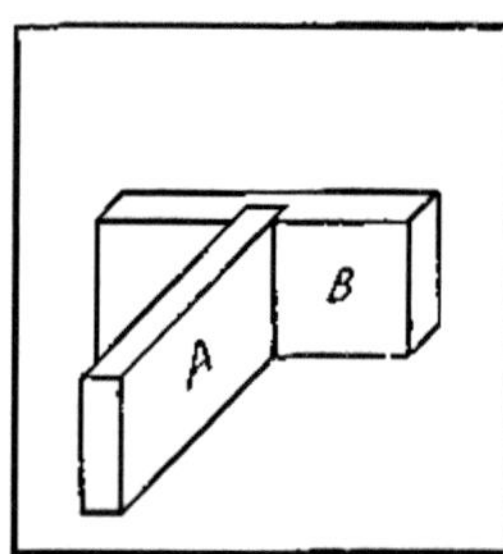


Figure 46.

Paragraph 61. The gained or housed joint is very similar to the plain butt joint except that in one piece of material (B) a gain, or dado, is cut the full size of the end of the other piece (A) This makes it possible for the end of the one piece to enter the gain and be supported on each side. This joint is usually assembled with nails or screws. It has an advantage over the plain butt joint in that it affords strength against downward pressure, for it does not depend entirely upon the nails or screws for its support.

This joint is used frequently in installing partitions in trays and boxes. It is used in various kinds of shelf construction, in building permanent shelving in store buildings, and in installing shelves in cabinet work, such as bookcases or china cabinets. To lay out this joint cut the end of the piece of material A perfectly square. With the try-square square a line across the face of the material B. Square another line across the face of the material B sufficiently distant from the first line to provide room for the thickness of material A. On each edge of material B gauge the depth of the gain, with a lead pencil and finger. If a marking gauge is used, do not gauge farther than is necessary and thus mar the edge of material B. With a try-square square the two lines on the edges to the gauge line. With a back saw saw on the two lines which are on the face of the material to the gauge line (it is well to saw on the inside of the mark so as to make sure the material A will fill the gain tightly). With a keen-edged chisel cut out the portion between the sawed lines, test with the edge of the try-square to make sure that the bottom of the gain is perfectly level. Assemble by bringing the end of the material A into the open gain, and nail through from the outside of the material B.

## CROSSLAP JOINT.

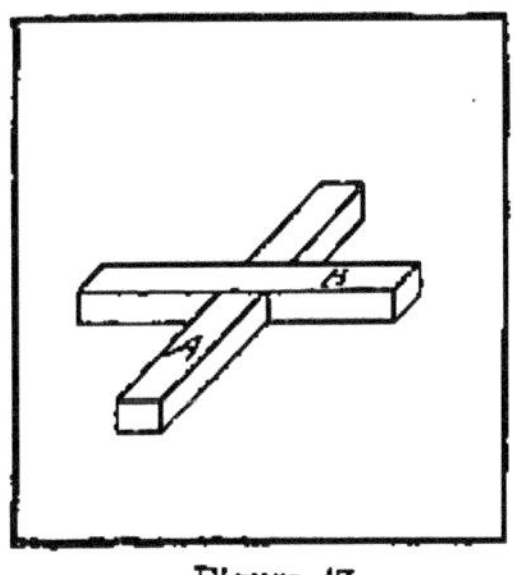


Figure 47.

**Paragraph 62.** The crosslap joint is sometimes called a half lap, because in making this joint the material is lapped by cutting out half the thickness from one piece, and the other half from the other. This joint is employed in various kinds of construction work where pieces of material running in different directions must cross.

## TO LAY OUT THE CROSSLAP JOINT.

In preparing a crosslap joint the first step is to make both pieces of material perfectly square. Then square a line across the working face of one of the pieces of material A at the position where the crosslap is to come. Lay the other piece of material B across the first piece with its working edge exactly even with the first line squared across, and with a sharp-pointed knife measure the width of the gain which is to be cut in A. At this point, with the try-square, square a second line across A. If this has been properly done the two lines will be just far enough apart to receive the width of the piece B. Square these lines down on each edge of A. With the marking gauge set to the depth which the gain is to be cut, carefully gauge the depth of the gain on each edge of the material. Exercise great care not to gauge beyond the pencil lines which are squared on the edges. With a back saw, saw on the two lines down to the gauge line. It is well to saw on the inside of the mark in order that the gain may not be too large. With a sharp chisel cut out the material between the two sawed lines, chiseling part way from one edge, and the remainder from the other edge to avoid splintering out. When the gain is cut in A, place B in the gain, and with the sharp point of a knife lay out the width of the gain to be cut in B. With the try-square carefully square these two lines across and also on both edges. With the marking gauge set exactly as it was when you made A, gauge the depth which the gain is to be cut in B. In making the piece B your gauging should be done not from the side on which your gain is to be cut, but from the opposite side in order to leave sufficient material to fill the gain which is cut in A. Cut this gain in the same manner in which you cut the gain in A. After the joint is assembled it may be well to plane both surfaces very carefully with a sharp plane set to take a very thin shaving.

## END HALF-LAP JOINT.

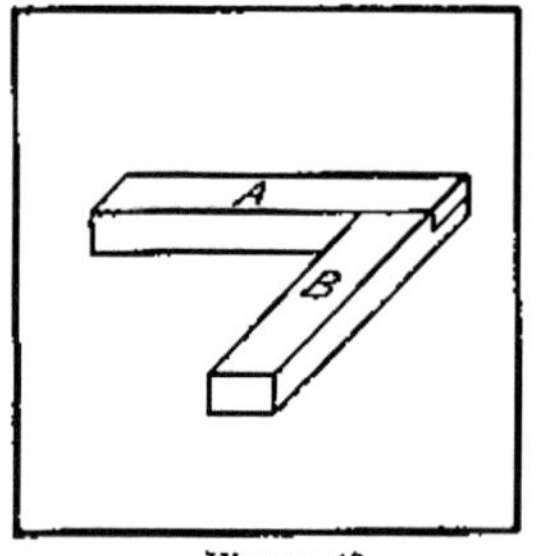

Figure 48.

**Paragraph 63.** The end half-lap joint is very similar to the crosslap joint. It takes its name from the fact that the material is cut in such a form that one piece laps over the other.

This joint is used in various kinds of frame construction. It is occasionally used in the making of cheap door frames or window screens. This joint is also sometimes used in making the corners of sill construction in small buildings.

## TO LAY OUT THE END HALF-LAP JOINT.

See that both pieces of material are perfectly square on all sides and on the ends which are to form the joints. Square a line across the face of piece A as far from the end as the width of piece B. Square this line down on each edge of piece A. With the marking gauge set to one-half the thickness of the piece, gauge the depth which the lap is to be cut. Gauge on both sides and across the end. With the back saw, saw down to the gauge line. Place the material in the vise and rip out this corner. When the first piece is finished (it should be carefully smoothed with a sharp chisel) lay it on piece B, and with the sharp point of a knife indicate on the working face where the line is to be squared across. Square this line down on both edges. With the marking gauge set at the same depth as it was when piece A was laid out, lay out the depth which the lap is to be cut in B. Bear in mind that the amount of material left on in B must be sufficient to fill the opening cut in A. For that reason the marking gauge must be used, not from the side from which the gain is to be cut, but from the opposite side. Gauge on both edges and the end. Saw out this lap in the same manner as you did in A. Carefully smooth with a sharp chisel. Assemble with glue or with nails or screws as the nature of the work may demand.

## PLAIN MITER JOINT.

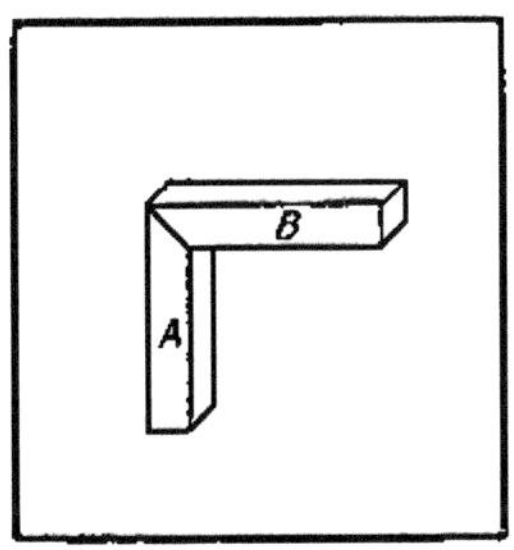

Figure 49.

Paragraph 64. The plain miter joint is the most frequently used in the construction of various kinds of rectangular frames, such as picture frames, window screens, frames of moulding in various trimmed work, panel work, and almost every kind of construction in which the rectangular frame is employed. The miter joint is very easily constructed, for it is usually sawed in a miter box. If a miter box is not available, this joint can be laid out by the use of the steel square. It is the regular half-pitch cut shown in Chapter II., Paragraph 24, and in Paragraph 75 of this chapter. The T-bevel should be set at the 45 degree angle. This is done by laying out the 45 degree angle with the steel square or compasses and setting the T-bevel on the line thus laid out.

## TO LAY OUT AND EXECUTE THE MITER JOINT.

Make sure that the material is perfectly square. With the T-bevel perfectly set, working from the working edge (on piece A), lay out the 45 degree angle. With the try-square, square this line down on each edge of the material. Hold the material in the bench vise or with the bench hook, and carefully saw these lines. If the material is of such a nature that it can be reversed, the other piece of material (piece B) may be turned around in such a way as to make the one cut answer for both pieces. This, however, cannot be done if the material is of such a nature as to have a face side, which must be up, as in the case of moulding. In this case it is necessary to make another cut in the same way in which this cut was made, except on the opposite end of the piece of material. Assemble the joint with glue, or with glue and brads, or with corrugated nails, as the nature of the work may demand.

## MITERED HALF-LAP JOINT.

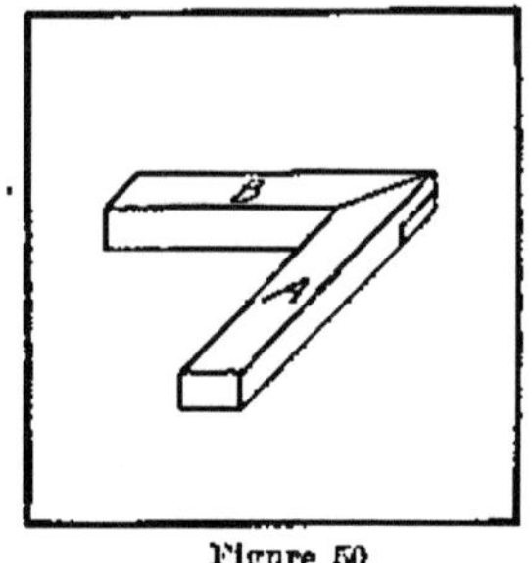


Figure 50.

**Paragraph 65.** The mitered half-lap joint is not used as commonly as the half-lap or mitered joint. However, it is sometimes desirable where the face of the work should show the appearance of a mitered joint, and a little more strength is desired than can be secured with the plain miter. This joint consists in half the thickness of the material being made into a miter joint while the remaining portion is cut to form a half lap.

This joint may be used in making window frames, small panel doors and almost any other sort of rectangular frame construction. It is sometimes used in picture frame construction, though not commonly, because the edge of the picture frame is in view and the half-lap joint would be rather unsightly. To lay out the half-lap joint be sure the material is exactly square. Piece A may be first cut in the miter box or laid out with the T-bevel and cut with the back saw at the regular miter cut (as shown in Paragraph 64). With the marking gauge set to one-half the thickness of the material, gauge the depth to which the lap is to be cut. At exactly the point where the inside of the miter starts square a line across one face of the material A. With a try-square, square this line down to the gauge line. With the back saw carefully saw out as indicated by the line just described. With a keen chisel smooth this work. Lay this joint in position on piece of material B and, with the sharp point of a knife, mark the point where the miter is to start. With the T-bevel lay out this miter. Square these lines down on both edges. With the marking gauge set exactly as it was when piece A was laid out, gauge the depth which is to be cut away in material B. Saw this miter down to the gauge line. (Notice that in this case you do not saw more than one-half way through.) Saw out this triangular piece as already laid out. Smooth with a keen chisel. If properly executed these two pieces of material should fit perfectly at a right angle. Assemble with glue and brads or as the nature of the work may demand.

## BLIND OR CLOSED MORTISE AND TENON.

Figure 51.

**Paragraph 66.** The closed mortise and tenon joint is one of the oldest and most commonly employed joints of woodwork. It is formed by cutting an opening, or mortise, in one piece of material B and shaping the end of another piece of material A to enter this opening. This joint is usually assembled by the use of a wood pin, which gives it great strength in every direction. It was formerly the most important joint in house, barn and bridge construction, because houses were originally built with large timber in the frame. This joint is not common in modern house construction because the large timbers have gone out of use. It is, however, used considerably yet in mill and bridge construction where timbers are employed.

## TO LAY OUT THE MORTISE AND TENON JOINT.

Be sure that the material is perfectly square. In laying out mortises a special gauge is generally used. This gauge is similar to an ordinary marking gauge, except that it has two points, both of which are adjustable. Set the mortising gauge so the two points will be as far apart as the size desired for the mortise and so the head of the marking gauge will be as far from the first point as the distance you desire the mortise from the working face. From the working face gauge the width of the mortise on the working edge of piece B. Determine the width which the mortise is to be and with a try-square, square these lines. In a blind mortise or tenon joint the depth of the mortise is not laid out, but you should determine how deep the mortise is to be and use a bit-gauge or some other device to determine how deep to bore. As the wood is to be cut away in forming the mortise, select a bit which will bore a hole about the size between the gauge lines. Bore as many holes as convenient without over-reaching the layout. With a sharp chisel cut out the wood to the gauge line. Be sure that the sides of the mortise are cut down exactly perpendicularly in every direction. Determine the length of the tenon and square a line this distance from the working end of material A on the working face.

In most projects the length of the tenon is determined by the nature of the work, the strength required, etc. With a try-square and lead pencil carefully square this line on both faces and edges of material A. With the mortising gauge set exactly as it was in laying out the mortise, gauge the width of the tenon across the end and down the edges to the square line. Hold material on the bench hook and with the back saw, saw down to the gauge line. Place the material in the vise and saw the tenon as illustrated in Chapter 2, Paragraph 14. If there is to be a relish on one or both sides of the tenon, lay out this relish and saw out with the back saw. Test the tenon to make sure that it exactly fills the mortise; pare with a keen chisel until it will enter the mortise without any danger of splitting. Remove the tenon from the mortise and bore a hole which is to receive the fastening pin. Bore this hole first through piece B, which contains the mortise, then in the tenon bore a hole a tiny bit closer to the shoulder than in the mortise. This will have a tendency to pull the tenon tightly into the mortise when the pin is driven. This process is called *draw boring.* It was always used in the framing of buildings in order to make sure that the joint would be as tight as possible when assembled.

## THROUGH MORTISE AND TENON JOINT.

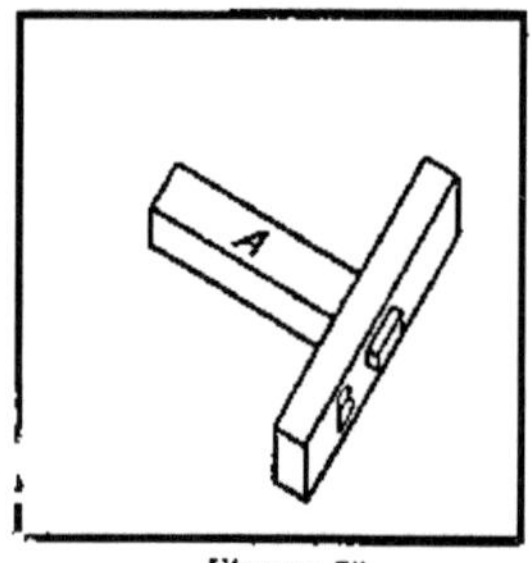

Figure 52.

**Paragraph 67.** The through mortise and tenon joint is very similar to the pinned mortise and tenon joint, with the exception that the mortise is cut entirely through the material B and the tenon A is allowed to extend so as to be exposed a short distance on the opposite side. This form of mortise and tenon construction is frequently used in cabinet work, where the exposed end of the tenon is treated in a decorative manner. This mortise and tenon joint is a little more difficult than the blind mortise and tenon because the joint is exposed on the opposite side and the mortise must fit the tenon perfectly in order to show good workmanship. This joint is laid out exactly like the blind mortise and tenon except that the mortise is laid out on both sides of the material B. In cutting, the work is done from both sides to avoid splintering out and to be sure that the mortise will be accurately cut and that the tenon will fill it properly. The tenon must also be formed with great care so as to make sure that it will properly fill the mortise.

## THE OPEN MORTISE AND TENON JOINT.

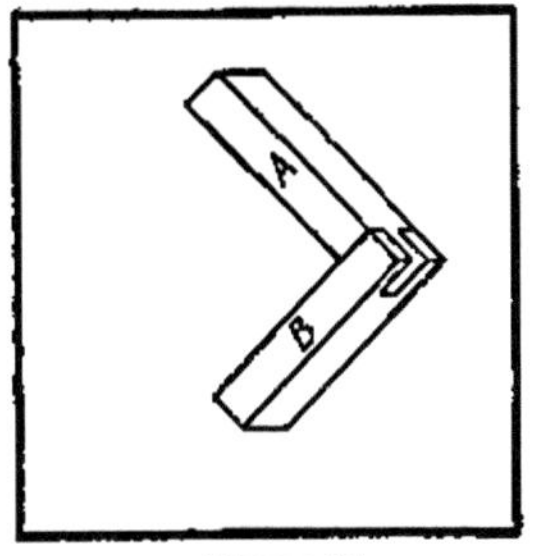

Figure 53.

**Paragraph 68.** The open mortise and tenon joint is used in the construction of rectangular frame work which employs heavy timbers. This joint, however, is not in very common use. It is very similar to the end half-lap joint, but is a little more complicated.

In laying out the open mortise and tenon joint the tenon piece A will be laid out and cut in the same manner as in cutting the tenon for the blind mortise and tenon joint. The mortise piece B is laid out with a mortising gauge in the same manner as any other mortise except that, since it is at the end of the material, instead of being bored and chiseled out it can be ripped down with the rip saw and cut out with a chisel.

## ROUND TENON.

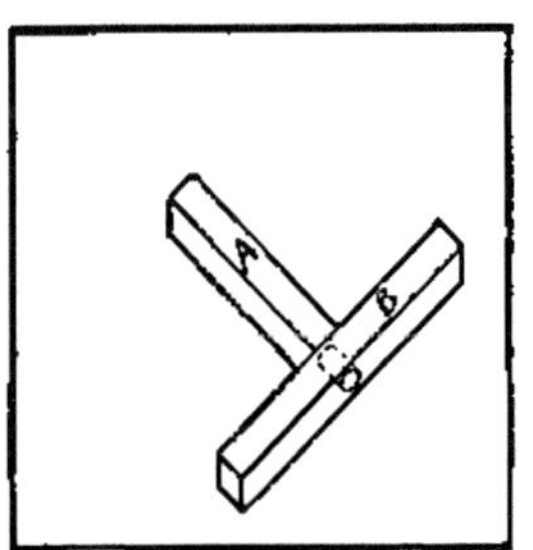

Figure 54.

**Paragraph 69.** The round tenon is used in joining materials where there is no great strain sidewise. It is rather easily constructed, but is not so substantial or rigid as the blind mortise and tenon, and for that reason it is not so common. It is used in wheel construction where the spoke joins the felly. It is frequently used on the end of materials where the principal pressure is downward with but little strain sidewise. For instance, in the legs of the camp stool.

## TO LAY OUT THE ROUND TENON CONSTRUCTION.

Decide the length the tenon is to be and square a line entirely around the material that distance from the end (piece A). Determine the diameter of the round tenon and set the mortising gauge with the two points as far apart as the desired diameter. Set the gauge with the head at the proper distance from the first point to lay out the tenon in the center of the material. Carefully gauge the tenon on the edge of the material. With the rip saw saw down to the squared line in the same manner in which you would saw any tenon. With the two points exactly the same distance apart set the head of the marking gauge so as to lay out the tenon the proper distance from the working edge and gauge the width of the tenon on each side of the tenon already sawed. Again saw down to the shoulders. This will form a square tenon. Find the center of this square tenon by drawing the diagonals on the end. Set the compasses and on the end of the square tenon lay out a circle the size of the desired round tenon. With a pocket-knife carefully cut away the corners and make the tenon round to the size indicated on the end. It should be finished with a wood file. In this joint the mortise is to be merely a round hole (piece B). It is bored with a brace and bit of the proper size. It might be well to bore this hole before the tenon is completed so it can be tested from time to time to make sure that it is made the exact size to fill the mortise snugly. This joint may be assembled with glue or a small brad may be driven through B into the tenon, as the nature of the work may indicate.

## KEYED MORTISE AND TENON.

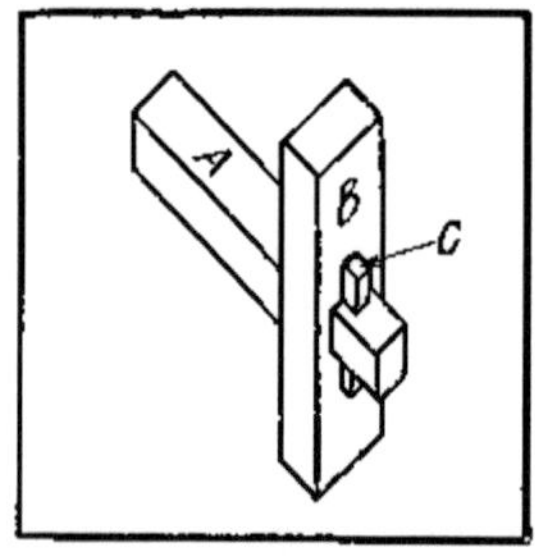

Figure 55.

**Paragraph 70.** The keyed mortise and tenon joint is a very old one. It was formerly used only in heavy construction work or where great strength was required. In recent years, however, it has found its way into a great many kinds of cabinet construction, where it is used for its artistic effect as well as for strength. There is no joint which will present greater strength than the keyed mortise and tenon. If it is properly proportioned it will withstand almost any kind of strain and cannot be torn apart until the material is split and almost absolutely destroyed. In the keyed mortise (B) and tenon (A) construction the laying out and execution are very similar to the through mortise and tenon, except that the tenon is cut very much longer so as to extend a sufficient distance to have a mortise cut in it and allow a key (C) to be used.

Lay out the mortise and the tenon as explained in Paragraph 66. Allow the tenon to extend through the mortise far enough to receive the mortise for the key and still leave sufficient wood to give the necessary strength. In designing the keyed mortise and tenon joint it is necessary to take into consideration how much strength will be required. In cabinet and artistic work of course strength is not an important point. Then one must consider the general appearance of the work. It is quite common to see rather heavy keyed tenons on a piece of work which is not subjected to a great strain, but because of the massive appearance which is desired throughout the work large tenons and keys are used. This is a matter of judgment and no definite rule can be given. Note: In cutting the mortise for the key and in preparing the key, be sure that the key tightens in such a way as to hold the two pieces of material closely together. The key must not tighten laterally or it will split the end of the tenon. It is well for the key to fit rather loosely this way, but to bind very snugly in the other direction. The size and shape of the key is a matter of taste. The key is sometimes cut in a scrolled or artistic form.

## LAPPED DOVE-TAILED JOINT.

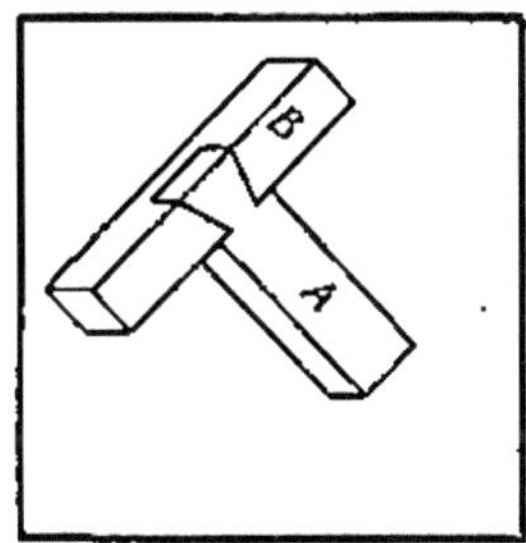


Figure 56.

Paragraph 71. The lapped dove-tail joint is simply a lapped joint in which the farther end of the tenon is wider than the portion that is next the shoulder. This makes it impossible for the joint to pull apart without splitting the material. The lapped dove-tail joint is not very common because it is rather difficult to construct and presents but few advantages, which are hardly sufficient to justify the efforts required in making it. It is very suitable in installing mullions or cross ties in any sort of large frame work. The dividing strips in large window screens would offer an opportunity for the application of this joint.

## TO LAY OUT THE LAP AND DOVE-TAIL.

The angle at which the dove-tail is cut is not material. Whatever angle is decided upon should be set on the T-bevel. The materials should be planed exactly square. On piece A cut the lap joint the same as when making an end half-lap (Paragraph 63). Then with the T-bevel lay out the angle of the dove-tail on the working face. With the back saw, saw down the shoulder and rip down the lines laid out with the T-bevel just as you would saw out a tenon. Lay this piece of material across the piece B in the desired position. With the sharp point of a knife indicate the width for the gain. With the T-bevel lay out the gain on the working face. (Sometimes this gain is laid out merely by marking on each side of the tenon. It is more desirable, however, to lay it out with the T-bevel in order to have it absolutely accurate.) Square these lines down on both edges of material B, with the marking gauge set exactly as it was used in laying out the tenon, gauge the depth which the gain is to be cut. Saw down to the gauge line, then with a sharp chisel pare out the gain. Assemble this joint with glue, brads, nails or screws as the nature of the work may indicate.

## DOWEL JOINT.

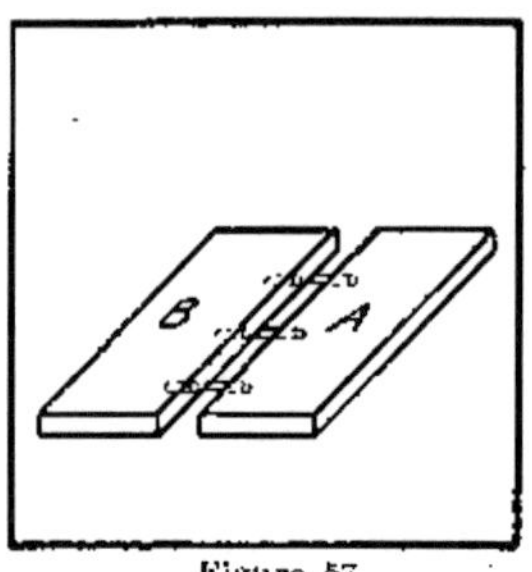

Figure 57.

**Paragraph 72.** In making up wide boards, such as table tops, drawing boards, or any other cabinet construction in which it is impractical to use one wide board, dowels are frequently used. The purpose of the dowels is to reinforce the glued joints. Dowels may be placed in the joint at any distance apart. In work subject to great strain the dowels are frequently placed within a few inches of each other. In other work they are placed farther apart. This must always be a matter of judgment. The size (diameter) of the dowel depends upon the thickness of the board to be joined. In 7/8" or 1" material, 1/4" or 3/8" dowels are commonly used, extending 1½" or 2" into the edge of each board. Dowels are usually covered with glue, thus when the edges of the board are glued together a very strong joint is made.

## TO LAY OUT AND BORE FOR DOWELS.

See Chapter II., Paragraphs 18 and 13. Saw short pieces of dowels just long enough to fill the depth of the holes in board A and extend enough to fill the holes in board B. Put some glue on the dowels and drive them into board A. Then to make sure that the dowels are not too long, measure the distance they extend and measure the depth of the holes in board B. Cover the dowels with glue, also glue the edges which are to join. Make sure that the face side of the two boards are turned in the same direction; drive the boards together. After the boards are driven together they should be clamped very tightly with a steel clamp. If you have no steel clamp, substitutes may be made by nailing some blocks at convenient distances apart on any rough piece of material and tightening with wedges. Dowel joints should be clamped twelve to twenty-four hours to give the glue a chance to harden.

## TONGUE AND GROOVE JOINT.

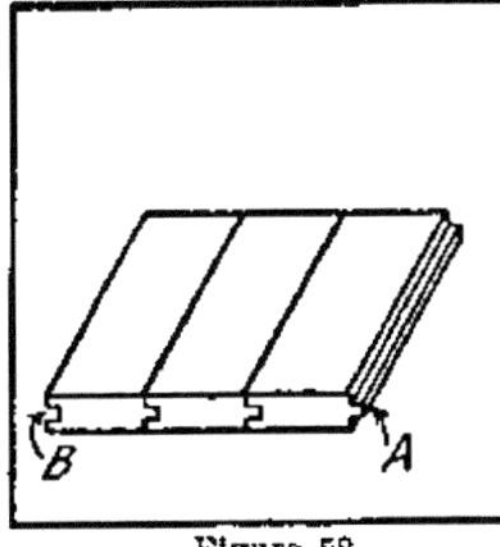


Figure 58.

**Paragraph 73.** The tongue and groove joint is very commonly used in joining the edges of boards. This joint is found in all kinds of flooring and ceiling. It is also used somewhat in joining boards in cabinet construction, such as in table tops, counter tops and in other places where wide boards are needed. It is not common to prepare a tongue and groove joint in the shop; material is usually purchased with the tongue and the groove already made; this is particularly true in flooring and ceiling. While the tongue and groove joint is not commonly made by hand, yet there are frequently occasions where it is necessary to do a little of this kind of work. For this reason the shop should be provided with a set of matching planes for the purpose of cutting the tongue and groove. One plane is so constructed as to cut the tongue while the other is formed to cut the groove (these planes are sometimes so constructed that the same plane does the work of both, one side being used for the tongue and the opposite side for the groove work).

## TO PREPARE TONGUE AND GROOVE.

First, see that your material is planed perfectly straight and square on the edges. Then place the material in the vise exactly as though you were going to plane the edge, and with the matching plane (which must be firmly held against the working face) plane a groove (B) on one edge of each piece of material. Plane a tongue (A) on the opposite edge of each piece. This joint can be assembled with glue or treated as the nature of the work may demand.

## HALVED SPLICE.

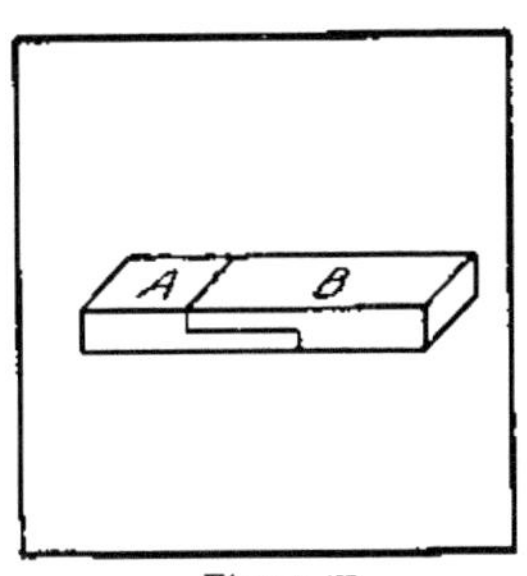


Figure 59.

**Paragraph 74.** The halved splice is used for the purpose of splicing materials in length. This joint is very similar to the half-lap joint except that the material continues in one direction rather than at right angles. In preparing this joint see that the material is planed perfectly square. Lay out the half-lap as explained in Paragraph 63. Assemble with glue and brads, or nails and screws, as the nature of the work may demand.

## SIMPLE HALF-PITCH CUT.

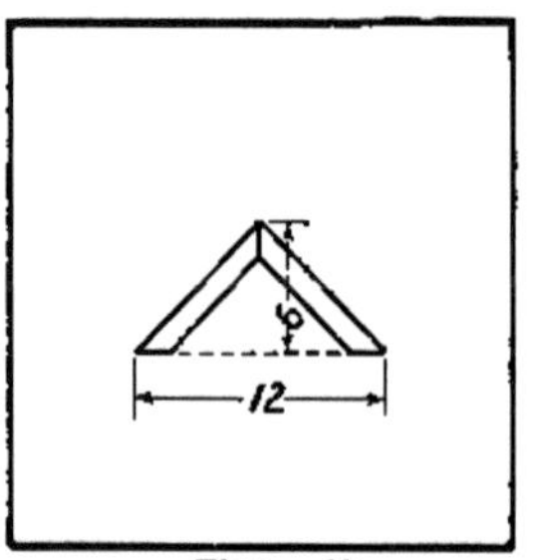

Figure 60.

**Paragraph 75.** In house or roof construction the cutting of rafters is a very essential matter. In simple roof work this is not difficult. Most roofs follow the regular standards of pitch, the most common being half, third and quarter-pitch. By the pitch of the roof is meant the relation of the elevation of the roof to the width of the building. A half-pitch roof is one in which the elevation of the rafters is one-half the width of the building. To illustrate: if a building is 12 ft. wide the elevation of the rafters would be one-half of 12, which is 6 ft. To lay out the half-pitch cut a steel square should be used, as explained in Chapter 2, Paragraph 24. In cutting the brace for a door or any other purpose the half-pitch cut would be laid out in exactly the same way.

## THIRD-PITCH CUT.

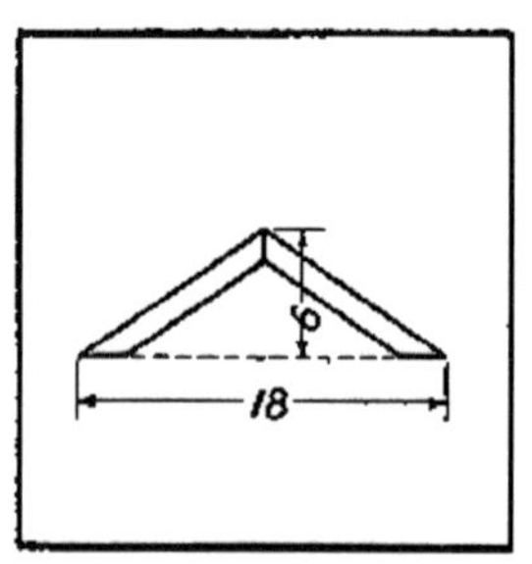

Figure 61.

**Paragraph 76.** A third-pitch roof is one in which the elevation of the rafters is one-third the width of the building. To illustrate: if a building is 18 ft. wide a third-pitch roof would be one in which the elevation to the point of the rafters would be one-third of 18 ft., which is 6 ft. To make this cut a steel square should be used, as indicated in Chapter 2, Paragraph 25.

## QUARTER-PITCH CUT.

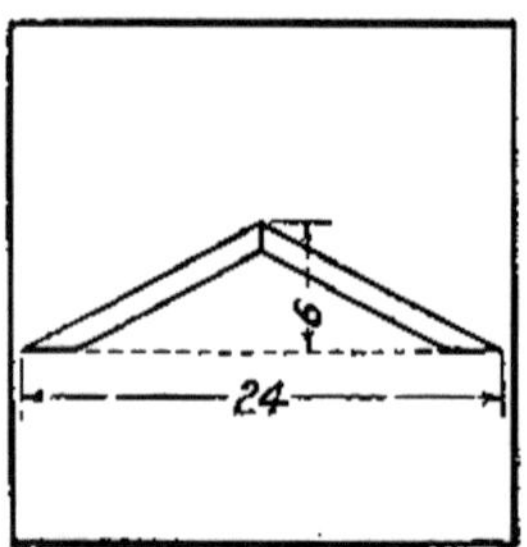

Figure 62.

**Paragraph 77.** A quarter-pitch roof is one in which the elevation of the rafters is one-fourth the width of the building. To illustrate: if the width of the building is 24 ft., the elevation of a quarter-pitch roof will be one-fourth of 24, which is 6 ft. This cut for a rafter would be laid out as indicated in Chapter 2, Paragraph 26.

Of course in roof construction there are a great many other rafter problems which arise, such as the cutting of valley, hip and jack rafters. As this information belongs purely to the carpenter's trade, it is not worth while taking it up here. The matter of getting the length of rafters is a simple problem which can be easily figured out in the arithmetic class by figuring the hypotenuse of a right triangle, in which the elevation is the altitude and one-half the width of the building is the base. Of course the carpenter has rules by which he is able to get the length of a rafter by the use of the steel square.

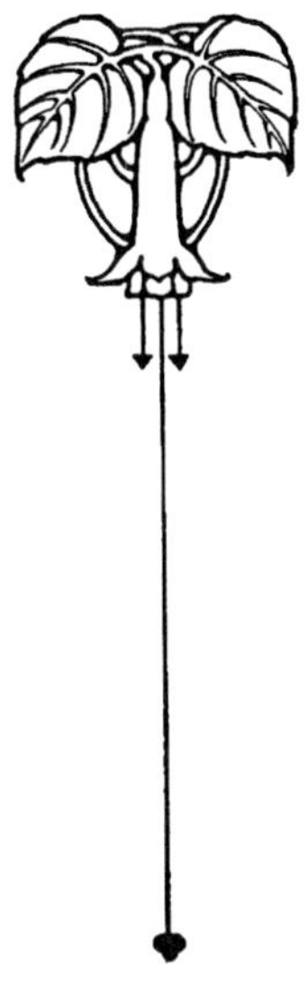

# CHAPTER VI

# TOOLS AND TOOL SHARPENING

## SAWS.

**Paragraph 78.** There are a great many kinds of saws, each of which is constructed for some sort of special work. It is not necessary that you should learn all about the different kinds of saws; however, there are a few points regarding the more common ones with which you should become familiar.

The ordinary hand saws, or panel saws, as they are sometimes called, are in most common use, and for that reason you will need to know about them. Hand saws are divided into two general classes, those that cut in the direction of the grain, called rip saws, and those that cut across the grain, known as cross-cutting saws. The principal distinguishing feature between the two classes of saws is the shape of the teeth, each having the teeth so shaped and filed as to perform its particular work most satisfactorily.

A mistake frequently made by beginners is that of attempting to use a rip saw for cross cutting purposes. On account of the shape of its teeth and the angle at which they are filed, a rip saw will not do satisfactory work in cutting across the grain of wood. You will understand this better after studying the illustration and the discussion which follows, and also making some practical experiments in the shop.

The cross-cutting saw is sometimes taken for ripping purposes. This is not such a bad mistake, for a cross-cutting saw will do fairly good work in the direction of the grain, although it will not cut so rapidly as the rip saw. In ripping material which is very knotty or cross grained a cross-cutting saw will often give very excellent results. On account of its being so necessary for you to select a saw which is fitted for the particular work which you expect to do, you must be able to distinguish between the cross-cutting and rip saws.

## RIP SAWS.

**Paragraph 79.** The following illustration (Figure 63) shows the appearance of the teeth of a rip saw. The size of the teeth is somewhat exaggerated so you may be able to recognize the essential features. At first glance you possibly would not distinguish the difference between the shape of these teeth and the teeth of a cross-cutting saw; therefore you must examine the illustration carefully, studying the appearance of the teeth from all the different views which are given.

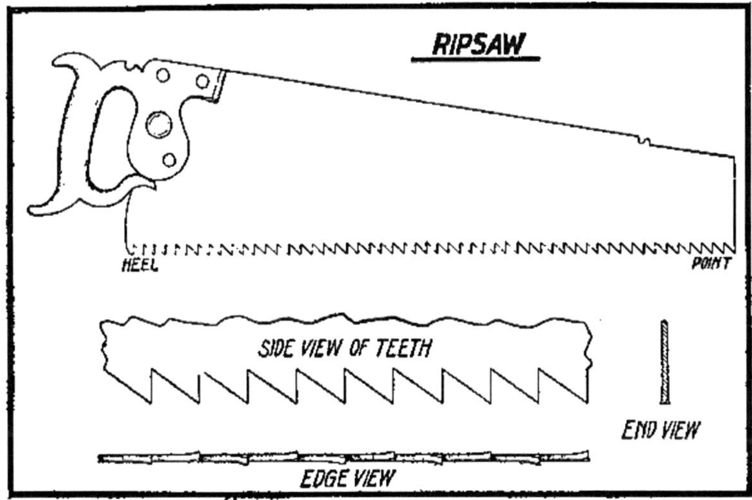


Figure 63.

In order that saws may run easily, and cut a wide enough groove, or kerf, as it is called, to allow the blade to run freely, the edge of the blade which has the teeth is usually a little thicker than the back edge of the blade. The teeth also are given "set"; that is, half the teeth (alternating) are turned slightly toward one side while the remaining half are turned toward the other side. This plan of setting the teeth has the effect of enabling the saw to cut a kerf sufficiently wide for the blade to run through smoothly.

Rip saw teeth are not given much set. However, they should have a little set, as shown in the end view of Figure 63. By examining a rip saw in the shop, noticing the set, the shape of the teeth, and experimenting with it, you will see clearly why it should always be used only for ripping purposes.

## CROSS-CUTTING SAWS.

**Paragraph 80.** The teeth of cross-cutting saws, instead of being filed square across like rip saw teeth, are filed at an angle, so that the cutting edge of each tooth approaches the wood very much in the manner of a keen knife blade. This is the feature which makes it possible for a cross-cutting saw to sever the fibers of wood and make a smooth cut across the grain. Figure 64 shows you the shape of the teeth of a cross-cutting saw.

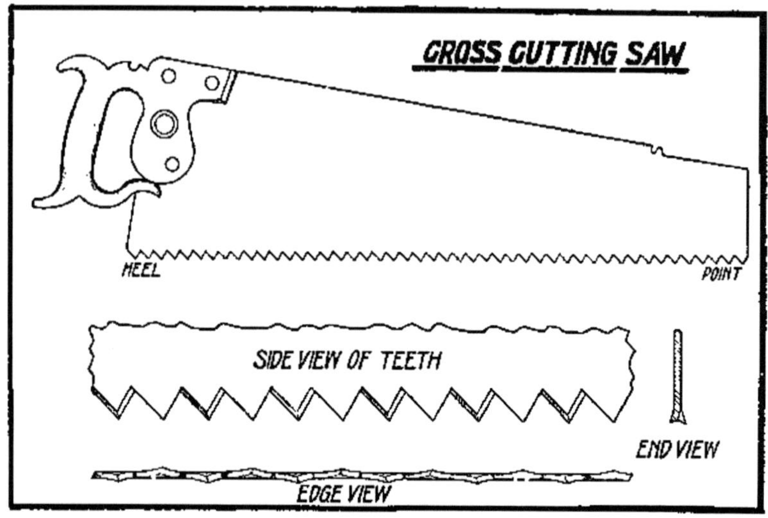


Figure 64.

You will observe that the front, or cutting edge, of each tooth leans slightly backward toward the heel of the saw. The side view shows that the teeth are beveled. This is done by filing them half from one side and the other half from the opposite side. The teeth are also given more set than was found in the rip saw. This may be seen from the edge and end view. A careful study of the characteristic features of cross-cutting saws, together with a little thoughtful experimenting in the shop, will enable you to understand these points fully.

## SAW FILING.

**Paragraph 81.** Saw filing is a very technical piece of work. It should not be attempted without considerable study; it is not to be expected that elementary students should file their own saws in the shop. This work should be done by the teacher or an expert saw filer. An inexperienced student is likely to damage a saw almost beyond repair in his early attempts at filing. NOTE: If it is thought advisable to attempt sawfiling in the school there should be a saw or two put aside for this purpose and used for practice work. No student should be permitted to attempt the work on any of the regular shop saws until he has acquired sufficient skill to be able to do it without danger of damage to the saw. It is not the purpose of this discussion to give detailed illustrations and instructions on the technical subject of saw dressing. A careful study of some of the references given in this text will offer valuable assistance along that line.

## CARE OF SAWS.

**Paragraph 82.** All saws should be kept perfectly clean, free from glue, rust or anything else which would give the sides of the saw a rough surface. Saws should be wiped frequently with an oiled rag (do not use linseed oil). If any spots of rust appear they should be rubbed off with powdered emery, pumice stone, or with a piece of well-worn sandpaper and a little oil. Care should be exercised never to allow the teeth of a saw to strike against any kind of metal, such as the vise jaw, a nail or a screw. If it is necessary to saw a board which is covered with dirt, cement, or any other substance which is likely to dull the saw, the board should be carefully cleaned along the line where the saw cut is to be made before the work is attempted. It is very much easier and cheaper to keep shop saws sharp and in good order by proper care than to have them re-sharpened.

## PLANES.

**Paragraph 83.** A plane is one of the most important tools which you must learn to handle. There are a great many different kinds and sizes of planes designed for different sorts of special work. In their principal features they are very similar. They all consist of some sort of sharp cutting blade firmly fastened in a suitable stock provided with a convenient handle. The planes in most common use, and no doubt the ones which you will find in your shop, are the block plane, smoothing plane and jack plane. In carpenter work and in cabinet-making there is frequently a need for a very long plane, known as a jointer. The only advantage which such a plane has over your bench plane, or jack plane, as it is sometimes called, is in length. The extra long stock of the jointer makes it especially suitable for planing straight edges on long strips for the edges of boards, which are to be dowled, or for fitting long doors which must be planed perfectly straight.

## THE JACK PLANE.

**Paragraph 84.** The old-fashioned jack plane, which was formerly used for all sorts of general purpose work, has almost entirely gone out of use. The jack plane was constructed with a large open throat, the blade was ground somewhat rounding so it could be set to take a very thick shaving without causing the corners of the blade to tear the wood. This plane was used to dress weather boarding, flooring and all sorts of heavy work, in the early days when all planing was done by hand. Now, this sort of planing is done by electric or steam power, so the old-fashioned jack plane has practically gone out of use. The word, however, is still used frequently in referring to the ordinary general purpose bench plane. This is the plane with which you will do a large portion of your work. An illustration and explanation will be given in this discussion.

## THE SMOOTHING PLANE.

**Paragraph 85.** The smoothing plane is shorter than the jack plane, but is otherwise very similar in construction. It is used on small work and to plane broad surfaces. The fact that it has a short stock makes it possible for it to follow the indentations on a surface and thus smooth it perfectly.

## BLOCK PLANE.

**Paragraph 86.** The block plane is very much smaller than the smoothing plane. Besides its size, it has certain other features which distinguish it from other planes and adapt it to the particular class of work which it is intended to do. Block planes are usually made almost entirely of iron. The particularly characteristic feature is the method of putting in the blade. A block plane blade has its bevel on the top side and the blade is not provided with a break bit. The purpose of this plane is to smooth the end of a board. You can readily see that since its purpose is to cut across the grain, it would not require a bit for the purpose of breaking the shavings.

## PARTS OF THE PLANE.

**Paragraph 87.** The following illustration shows a modern iron plane, which is typical of the present-day method of plane construction. This is a No. 5 bench plane, which you have just learned is frequently called a jack plane. In size and general construction it is adapted to almost any kind of general purpose work for which you will require a plane in the shop. It is long enough to render good service as a jointer and for the class of smoothing work which you will need to do it will be very convenient.

While this style of plane has a great many different parts, there are really only a few with which you need to concern yourself. Such parts as the handle, the knob and the bottom or sole, are so evident that they are not pointed out to you in the illustration. You should study Figure 65 with your bench plane before you and thus thoroughly familiarize yourself with the nature and function of each of the parts which are pointed out in this illustration.

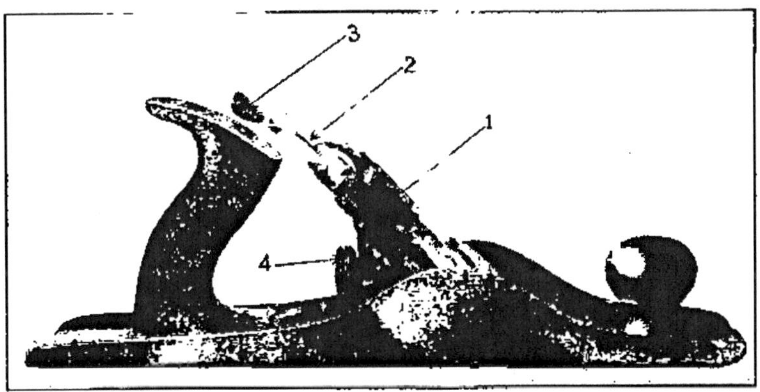


Figure 65.

Arrow No. 1 points out the clamp iron, the purpose of which is to hold the blade, or bit, firmly in position. Notice that this clamp is fastened by a little lever at the top. To loosen the clamp for the purpose of removing the bit the little lever should be raised. This portion of the plane is frequently broken by beginning students because they attempt to force down the lever when the blade is not in its proper position. It should not require much force to push down the lever; if you are having such difficulty with your plane make sure that the plane blade is resting properly in its position and that there are no chips under it. If the lever still refuses to operate properly, the little screw which holds the clamp in position may be slightly loosened. However, this screw should not often require adjusting.

Arrow No. 2 points out the plane blade, or plane iron, as it is sometimes called. This plane iron is composed of two parts, firmly clamped together by a set screw. If you remove the clamp and take out the plane iron you will find that the cutting blade is clamped in the stock, with the bevel on the bottom side of the blade; the cap iron, or break bit, as it is more properly called, is fastened to the blade on the top side. Before separating the break bit from the cutting blade, you should notice the manner in which the two blades are adjusted. If the plane is set for fine finishing work the edge of the break bit will come very close to the edge of the cutting blade (perhaps within 1/64 of an inch). If the plane is set for rougher work, where it will be required to take a thick shaving in planing away stock, then the break bit will be considerably farther from the cutting edge, perhaps as much as 1/16 of an inch, or even more. A little experimenting will enable you to adjust the break blade properly for any kind of work which you may care to do. You should be very careful when putting the break blade in position to avoid striking it against the cutting edge of the blade.

Arrow No. 3 points out the adjusting lever. The purpose of this lever is to adjust the plane blade so that it will extend through the throat of the plane evenly at each side. If one corner of the bit extends too far through, push the lever the proper direction to adjust it. By examining the sole of the plane and watching the movement of the blade as you move the adjusting lever you will learn just how to control it.

Arrow No. 4 points out the adjusting nut which regulates the depth of the plane blade and thus controls the thickness of the shaving to be cut. By turning this bronze nut either to the right or to the left, the blade will be raised or lowered. You will have to experiment with your own plane in order that you may know just how to adjust the blade with this nut.

A mistake frequently made by beginners is in attempting to cut too thick a shaving; where a thick shaving is removed the wood is not left perfectly smooth. You should adopt the rule of keeping your plane blades very sharp and set to take only a very thin shaving. This will insure good work and the proper use of the tool.

In laying down a plane it should be laid on its side rather than on its sole. In laying it on the sole there is danger of nicking the extreme cutting edge of the bit which is extending through the throat. If, after thoroughly studying these points regarding your plane, you are, for any reason, unable to get satisfactory results, you should consult someone who is thoroughly familiar with plane construction. It is not well for you to attempt the adjustment of any of the parts other than those already explained.

## PLANE SHARPENING.

Paragraph 88. As it is impossible to do satisfactory work with a dull plane, you must learn to sharpen your plane blades. This is not a difficult task, and if thoughtfully approached will give you no trouble. It should be a source of great satisfaction for you to be able to keep your tools in excellent shape. In plane sharpening there are just a few points which you should bear in mind—first, a plane blade should be perfectly square on its cutting edge. Test with the try-square to make sure this is true. The extreme corners should be rounded very slightly to prevent them from scratching the wood unduly when the plane is used. This matter of rounding the blade is such a small point that you need give it but little attention. You should rather take precaution not to round the blade too much. Adopt the rule of testing the blade with a try-square and making it straight while whetting.

The plane blade should be sharpened at a continuous bevel; that is, the angle of sharpening should not vary and should not be rounded in the least. It will require some practice to be able to bevel a plane blade in this manner.

## GRINDING.

Paragraph 89. For a great many years grinding on a grindstone has been the standard method of sharpening chisel and plane blades. If your shop is equipped with a grindstone you will find it convenient for this purpose. Be sure to use water on the stone while grinding. The purpose of the water is to wash away the little particles of steel as they are ground from the edge of the tool. If water is not used this steel will imbed itself in the face of the stone and will thus hinder the grinding process. The water also serves another very important purpose. It prevents friction, and thus avoids heating the plane blade. Never grind an edged tool on a dry grindstone. The surface of the grindstone must be kept smooth and straight, in order that plane blades and wide chisels may be squarely ground. If it is necessary to grind a cold chisel, screw driver, punch, or any irregular shaped tool, it should be done on the side of the grindstone to avoid abusing the face. In grinding a blade, hold it at a constant angle in order to give it a true bevel, as has been explained. This angle will vary, depending upon the kind of work for which the blade is being sharpened. If you expect to do considerable rough work on hard and knotty material, the plane blade should not be ground too thin; that is, there should be a thicker bevel than if you were preparing it for soft wood or fine finishing purposes. A very satisfactory angle for a general purpose plane is about 27 or 30 degrees. When you remove the blade from the stone to examine it, be sure to put it back in position at exactly the same angle.

You cannot completely sharpen a blade on a grindstone. When the bevel has been completed and all of the nicks have been ground out, you will find the cutting edge is very rough and will possibly be turned up slightly in the form of a wire edge. This indicates that the grinding is done and that you should finish sharpening the plane blade on a whetstone.

## WHETTING.

**Paragraph 90.** The final sharpening of the blade must be done on a fine whetstone of some sort. This may be a natural stone or an artificial stone made of carborundum. For the finishing work use a stone of fine grit. See that the face of the stone is perfectly clean and use plenty of oil during the whetting process. Do not use linseed oil on any kind of whetstone. It will not only fail to give satisfactory results, but will render the stone unfit for use. Use machine oil, which may be thinned with kerosene. The oil on the whetstone is to serve the same purpose as the water on the grindstone.

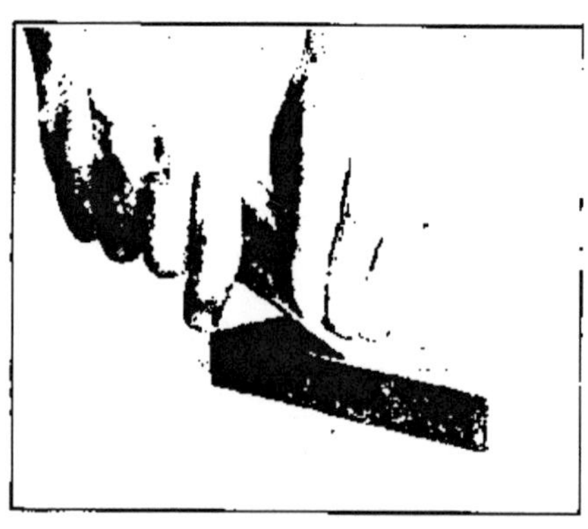

Figure 66.

Grasp the plane blade firmly with the right hand; let the fingers of the left hand rest on top of the blade, as shown in Figure 66. Whet with a backward and forward motion covering the entire length of the stone. Be sure to keep the angle constant. In order to do this you must not use a rocking motion. Some mechanics whet a blade with a rotary, or circular motion, but this plan is not to be recommended, for it is less likely to produce a true angle and a perfectly square cutting edge. Examine frequently to see that the whetting is being done on the extreme point, or cutting edge of the bevel; that is, the whetting will be done at a little greater angle than the grinding is done. When a very fine wire edge appears, lay the blade flat on its straight side and draw it across the stone, using great precaution not to raise the opposite end of the blade, but to keep it perfectly flat. (See Figure 67). After the edge has been made as keen as possible on the oil stone give it a few strokes, stropping fashion, on a piece of leather, which should be kept in the shop for that purpose. If this has been properly done, the plane blade should be keen enough to shave. If you have not secured such results it will be well to find the difficulty and try it again.

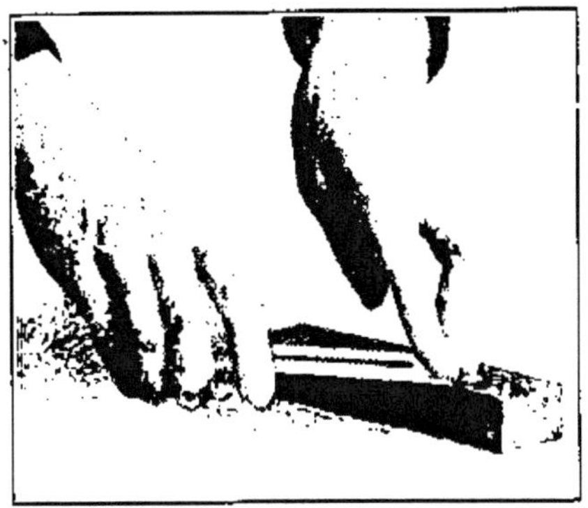

Figure 67.

## BEVELING ON A CARBORUNDUM STONE.

**Paragraph 91.** If your shop is not equipped with a grindstone, you will be able to get very satisfactory results by the use of a rather coarse carborundum stone. This is merely a whetstone with coarse grit which enables it to cut very rapidly. It should be used in the exact manner of the whetstone just explained. In purchasing a carborundum stone for the shop it is best to provide a stone which has coarse grit on one side and fine on the other. This makes it convenient to use the coarse side of the stone in cutting down and forming the desired bevel on a chisel or plane blade. The stone may then be turned over and the final whetting completed, as already explained.

## SHARPENING CHISELS.

**Paragraph 92.** Chisels are sharpened in almost exactly the same way as plane blades. The length of the bevel of the chisel will depend on the kind of work which it is to do. For heavy mortising or work in hard wood, a chisel should not be ground too thin, or it will not stand the strain. For working soft wood it is very desirable that chisels be ground to a long, thin bevel. This makes it possible for them to cut very smoothly. The bevel should be formed on the grindstone or carborundum stone at a constant angle, as already explained. The wire edge should be removed and the final cutting edge produced on a fine whetstone, after which the chisel should be stropped on leather in the same manner as the plane blade.

## SHARPENING KNIVES.

**Paragraph 93.** Sloyd knives, pocket knives, butcher knives, and in fact almost all tools which belong to the general type of knives, may be sharpened in the manner already explained. These tools are, however, beveled on both sides; the shape and length of the bevel is determined in each case by the kind of work which is to be done with the tool.

## CARE OF SHARPENING EQUIPMENT.

**Paragraph 94.** Somewhere in the shop there should be a definite place to keep the sharpening stone. A small table, or shelf on the wall, is very satisfactory for this purpose. The shelf or table should be at a convenient height and the stone should be either imbedded in the shelf top, or there should be small cleats so nailed as to form a receptacle for the stone to hold it reasonably solid when in use. The stone should not be carried about from bench to bench or place to place in the shop. The sharpening should all be done at the bench or table provided for that purpose. A can of suitable oil should be kept near the stone. A small try-square should hang at a convenient place so it can be readily used to test the blades which are being sharpened. A piece of leather to serve as a strop should be securely glued to a strip of wood and should form a part of the sharpening table equipment. The importance of tool sharpening makes it necessary that provisions be made to encourage students in undertaking the work. They will not be enthusiastic about sharpening their tools, unless suitable sharpening equipment is provided, and kept in good condition.

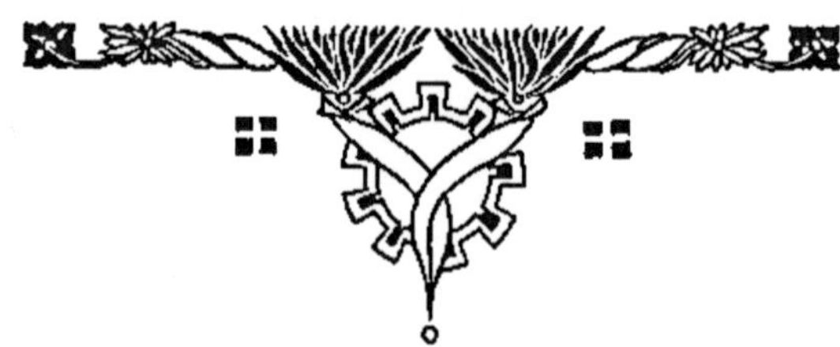

CPSIA information can be obtained at www.ICGtesting.com
Printed in the USA
LVOW08s0155040316

477751LV00001B/58/P